The Economics of Information and Uncertainty

A Conference Report
Universities–National Bureau
Committee for Economic Research

Number 32

National Bureau of Economic Research

The Economics of Information and Uncertainty

Edited by John J. McCall

The University of Chicago Press

Chicago and London

JOHN J. MCCALL is professor of economics at the University of California, Los Angeles, and a consultant at the RAND Corporation. He is the author (with Dale Jorgenson and Roy Radner) of *Optimal Replacement Policy* and *Income Mobility, Racial Discrimination, and Economic Growth* and the editor (with Steve Lippman) of *Studies in the Economics of Search*.

The University of Chicago Press, Chicago 60637
The University of Chicago Press, Ltd., London

Library of Congress Cataloging in Publication Data
Main entry under title:

The Economics of information and uncertainty.

(A Conference report / Universities—National
Bureau Committee for Economic Research ; no. 32)
   Bibliography: p.
   Includes indexes.
   1. Uncertainty (Information theory)—Congresses.
2. Risk—Congresses.   3. Economics—Decision
making—Statistical methods—Congresses.   I. McCall,
John Joseph, 1933-   . II. Series: Conference
report (Universities—National Bureau Committee for
Economic Research)
HB133.E34   338.5   81-15930
ISBN 0-226-55559-3   AACR2

Contents

Prefatory Note

This volume contains the papers presented at the Conference on the Economics of Information and Uncertainty held in Boston, 14–16 June 1979, sponsored by the Universities–National Bureau Committee for Economic Research. Funds for the conference were provided by the National Science Foundation; we are indebted for its support. We also thank John J. McCall, who served as chairman of the conference and editor of this volume.

Executive Committee, June 1979
Edwin S. Mills, chairman
Irma Adelman
Richard Bird
Robert Eisner
Dudley G. Luckett
Leonard W. Weiss
Robert E. Lipsey, NBER
representative

Introduction

John J. McCall

The papers in this volume were presented at a conference on the economics of information and uncertainty held in Boston in June of 1979 and sponsored by the Universities–National Bureau Committee for Economic Research.[1] The papers cover a broad range of topics and at first glance may appear unrelated. Of course, each of the papers is concerned with a particular aspect of either the economics of information or the economics of uncertainty, but this, in itself, is a relatively weak link. There is, however, a fundamental theme that does create strong interactions among these essays, namely, the role of incentives, risk, and risk sharing in organizational structure. Since this theme permeates and unifies much of the recent literature on the economics of uncertainty,[2] we begin this introduction with an elaboration of its origins and ramifications.

This basic theme has received considerable attention in three different literatures: the theory of finance, organization theory, and the economics of insurance. In the recent literature on organization theory and insurance, the intersection between the set of organizational concepts and the set of insurance concepts is so large that it is no longer useful to distinguish between these two disciplines. Thus, in our discussion of organization theory we see that topics like moral hazard and adverse selection, which formerly belonged exclusively to insurance theory, are precisely the problems that have vivified the new organizational research.

John J. McCall is professor of economics at the University of California, Los Angeles.

The theory of finance was one of the first to recognize the importance of uncertainty in comprehending economic behavior. This is not surprising since the stock market cannot be ignored by financial analysts. The first tasks of finance were to explain the stochastic behavior of the stock market and its role in a capitalist economy. Thus, Bachelier, by inventing Brownian motion to explain stock price fluctuations, and Arrow, by perceiving the risk sharing function of the stock market, laid the groundwork for modern finance.

Arrow pointed to the stock market as the main institution for shifting the risks of business from entrepreneurs to the general public. Individuals can diversify their portfolios to achieve an acceptable level of expected return for a given level of risk. This ability to pool risks enables firms to undertake projects that would otherwise be unacceptable. Thus, society is better off. The stock market is not a perfect risk pooling entity like the futures market. It is unable to separate production and risk, leaving the former to the manager and transferring the latter to the general public. Instead, with the issuance of stock the firm's owners and managers are separated and the profit maximizing incentives of the managers are diluted. Thus, the inability of stockholders to monitor managers' efforts gives rise to a moral hazard problem.

The study of stock market fluctuations and the stock market as a risk pooling institution has led to important contributions like the capital asset pricing model, the options pricing model, the efficient market hypothesis, the Modigliani-Miller theorem, and recent research on the theory of the firm.[3] This last endeavor has given us new concepts like spanning and unanimity from which an entirely new perspective for evaluating a firm's behavior has emerged.

Several of the papers in this volume make important contributions to finance. In the past, ideas have tended to move from finance to economics. In his paper Brock returns the favor and shows how some of the recent economic research in growth theory and rational expectations can be used to enrich the extant financial models. Kreps conducts an intensive study of the Black-Scholes option pricing model and shows that its power depends on some very delicate properties that are not robust. Kihlstrom and Laffont extend the theory of the firm by including stockholders as decision makers. The efficiency of the ensuing competitive allocation of risk and capital is studied in detail. Grossman and Hart, by demonstrating how the financial structure of the corporation affects the incentives of the managers, suggest how the market resolves the moral hazard problem with the issuance of stock.

From our discussion of the finance literature it is clear that stochastic considerations have led to a reformulation of the theory of the firm. There is, of course, another vast literature on organization theory which has joined with the finance literature in promulgating this "new" theory of the firm. Let us spend a moment reviewing this organizational literature.[4]

The basic problem in any organization from the beehive to IBM is to design decision making procedures that are "best" for achieving organizational goals. There are two reasons why this problem is difficult and interesting. First, members of the organization may possess individual goals that are quite different from the primary goal of the organization. Second, the decision making procedures must be based on incomplete information. From this description it is clear that organizational decision making takes place in an agency setting. Thus, the problems arise because of the divergence of incentives between the organization (principal) and its members (agents) as well as the differential cost of obtaining pertinent information.[5] For example, the manager observes an outcome that depends on the state of nature and the actions of the agent. Usually it is costly to distinguish the state of nature from these actions. If this cost is not incurred, the manager is unable to determine the relative contribution of each to the outcome. Since rewards are based on the outcome, the manager would surely like to separate the outcome into the part attributable to the actions of the agent and the part due to the state of nature. This is, of course, the essence of the moral hazard problem. Among the more "specific" results in this area are the recent ones of Harris and Raviv (1979). They demonstrate that monitoring the agent does not pay if the agent is risk neutral or if the relation between his action and the outcome is freely observable. When monitoring does pay, they show that "any Pareto optimal contract can be approximated by an 'all-or-nothing' type of contract." If the action is "acceptable," the agent is paid; otherwise he receives nothing.

In any firm there are at least three distinct groups of participants: stockholders, managers, and owners of nonmanagerial inputs. The three groups voluntarily collaborate in pursuit of a common goal. The common goal that binds these groups must be strong enough to withstand the disintegrating forces that are unleashed when each group pursues its own objective and each individual looks to his own welfare. Even when the common bond is sufficiently strong to preserve the integrity of the organization, the problems of decision making under uncertainty remain.

Because decisions must be based on imperfect information, the organization's welfare is always in jeopardy. A decision that was best in an *ex ante* sense may nevertheless impose great costs on the organization and indeed may even lead to its demise. These hazards or risks, which are fundamental and intrinsic to life as we know it, are allocated among the members of the organization. This allocation must be conducted in such a way that individual incentives are preserved. In order to obtain a proper allocation, due regard must be given to the timing of information, the risk preferences of the organization's members, and the role of chance factors in determining outcomes. In many applications it is difficult if not impossible to "give due regard." It is especially hard to distinguish between the roles of chance and individual effort in determining outcomes. It is natural to attribute good outcomes to our personal effort while blaming fickle nature for untoward events. An appropriate allocation can be accomplished by means of the Pareto optimal contracting that was discussed in the theory of agency. Thus, in certain circumstances it will be in the interest of the employees to subject themselves to monitoring in order to control shirking and to dismissal if their conduct deviates from an agreed-upon norm.

The literature on decision making in organizations has till recently concentrated on the informational problem and assumed that all members possessed a common objective function. In their seminal work Marschak and Radner (1972) studied the behavior of organizations by developing a theory of teams. They recognized that the members of any organization differ in three important respects: first, they control different actions; second, they each have access to different information on which they base their actions; and third, they have different goals. Their theory of teams concentrates on the first two differences and for all practical purposes ignores differences in goals. Thus restricted, their analysis derives the optimal decision function for a particular information structure and evaluates alternative information structures.

The major point made by Alchian and Demsetz (1972) is that the genesis of the capitalist firm is founded on imperfect information. They emphasize that the firm is not a jail in which conflicts are resolved by decree. Members of the firm—employers and employees—are voluntary participants in a cooperative venture. But why all this confusion about the control that the boss exercises over the worker's welfare? Alchian and Demsetz argue that this control is not dictatorial but instead jointly agreed to by both employee and employer. The essence of the control is the monitoring function performed by management. Monitoring is necessary because the firm's production function depends on team output. In the absence of monitoring some team members would shirk. The main function of management is to deter shirking by monitoring inputs and firing malingerers. Management's reward for this monitoring takes the form of a residual claim on output.

In their recent paper Jensen and Meckling (1976) show how the financial structure of the firm is affected by moral hazard. They first study the moral hazard associated with the issuance of stock. If the manager owns the entire firm in the sense that he is the only stockholder, his decisions will be such as to maximize his utility. Assume that his utility derives from both pecuniary and nonpecuniary returns. The nonpecuniary returns flow from Alchian amenities like thick rugs, friendly staff, etc. Now suppose that he sells some fraction α of his stock to outsiders. The outsiders and the manager have identical incentives with respect to pecuniary returns, but the outsiders do not share in the nonpecuniary returns. This gives rise to moral hazard and monitoring because the manager captures the full benefit of the nonpecuniary returns whereas he only pays $(1 - \alpha)$ for their total and marginal cost. As α increases, his incentive to spend resources on perquisites also increases and of course the outsiders will have a greater incentive to monitor the manager's behavior. The difference between the value of the solely owned firm and one in which the manager owns $(1 - \alpha)$ measures the cost of agency (apart from the tax benefits associated with the perquisites).

A similar moral hazard problem exists for debt. Suppose that the owner-manager has a small amount invested in the firm and relies on bondholders to finance the rest. Since he is the residual claimant, the smaller his stake in the enterprise relative to that of the bondholders, the greater his incentive to undertake investments that have high payoffs if successful. When such an investment is a success, he pays the bondholder a *fixed* fee and the owner gets the residual. If the investment fails, most of the cost is borne by the bondholders. Thus, it behooves the bondholders to police the manager's behavior.

Three of the papers in this volume address various aspects of the moral hazard problem that afflicts organizational decision making. The paper by Green extends the theory of teams to the situation where the two participants in decision making do not have identical utility functions. One participant gathers information and transmits it to the other, who makes the decision. Because of the different utility functions, it may pay the collector of information to dissemble. Green measures the value of information and shows that the value of improved information may be negative. Grossman and Hart show how the threat of bankruptcy can mitigate the moral hazard created by the inability of stockholders to monitor the manager's effort. Mortensen is concerned with the genesis of organizations. How do the members of an organization find one another? This is characterized as a problem of search. Mortensen shows how the allocation of the organization's output among its members affects the intensity with which they search. An externality occurs because the searcher in picking his search intensity only considers his own expected benefit from the match. Mortensen shows how contracts can be designed to solve this incentive problem.

Carlton, and Porter and Spence study other aspects of the theory of the firm. Carlton shows that the presence of uncertainty may alter our attitude toward monopoly. In particular, he argues that under uncertainty a market structure that has both monopolistic and competitive features may be preferable to either pure monopoly or pure competition. Porter and Spence present a practical application of organization theory that illustrates how an organization makes decisions under uncertainty when there is a high degree of dependence between its actions and those of its rivals. Previous discussions focused on organizations operating within a competitive environment. Thus, conflict among firms and strategic considerations were absent. The papers by Carlton, and Porter and Spence investigate situations in which strategic considerations can no longer be ignored. In Porter and Spence's paper, the market structure is oligopolistic and the reactions of firms to their competitors is crucial. In Carlton's paper the market is monopolistic with a competitive fringe, and limit pricing is one of the strategic devices used by the monopolist.

We conclude the introduction with a more detailed summary of each essay.

The paper "Asset Prices in a Production Economy," by William A. Brock, generalizes the capital asset pricing model in two directions. First, it is made dynamic by constructing an intertemporal model; second, this dynamic model is formulated in a general equilibrium framework. Brock's intertemporal general equilibrium model is obtained by an artistic linkage of several relatively independent contributions in finance and economics. These include the stochastic growth model of Brock-Mirman, Merton's intertemporal capital asset pricing model, Lucas's asset pricing model, and Ross's arbitrage theory of asset pricing. The equilibrium concept is one of rational expectations. While the paper is very theoretical, Brock's goal is to answer basic economic questions like the effect of increased progessivity in income taxes on the relative prices of risky assets. Empirical research utilizing Brock's framework strikes me as very important. Depending upon one's perspective this work can be viewed as enriching the thriving finance theory "industry" or as arresting the decline of the growth theory "industry" by embedding market institutions into the standard stochastic growth models.

Dennis W. Carlton's paper, "Planning and Market Structure," evaluates alternative market organizations according to their ability to plan production in response to information about consumer demands. Carlton adopts a Schumpeterian stance and argues that the incentives in competitive markets are such that the acquisition of information about demand uncertainty is inefficient. Unlike the competitive firm, a monopoly does have incentives to gather this information and adjust its production accordingly. However, Carlton shows via an example that the benefits accruing to a monopolist from planning are unlikely to offset the monopoly's deadweight loss. Thus, even in the presence of imperfect information a competitive market structure may be preferred to a monopoly. Carlton then introduces a market composed of a dominant firm, which may be a cartel, and a competitive fringe. He shows that this mixed market structure is preferable to either pure competition or pure monopoly. In the mixed structure the incentives for planning reside in the dominant firm, so society reaps the planning benefits of monopoly. At the same time, the deadweight loss of monopoly is reduced by the discipline imposed by the competitive fringe. In its effort to control the size of the competitive fringe, the dominant firm pursues a policy that looks like predatory pricing but is socially superior to the policy of either pure competition or pure monopoly.

The paper "Statistical Decision Theory Requiring Incentives for Information Transfer," by Jerry Green, studies the transfer of information within an organization. The organization is composed of two members. The distinguishing assumption of Green's analysis is that the utility functions of the two members are different. Thus, it may be optimal for the first agent to adjust the information before transmission. For this environment Green shows that, with two actions and two observations, either the information is valueless or a first-best can be achieved. If there are more than two actions, a randomized strategy may be optimal. The randomized strategy is remarkable in that positive probabilities may be attached to dominated actions. The reason for this is that such a strategy by the decision maker may induce veracity in his otherwise unreliable colleague. Green then proves that the decision maker may not want to improve the information structure of his unreliable agent; i.e., the value of "better" information, in the Blackwell sense, may be negative. Green concludes on a positive note by showing that, when there are only two possible observations, the value of improving the agent's information to the decision maker is necessarily nonnegative.

In "Corporate Financial Structure and Managerial Incentives," Sanford J. Grossman and Oliver D. Hart develop a new equilibrium concept to resolve the conflict that exists between the managers of a firm and the firm's stockholders. This conflict is another manifestation of the moral hazard problem. In general, shareholders will not be able to monitor management's actions *and* management's objective function may be quite different from that of the shareholders. The threat of takeover and management compensation schemes like stock options mitigate this moral hazard. Grossman and Hart suggest a third method, viz., the issuance of debt, which, by creating a probability of bankruptcy, an event which is assumed to impose high costs on management, induces the managers to take actions that reduce the bankruptcy probability. Of course, that probability is minimized when the managers maximize profits. Thus, if the costs of bankruptcy are sufficiently high, the issuance of debt eliminates the moral hazard problem. Grossman and Hart show how this resolution occurs in a mature corporation where the financial structure is determined by the management. The market value of the firm is positively related to its level of debt. But managers benefit from high market value because their compensation may be related to market value, because the probability of takeover is nonincreasing in market value, and because the cost of raising additional capital is nonincreasing in market value.

In their paper "A Competitive Entrepreneurial Model of a Stock Market," Richard E. Kihlstrom and Jean-Jacques Laffont adopt Diamond's notion of efficiency and extend results like his to circumstances in which technologies do not exhibit stochastic constant returns to scale. In their model, firms are created and run by entrepreneurs who maximize expected utility. The entrepreneurs are permitted to make personal portfolio decisions in addition to the financial decisions that they make as managers. The firm is competitive in that it is a price taker in all markets. Entry is restricted only by the fixed fee that each entrant must pay. Furthermore, there are infinitely many individuals, each of which belongs to one of several types. Any individual is a potential entrepreneur. A final condition for competition is that returns across firms be stochastically dependent. One of the consequences of their model is that whether or not an individual becomes an entrepreneur is a matter of indifference in equilibrium. A necessary condition for this indifference is the absence of arbitrage opportunities in equilibrium. This will be the case when the Miller-Modigliani theorem obtains and the market value of the resources devoted to a firm equals its equilibrium value.

The authors introduce a special kind of rational expectations called "classical expectations" and prove that, when these expectations hold, an equilibrium exists. This equilibrium has several interesting properties. The optimal portfolio of an individual possesses a nondiversification property in that for entrepreneurs it includes shares in his own firm or in firms that are managed like his, whereas for nonentrepreneurs it includes shares in firms that are managed like firms he would establish. Another equilibrium property is that the number of types of firms equals the number of types of individuals in the economy. Each type of individual holds shares only in firms created by entrepreneurs of the same type. Kihlstrom and Laffont refer to this as a clientele effect and show that it results in unanimous agreement among shareholders in the firm's goals. The equilibrium presented reduces to Diamond's when the technology has stochastic constant returns to scale. Furthermore, the model reduces to the perfectly competitive equilibrium when uncertainty is eliminated. Finally, the model reveals that a stock market will be necessary only when all three of the following conditions are satisfied: costs of entry are fixed, and uncertainty and risk aversion are present for a large number of investors. In the absence of any one of these conditions, the economy achieves the same allocation without a stock market.

In "Multiperiod Securities and the Efficient Allocation of Risk: A Comment on the Black-Scholes Option Pricing Model," David M. Kreps conducts a sophisticated mathematical analysis of the Black-Scholes option pricing model. A Debreu-style economy is presented in which the Black-Scholes prices, which are exogenous in their model, are now endogenously determined. In this general equilibrium setting, Kreps specifies a necessary and sufficient condition for this Debreu economy to possess a complete set of markets. Of course, when this condition is satisfied, the equilibrium allocation corresponding to these equilibrium option prices is Pareto efficient. Unfortunately, the necessary and sufficient conditions involve the equilibrium prices. Kreps then examines the robustness of this model and asks whether, for small deviations from these necessary and sufficient conditions, the resulting economy will possess markets that are approximately complete and the allocation of risk will be approximately efficient. Answers to these questions are quite difficult. The following summary statement by Kreps is most illuminating:

> Frequent trading makes it *possible* for a few securities to span many states of nature. Whether markets are "perfectly" complete depends critically on the fine structure of the way in which uncertainty resolves. But the condition required for complete markets is not "nearly" required for "approximately" complete markets. If equilibrium prices approximate an ideal model in a fairly coarse sense, and if that ideal model has perfectly complete markets, then markets in the original model will give nearly efficient equilibrium allocations. Thus if actual security prices behave "like" those in the Black-Scholes model (meaning here the general class of diffusion process models for which markets are complete), risk is allocated approximately efficiently.

In his paper "The Matching Process as a Noncooperative Bargaining Game," Dale T. Mortensen investigates the formation of organizations. There is imperfect information in that the identities and/or locations of potential members are not known in advance. Information about potential members is acquired by search. The rule for dividing the surplus of any match among its members affects the intensity with which prospective members search. Matched agents do not search, and the rate at which matches form is endogenously determined by the search intensities selected by unmatched agents. Mortensen shows that in general the joint Nash choice of such intensities and the associated matching process are inefficient. In his quest for efficiency Mortensen considers linear and quadratic matching technologies. In the first the probability of forming a match in a small period of time is independent of the number of unmatched agents. In the second this probability is proportional to the number of unmatched agents.

Given a linear technology, the search intensities selected by unmatched agents are too low to achieve efficiency. The choice of a search intensity is not affected by the rewards received by the other number of the match. Mortensen shows that, if the agent responsible for the match receives all of its surplus, joint wealth is maximized by the Nash choice of such intensities. However, this arrangement fails to achieve efficiency for the quadratic technology. In addition to the externality just discussed for the linear case, there is a second externality present in the quadratic technology: more intensive search reduces the probability of meeting an unmatched agent. Thus, by this second externality individuals search too much. Mortensen shows that efficiency is restored when the agent responsible for the match, the matchmaker, receives a fraction f of the surplus, where $\frac{1}{2} \leq f \leq 1$. Finally, Mortensen demonstrates that for both technologies there is a unique division of the match's surplus such that all unmatched agents search efficiently.

In their paper "The Capacity Expansion Process in a Growing Oligopoly: The Case of Corn Wet Milling," Michael E. Porter and A. Michael Spence vividly describe how uncertainty affects economic decision making. How should a firm in an evolving oligopolistic industry augment its productive capacity? The cost of not making such additions when it should is that its industry position will erode. On the other hand, overexpansion will also have a deleterious effect on profits. Factors that should be incorporated in this decision include the following: stochastic lead times with large expected values, expectations about future demand, and the usual strategic considerations that are characteristic of oligopolistic industries. Porter and Spence conduct their study of the capacity expansion decision for the corn wet milling industry. They conclude from this analysis that it is possible to calculate the most likely capacity decisions for firms in an expanding oligopolistic industry. The equilibrium concept used in making this calculation is one of rational expectations. They consider the study of expectations formation an extremely important topic of future research. Another significant finding is that a strategy of preemptive investment is rendered unattractive by the presence of uncertainty. Thus, uncertainty eliminates outcomes in which a large market share is lodged in a few firms.

Notes

1. For their help in organizing the conference, I am indebted to Buz Brock, Rich Kihlstrom, Steve Lippman, Dale Mortensen, Chris Mortensen, Mike Rothschild, Mike Spence, and George Stigler.

2. For two recent surveys of this literature, see Hirshleifer and Riley (1979) and Lippman and McCall (1981). The reader may also wish to consult the proceedings of two previous conferences on the economics of information published in the *Quarterly Journal of Economics*, November 1976, and the *Review of Economic Studies*, October 1977. See also Diamond and Rothschild (1978).

3. For excellent surveys of this recent research, see Baron (1979) and Kreps (1979).

4. For a glimpse of this literature, see "Symposium on the Economics of Internal Organizations" (1975).

5. See Arrow (1964), Harris and Raviv (1979), Hurwicz and Shapiro (1977), Ross (1973), Shavell (1979), and Stiglitz (1974, 1975).

References

Alchian, A., and Demsetz, H. 1972. Production, information costs, and economic organization. *American Economic Review* 62: 777–95.

Arrow, K. 1964. Control in large corporations. *Managament Science* 10: 397–408.

———. 1971. *Essays in the theory of risk bearing*. Chicago: Markham.

Baron, D. 1979. Investment policy, optimality, and the mean-variance model. *Journal of Finance* 34: 206–32.

Diamond, P., and Rothschild, M. 1978. *Uncertainty in economics*. New York: Academic Press.

Harris, M., and Raviv, A. 1979. Optimal incentive contracts with imperfect information. *Journal of Economic Theory* 20: 231–59.

Hirshleifer, M., and Riley, J. 1979. The analytics of uncertainty and information—an expository survey. *Journal of Economic Literature* 17: 1375–1421.

Hurwicz, L., and Shapiro, L. 1977. Incentive structures maximizing residual gain under incomplete information. Discussion Paper 77–83, April. University of Minnesota.

Jensen, M., and Meckling, W. 1976. Theory of the firm. *Journal of Financial Economics* 3: 305–60.

Kreps, D. 1979. *Three essays on capital markets*. Technical Report 298. Stanford University.

Lippman, S., and McCall, J. 1981. The economics of uncertainty: Selected topics and probabilistic methods. In Arrow, K.J., and Intriligator, M.D., eds., *Handbook of mathematical economics*. Amsterdam: North-Holland.

Marschak, J., and Radner, R. 1972. *The theory of teams*. New York: Wiley.

Mirrlees, J. 1976. The optimal structure of incentives and authority within an organization. *Bell Journal of Economics* 7: 105–31.

Radner, R. 1961. The evaluation of information in organizations. In Neyman, J., ed., *Proceedings of the Fourth Berkeley Symposium on Mathematics, Statistics, and Probability*, vol. 1. Berkeley and Los Angeles: University of California Press.

Ross, S. 1973. The economic theory of agency: The principal's problem. *American Economic Review* 63: 134–139.

Shavell, S. 1979. Risk sharing and incentives in the principal and agent relationship. *Bell Journal of Economics* 10: 55–73.

Stiglitz, J. 1974. Risk sharing and incentives in sharecropping. *Review of Economic Studies* 41: 219–56.

———. 1975. Incentives, risk, and information: Notes toward a theory of hierarchy. *Bell Journal of Economics* 5: 552–79.

Symposium: The economics of information. 1976. *Quarterly Journal of Economics* 90: 591–666.

Symposium on economics of information. 1977. *Review of Economic Studies* 44: 389–601.

Symposium on the economics of internal organization. 1975. *Bell Journal of Economics* 6: 163–280.

1   Asset Prices in a Production Economy

William A. Brock

1.1   Introduction

This paper develops an intertemporal general equilibrium theory of capital asset pricing.[1] It is an attempt to put together ideas from the modern finance literature and the literature on stochastic growth models. In this way we will obtain a theory that ultimately is capable of addressing itself to general equilibrium questions such as: (1) What is the impact of an increase in the corporate income tax upon the relative prices of risky stocks? (2) What is the impact of an increase in progressivity of the personal income tax upon the relative price structure of risky assets? (3) What conditions on tastes and technology are needed for the validity of the Sharpe-Lintner certainty equivalence formula and the Ross (1976) arbitrage theory and so forth?

The theory presented here derives part of its inspiration from Merton (1973). However, as pointed out by Hellwig (undated), Merton's intertemporal capital asset pricing model (ICAPM) is not a general equilibrium theory in the sense of Arrow-Debreu (i.e., the *technological* sources of uncertainty are not related to the equilibrium prices of the risky assets in Merton). We do that here and preserve the empirical tractability of Merton's formulation.

Basically what is done here is to modify the stochastic growth model of Brock and Mirman (1972) in order to put a nontrivial investment decision into the asset pricing model of Lucas (1978). This is done in such a way as to preserve the empirical tractability of the Merton formulation and at the same time determine the risk prices derived by Ross (1976) in his arbitrage theory of asset pricing. Ross's price of systematic risk k at date t

William A. Brock is associated with California Institute of Technology, the University of Chicago, and the University of Wisconsin, Madison.

denoted by λ_{kt} which is induced by the source of systematic risk $\tilde{\delta}_{kt}$ is determined by the covariance of the marginal utility of consumption with $\tilde{\delta}_{kt}$. In this way Ross's λ_{kt} are determined by the interaction of sources of production uncertainty and the demand for risky assets. Furthermore, our model provides a context in which conditions may be found on tastes and technology that are sufficient for equilibrium returns to be a linear function of the uncertainty in the economy. Linearity of returns is necessary for Ross's theory.

The paper proceeds as follows. Section 1.1 is the introduction. Section 1.2 presents an N process version of the 1 process stochastic growth model of Brock and Mirman (1972). The N process growth model will form the basis for the quantity side of the asset pricing model developed in section 1.3.

In section 1.2 it is indicated that optimum paths generated in the N process model are described by time independent continuous optimum policy functions à la Bellman. A functional equation is developed that determines the state valuation function using methods that are standard in the stochastic growth literature. It is also indicated that for any initial state the optimum stochastic process of investment converges in distribution to a limit distribution independent of the initial state. The detailed analysis of these questions is done in Brock (1979).

Section 1.3 converts the growth model of section 1.2 into an asset pricing model by introducing competitive rental markets for the capital goods and introducing a market for claims to the pure rents generated by the ith firm $i = 1, 2, \ldots, N$. Each of the N processes is identified with one "firm." Firms pay out rentals to consumers. The residual is pure rent. Paper claims to the pure rent generated by each firm i and a market for these claims is introduced along the lines of Lucas (1978).

Equilibrium is defined using the concept of rational expectations as in Lucas. That is, both sides of the economy possess subjective distributions on pure rents, capital rental rates, and share prices. Both sides draw up demand and supply schedules conditioned on their subjective distributions. Market clearing introduces an objective distribution on pure rents, capital rental rates, and share prices. A rational expectations equilibrium (REE) is defined by the requirement that the objective distribution equal the subjective distribution at each date. I hasten to add that no problems of incomplete information will be dealt with in this paper.

In section 1.3 it is shown using recent results of Benveniste and Scheinkman (1977) that the quantity side of an REE is identical to the quantity side of the N process growth model developed in section 1.2. The key idea used is the Benveniste-Scheinkman result that the standard transversality condition at infinity is *necessary* as well as sufficient for an infinite horizon concave programming problem.

The financial side of the economy is now easy to develop. A unique asset pricing function for stock i of the form $P_i(y)$ is shown to exist by use of a contraction mapping argument along the lines of Lucas.

Section 1.4 uses a special case of the model in section 1.3 to develop an intertemporal general equilibrium theory that determines the risk prices of Ross endogenously. Capital asset pricing formulas such as the Sharpe-Lintner certainty equivalence (SL) formula are derived in section 1.4. It is shown there that the SL formula can be derived only if the asset pricing function is linear in the state variable.

The convergence result in section 1.2 allows stationary time series methods based on the mean ergodic theorem to be used to estimate the risk prices of Ross, provided that the economy is in stochastic steady state.

In section 1.5 an explicit example of the N process model is solved for the optimum in closed form. The asset pricing function $P_i(y)$ turns out to be linear in output y for this case. The risk prices of Ross can also be calculated in closed form for the example.

Finally, the appendixes develop technical results that are needed but somewhat tangential to the main issue addressed in each section.

1.1.1 Notations

Equations are numbered consecutively within each section. Thus, for example, equation 2 in section 1.3 is written "(3.2)." Assumptions, theorems, lemmas, and remarks are numbered consecutively within each section. For example, assumption 2 in section 1.3 will be written "assumption 3.2."

The convention is the same in the appendixes except that "A" appears to separate entities from those in the main text. For example, assumption 2 in the appendix to section 1.3 will be written "assumption A3.2."

Finally, we should mention that after this paper was written we found the papers by Cox, Ingersoll, and Ross (1978) and by Prescott and Mehra (1977) which are similar in spirit to this paper. Other related papers are Johnsen (1978) and Richard (1978). Nevertheless, the question addressed and the methods used differ substantially in all of these papers.

1.2 The Optimal Growth Model

Since the model to be given below is studied in detail in Brock (1979), we shall be brief where possible.

The model is given by

$$(2.1) \qquad \max E_1 \sum_{t=1}^{\infty} \beta^{t-1} u(c_t),$$

$$(2.2) \qquad \text{s.t. } c_{t+1} + x_{t+1} - x_t = \sum_{i=1}^{N} [g_i(x_{it}, r_t) - \delta_i x_{it}],$$

$$(2.3) \qquad x_t = \sum_{i=1}^{N} x_{it}, x_{it} \geqq 0, i = 1, 2, \ldots, N, t = 0, 1, 2, \ldots,$$

$$(2.4) \qquad c_t \geqq 0, t = 1, 2, \ldots,$$

$$(2.5) \qquad x_0, x_{i0}, i = 1, 2, \ldots, N, r_0 \text{ historically given,}$$

where E_1, β, u, c_t, x_t, g_i, x_{it}, r_t, and δ_i denote mathematical expectation conditioned at time 1, discount factor on future utility, utility function of consumption, consumption at date t, capital stock at date t, production function of process i, capital allocated to process i at date t, random shock which is common to *all* processes i, and depreciation rate for capital installed in process i, respectively.

The space of $\{c_t\}_{t=1}^{\infty}$, $\{x_t\}_{t=1}^{\infty}$ over which the maximum is being taken in equation (2.1) needs to be specified. Obviously, decisions at date t should be based only upon information at date t. In order to make the choice space precise, some formalism is needed. We borrow from Brock and Majumdar (1978) at this point.

The *environment* will be represented by a sequence $\{r_t\}_{t=1}^{\infty}$ of real vector valued random variables which will be assumed to be independently and identically distributed. The common distribution of r_t is given by a measure $\mu: \mathcal{B}(R^m) \to [0,1]$, where $\mathcal{B}(R^m)$ is the Borel σ-field of R^m. In view of a well-known one-to-one correspondence (see, e.g., Loéve 1963, pp. 230–31), we can adequately represent the environment as a measure space $(\Omega, \mathcal{F}, \nu)$, where Ω is the set of all sequences of real m vectors, $\mathcal{F}$ is the σ-field generated by cylinder sets of the form

$$\underset{t=1}{\overset{\infty}{\pi}} A_t,$$

where

$$A_t \in \mathcal{B}(R^m), \qquad t = 1, 2, \ldots$$

and

$$A_t = R^m$$

for all but a finite number of values of t. Also ν (the stochastic law of the environment) is simply the product probability induced by μ (given the assumption of independence).

The random variables r_t may be viewed as the tth coordinate function on Ω; i.e., for any $\omega = \{\omega_t\}_{t=1}^{\infty} \in \Omega$, $r_t(\omega)$ is defined by

$$r_t(\omega) = \omega_t.$$

We shall refer to ω as a possible state of the environment (or an environment sequence) and to ω_t as the environment at date t. In what follows, $\mathcal{F}_t$ is the σ-field guaranteed by partial histories up to period t, (i.e., the smallest σ-field generated by cylinder sets of the form

$$\underset{\tau=1}{\overset{\infty}{\pi}} A_\tau,$$

where A_t is in $\mathcal{B}(R^m)$ for all t, and $A_\tau \in R^m$ for all $\tau > t$). The σ-field $\mathcal{F}_t$ contains all of the information about the environment which is available at date t.

In order to express precisely the fact that decisions c_t, x_t only depend upon information that is available at the time the decisions are made, we simply require that c_t, x_t be measurable with respect to $\mathcal{F}_t$.

Formally the maximization in (2.1) is taken over all stochastic processes $\{c_t\}_{t=1}^\infty$, $\{x_t\}_{t=1}^\infty$ that satisfy (2.2)–(2.5) and such that for each $t = 1$, $2, \ldots$, c_t, x_t are measurable with respect to $\mathcal{F}_t$. Call such processes "admissible."

Existence of an optimum $\{c_t\}_{t=1}^\infty$, $\{x_t\}_{t=1}^\infty$ may be established by imposing an appropriate topology $\mathcal{T}$ on the space of admissible processes such that the objective (2.1) is continuous in this topology and the space of admissible processes is $\mathcal{T}$-compact. While it is beyond the scope of this article to discuss existence, presumably a proof can be constructed along the lines of Bewley (1972).

The notation almost makes the working of the model self-explanatory. There are N different processes. At date t it is decided how much to consume and how much to hold in the form of capital. It is assumed that capital goods can be costlessly transformed into consumption goods on a one-for-one basis. After it is decided how much capital to hold then it is decided how to allocate the capital across the N processes. After the allocation is decided nature reveals the value of r_t, and $g_i(x_{it}, r_t)$ units of new production are available from process i at the end of period t. But $\delta_i x_{it}$ units of capital have evaporated at the end of t. Thus, the net new produce is $g_i(x_{it}, r_t) - \delta_i x_{it}$ from process i. The total produce available to be divided into consumption and capital stock at date $t+1$ is given by

$$(2.6) \quad \sum_{i=1}^N [g_i(x_{it}, r_t) - \delta_i x_{it}] + x_t = \sum_{i=1}^N [g_i(x_{it}, r_t) + (1 - \delta_i)x_{it}]$$

$$\equiv \sum_{i=1}^N f_i(x_{it}, r_t) \equiv y_{t+1},$$

where

$$(2.7) \quad f_i(x_{it}, r_t) \equiv g_i(x_{it}, r_t) + (1 - \delta_i)x_{it}$$

denotes the total amount of produce emerging from process i at the end of period t. The produce y_{t+1} is divided into consumption and capital stock at the beginning of date $t+1$, and so on it goes.

Note that we are assuming that it is costless to install capital into each process i and it is costless to allocate capital across processes at the beginning of each date t.

The objective of the optimizer is to maximize the expected value of the discounted sum of utilities over all consumption paths and capital allocations that satisfy (2.2)–(2.5).

In order to obtain sharp results we will place restrictive assumptions on this problem. We collect the basic working assumptions into one place:

Assumption 2.1. The functions $u(\cdot), f_i(\cdot)$, are all concave, increasing, and twice continuously differentiable.

Assumption 2.2. The stochastic process $\{r_t\}_{t=1}^{\infty}$ is independently and identically distributed. Each r_t: $(\Omega, \mathcal{B}, \mu) \rightarrow R^m$, where $(\Omega, \mathcal{B}, \mu)$ is a probability space. Here Ω is the space of elementary events, $\mathcal{B}$ is the σ-field of measurable sets with respect to μ, and μ is a probability measure defined on subsets $B \subseteq \Omega$, $B \in \mathcal{B}$. Furthermore, the range of r_t, $r_t(\Omega)$, is *compact*.

Assumption 2.3. For each $\{x_{i1}\}_{i=1}^{N}$, r_1 the problem (1) *has* a unique optimal solution (unique up to a set of realizations of $\{r_t\}$ of measure zero).

Notice that assumption 2.3 is implied by assumption 1 and *strict* concavity of u, $\{f_i\}_{i=1}^{N}$. Rather than try to find the weakest possible assumptions sufficient for uniqueness of solutions to (2.1), it seemed simpler to reveal the role of uniqueness in what follows by simply *assuming* it. Furthermore, since we are not interested in the study of existence of optimal solutions in this article, we have simply assumed that also.

By assumption 2.3 we see that to each output level y_t, optimum c_t, x_t, x_{it}, given y_t, may be written

(2.8) $$c_t = g(y_t), x_t = h(y_t), x_{it} = h_i(y_t).$$

The optimum policy functions $g(\cdot)$, $h(\cdot)$, $h_i(\cdot)$ do not depend upon t because the problem given by (2.1)–(2.5) is time stationary.

Another useful optimum policy function may be obtained. Given x_t, r_t assumption 2.3 implies that the optimal allocation $\{x_{it}\}_{i=1}^{N}$ and next periods' optimal capital stock x_{t+1} is unique. Furthermore, these may be written in the form

(2.9) $$x_{it} = a_i(x_t, r_{t-1}),$$

(2.10) $$x_{t+1} = H(x_t, r_t).$$

Equations (2.9), (2.10) contain r_{t-1}, r_t, respectively, because the allocation decision is made after r_{t-1} is known but before r_t is revealed but the capital-consumption decision is made after y_{t+1} is revealed (i.e., after r_t is known).

Equation (2.10) looks very much like the optimal stochastic process studied by Brock and Mirman, and Mirman and Zilcha. It was shown in Brock and Mirman (1972, 1973) for the case $N = 1$ that the stochastic difference equation (2.10) converges in distribution to a unique limit distribution independent of initial conditions. We show in Brock (1979) that the same result may be obtained for our N process model by following the argument of Mirman and Zilcha. We collect some facts here that are established in Brock (1979).

Result 2.1. Adopt assumption 2.1. Let $U(y_1)$ denote the maximum value of the objective in (2.1) given initial resource stock y_1. Then $U(y_1)$ is concave and nondecreasing in y_1, and for each $y_1 > 0$ the derivative $U'(y_1)$ exists and is nonincreasing in y_1.

Proof. Mirman and Zilcha (1977) prove in their equation (2) that

$$U'(y_1) = u'(g(y_1)), \qquad \text{for } y_1 > 0,$$

for the case $N = 1$. The same argument may be used here. The details are left to the reader.

Remark 2.1. Equation (a) shows that $g(y_1)$ is nondecreasing since $u''(c) < 0$ and $U'(y)$ is nonincreasing in y as a result of the concavity of $U(\bullet)$.

Result 2.2. Adopt assumption 2.1. Also assume that units of utility may be chosen so that $u(c) \geq 0$, for all c. Furthermore, assume that along optima,

$$E_1 \beta^{t-1} U(y_t) \to 0, \qquad \text{as } t \to \infty.$$

If $\{c_t\}_{t=1}^\infty, \{x_t\}_{t=1}^\infty, \{x_{it}\}_{i=1}^N, t = 1, 2, \ldots,$ is optimal, the following conditions must be satisfied: for each i, t

$(2.10a)$ $\qquad u'(c_t) \geq \beta E_t\{u'(c_{t+1}) f_i'(x_{it}, r_t)\},$

$(2.10b)$ $\qquad u'(c_t) x_{it} = \beta E_t\{u'(c_{t+1}) f_i'(x_{it}, r_t) x_{it}\},$

and

$(2.10c)$ $\qquad \lim_{t \to \infty} E_1\{\beta^{t-1} u'(c_t) x_t\} = 0.$

Proof. The proof proceeds much like the proof of lemma 3.1, which is given in section 1.3 below. For details see Brock (1979).

Lemma 2.1. Assume that $u'(c) > 0$, $u''(c) < 0$, $u'(0) = +\infty$. Furthermore, assume that $f_j(0, r) = 0$, $f_j'(x, r) > 0$, $f_j''(x, r) \leq 0$ for all values of r. Also, suppose that there is a set of r values with positive probability such that f_j is strictly concave in x. Then the function $h(y)$ is continuous in y, increasing in y, and 0 when $y = 0$.

Proof. See Brock (1979).

Now by assumption 2.3 and equations (2.8)–(2.10) it follows that y_{t+1} may be written

(2.11) $\qquad y_{t+1} = F(x_t, r_t).$

Following Mirman and Zilcha (1977), define

(2.12) $\qquad \underline{F}(x) \equiv \min_{r \in R} F(x, r), \quad \overline{F}(x) \equiv \max_{r \in R} F(x, r),$

where R is the range of the random variable

$$r:(\Omega, \mathscr{B}, \mu) \to R^m,$$

which is compact by assumption 2.2. The following lemma shows that $\underline{F}$, $\overline{F}$ are well defined.

Lemma 2.2. The function $F(x,r)$ is continuous in r.

Proof. See Brock (1979).

Let $\underline{x}$, $\bar{x}$ be *any* two fixed points of the functions

(2.13) $$\underline{H}(x) \equiv h(\underline{F}(x)), \overline{H}(x) \equiv h(\overline{F}(x)),$$

respectively. Then

Lemma 2.3. Any two fixed points of the pair of functions defined in (2.13) must satisfy

(2.14) $$\underline{x} \leq \bar{x}.$$

Proof. See Brock (1979).

We may apply arguments similar to Brock and Mirman (1972) and prove

Theorem 2.1: There is a distribution function $F(x)$ of the optimum aggregate capital stock x such that

$$F_t(x) \to F(x)$$

uniformly for all x: Furthermore, $F(x)$ does not depend on the initial conditions (x_0, r_0).

Proof. See Brock (1979).

Here

(2.15) $$F_t(x) \equiv \text{prob}\{x_t \leq x\}.$$

Theorem 2.1 shows that the distribution of optimum aggregate capital stock at date t, $F_t(x)$, converges pointwise to a limit distribution $F(x)$.

Theorem 2.1 is important because we will use the optimal growth model to construct equilibrium asset prices and risk prices. Since these prices will be time stationary functions of x_t and since x_t converges in distribution to F, we will be able to use the mean ergodic theorem and stationary time series methods to make statistical inferences about these prices on the basis of time series observations.

1.2.1   The Price of Systematic Risk

Steve Ross (1976) produced a theory of capital asset pricing that showed that the assumption that all systematic risk free portfolios earn the risk free rate of return plus the assumption that asset returns are generated by a K factor model leads to the existence of "prices" $\lambda_0, \lambda_1, \lambda_2,$ . . . , λ_K on mean returns and on each of the K factors. These prices satisfied the property that expected returns $E\widetilde{\mathfrak{X}}_i \equiv a_i$ on each asset i were a linear function of the standard deviation of the returns on asset i with respect to each factor k; i.e.,

$$(2.16) \qquad a_i = \lambda_0 + \sum_{k=1}^{K} \lambda_k b_{ki}, \qquad i = 1, 2, \ldots, N,$$

where the original model of asset returns is given by

$$(2.17) \qquad \widetilde{\mathfrak{X}}_i = a_i + \sum_{k=1}^{K} b_{ki}\widetilde{\delta}_k + \widetilde{\epsilon}_i, \qquad i = 1, 2, \ldots, N.$$

Here $\widetilde{\mathfrak{X}}_i$ denotes random ex ante anticipated returns from holding the asset one unit of time; $\widetilde{\delta}_k$ is systematic risk emanating from factor k; $\widetilde{\epsilon}_i$ is unsystematic risk specific to asset i; and a_i, b_{ki} are constants. Assume that the means of $\widetilde{\delta}_k$, $\widetilde{\epsilon}_i$ are zero for each k, i; that $\widetilde{\epsilon}_1, \ldots, \widetilde{\epsilon}_N$ are independent; and that $\widetilde{\delta}_k$, $\widetilde{\epsilon}_i$ are uncorrelated random variables with finite variances for each k, i.

Ross proved that $\lambda_0, \lambda_1, \ldots, \lambda_K$ exist that satisfy (2.16) by forming portfolios $\eta \in R^N$ such that

$$(2.18) \qquad \sum_{i=1}^{N} \eta_i = 0,$$

by constructing the η_i such that the coefficients of each $\widetilde{\delta}_k$ in the portfolio returns

$$(2.19) \qquad \sum_{i=1}^{N} \eta_i \widetilde{\mathfrak{X}}_i = \sum_{i=1}^{N} \eta_i [a_i + \sum_{k=1}^{K} b_{ki}\widetilde{\delta}_k + \widetilde{\epsilon}_i]$$

$$= \sum_{i=1}^{N} \eta_i a_i + \sum_{k=1}^{K} (\sum_{i=1}^{N} b_{ki}\eta_i)\widetilde{\delta}_k + \sum_{i=1}^{N} \eta_i \widetilde{\epsilon}_i$$

are zero, and by requiring that

$$(2.20) \qquad \sum_{i=1}^{N} \eta_i a_i = 0$$

for all such systematic risk free zero wealth portfolios.

Here (2.18) corresponds to the zero wealth condition. The condition,

$$(2.21) \qquad 0 = \sum_{i=1}^{N} b_{ki}\eta_i, \qquad k = 1, 2, \ldots, K,$$

corresponds to the systematic risk free condition. Actually Ross did not require that (2.20) hold for *all* zero wealth systematic risk free portfolios but only for those that are "well diversified" in the sense that the η_i are of comparable size so that he could use the assumption of independence of $\widetilde{\epsilon}_1, \ldots, \widetilde{\epsilon}_N$ to argue that the random variable

$$\sum_{i=1}^{N} \eta_i \widetilde{\epsilon}_i$$

was "small" and hence bears a small price in a world of investors who would pay a positive price only for the avoidance of risks that could *not* be diversified away.

Out of this type of argument Ross argues that the condition: for all $\eta \in R^N$

$$(2.22a) \qquad \sum_{i=1}^{N} \eta_i = 0, \ \sum_{i=1}^{N} \eta_i b_{ki} = 0, \ k = 1, 2, \ldots, K,$$

implies that in *equilibrium*

$$(2.22b) \qquad \sum_{i=1}^{N} \eta_i a_i = 0$$

should hold.

All that (2.22) says is that zero wealth, zero systematic risk portfolios should earn a zero mean rate of return. Condition (2.22) is economically compelling because in its absence rather obvious arbitrage opportunities appear to exist.

Whatever the case, (2.22) implies that there exists $\lambda_0, \lambda_1, \lambda_2, \ldots, \lambda_K$ such that (2.16) holds and the proof is just simple linear algebra. Notice that Ross made no assumptions about mean variance investor utility functions or normal distributions of asset returns common to the usual Sharpe-Lintner type of asset pricing theories which are standard in the finance literature.

However, Ross's model, like the standard capital asset pricing models in finance, does not link the asset returns to underlying sources of uncertainty. Our growth model will be used as a module in the construction of an intertemporal general equilibrium asset pricing model where relationships of the form (2.17) are determined within the model and hence the $\lambda_0, \lambda_1, \ldots, \lambda_K$ will be determined within the model as well. Such a model of asset price determination preserves the beauty and empirical tractability of the Ross-Sharpe-Lintner formulation, but at the same time will give us a context where we can ask general equilibrium questions such as, What is the impact of an increase of the progressivity of the income tax on the demand for and supply of risky assets and the $\lambda_0, \lambda_1, \ldots, \lambda_K$?

Let us get on with relating the growth model to (2.16). For simplicity assume all processes i are active (i.e., (2.10a) holds with equality). We record (2.10a) here for convenience.

$$(2.23) \qquad u'(c_t) = \beta E_t \{u'(c_{t+1}) f_i'(x_{it}, r_t)\}.$$

Now (2.17) is a special hypothesis about asset returns. What kind of hypothesis about "technological" uncertainty corresponds to (2.17)? Well, as an example, put for each $i = 1, 2, \ldots, N$

$$(2.24) \ f_i(x_{it}, r_t) \equiv (A_{it}^0 + A_{it}^1 \tilde{\delta}_{1t} + A_{it}^2 \tilde{\delta}_{2t} + \ldots + A_{it}^K \tilde{\delta}_{Kt}) f_i(x_{it}) \equiv r_{it} f_i(x_{it}),$$

where

$$A_{it}^k \equiv A_i^k$$

are constants and

$$\{\tilde{\delta}_{kt}\}_{t=1}^{\infty}$$

are independent and identically distributed random variables for each k and for each k, t the mean of $\tilde{\delta}_{kt}$ is zero, the variance is finite, and $\tilde{\delta}_{st}$ is independent of $\tilde{\delta}_{kt}$ for each s, k, t. Furthermore, assume that $f(\cdot)$ is concave, increasing, and twice differentiable, that $f'(0) = +\infty$, that $f'(\infty) = 0$, and that there is a bound ϵ_0 such that

$$r_{it} > \epsilon_0 > 0$$

with probability 1 for all t_1. These assumptions are stronger than necessary, but will enable us to avoid concern with technical tangentialities. Define, for all t,

$$\tilde{\delta}_{0t} \equiv 1,$$

so that we may sum from $k = 0$ to K in (2.25) below.

Insert (2.24) into (2.23) to get for all t, k, i

$$(2.25) \qquad u'(c_t) = \beta E_t\{u'(c_{t+1})(\sum_{k=0}^{K} A_{it}^k \tilde{\delta}_{kt})f_i'(x_{it})\}$$

$$= \sum_{k=0}^{K} ([A_{it}^k f_i'(x_{it})]E_t\{\beta u'(c_{t+1})\tilde{\delta}_{kt}\}).$$

Now set (2.25) aside for a moment and look at the marginal benefit of saving one unit of capital and assigning it to process i at the beginning of period t. At the end of period t, r_t is revealed and extra produce

$$(2.26) \qquad \mathcal{Y}_{it} \equiv A_{it}^0 f_i'(x_{it}) + \sum_{k=1}^{K} A_{it}^k f_i'(x_{it})\tilde{\delta}_{kt}$$

emerges.

Putting

$$(2.27) \qquad a_i \equiv A_{it}^0 f_i'(x_{it}), b_{ki} \equiv A_{it}^k f_i'(x_{it}), \tilde{\delta}_{kt} = \tilde{\delta}_k,$$

equation (2.26) is identical with Ross's (2.17) with $\tilde{\epsilon}_i \equiv 0$. We proceed now to generate the analogue to (2.16) in our model. Turn back to (2.25). Rewrite (2.25) using (2.27) thus:

$$(2.28) \qquad u'(c_t) = \sum_{k=1}^{K} b_{ki} E_t\{\beta u'(c_{t+1})\tilde{\delta}_{kt}\} + a_i E_t\{\beta u'(c_{t+1})\}.$$

Hence,

$$(2.29) \quad a_i = \frac{u'(c_t)}{\beta E_t\{u'(c_{t+1})\}} \sum_{k=1}^{K} b_{ki}(E_t\{u'(c_{t+1})\tilde{\delta}_{kt}\}/E_t\{u'(c_{t+1})\})$$

so that $\lambda_0, \lambda_1, \ldots, \lambda_K$ defined by

$$(2.30) \quad \lambda_0 \equiv u'(c_t)/\beta E_t\{u'(c_{t+1})\}, \quad -\lambda_k \equiv E_t\{u'(c_{t+1})\tilde{\delta}_{kt}\}/E_t\{u'(c_{t+1})\}$$
$$= \lambda_0 \text{ covariance } [\beta u'(c_{t+1})/u'(c_t), \tilde{\delta}_{kt}]$$

yields

$$(2.31) \qquad\qquad a_i = \lambda_0 + \sum_{k=1}^{K} b_{ki}\lambda_k.$$

Here t subscripts have been dropped.

These results are extremely suggestive and show that the model studied in this section may be quite rich in economic content. Although the model is a normative model, in the next section we shall turn it into an equilibrium asset pricing model so that the λ_k become equilibrium risk prices. Let us explore the economic meanings of (2.30) in some detail.

Suppose that $K = 1$ and that there is a risk free asset N in the sense that

$$(2.32) \qquad\qquad b_{N1} \equiv A_{Nt}^1 f'(x_{Nt}) = 0;$$

i.e.,

$$(2.33) \qquad\qquad A_{Nt}^1 = 0.$$

Then by (2.33)

$$(2.34) \qquad\qquad a_N = \lambda_0, a_i = a_N + b_{1i}\lambda_1$$

so that for all $i, j \neq N$

$$(2.35) \qquad\qquad (a_i - a_N)/b_{1i} = (a_j - a_N)/b_{1j}.$$

The second part of equation (2.34) corresponds to the security market line which says that expected return and risk are linearly related in a one-factor model. Equation (2.35) corresponds to the usual Sharpe-Lintner-Mossin capital asset pricing model result that in equilibrium the "excess return" per unit of risk must be equated across all assets.

The economic interpretation of λ_0 given in (2.30) is well known and needs no explanation here. Look at the formula for λ_k. The covariance of the marginal utility of consumption at time $t + 1$ with the zero mean finite variance shock $\tilde{\delta}_{kt}$ appears in the numerator. Since output increases when $\tilde{\delta}_{kt}$ increases and since

$$c_{t+1} = g(y_{t+1})$$

doesn't decrease when y_{t+1} increases, this covariance is likely to be negative so that the sign of λ_k is positive. We will look into the determinants of the magnitudes of $\lambda_0, \lambda_1, \ldots, \lambda_K$ in more detail later. Let us show how our model may be helpful in the empirical problem in estimating the $\lambda_0, \lambda_1, \ldots, \lambda_K$ from time series data.

First, how is one to close Ross's model (2.17) since the $\mathscr{L}_i$ are *subjective*? The most natural way to close the model in markets as well organized as United States securities markets would seem to be rational expectations: the subjective distribution of $\mathscr{L}_i$ is equal to the actual or objective distribution of $\mathscr{L}_i$. We shall show that our asset pricing model under rational expectations which is developed below generates the same solution as the normative model discussed above. Hence, the convergence theorem implies that $\{x_t, c_t, x_{1t}\ x_{2t}, \ldots, x_{Nt}\}_{t=1}^{\infty}$ converges to a stationary stochastic process.

Thus, the mean ergodic theorem, which says very loosely that the *time* average of any function G of a stationary stochastic process equals the *average* of G over the stationary distribution of that process, allows us to apply time series methods developed for stationary stochastic processes to estimate $\lambda_0, \lambda_1, \ldots, \lambda_K$. Let us turn to development of the asset pricing model.

1.3   An Asset Pricing Model

In this section we reinterpret the model of section 1.2 and add to it a market for claims to pure rents so that it describes the evolution of equilibrium context in which to discuss the martingale property of capital asset prices, but also our model will contain a nontrivial investment decision and a nontrivial market for claims to pure rents (i.e., a stock market), as well as a market for the pricing of the physical capital stock.

We believe that there is a considerable benefit in showing how to turn optimal growth models into asset pricing models. This is so because there is a large literature on stochastic growth models which may be carried over to the asset pricing problem with little effort. Although the model presented here is somewhat artificial, we believe that studying it will yield techniques that can be used to study less artificial models.

We will build an asset pricing model much like that of Lucas (1978). The model contains one representative consumer whose preferences are identical to the planner's preferences given in equation (2.1). The model contains N different firms which rent capital from the consumption side at rate R_{t+1} at each date so as to maximize

$$(3.1) \qquad \pi_{it+1} \equiv f_i(x_{it}, r_t) - R_{i,t+1} x_{it}.$$

Notice that it is assumed that each firm i makes its decision to hire x_{it} *after* r_t is revealed. Here $R_{i,t+1}$ denotes the rental rate on capital prevailing in industry i at date $t+1$. It is to be determined within the model. These "rental markets" are rather artificial. They are introduced in order to obtain lemma 3.2 below.

The model will introduce a stock market in such a way that the real quantity side of the model is the same as that of the growth model in equilibrium. Our model is closed under the assumption of rational expectations. The quantity side of the model is essentially an Arrow-Debreu model as is the model of Lucas. That is, we will introduce securities markets in such a way that there are enough securities such that any equilibrium is a Pareto optimum. However, there is a separate market where claims to the rents (3.1) are competitively traded. In Arrow-Debreu the rents are redistributed in a lump sum fashion.

Market institutions may be introduced into the model of section 1.2 in an alternative manner than that done here in section 1.3. This alternative formulation enables us to link the theory up with the Modigliani-Miller (MM) formulation in their famous article on the variance of firm value to dividend policy. We sketch this alternative model in the appendix to section 1.3.

The model is in the spirit of Lucas's model, where each firm i has outstanding one perfectly divisible equity share. Ownership of $\alpha\%$ of the equity shares in firm i at date t entitles one to $\alpha\%$ of profits of the firm i at date $t+1$. Equilibrium asset prices and equilibrium consumption, capital, and output are determined by optimization under the hypothesis of rational expectations much as in Lucas. Let us get on with the model.

1.3.1.   The Model

There is one representative consumer (or a "representative standin," as Lucas calls him) that is assumed to solve

$$(3.2) \qquad \max E_1 \sum_{t=1}^{\infty} \beta^{t-1} u(c_t)$$

subject to

$$(3.3) \quad c_t + x_t + \underset{\sim}{P}_t \cdot \underset{\sim}{Z}_t \le \underset{\sim}{\pi}_t \cdot \underset{\sim}{Z}_{t-1} + \underset{\sim}{P}_t \cdot \underset{\sim}{Z}_{t-1} + \sum_{i=1}^{N} R_{it} x_{i,t-1} \equiv y_t,$$

$$(3.4) \quad c_t \ge 0, x_t \ge 0, \underset{\sim}{Z}_t \ge 0, x_{it} \ge 0, \qquad i = 1, 2, \ldots, N, \text{ all } t,$$

$$(3.5) \quad c_1 + x_1 + \underset{\sim}{P}_1 \cdot \underset{\sim}{Z}_0 \le \underset{\sim}{\pi}_1 \cdot \underset{\sim}{Z}_0 + \underset{\sim}{P}_1 \cdot \underset{\sim}{Z}_0 + \sum_{i=1}^{N} R_{i1} x_{i0} \equiv y_1,$$

$$Z_0 \equiv 1, R_{i1} \equiv f_i'(x_{i0}, r_0), \pi_{i1} \equiv f_i'(x_{i0}, r_0) - f_i'(x_{i0}, r_0) x_{i0}, x_0, \{x_{i0}\}_{i=1}^{N}$$

given, where c_t, x_t, P_{it}, Z_{it}, π_{it}, R_{it} (all assumed measurable $\mathscr{F}_t$) denote consumption at date t, total capital stock owned at date t by the consumer, price of one share of firm i at date t, number of shares of firm i owned by the individual at date t, profits of firm i at date t, and rental factor (i.e., $R_{it} \equiv$ principal plus interest) obtained on a unit of capital leased to firm i. Here "$\cdot$" denotes scalar product.

Firm i is assumed to hire x_{it} so as to maximize (3.1).[2] The consumer is assumed to lease capital x_{it} at date t to firm i before r_t is revealed. Hence $R_{i,t+1}$ is uncertain at date t. The consumer, in order to solve his problem at date 1 must form expectations on $\{P_{it}\}_{t=1}^{\infty}$, $\{R_{it}\}_{t=1}^{\infty}$, $\{\pi_t\}_{t=1}^{\infty}$ and maximize (3.2) subject to (3.3)–(3.5). In this way notional demands for consumption goods and equities as well as notional supplies of capital stocks and capital services to each of the N firms are drawn up by the consumer side of the economy. Similarly for the firm side. We close the model with

Definition. The stochastic process $\mathscr{R} \equiv \langle\{\bar{P}_{it}\}_{t=1}^{\infty}, \{\bar{R}_{it}\}_{t=1}^{\infty}, \{\bar{\pi}_{it}\}_{t=1}^{\infty};$ $\{\bar{x}_{it}\}_{t=1}^{\infty}, \{\bar{Z}_{it}\}_{t=1}^{\infty}, i = 1, 2, \ldots, N, \{\bar{c}_t\}_{t=1}^{\infty}, \{\bar{x}_t\}_{t=1}^{\infty}\rangle$ is a *rational expectations equilibrium* (REE) if, facing $\mathscr{P} \equiv \langle\{\bar{P}_{it}\}_{t=1}^{\infty}, \{\bar{R}_{it}\}_{t=1}^{\infty}, \{\bar{\pi}_{it}\}_{t=1}^{\infty}\rangle$, the consumer solves (3.2) and chooses

$$(3.6) \qquad x_t = \bar{x}_t, \; x_{it} = \bar{x}_{it}, \; c_t = \bar{c}_t, \; Z_{it} = \bar{Z}_{it} \qquad \text{a.e.,}$$

and the ith firm solves (3.1) and chooses

$$(3.7) \qquad x_{it} = \bar{x}_{it},$$

and furthermore

(3.8) (asset market clears) $\bar{Z}_{it} \leq 1, \text{if } \bar{Z}_{it} < 1, \bar{P}_{it} = 0$ a.e.,

(3.9) (goods market clears) $\bar{c}_t + \bar{x}_t = \sum\limits_{i=1}^{N} f_i(\bar{x}_{i,t-1}, r_{t-1})$ a.e.,

(3.10) (capital market clears) $\sum\limits_{i=1}^{N} \bar{x}_{it} = \bar{x}_t$ a.e.

Here "a.e." means "almost everywhere." This ends the definition of REE that we will use in this paper.

It is easy to write down first-order necessary conditions for an REE. Let us start on the consumer side first. We drop upper bars to ease typing. At date t, if the consumer buys a share of firm i, the cost is P_{it} units of consumption goods. The marginal cost at date t in utils foregone is $u'(c_t)P_{it}$. At the end of period t, r_t is revealed and $P_{i,t+1}, \pi_{i,t+1}$ become known. Hence, the consumer obtains

$$(3.11) \qquad u'(c_{t+1}) \, (P_{i,t+1} + \pi_{i,t+1})$$

extra utils at the beginning of $t+1$ if he collects $\pi_{i,t+1}$ and sells the share "exdividend" at $P_{i,t+1}$. But these utils are uncertain and are received one period into the future. The expected present value of utility gained at $t+1$ is

$$(3.12) \qquad \beta E_t\{u'(c_{t+1}) \, (P_{i,t+1} + \pi_{i,t+1})\}.$$

Consumer equilibrium in the market for asset i requires that the marginal opportunity cost at date t be greater than or equal to the present value of the marginal benefit of dividends and exdividend sale price at date $t+1i$:

$(3.13a)$ $P_{it}u'(c_t) \geq \beta E_t\{u'(c_{t+1}) \, (\pi_{i,t+1} + P_{i,t+1})\}$ a.e.

$(3.13b)$ $P_{it}u'(c_t)Z_{it} = \beta E_t\{u'(c_{t+1}) \, (\pi_{i,t+1} + P_{i,t+1})\}Z_{it}$ a.e.

Similar reasoning in the rental market yields

(3.14a) $$u'(c_t) \geqq \beta E_t \{u'(c_{t+1}) (R_{i,t+1})\} \qquad \text{a.e.}$$

(3.14b) $$u'(c_t)x_{it} = BE_t\{u'(c_{t+1}) (R_{i,t+1})\}x_{it} \qquad \text{a.e.}$$

It would be nice if the first-order necessary conditions (3.13)–(3.14) characterized consumer optima. But it is well known that a "transversality condition" at infinity is needed in addition to completely characterize optima. Recent work by Benveniste and Scheinkman (1977) allows us to prove

Lemma 3.1: Adopt assumption 2.1. Furthermore, assume that $\mathcal{P}$ is such that $W(y_t,t) \to 0$, $t \to \infty$, where $W(y_t,t)$ is defined by

(3.15) $$W(y_t,t) = \max E_1 \sum_{s=t}^{\infty} \beta^{s-1}u(c_s)$$

subject to (3.3)–(3.5) with t replaced by s and 1 replaced by t. Here y_t denotes the right-hand side (R.H.S.) of (3.3). Then, given $\{P_{it}\}_{t=1}^{\infty}$, $\{\pi_{it}\}_{t=1}^{\infty}$, $\{R_{it}\}_{t=1}^{\infty}$, $i = 1, 2, \ldots N$ optimum solutions $\{Z_{it}\}_{t=1}^{\infty}$, $\{x_{it}\}_{t=1}^{\infty}$, $i = 1, 2, \ldots, N$, $\{c_t\}_{t=1}^{\infty}$, $\{x_t\}_{t=1}^{\infty}$ to the consumer's problem (3.2) subject to (3.3)–(3.5) are *characterized* by (3.13)–(3.14) and

(3.16) TVC_∞ (equity market) $\lim\limits_{t\to\infty} E_1 \{\beta^{t-1}u'(c_t) \underline{P}_t \cdot \underline{Z}_t\} = 0,$

(3.17) TVC_∞ (capital market) $\lim\limits_{t\to\infty} E_1 \{\beta^{t-1}u'(c_t) x_t\} = 0.$

Proof: Suppose $\{\underline{\bar{Z}}_t\}, \{\bar{c}_t\}, \{\bar{x}_t\}$ satisfies (3.13)–(3.17), and let $\{\underline{Z}_t\}, \{c_t\}, \{x_t\}$ be any stochastic process satisfying the same initial conditions and (3.3)–(3.5). Compute for each T an upper bound to the shortfall:

(3.18) $$E_1\{\sum_{t=1}^{T} \beta^{t-1}u(c_t) - \sum_{t=1}^{T} \beta^{t-1}u(\bar{c}_t)\}$$

(3.19) $$\leqq E_1\{\sum_{t=1}^{T} \beta^{t-1}u'(\bar{c}_t)(c_t - \bar{c}_t)\}$$

(3.20) $$= E_1\{\sum_{t=1}^{T} \beta^{t-1}u'(\bar{c}_t)[\underline{\pi}_t \cdot \underline{Z}_{t-1} + \underline{P}_t \cdot \underline{Z}_{t-1} + \sum_{i=1}^{N} R_{it}x_{i,t-1}$$

$$- \underline{P}_t \cdot \underline{Z}_t - x_t - \underline{\pi}_t \cdot \underline{\bar{Z}}_{t-1} - \underline{P}_t \cdot \underline{\bar{Z}}_{t-1} - \sum_{i=1}^{N} R_{it}\bar{x}_{i,t-1}$$

$$+ \underline{P}_t \cdot \underline{\bar{Z}}_t + \bar{x}_t]\}$$

(3.21) $$= E_1 \{\beta^{T-1}u'(\bar{c}_T)[\underline{P}_T \cdot (\underline{\bar{Z}}_T - \underline{Z}_T) + \bar{x}_T - x_T]\}$$

(3.22) $$\leqq E_1 \{\beta^{T-1}u'(\bar{c}_T)[\underline{P}_T \cdot (\underline{\bar{Z}}_T + \bar{x}_T]\} \to 0, T \to \infty.$$

Here equations (3.13)–(3.14) were used to telescope out the middle terms in the series of R.H.S. (3.20).

The terms corresponding to date 1 cancel each other because the initial conditions are the same. Hence, only the terms of R.H.S. (3.21) remain of all the terms of R.H.S. (3.19) and (3.20). That R.H.S. (3.21) has an asymptotic upper bound of zero follows from (3.16), (3.17), and the nonnegativity of Z_T, x_T. This shows that (3.13)–(3.14), (3.16)–(3.17) imply optimality. Notice that no assumptions on $W(y_t,t)$ are needed to get this side of the proof.

Now let $\{\bar{Z}_t\}$, $\{\bar{c}_t\}$, $\{\bar{x}_t\}$ be optimal given $\{P_t, R_t, \pi_t\}$. Since $u'(0) = +\infty$ implies that $\bar{c}_t > 0$ a.e. and W is differentiable at $\bar{y}_t$, we have by concavity of W, and $u \geq 0$ (dropping upper bars from this point on),

(3.23) $W(y_t,t) \geq W(y_t,t) - W(y_t/2,t) \geq W'(y_t,t)(y_t/2) = \beta^{t-1}u'(c_t)y_t/2$.

Hence,

(3.24) $E_1 W(y_t,t) \to 0, t \to \infty$ implies $E_1 \beta^{t-1}u'(c_t)y_t \to 0, t \to \infty$.

But

(3.25) $y_t \equiv \pi_t \cdot Z_{t-1} + P_t \cdot Z_{t-1} + \sum_i R_{it}x_{i,t-1}$

so that, by the first-order necessary conditions,

(3.26) $E_1 \beta^{t-1}u'(c_t)((\pi_t + P_t) \cdot Z_{t-1} + \sum_i R_{it}x_{i,t-1})$

$= E_1 \beta^{t-2}u'(c_{t-1})P_{t-1} \cdot Z_{t-1} + E_1 \beta^{t-2}u'(c_{t-1})x_{t-1}$

because (in more detail) (3.13a)–(3.14b) imply

(3.27) $x_{i,t-1}u'(c_{t-1}) = \beta E_{t-1}\{u'(c_t)R_{it}\}x_{i,t-1}$,

(3.28) $\beta^{-1}x_{t-1}u'(c_{t-1}) = E_{t-1}\{u'(c_t)(\sum_i R_{it}x_{i,t-1})\}$,

(3.29) $P_{i,t-1}u'(c_{t-1})Z_{i,t-1} = \beta E_{t-1}\{u'(c_t)(\pi_{it} + P_{it})Z_{i,t-1}\}$,

(3.30) $\beta^{-1}u'(c_{t-1})P_{t-1} \cdot Z_{t-1} = E_{t-1}\{u'(c_t)(\pi_t \cdot Z_{t-1} + P_t \cdot Z_{t-1})\}$.

Hence, because $P_{t-1} \geq 0$, $Z_{t-1} \geq 0$, and $x_{t-1} \geq 0$, (3.24) implies

(3.31) $E_1 \beta^{t-2}u'(c_{t-1})P_{t-1} \cdot Z_{t-1} \to 0, \qquad t \to \infty$,

(3.32) $E_1 \beta^{t-2}u'(c_{t-1})x_{t-1} \to 0, \qquad t \to \infty$,

as was to be shown.

The first part of this argument follows Malinvaud (1953), and the second part is adapted from Benveniste and Scheinkman (1977). Lemma 3.1 is important because it shows that (3.13)–(3.14), (3.16), (3.17) *characterize* consumer optima.

Remark 3.1. The assumption that $E_1W(y_t, t) \to 0, t \to \infty$, restrains $\mathcal{P}$. It requires that $\mathcal{P}$ be such that along any path in $\mathcal{P}$ utils cannot grow faster than β^t on the average. A general sufficient condition on $\mathcal{P}$ for $E_1W(y_t,t)$

→ 0 can be given by what should be a straightforward extension of the methods of Brock and Gale (1970) and McFadden (1973) to our setup.

An obvious sufficient condition is that the utility function be bounded, i.e., that there be numbers $\underline{B} < \bar{B}$ such that for all $c \geq 0$

$$\underline{B} \leq u(c) \leq \bar{B}.$$

Remark 3.2. The method used here of introducing a stock market into this type of model where an investment decision is present was first developed by Scheinkman (1977) in the certainty case.

A basic lemma is

Lemma 3.2 (i). Let $X = \langle \{\bar{c}_t\}_{t=1}^{\infty}, \{\bar{x}_{it}\}_{t=1}^{\infty}, \{\bar{x}_t\}_{t=1}^{\infty} \rangle$ solve the optimal growth problem (1.1); then define

(3.33) $\bar{R}_{it+1} \equiv f_i'(\bar{x}_{it}, r_t), \quad \bar{\pi}_{i,t+1} \equiv f_i(\bar{x}_{it}, r_t) - f_i'(\bar{x}_{it}, r_t)\bar{x}_{it}.$

Then let $\{\bar{P}_{it}\}_{t=1}^{\infty}, i = 1, 2, \ldots, N$, satisfy (3.27), (3.29), and (3.31). Put

(3.34) $\bar{Z}_{it} = 1,$

Then $\langle \{\bar{P}_{it}\}_{t=1}^{\infty}, \{\bar{R}_{it}\}_{t=1}^{\infty}, \{\bar{\pi}_{it}\}_{t=1}^{\infty}, \{\bar{x}_{it}\}_{t=1}^{\infty}, \{\bar{Z}_{it}\}_{t=1}^{\infty}, i = 1, 2, \ldots, N,$
$\{\bar{c}_t\}_{t=1}^{\infty}, \{\bar{x}_t\}_{t=1}^{\infty} \rangle \equiv \mathfrak{R}$ is an REE.

Lemma 3.2(ii). Let $\mathfrak{R}$ be an REE. Then X solves the optimal growth problem (1.1).

Proof. The proof of this is straightforward and is done in the appendix to section 1.3. Lemma 3.2 is central to this paper because it shows that the quantity side of any competitive equilibrium may be manufactured from solutions to the growth problem. This fact will enable us to identify the Ross prices, for example. Furthermore, it will be used in the existence proof of an asset pricing function which is developed below.

Turn back to the discussion of the relationship between the growth model of section 1.2 and the risk prices of Ross. This will facilitate the economic interpretation of an REE stochastic process

$$\{\bar{R}_{it}\}_{t=1}^{\infty}, \{\bar{P}_{it}\}_{t=1}^{\infty}, \{\bar{\pi}_{it}\}_{t=1}^{\infty}.$$

Drop upper bars off equilibrium quantities from this point on in order to simplify notation. Assume that conditions are such that all asset prices are positive with probability 1 in equilibrium. Then $\bar{Z}_{it} = 1$ with probability 1, and from (3.29) we get for each t

(3.35) $u'(c_t) = \beta E_t\{u'(c_{t+1})\mathfrak{X}_{it}\}, \mathfrak{X}_{it} \equiv (P_{i,t+1} + \pi_{i,t+1})/P_{it}.$

Now because profit maximization implies $f_i'(x_{it}, r_t) = R_{i,t+1}$,

(3.36) $\pi_{i,t+1} = f_i(x_{it}, r_t) - f_i'(x_{it}, r_t)x_{it}.$

Turning to the rental market, suppose that all processes are used with probability 1. Then (3.36) and (3.37) give us for each i, t

(3.37) $u'(c_t) = \beta E_t\{u'(c_{t+1})f_i'(x_{it}, r_t)\}.$

Examine the specification

(3.38) $$f_i(x_{it}, r_t) = (\sum_{k=0}^{K} A_{it}^k \tilde{\delta}_{kt}) f_i(x_{it}) \equiv r_{it} f_i(x_{it})$$

developed in section 1.2. Now (2.28), (3.37), and (3.35) imply

(3.39) $$u'(c_t) = \sum_{k=1}^{K} b_{kit} E_t\{\beta u'(c_{t+1}) \tilde{\delta}_{kt}\} + a_{it} E_t\{\beta u'(c_{t+1})\}$$

$$= \beta E_t\{u'(c_{t+1}) \tilde{\mathscr{X}}_{it}\}.$$

We are *not* entitled to write returns $\mathscr{X}_{it}$ defined by (3.35) in the linear Ross form (2.17) unless $P_i(y_{t+1})$ is linear in y_{t+1}, even for the specification (3.38) above. An example will be presented in section 1.5 below where $P_i(y_{t+1})$ turns out to be linear in y_{t+1}. But first we must show that an asset pricing function exists.

1.3.2   Existence of an Asset Pricing Function

Since in equilibrium the quantity side of our asset pricing model is the same as the N process growth model, we may use the facts collected in section 1.2 about the N process growth model to prove the existence of an asset pricing function $P(y)$ in much the same way as Lucas (1978).

To begin with, let us assume
Assumption 3.1. Assume for all $r \in R$,

$$(a) f_i'(0, r) = +\infty, \qquad i = 1, 2, \ldots, N,$$

$$(b) \pi_i(x, r) \equiv f_i(x, r) - f_i'(x, r) x > 0 \text{ for all } x > 0.$$

Assumption 3.1(a) implies that (3.14a) holds with equality in equilibrium. Also, assumption 3.1(b) implies (3.13a) holds with equality in equilibrium. Let us search as does Lucas for a bounded continuous function $P_i(y)$ such that in equilibrium

(3.40) $P_{it} u'(c_t) = P_i(y_t) u'(c_t) = \beta E_t\{u'(c_{t+1})(\pi_{i,t+1} + P_i(y_{t+1}))\}.$

Convert the foregoing problem into a fixed point problem. Note first from section 1.2 that

(3.41) $$u'(c_t) = U'(y_t) \qquad t = 1, 2, \ldots,$$

(3.42) $$\pi_{i,t+1} = f_i(x_{it}, r_t) - f_i'(x_{it}, r_t) x_{it} \equiv \pi_i(x_{it}, r_t) = \pi_i(\eta_i(x_t)x_t, r_t)$$

$$= \pi_i[\eta_i(h(y_t))h(y_t), r_t] \equiv J_i(y_t, r_t),$$

(3.43) $$y_{t+1} = \sum_{j=1}^{N} f_j(\eta_j(x_t)x_t, r_t) = \sum_{j=1}^{N} f_j(\eta_j(h(y_t))h(y_t), r_t] \equiv Y(y_t, r_t).$$

Put

(3.44) $$G_i(y_t) \equiv \beta \int_{r \in R} U'[Y(y_t, r)] J_i(y_t, r) \mu(dr),$$

(3.45) $$F_i(y_t) \equiv P_i(y_t)U'(y_t),$$

(3.46) $$(T_iF_i)(y_t) \equiv G_i(y_t) + \beta \int_{r \in R} F_i[Y(y_t, r)]\mu(dr).$$

Then, for each i, (3.40) may be written as

(3.47) $$F_i(y_t) = (T_iF_i)(y_t).$$

Problem (3.47) is a fixed point problem in that we search for a function F_i that remains fixed under operator T_i. In order to use the contraction mapping theorem to find a fixed point F_i, we must show first that T_i sends the class of bounded continuous functions on $[0,\infty)$, call it $C[0,\infty)$, into itself. The results of section 1.2 established that all of the functions listed in (3.41)–(3.46) are continuous in y_t. We need

Lemma 3.3. If $U(y)$ is bounded on $[0,\infty)$, then $G_i(y)$ is bounded.
Proof. First, by concavity of U we have

(3.48) $$U(y) - U(0) \geq U'(y)(y - 0) = U'(y)y.$$

Hence, there is B such that

(3.49) $$U'(y)y \leq B \text{ for all } y \in [0,\infty).$$

Second,

$$\int_R U'[Y(y,r)]J_i(y,r)\mu(dr) = \int_R U'[Y(y,r)]Y(y,r)J_i(y,r)/Y(y,r)\mu(dr)$$

$$\leq B \int J_i(y,r)/Y(y,r)\mu(dr) \leq B$$

since $f_i' \geq 0$ implies

$$f_i - f_i'x_{it} \equiv J_i \leq f_i, \quad Y \equiv \sum_{j=1}^{N} f_j, \quad J_i/Y \leq 1.$$

Thus, G_i is bounded by βB. This ends the proof.
We must show that if

(3.50) $$\|F_i\| \equiv \sup_{y \in [0,\infty)} |F_i(y)|$$

is chosen to be the norm on $C[0,\infty)$, then T_i is a contraction with modulus β. It is a well-known fact that $C(0,\infty)$ endowed with this norm is a Banach space.

Lemma 3.4. $T_i: C[0,\infty] \to C[0,\infty)$ is a contraction with modulus β.
Proof. We must show that for any two elements A, B in $C[0,\infty)$

(3.51) $$\|T_iA - T_iB\| \leq \beta\|A - B\|.$$

Now for $y \in [0,\infty)$ from (3.46) we have

(3.52) $$|T_iA(y) - T_iB(y)| = \beta|\int(A[Y(y,r)] - B[Y(y,r)])\mu(dr)|$$

$$\leq \beta\int|A(y') - B(y')|\mu(dr)$$

$$\leq \beta \int \sup_{y' \text{ in } [0,\infty)} |A(y') - B(y')| \, \mu(dr) = \beta \|A - B\|.$$

Take the supremum of the left-hand side (L.H.S.) of (3.52) to get

(3.53) $\|T_i A - T_i B\| \leq \beta \|A - B\|.$

This ends the proof.

Theorem 3.1. For each i there exists exactly one asset pricing function of the form $P_i(y)$ where $P_i \in C[0,\infty)$.

Proof. Apply the contraction mapping theorem to produce a fixed point $\bar{F}_i(y) \in C[0,\infty)$. Put

(3.54) $P_i(t) = \bar{F}_i(y)/U'(y).$

It is clear that $P_i(y)$ satisfies (3.40). Furthermore, by the very definition of T_i any $P_i(y)$ that satisfies (3.40) is such that $P_i(\bullet)U'(\bullet) \equiv \bar{F}_i(\bullet)$ is a fixed point of T_i. This ends the proof.

Remark 3.3. Assumption 3.1(a) is not needed for the existence theorem. Assumption 3.1(b) is needed in the theorem so that (3.40) holds with equality.

Our proof of existence, as does Lucas's, leaves begging the question of whether there exist equilibria that are not stationary, that is, equilibria that cannot be written in the form of $P_i(y)$ for some time stationary function $P_i(\bullet)$.

Indeed, the papers of Cass, Okuno, and Zilcha (1979) and Gale (1973) have brought out in a dramatic way the multitude of non–time stationary equilibria that exist in overlapping generations models. If we applied the above fixed point method to overlapping generations models, we would only find the time stationary equilibria. Calvo (1979) and Wilson (1978) show that the same problem may arise even in infinite horizon monetary models with only one agent type.

Fortunately for our case we may use the necessity of the transversality condition (3.16) to show that there is only one equilibrium.

Theorem 3.1'. Assume the hypothesis of theorem 3.1. For each i, t, there is only one equilibrium asset price P_{it} and it can be written in the form $P_i(y_t)$.

Proof. Look at (3.13a) and develop a recursion as is done in (A3.13) below. We get

$$P_{i1} = E_1 \sum_{s=2}^{T} \Pi_s \pi_{is} + E_1 \Pi_T P_{iT}.$$

We must first show that (3.16) implies

$$E_1 \Pi_T P_{iT} \to 0, \qquad T \to \infty.$$

In order to see this, first note that $Z_{i1} = 1$ in equilibrium. Also by definition of Π_t

$$E_1\Pi_t P_{it} = E_1\{[\beta^{t-1}u'(c_t)/u'(c_1)]P_{it}\}$$
$$= (1/u'(c_1))E_1\{\beta^{t-1}u'(c_t)P_{it}\} \to 0, \qquad t \to \infty.$$

The last statement follows directly from (3.16) since $Z_{it} = 1$ in equilibrium.

Second, we must know the values of Π_s, π_{is}. But lemma 3.1 tells us that the quantity side of the growth model is the same as the quantity side of the "market" model in equilibrium. Hence, the solution of the growth problem (2.1) determines the values of Π_s, π_{is} for all i, s.

Finally, P_{i1} is given by

(3.55) $$P_{i1} = E_1 \sum_{s=2}^{\infty} \Pi_s \pi_{is}, \qquad i = 1, 2, \ldots, N.$$

The same argument may be used to show that

$$P_{it} = E_t \sum_{s=t+1}^{\infty} \Pi_s \pi_{is}, \qquad i = 1, 2, \ldots, N, \quad t = 1, 2, \ldots$$

This ends the proof.

Remark 3.4. We cannot overemphasize the fact that the methods of proof used in theorem 3.1 will not characterize *all* of the equilibria in general. Such methods are incapable of proving uniqueness of equilibria. In fact, one of the main contributions of our paper is to develop methods of analysis that characterize *all* equilibria.

Remark 3.5. It is interesting to note that (3.55) was derived by Johnsen (1978). He did it by iterating (3.47). Given any initial approximation, the contraction mapping theorem implies that the sequence of nth iterates converges to the unique solution $P_i(y)$ as $n \to \infty$. It is important to note, as pointed out earlier, that there are examples where there are equilibria of a non–time stationary form. In such cases, the approximation method will not get *all* of the equilibria.

1.4   Certainty Equivalence Formulas

What we shall do in this section is to use the asset pricing model of section 1.3 to construct a Sharpe-Lintner formula for the pricing of common stocks. In equilibrium our formula must hold. Furthermore, the data used in the formula to discount future profits are observable. The closest analogue to it seems to be that of Rubenstein (1976) in that Rubenstein relates the "price of risk" to tastes and technology.

The formula will be derived from the following special case of the model of section 1.3:

(4.1) $$f_i(x_{it}, r_t) \equiv \bar{f}_i(x_{it})(A_i^0 + A_i^1\tilde{\delta}_t), A_i^0 > 0.$$

In other words, put $K = 1$ in (3.38). Here $\{\tilde{\delta}_t\}_{t=1}^{\infty}$ is an independent and identically distributed sequence of random variables with zero mean and finite variance σ^2. The numbers A_i^0, A_i^1 and the random variables $\tilde{\delta}_t$ are assumed to satisfy the following: there is $\epsilon_0 > 0$ such that for each t

(4.2) $\text{prob}\,(A_i^0 + A_i^1\tilde{\delta}_t \geq \epsilon_0) = 1$.

Optimum profits are given by

(4.3) $\pi_i(x_{it}, r_t) = \bar{f}_i(x_{it})(A_i^0 + A_i^1\tilde{\delta}_t) - \bar{f}_i'(x_{it})x_{it}(A_i^0 + A_i^1\tilde{\delta}_t) \equiv \bar{\pi}_i(x_{it})(A_i^0\tilde{\delta}_t).$

In order to shorten the notational burden in the calculations below, put

(4.4) $f_i(x_{it}, r_t) = \mu_{it} + \sigma_{it}\tilde{\delta}_t,$

(4.5) $f_i'(x_{it}, r_t) = \mu_{it}' + \sigma_{it}'\tilde{\delta}_t,$

(4.6) $\pi_i(x_{it}, r_t) = \bar{D}_{it} + V_{it}\tilde{\delta}_t,$

where

(4.7) $\mu_{it} \equiv \bar{f}_i(x_{it})A_i^0, \sigma_{it} \equiv \bar{f}_i(x_{it})A_i^1, \mu_{it}' = \bar{f}_i'(x_{it})A_i^0, \sigma_{it} = \bar{f}_i'A_i^1,$

$\bar{D}_{it} = \bar{\pi}_i(x_{it})A_i^0, V_{it} = \bar{\pi}_i(x_{it})A_i^1.$

All quantities will be evaluated at equilibrium levels unless otherwise noted. The notation is meant to be suggestive with $\bar{D}_{it}$ standing for average dividends or profits expected at date t, V_{it} standing for the coefficient of variability of profits with respect to the process $\{\tilde{\delta}_t\}_{t=i}^\infty$, and so forth. For a specific parable think of the $\{\tilde{\delta}_t\}_{t=1}^\infty$ process as "the market." Then production and profits in all industries $i = 1, 2, \ldots, N$ are affected by the market. High values of $\tilde{\delta}_t$ correspond to "booms" and low values to "slumps." Industries i with $A_i^1 > 0$ are procyclical. Those with $A_i^1 < 0$ are countercyclical, and those with $A_i^1 = 0$ are a-cyclical.

Assumption 4.1. There is at least one industry, call it N, that is a-cyclical. The Nth industry will be called *risk free*. For emphasis we will sometimes say that N is *systematic risk free*.

In order that all industries be active in equilibrium and that output remain bounded we shall assume

Assumption 4.2(i). $\bar{f}_i'(0) = +\infty$, $i = 1, 2, \ldots, N$,

Assumption 4.2(ii). $\bar{f}_i'(\infty) = 0$, $i = 1, 2, \ldots, N$.

Assumption 4.2(i) guarantees that all $x_{it} > 0$ along an equilibrium. Assumption 4.2(ii) implies there is a bound B such that $x_{it} \leq B$ with probability 1 for all i, t.

Although concavity of $f(x)$ and $f(0) = 0$ imply optimum profits are nonnegative, we shall require that profits are positive for each $x > 0$; i.e.,

Assumption 4.3. For all $x > 0$, $\pi_i(x) \equiv \bar{f}_i(x) - \bar{f}_i'(x)x > 0$.

Assumption 4.3 will be used to show that equity prices are positive in equilibrium.

By the first-order necessary conditions of equilibrium (3.13)–(3.14), (4.2), and assumptions 4.2(i) and 4.3, it follows that

(4.8) $\qquad P_{it}u'(c_t) = \beta E_t\{u'(c_{t+1})(\pi_{i,t+1} + P_{i,t+1})\}$

(4.9) $\quad u'(c_t) = \beta E_t\{u'(c_{t+1})R_{i,t+1}\} = \beta E_t u'(c_{t+1})\mu'_{it} + \beta E_t(u'(c_{t+1})\tilde{\delta}_t)\sigma'_{it}.$

The R.H.S. of (4.9) follows from (4.5). It is clear from assumption 4.3 that equity prices are positive since $\pi_{i,t+1}$ is positive with probability 1. Hence, both (4.8) and (4.9) are equalities and $Z_{it} = 1$.

The $P = PDV$ formula will be derived from (4.8), (4.9) by recursion. Use (4.3), (4.6) to get

(4.10) $\qquad\qquad\qquad \pi_{i,t+1} = \bar{D}_{it} + V_{it}\tilde{\delta}_t.$

In order to shorten notation put $u'(c_{t+1}) = u'_{t+1}$ for all t. From (4.8), (4.10) we get

(4.11) $\quad P_{it}u'(c_t) = \beta E_t u'_{t+1}\bar{D}_{it} + \beta E_t(u'_{t+1}\tilde{\delta}_t)V_{it} + \beta E_t\{u'_{t+1}P_{i,t+1}\}.$

Notice that $\mu'_{it}, \sigma'_{it}, \bar{D}_{it}, V_{it}$ are (in theory, at least) observable. Hence, if we recurse (4.11) forward by replacing t by $t+1$ in (4.8) and inserting the result into (4.11), we can use (4.9) to solve for

(4.12) $\quad E_t m_t \equiv \dfrac{\beta E_t u'_{t+1}}{u'_t}, E_t n_t \equiv \dfrac{\beta E_t(u'_{t+1}\tilde{\delta}_t)}{u'_t}, m_t \equiv \dfrac{\beta u'_{t+1}}{u'_t}, n_t \equiv \dfrac{\beta u'_{t+1}\tilde{\delta}_t}{u'_t}$

in terms of μ'_{it}, σ'_{it} and build up a $P = PDV$ formula for P_{it}.

Let us continue. From (4.11) we get

(4.13) $P_{it} = E_t m_t \bar{D}_{it} + E_t n_t V_{it} + \beta E_t\{u'_{t+1}P_{i,t+1}\}/u'_t = E_t m_t \bar{D}_{it} + E_t n_t V_{it}$

$\qquad + E_t\{m_t[E_{t+1}m_{t+1}\bar{D}_{i,t+1} + E_{t+1}n_{t+1}V_{i,t+1} + \beta E_{t+1}(u'_{t+2}P_{i,t+2})/u'_{t+1}]\}$

$\qquad = E_t m_t \bar{D}_{it} + E_t n_t V_{it} + E_t\{m_t E_{t+1}m_{t+1}\bar{D}_{i,t+1} + m_t E_{t+1}n_{t+1}V_{i,t+1}\} + \cdots$

$\qquad\qquad + E_t\{m_t E_{t+1}m_{t+1}\ldots E_{t+T}(m_{t+T}\bar{D}_{i,t+T})\}$

$\qquad\qquad + E_t\{m_t E_{t+1}m_{t+1}\ldots E_{t+T-1}m_{t+T-1}E_{t+T}n_{t+T}V_{i,t+T}\}$

$\qquad\qquad + E_t\{m_t E_{t+1}m_{t+1}\ldots E_{t+T}(m_{t+T}P_{i,t+T+1})\}.$

For the next move we need

Assumption 4.4. The utility function $u(\cdot)$ is such that for all $\{P_{it}, \pi_{it}, R_{it}\}_{t=1}^{\infty}, i = 1, 2, \ldots, N$, the TVC_{∞} is *necessary* for a consumer's maximum. Note that, as was pointed out in remark 3.1, boundedness of $u(\cdot)$ is sufficient for assumption 4.4. Now the TVC_{∞} implies that

(4.14) $\qquad E_t\{m_t E_{t+1}m_{t+1}\ldots E_{t+T}(m_{t+T}P_{i,t+T+1})\} \to 0, T \to \infty.$

By (4.9) we get for each t

(4.15) $\qquad\qquad\qquad 1 = E_t m_t \mu'_{it} + E_t n_t \sigma'_{it}.$

Therefore, if $\sigma'_{Nt} \equiv 0$, (4.15) implies

(4.16) $E_t m_t = 1/\mu'_{Nt}, E_t n_t = [(\mu'_{Nt} - \mu'_{it})/\sigma'_{it}](1/\mu'_{Nt}) \equiv -\Delta_t/\mu'_{Nt}.$

Note here that Δ_t is the excess marginal return over the risk free marginal return divided by marginal risk. Also μ'_{Nt} is principal plus interest obtained by employing a marginal unit in process N. It is important to observe that Δ_t is independent of i. Furthermore, the Ross risk price λ_t is determined by $\lambda_t = \Delta_t$. This follows from (2.30) and (4.16).

Turn now to the K factor case. In the K factor case, put

(4.17) $f_i(x_{it}, r_t) \equiv \bar{f}_i(x_{it})(\sum_{k=0}^{K} A_i^k \widetilde{\delta}_{t+1}^k), \widetilde{\delta}_{t+1}^0 \equiv 0, A_i^0 > 0.$

Put the same assumptions on the data as in section 1.3. Then as in (4.4), (4.5), (4.6) we may write

(4.18) $f_i(x_{it}, r_t) = \mu_{it} + \sum_{k=1}^{K} \sigma_{it}^k \widetilde{\delta}_{t+1}^k,$

(4.19) $f_i'(x_{it}, r_t) = \mu'_{it} + \sum_{k=1}^{K} \sigma_{it}'^k \widetilde{\sigma}_{t+1}^k,$

(4.20) $\pi_i(x_{it}, r_t) = \bar{D}_{it} + \sum_{k=1}^{K} V_{it}^k \widetilde{\delta}_{t+1}^k \equiv \pi_{i,t+1},$

where the entities in (4.18)–(4.20) are defined as in (4.7). Keep the same assumptions as above. Then (4.8), (4.9) become

(4.21) $P_{it}u_i' = \beta E_t\{u'_{t+1}(\bar{D}_{it} + \sum_{k=1}^{K} V_{it}^k \widetilde{\delta}_{t+1}^k) + u'_{t+1}P_{i,t+1}\},$

(4.22) $u_t' = \beta E_t\{u'_{t+1}(\mu'_{it} + \sum_{k=1}^{K} \sigma_{it}'^k \widetilde{\delta}_{t+1}^k)\}.$

Define

(4.23) $m_t \equiv (\beta u'_{t+1})/u_t', n_t^k \equiv (\beta u'_{t+1}\widetilde{\delta}_{t+1}^k)/u_t'.$

Then, letting N be a free risk process (i.e., $\sigma_{Nt}'^k \equiv 0$, for all k, t), we get

(4.24) $E_t m_t = 1/\mu'_{Nt}$

and for each i

(4.25) $1 = (E_t m_t)\mu'_{it} + \sum_{k=1}^{K} \sigma_{it}'^k(E_t n_t^k) = \mu'_{it}/\mu'_{Nt} + \sum_{k=1}^{K} \sigma_{it}'^k(E_t n_t^k).$

Hence, from (4.25) it follows that

(4.26) $(\mu'_{Nt} - \mu'_{it})/\mu'_{Nt} = \sum_{k=1}^{K} \sigma_{it}'^k(E_t n_t^k),$ $i = 1, 2, \ldots, N.$

It is assumed that a unique solution of (4.26) for $E_t n_t^k$ exists and is defined by

(4.27) $E_t n_t^k \equiv -\Delta_t^k/\mu'_{Nt}.$

Also, the Ross price of systematic risk k, λ_{kt} satisfies $\lambda_{kt} = \Delta_t^k$. This last equality follows from (2.30) and (4.27). From (4.8) we get (putting $\xi_{it} \equiv \bar{D}_{it} - V_{it}\Delta_t$)

(4.28) $P_{it} = \xi_{it}/\mu'_{Nt} + E_t\{[\frac{\beta u'_{t+1}}{u'_t}\mu'_{Nt}](P_{i,t+1})\}\mu'_{Nt} \equiv \{\xi_{it} + E_t\hat{P}_{i,t+1}\}/\mu'_{Nt}.$

Hence,

(4.29) $$E_t\hat{P}_{i,t+1} + \xi_{it} = \mu'_{Nt}P_{it}.$$

Equation (4.29) says that investing P_{it} in the stock market must give the same expected return after paying for the services of risk bearing as investing it in the risk free process. It states that the stock market is a "fair game," taking into account the opportunity cost of funds and the cost of risk bearing.

Clearly, restrictive assumptions on tastes and technology are necessary to get a martingale. Also, only for specific preferences is equation (4.29) testable. Its violation would signal "market inefficiency" in our model world.

A far better test would be based on (3.55). But even verification of (3.55) would not test Pareto optimality of the stock market allocation. This is so because there may exist heterogeneous consumer economies (e.g., overlapping generations models) where (3.55) holds, but the allocation is not Pareto optimal. This question remains to be investigated.

It is worth pointing out here that if the random variable

(4.30) $$(\beta u'_{t+1}/u'_t)\mu'_{Nt} \equiv I_t$$

is independent of $P_{i,t+1}$ at date t, then (4.16) implies that (4.29) may be rewritten

(4.31) $$E_t P_{i,t+1} + \xi_{it} = \mu'_{Nt}P_{it}.$$

Equation (4.31) contains no subjective entities—unlike (4.29). The problem of deriving equations like (4.31) that contain no entities that are subjective and hence are directly testable is solved abstractly by (3.55). Perhaps a formula analogous to (4.31) exists that holds in, at least, an approximate sense.

1.4.1   A Testable Formula

In what follows a simple formula is developed under the hypothesis of linearity of the asset pricing functions $P_i(y)$. An example where $P_i(y)$ is linear is given in section 1.5 below.

Theorem 4.1. Adopt assumptions 4.1–4.4. Furthermore, assume that there are constants K_i, L_i such that

(4.32) $$P_i(y) = K_iy + L_i, \qquad i = 1,2,\ldots,N.$$

Then, for each t,i

$$(4.33) \qquad \mu'_{Nt}P_{it} = E_t P_{i,t+1} - \sum_{k=1}^{K} \Delta_t^k S_{it}^k + E_t \pi_{i,t+1} - \sum_{k=1}^{K} \Delta_t^k V_{it}^k$$

must hold. Here by (4.32) and (4.20) we may write

$$(4.34) \qquad P_{i,t+1} \equiv P_i(y_{t+1}) \equiv \bar{P}_{it} + \sum_{k=1}^{K} S_{it}^k \tilde{\delta}_{t+1}^k, \bar{P}_{it} \equiv E_t P_{i,t+1},$$

$$(4.35) \qquad \pi_{i,t+1} \equiv \bar{D}_{it} + \sum_{k=1}^{K} V_{it}^k \tilde{\delta}_{t+1}^k, \bar{D}_{it} \equiv E_t \pi_{i,t+1},$$

where $E_t P_{i,t+1}$, $E_t \pi_{i,t+1}$, S_{it}^k, V_{it}^k do *not* depend upon y_{t+1} but depend on $(x_{1t}, \ldots, x_{Nt})$ only.

Proof. In order to establish (4.33) it must be shown that (4.34), (4.35) hold. By (4.17) and the definition of y_{t+1} we have

$$(4.36) \qquad y_{t+1} \equiv \sum_{j=1}^{N} f_j(x_{j+1}, r_t) = \sum_j \bar{f}_j(x_{jt}) \left(\sum_{k=0}^{K} A_j^k \tilde{\delta}_{t+1}^k \right)$$

$$= L(y_t) + \sum_{k=1}^{K} M^k(y_t)\tilde{\delta}_t^k.$$

Hence, y_{t+1} is a linear combination of the shocks $\tilde{\delta}_{t+1}^k$ with weights that depend only upon $(x_{1t}, \ldots, x_{Nt})$. So also is $P_{i,t+1}$. Thus, (4.34) holds for appropriate S_{it}^k since $P_{i,t+1}$ is linear in y_{t+1}. Equation (4.20) is identical to (4.35).

Divide both sides of (4.21) by u'_t to get

$$(4.37) \qquad P_{it} = E_t\{m_t(\bar{D}_{it} + \sum_{k=1}^{K} V_{it}^k \tilde{\delta}_{t+1}^k)\} + E_t\{m_t P_{i,t+1}\}.$$

Put, using (4.23),

$$(4.38) \qquad \bar{m}_t \equiv E_t m_t, \bar{n}_t^k \equiv E_t n_t^k.$$

By (4.37) and (4.34) we have

$$P_{it} = \bar{m}_t \bar{D}_{it} + \sum_{k=1}^{K} V_{it}^k \bar{n}_t^k + E_t\{m_t(\bar{P}_{it} + \sum_{k=1}^{K} S_{it}^k \tilde{\delta}_{t+1}^k)\}$$

$$= \bar{m}_t \bar{D}_{it} + \sum_{k=1}^{K} V_{it}^k \bar{n}_t^k + \bar{m}_t \bar{P}_{it} + \sum_{k=1}^{K} S_{it}^k \bar{n}_t^k.$$

But (4.24) and (4.27) imply

$$\mu'_{Nt}P_{it} = \bar{D}_{it} + \bar{P}_{it} - \sum_{k=1}^{K} \Delta_t^k(V_{it}^k + S_{it}^k).$$

This ends the proof.

It is worth pointing out that, although (4.33) contains no subjective entities and, hence, is *directly testable*, it was derived under the strong hypothesis of linearity of the asset pricing function $P_i(y_{t+1})$. The linearity hypothesis was needed to be able to write the one-period returns $\mathcal{Z}_{it}$ to holding asset i in the linear form (2.17) of Ross. The linear form of $\mathcal{Z}_{it}$ was used, in turn, to derive (4.33). We suspect that strong conditions will be required on utility and technology to be able to write equilibrium asset returns in the form (2.17). Hence, (4.33) is not general: it holds only as a linear approximation. Thus, it is likely to hold in continuous time relatives of our model.

The economic content of (4.33) is compelling. It is a standard "no arbitrage profits" condition. The price of risk bearing over the time interval $t,t+1$ sells for Δ_t^k per unit of risk of type k. At date t, risk emerges from two sources: (i) $\pi_{i,t+1}$, and (ii) $P_{i,t+1}$. Profits contain V_{it}^k units of risk of type k. The price of stock i at date $t+1$ contains S_{it}^k units of risk of type k. Hence, the total cost of risk bearing from all sources of risk for all types of risk is

$$\sum_{k=1}^{K} \Delta_t^k(V_{it}^k + S_{it}^k).$$

Thus, (4.33) just says that the risk free earnings from an investment of P_{it} must equal the sum of risk adjusted sale value of stock i at date $t+1$ and risk adjusted profits.

Remark. The formula (4.33) is exactly the Sharpe-Lintner formula of finance. While the formula itself is textbook knowledge, the advantage of deriving it from a general equilibrium model is that we can study exactly what conditions on tastes and technology are required for its validity. Namely, tastes and technology must be such that the asset pricing function is linear in y.

A set of approximate formulas of "accuracy" a may be derived from (4.37) by expanding

$$(4.39) \qquad P_{i,t+1} \equiv P_i(y_{t+1}) = P_i[L(y_t) + \sum_{k=1}^{K} M^k(y_t)\tilde{\delta}_t^k]$$

in a Taylor series about $L(y_t)$ and discarding terms of order higher than a. The Sharpe-Lintner formula (4.33) corresponds to $a = 1$. In order to see how this type of development goes, we calculate the case $a = 2, K = 1$ and discard terms of order higher than 2. Doing this, we get, putting $M^1(y) = M(y)$,

$$(4.40) \qquad P_i[L(y_t) + M(y_t)\tilde{\delta}_t] = P_i[L(y_t)] + P_i'[L(y_t)]M(y_t)\tilde{\delta}_t$$
$$+ \frac{1}{2}P_i''[L(y_t)]M^2(y_t)\tilde{\delta}_t^2.$$

Inserting (4.40) into (4.37), we get for $i = i,2,\ldots,N$

$$(4.41) \quad P_i(y_t) \equiv P_{it} = \bar{m}_t\bar{D}_{it} + \bar{n}_t V_{it} + \bar{m}_t P_i[L(y_t)] + \bar{n}_t P_i'[L(y_t)]M(y_t)$$
$$+ \bar{o}_t \frac{1}{2}P_i''[L(y_t)]M^2(y_t),$$

where

$$(4.42) \qquad \bar{o}_t \equiv E_t(m_t \tilde{\delta}_t^2).$$

Since (4.41) holds for all i, the subjective entities $\bar{m}_t$, $\bar{n}_t$, $\bar{o}_t$ may be expressed in terms of observables as before in the $a = 1$ case.

Space limitations prevent us from pursuing the development of asset pricing formulas further.

1.5 Example

In this section we present a solved example where equilibrium returns are linear in the stocks. Let the data be given by

$$(5.1) \qquad u(c) = \log c,$$

$$(5.2) \qquad f_i(x_i, r) = A_i(r)x_i^\alpha, i = 1, 2, \ldots, N, 0 < \alpha < 1.$$

We shall assume that for all i

$$A_i(r) > 0 \text{ for all } r \in R$$

and $A_i(r)$ is continuous in r. Since R is compact, each $A_i(r)$ has a positive lower bound $\underline{A}_i > 0$.

First-order necessary conditions (1.10a), (1.10b) become for all t

$$(5.3a) \qquad \frac{1}{c_t} \geq \beta \alpha E_t \{ \frac{1}{c_{t+1}} A_i(r_t) x_{it}^{\alpha-1} \},$$

$$(5.3b) \qquad \frac{1}{c_t} x_{it} = \beta \alpha E_t \{ \frac{1}{c_{t+1}} A_i(r_t) x_{it}^{\alpha-1} \} x_{it}, \qquad i = 1, 2, \ldots, N,$$

$$(5.3c) \qquad \lim_{t \to \infty} E_1 \{ \frac{\beta^{t-1}}{c_t} x_t \} = 0.$$

Conjecture an optimum solution of the form

$$(5.4) \qquad c_t = (1 - \lambda)y_t, x_t = \lambda y_t, x_{it} = \eta_i x_t, \sum_{i=1}^{N} \eta_i = 1,$$

where

$$(5.5) \qquad \lambda > 0, \eta_i \geq 0, \qquad i = 1, 2, \ldots, N.$$

Insert (5.4) into (5.3a); solve (5.3b) for λ, $\{\eta_i\}_{i=1}^{N}$; and check that (5.3c) is satisfied. Doing this, we get

$$(5.6) \qquad \frac{1}{(1-\lambda)y_t} \geq \beta \alpha E_t \left\{ \frac{1}{(1-\lambda)y_{t+1}} A_i(r_t) x_{it}^{\alpha-1} \right\}$$

iff (if and only if)

$$\frac{1}{y_t} \geq \beta \alpha E_t \left\{ \frac{A_i(r_t)}{\sum_{j=1}^{N} A_j(r_t)x_{jt}^\alpha} x_{it}^{\alpha-1} \right\}$$

iff

$$\frac{1}{y_t} \geq \beta\alpha E_t \left\{ \frac{\eta_i^{\alpha-1} x_t^{\alpha-1} A_i(r_t)}{\sum\limits_{j=1}^{N} A_j(r_t)\eta_j^{\alpha} x_t^{\alpha}} \right\}$$

iff

$$\frac{1}{y_t} \geq \beta\alpha E_t \left\{ \frac{A_i(r_t)}{\sum\limits_{j=1}^{N} A_j(r_t)\eta_j^{\alpha}} \right\} \frac{\eta_i^{\alpha-1}}{x_t} \equiv \beta\alpha\eta_i^{\alpha-1} \Gamma_i / x_t$$

iff

(5.7) $$x_t \geq \beta\alpha\eta_i^{\alpha-1} \Gamma_i y_t.$$

Set (5.7) aside for the moment. From (5.3b), following the same steps that we used to get (5.7), we are led to

(5.8) $$\frac{x_{it}}{y_t} = \beta\alpha\eta_i^{\alpha} \Gamma_i$$

iff

(5.9) $$x_{it} = \beta\alpha\eta_i^{\alpha} \Gamma_i y_t = \eta_i x_t.$$

Hence, (5.7) holds with equality for all t,i. Since it is well known and is easy to see that for $N = 1$

$$\lambda = \beta\alpha,$$

it is natural to conjecture for $N \geq 1$ that

(5.10) $$\lambda = \beta\alpha, \eta_i^{\alpha-1} \Gamma_i = 1, \qquad i = 1, 2, \ldots, N,$$

and test (5.3c). If (5.10) satisfies (5.3c), then we have found an optimum solution and hence *the* unique optimum solution.

Continuing, we have

(5.11) $$\Gamma_i \equiv E\left[\frac{A_i(r)}{\sum\limits_{j=1}^{N} A_j(r)\eta_j^{\alpha}} \right] = \eta_i^{1-\alpha}, \quad \sum\limits_{j=1}^{N} \eta_j = 1.$$

It is shown in the appendix to section 1.5 that (5.11) has a unique solution $\{\bar{\eta}_i\}_{i=1}^{N}$.

It is straightforward to check that (5.4) with $\bar{\lambda} \equiv \alpha\beta$, $\eta_i \equiv \bar{\eta}_i$, $i = 1, 2, \ldots, N$, generates a solution that not only satisfies (5.3a), (5.3b) by construction but also satisfies (5.3c). We leave this to the reader.

Let us use the solution to calculate an example of an equilibrium asset price function from the work of section 1.3. From (3.13a) and (3.37) we get

$$(5.12) \quad E_t[u'(c_{t+1})(P_{i,t+1} + \bar{\pi}_{i,t+1})/\bar{P}_{it}] = E_t[\alpha A_i(r_t)\bar{x}_{it}^{\alpha-1}u'(c_{t+1})]$$

$$= E_t[\alpha A_i(r_t)\bar{\eta}_i^{\alpha-1}\bar{x}_t^{\alpha-1}u'(c_{t+1})],$$

$$(5.13) \quad \bar{\pi}_{i,t+1} = A_i(r_t)\bar{x}_{it}^{\alpha} - \alpha A_i(r_t)\bar{x}_{it}^{\alpha-1}\bar{x}_{it}$$

$$= (1-\alpha)A_i(r_t)\bar{x}_{it}^{\alpha} = (1-\alpha)A_i(r_t)\bar{\eta}_i^{\alpha}\bar{x}_t^{\alpha}.$$

Hence, the first-order necessary condition for an asset pricing function of the form $P_{it} = P_i(y_t)$ becomes for $u(c) = \log c$, using $c_t = (1 - \lambda y_t$,

$$(5.14) \quad P_i(y_t)/y_t = \beta E_t\{(P_i(y_{t+1}) + \pi_{i,t+1})/y_{t+1}\}.$$

Equations (5.13) and (5.14) give us

$$(5.15) \quad P_i(y_t)/y_t = \beta E_t\{(1-\alpha)A_i(r_t)\bar{\eta}_i^{\alpha}\bar{x}_t^{\alpha}/[\sum_{j=1}^{N} A_i(r_t)\bar{\eta}_j^{\alpha}\bar{x}_t^{\alpha}]$$

$$+ P_i(y_{t+1})/y_{t+1}\} \equiv \beta(1-\alpha)\bar{\eta}_i$$

$$+ \beta E_t\{P_i(y_{t+1})/y_{t+1}\}, \qquad i = 1, 2, \ldots, N.$$

Here by (5.11)

$$(5.16) \quad \bar{\eta}_i = E_t\{A_i(r_t)\bar{\eta}_i^{\alpha}/(\sum_{j=1}^{N} A_j(r_t)\bar{\eta}_j^{\alpha})\}.$$

The system of equations (5.15) is in particularly suitable form for the application of the contraction mapping theorem to produce a unique fixed point $\bar{P}(y) \equiv (\bar{P}_1(y), \ldots, \bar{P}_N(y))$ that solves (5.15). Rather than do this, we just conjecture a solution of the form

$$(5.17) \quad \bar{P}_i(y) = \bar{K}_i y, \qquad i = , 2, \ldots, N,$$

and find $\bar{K}_i$ from (5.15) by equating coefficients. Obviously from (5.15) $\bar{K}_i$ satisfies

$$(5.18) \quad \bar{K}_i = \beta(1-\alpha)\bar{\eta}_i + \beta\bar{K}_i, \qquad i = 1, 2, \ldots, N,$$

so that

$$(5.19) \quad \bar{K}_i = (1-\beta)^{-1}\beta(1-\alpha)\bar{\eta}_i, \qquad i = 1, 2, \ldots, N.$$

Since R.H.S. (5.15) is a contraction of modulus β on the space of bounded continuous functions on $[0, \infty)$ with values in R^N, the solution (5.17) is the only solution such that each $P_i(y)/y$ is bounded and continuous on $[0, \infty)$.

We now have a solved example. It is interesting to examine the dependence of $P_i(y)$ on the problem data from (5.17), (5.19).

First, in the one asset case we find $\eta_N = 1$ from (5.16) so that

$$(5.20) \quad P(y) = \frac{\beta}{1-\beta}(1-\alpha)y.$$

Hence, (i) the asset price decreases as the elasticity of output with respect to capital input increases; (ii) the variance of output has no effect on the asset price function; and (iii) the asset price increases, when β increases.

Result (i) follows because profit's share of national output is inversely related to α. One would expect (ii) from the log utility function. One would expect (iii) because as β increases, the future is worth more relative to the present—hence, savings should increase, forcing asset prices to rise.

Furthermore, (5.20) says that asset price increases as y increases.

Secondly, in the multiasset deterministic case we have

$$(5.21) \qquad P(y) = \frac{\beta}{1 - \beta}(1 - \alpha)\bar{\eta}_i y, \qquad i = 1, 2, \dots, N,$$

where $\bar{\eta}_i$ is given by equation (A5.4) in the appendix to section 1.5. We can see that if the coefficient A_i measures the *productivity* of firm i using the common technology x^α so that output of i is $A_i x^\alpha$, then firms that are *relatively* more productive bear higher relative prices for their stock. *Absolute* productivity does not affect relative prices. This is so because $\bar{\eta}_i$ is homogenous of degree zero in $(A_i, \dots, A_N)$.

This is again one of those results that looks intuitively clear after hindsight has been applied. The consumers in this economy have no other alternative but to lease capital or to invest in stock in the N firms. Hence, if the productivity of all of them is halved, the constellation of asset price relatives will not change although output will drop. This type of result is specific to the log utility and Cobb-Douglas production technologies.

The technique of Mirman and Zilcha (1975) may be applied to find the closed form solution for the limit distribution F mentioned in section 1.2. Once F is known the limit distribution of asset prices may be found from (3.40) and the limit distribution of Ross's risk prices may be calculated, from (2.30). We leave that to the reader.

1.6 Summary, Conclusions, Comments and Suggestions for Further Research

Most of the results of this paper are summarized in section 1.1. Therefore, we will first comment on what we think has been done here. What has been done is to turn normative stochastic growth theory into positive theory by introducing market institutions into received stochastic growth theory.

Furthermore, we have specialized the model so that received stochastic growth theory may be modified to generate the recursive structure that is so useful for preserving the empirical tractability of Merton's (1973) ICAPM. This has been done in such a way as to link our theory up with the K factor arbitrage theory of Ross (1976).

The reader may ask, Why not decentralize the N process growth model along the lines of Arrow-Debreu where the pure rents are redistributed lump sum, assume constant returns to scale so that pure rents are zero, and price the capital stock along Arrow-Debreu lines? The reason we did not do this is because it has already been done in the stochastic growth literature for the general N process multisector case. However, implications of this type of model for *finance* have not yet been explored in any great detail. But what we have done here may easily be modified to include this case.

This literature has been surveyed by Roy Radner (1974). It was pointed out in my comment on Radner (Brock 1974) that simple stochastic growth models could be turned into "rational expectations models" by introducing a representative firm and consumer and finding decentralizing prices for them along standard Malinvaud (1953) lines provided that the *initial* Malinvaud price is chosen so that the consumer's transversality condition at infinity is satisfied. For Malinvaud prices, see, for example, the papers in Los and Los (1974) on "stimulating prices" for the Russian literature and Zilcha (1976) and his references for the Western literature.

By our modification of the Malinvaud price technique mentioned above, all stochastic growth models may be turned into rational expectations models by introducing a representative consumer who has the same preferences as the planner in the growth model and using the resulting "decentralizing prices" as the rational expectations prices. After choosing the *initial* Malinvaud price so that the TVC_∞ holds for the representative consumer, growth models become "asset pricing models" by this device.

More advances should be expected along the lines of introducing imperfect information and inquiring into what rules firm managers should follow in order to maximize equilibrium welfare of the representative consumer when some contingency markets are absent.

Existing results on stochastic stability in the multisectoral growth literature could be used to extend the stochastic stability theorem that was presented here to the multisector case.

It should be straightforward to extend the pricing results themselves to the multisector case.

More difficult and more interesting would be to introduce heterogeneous consumers so that borrowing on future income might be introduced and investigate the impact of this new institution on the price of risk. For example, in a finite horizon model where the individual is constrained to plans that require only that the expected wealth at horizon T conditioned at date 1 be nonnegative, one suspects that the price of risk may be small and the security market line may be quite flat. But care must be taken since "for each lender there must a borrower be." Thus, the institutional requirements on wealth at date T and the penalties for insolvency should have an impact on the price of risk. Furthermore, following the same line of reasoning, the work of Truman Bewley (1977) on the self-insurance behavior embedded in the permanent income hypothesis of Milton Friedman via borrowing and lending leads to the belief that the security market line (SML) generated by such a modification of our model will be flatter than the SML predicted by the standard capital asset pricing model (CAPM). This observation may provide an additional clue to why the observed SML is flatter than the SML predicted by the CAPM. See Merton (1973) and Fama (1976) for a discussion of this issue. What we have said here about the issue is highly speculative at best.

We close this paper with the hope that the methods developed here should be of some use to economics and finance.

Appendix to Section 1.3

Let us prove lemma 3.2 first. Let X solve the optimal growth problem (1.1). It is obvious that $\mathcal{R}$ satisfies the first-order necessary conditions for an REE by its very definition. What is at issue is the TVC_∞ (3.16), (3.17). Put

(A3.1)
$$V(x_{t-1}, t-1) \equiv \max E_1 \sum_{s=t}^{\infty} \beta^{s-1} u(c_s),$$

$$\text{s.t. } c_s + x_s = \sum_{j=1}^{N} f_j(x_{j,s-1}, r_{s-1}),$$

(A3.2)
$$\sum_{j=1}^{N} x_{js} \equiv x_s, x_{js} \geq 0, j = 1, 2, \ldots, N, c_s \geq 0, x_s \geq 0,$$

$$s = t, t+1, \ldots, x_{t-1} \text{ given.}$$

Then, following a similar argument as that in (3.23)–(3.32), we have, since u is bounded, that for any $x_t \geq 0$, $V(x_t, t) \to 0$, $t \to \infty$, and

(A3.3)
$$V(x_t, t) \geq V(x_t, t) - V(x_t/2, t) \geq V'(x_t, t) x_t/2$$

$$= E_1\{\beta^t u'(c_{t+1}) f_i'(x_{it}, r_t) x_t/2\} = E_1\{\beta^{t-1} u'(c_t) x_t/2\} \geq 0.$$

Since the L.H.S. of (A3.3) must go to zero, the R.H.S. must also. Hence,

(A3.4)
$$E_1\{\beta^{t-1} u'(c_t) x_t\} \to 0, \qquad t \to \infty,$$

along any optimum program. This establishes (3.17).

What about (3.16)? Here the stochastic process $\{\bar{P}_{it}\}_{t=1}^{\infty}$ was assumed to have been constructed from the quantity side of the model by use of (3.29) so that the TVC_∞ (3.31) was satisfied. Hence, TVC_∞ (3.16) is satisfied by the very construction of $\{\bar{P}_{it}\}_{t=1}^{\infty}$. This establishes the implication: (i) implies (ii).

In showing that (ii) implies (i) it is clear that the first-order necessary conditions for the quantity side of an REE boil down to the first-order conditions for the optimal growth problem. What must be established is the TVC_{∞} (A3.4). But this follows from (3.17) of lemma 3.1. This ends the proof of lemma 3.2.

Remark A3.1. Lemma 3.2 is not really useful as it stands because, given the quantity side of the growth model, it was assumed that $\{\bar{P}_{it}\}$ was constructed from use of (3.29) so that (3.31) held. How can we be sure that such a solution to the stochastic difference equation (3.29) exists even though $Z_{it} = 1$ for all i, t and π_t is given by (3.33) from the quantity side of the growth problem? Even though we have assumed that pure rents are positive so that equity prices must be positive in *any* equilibrium so that $Z_{it} = 1$ for all i, t, there is still a problem to show that a solution of (3.29) exists such that (3.31) holds.

Theorems 3.1 and 3.1′ take care of this problem. They establish the existence of a solution of (3.29) that satisfies (3.31) under mild restrictions on the quantity side of the growth problem. The reason theorem 3.1 can be used is that standard arguments (see Brock and Mirman 1972; Mirman and Zilcha 1975, 1976, 1977) using dynamic programming establish that the quantity side of the growth model is recursive. Hence, the quantity side of any REE must be recursive too.

Appendix to Section 1.5

It is straightforward to show by direct calculation that for the example of section 1.5 the solution to the Bellman equation

(A5.1) $U(y_1) = \max\{u(y_1 - x_1) + \beta EU[\sum_j f_j(x_{j1}, r_1]\}$

is of the form

(A5.2) $U(y_1) = K_1 + [1/(1 - \alpha\beta)] \log y_1$

for some constant K_1.

Hence, for any given x_t the allocation functions $x_{it} \equiv \eta_i(x_t)$ are given by solving the problem

(A5.3) $\max \int \log\left[\sum_{i=1}^{N} A_i(r_t)\eta_i^{\alpha} x_t \right]\mu(dr_t),$

$$\text{s.t. } \eta_i \geq 0, i = 1, 2, \ldots, N, \sum_{i=1}^{N} \eta_i = 1.$$

But the solution η to problem (A5.3) is the same as the solution η to the problem

(A5.4) $$\max \int \log [\, \sum_{i=1}^{N} A_i(r_t)\eta_i^\alpha]\mu(dr_t)$$

because the log function is multiplicatively additive.

By strict concavity and monotonicity of the logarithm there is just one solution η to (A5.4). It may be readily studied by use of (A5.4), and we leave this to the reader.

Alternative Setup Where Firms Carry Capital and Maximize Value

Let equity i now represent a claim on the dividends of firm i. Also, let Z_{it}, d_{it}, and x_{it} be chosen by the firm. The budget constraint of firm i is

(A5.5) $$P_{it}(Z_{it} - Z_{i,t-1}) + g_i(x_{i,t-1},r_{t-1})$$
$$= x_{it} - x_{i,t-1} + \delta_i x_{i,t-1} + d_{i,t-1}Z_{i,t-1}.$$

Here the new symbol d_{it} denotes dividends per share paid at the end of period t. We will *derive* an expression for the value of the firm from the consumer side of the model.

The budget equation for the consumer is from (3.3):

(A5.6) $$c_t + \underline{P}_t \cdot (\underline{Z}_t - \underline{Z}_{t-1}) \leq \underline{d}_{t-1} \cdot \underline{Z}_{t-1} \equiv y_t.$$

The consumer faces $\{\underline{P}_t\}$, $\{d_{it}\}$ parametrically and maximizes (3.2) subject to (A5.6) and $\underline{Z}_t \geq 0$, $t = 1,2\ldots$ Note that we do not allow short selling. There is not enough space to treat short selling.

Arguments analogous to those of section 1.3 allow us to show that the necessary and sufficient conditions for a solution to the consumer's problem are

(A5.7) $$P_{it} \geq E_t\{\Gamma_{t+1}(d_{it} + P_{i,t+1})\},$$

(A5.8) $$P_{it}Z_{it} = E_t\{\Gamma_{t+1}(d_{it} + P_{i,t+1})\}Z_{it},$$

(A5.9) $$\lim_{t \to \infty} E_1\{\beta^{t-1}u'(c_t)\underline{P}_t \cdot \underline{Z}_t\} = 0.$$

Here Γ_{t+1} is defined by

(A5.10) $$\Gamma_{t+1} = \beta u'(c_{t+1})/u'(c_t).$$

Equation (A5.8) may be rewritten to derive a recursion for the value of the firm

(A5.11) $$V_{it} \equiv P_{it}Z_{it}.$$

We have from (A5.5), (A5.8)

(A5.12) $V_{it} \equiv P_{it}Z_{it} = E_t\{\Gamma_{t+1}(d_{it}Z_{it} + P_{i,t+1}Z_{it+1} + P_{i,t+1}Z_{it}$

$$- P_{i,t+1}Z_{i,t+1})\} = E_t\{\Gamma_{t+1}(V_{i,t+1} + d_{it}Z_{it}$$

$$- P_{i,t+1}(Z_{i,t+1} - Z_{it}))\} = E_t\{\Gamma_{t+1}(V_{i,t+1}$$

$$+ g_i(x_{it}, r_t) - (x_{i,t+1} - x_{it} + \delta_i x_{it}))\} \equiv E_t\{\Gamma_{t+1}(V_{i,t+1} + N_{i,t+1})\}.$$

The L.H.S. and extreme R.H.S of (A5.12) correspond to Modigliani-Miller's (MM) equation (5) (Miller and Modigliani 1961, p. 414). They use this equation to demonstrate that the firm's value is invariant to dividend policy. The same conclusion obtains in our general equilibrium model. In order to see it, develop the recursion

(A5.13) $V_{i1} = E_1\{\Gamma_2(V_{i2} + N_{i2})\} = E_1(\Gamma_2 N_{i2}) + E_1(\Gamma_2\Gamma_3 N_{i2})$

$$+ E_1(\Gamma_2\Gamma_3 V_{i3}) = \ldots = E_1(\Gamma_2 N_{i2}) + \ldots$$

$$+ E_1(\prod_{s=2}^{s=T} \Gamma_s N_{iT}) + E_1\{(\prod_{s=2}^{s=T} \Gamma_s)V_{iT}\}.$$

The $\{\Gamma_t\}$ sequence is a sequence of random discount factors. They were exogenously given in MM's model and were not endogenously determined by tastes and technology as in our setup. Hence, in order to get the invariance result, MM had to *assume* that dividend policy did not affect them.

More fundamentally, however, in order to get their invariance result, MM had to *assume* that

(A5.14) $$\lim_{T \to \infty} E_1\{(\prod_{s=2}^{s=T} \Gamma_s)V_{iT}\}$$

was not affected by dividend policy.

We can demonstrate that the consumer's TVC_∞ implies the limit (A5.14) is zero in equilibrium as soon as we define equilibrium.

Definition.[3] A rational expectations equilibrium (REE) is a stochastic process $\mathcal{R} \equiv \langle \{\bar{P}_{it}\}_{t=1}^\infty, \{\bar{x}_{it}\}_{t=1}^\infty, \{\bar{Z}_{it}\}_{t=1}^\infty, \{\bar{d}_{it}\}_{t=1}^\infty, i = 1,2,\ldots,N; \{\bar{c}_t\}_{t=1}^\infty, \{\bar{\Gamma}_t\}_{t=2}^\infty \rangle$ if, facing $\mathcal{P} \equiv \langle \{\bar{P}_{it}\}_{t=1}^\infty, \{\bar{d}_{it}\}_{t=1}^\infty \rangle$, the consumer chooses

(A5.15) $c_t = \bar{c}_t, Z_{it} = \bar{Z}_{it}, t = 1,2,\ldots; i = 1,2,\ldots,N,$

and if, facing $\{\bar{\Gamma}_t\}_{t=2}^\infty$, the ith firm chooses

(A5.16) $x_{it} = \bar{x}_{it}, t = 1,2,\ldots,$

and the ith firm accommodates the optimum investment plan (A5.16) by setting

(A5.17) $Z_{it} = \bar{Z}_{it}, d_{it} = \bar{d}_{it}, t = 1,2,\ldots$

Firms are assumed to solve

(A5.18) $\max \bar{V}_{i1} - x_{i1}$ s.t. $x_{it} \geq 0, t = 1, 2, \ldots,$

where

(A5.19) $\bar{V}_{i1} \equiv E_1\{ \sum_{T=2}^{\infty} (\prod_{s=2}^{s=T} \bar{\Gamma}_s N_{iT}) \}.$

Furthermore, a firm's expectations on the sequence of random discounts must be "rational" in the sense that

(A5.20) $\bar{\Gamma}_s = \beta u'(\bar{c}_s)/u'(\bar{c}_{s-1}), \qquad s = 2, 3, \ldots$

Finally, material balance must obtain:

(A5.21) $\bar{c}_t + \bar{x}_t = \sum_{i=1}^{N} f_i(\bar{x}_{i,t-1}, r_{t-1}), \sum_{i=1}^{N} \bar{x}_t, t = 1, 2, \ldots$

This ends the definition of REE.

It is fairly straightforward to use the argument used in section 1.3 to demonstrate that necessity of the TVC_∞ from the consumer's side implies that the limit in (A5.14) is zero in equilibrium. It is also fairly straightforward to show that $\langle \bar{c}_t, \bar{x}_t, \{\bar{x}_{it}\}_{i=1}^{N} \rangle_{t=1}^{\infty}$ is equilibrium if it solves the problem (2.1). Furthermore, the fixed point argument that was applied to (3.40) to produce the asset pricing function of section 1.3 may be adapted to produce a value function $V_i(y_t)$ from the recursion (A5.12).

Hence, value is independent of dividend policy. The function $V_i(y_t)$ may be used in conjunction with the "policy function form" of (A5.12)

(A5.22) $V_i(y_t) = E_t\{\Gamma_{t+1}(V_i(y_{t+1}) + N_i(y_{t+1}))\}$

to develop valuation formulas for the firm as we did in sections 1.3 and 1.4 above.

For example, at date t, y_{t+1} is a random variable. Suppose following the development in section 1.4 that y_{t+1} may be written

(A5.23) $y_{t+1} = \bar{y}_t + \sum_{k=1}^{K} \Psi_t^k \tilde{\delta}_t^k.$

Follow the development in (4.39)–(4.32), expanding V_i, N_i in Taylor series about $\bar{y}_t$, keeping only first-order terms, we get

(A5.24) $V_i(y_t) = E_t\{\Gamma_{t+1}(V_i(\bar{y}_t)) + (\sum_{k=1}^{K} \Psi_t^k \tilde{\delta}_t^k) V_i'(\bar{y}_t) + N_i(\bar{y}_t)$

$+ (\sum_{k=1}^{K} \Psi_t^k \tilde{\delta}_t^k) N_i'(\bar{y}_t) \}$

$= \bar{\Gamma}_{t+1}(V_i(\bar{y}_t) + N_i(\bar{y}_t)) + \sum_{k=1}^{K} \bar{\Theta}_{t+1}^k \Psi_t^k)(V_i'(\bar{y}_t) + N_i'(\bar{y}_t)),$

where

(A5.25) $\bar{\Gamma}_{t+1} \equiv E_t \Gamma_{t+1}, \bar{\Theta}_{t+1}^k \equiv E_t(\Gamma_{t+1}\tilde{\delta}_t^k).$

Formula (A5.24) is the Sharpe-Lintner formula for firm value.

Banz and Miller (1978), Breedon and Litzenberger (1978) (BMBL) propose a procedure that can be used to estimate $\{\Gamma_t\}$ from market data. Hence we may use their methods to implement (A5.22) empirically. We mention their methods here not only to implement (A5.22) empirically, but also to counter the objection that firms have no way of inferring $\{\Gamma_t\}$ from consumer behavior and, hence, there is no operational way that firms can solve (A5.18).

The BMBL idea is to use option pricing theory to price Arrow-Debreu elementary securities. Prices of these securities at date t reveal the marginal rate of substitution between goods at date t and date event pairs at $t+1$. Since Γ_{t+1} is this marginal rate of substitution, therefore it is revealed. Furthermore, in recursive systems like ours which can be written as functions of a state variable the number of Arrow-Debreu securities that are needed to reveal $\{\Gamma_t\}$ can be greatly reduced.

The prices of the Arrow-Debreu securities that are needed to reveal $\{\Gamma_t\}$ may be found to any degree of accuracy desired by writing options that pay off on certain intervals of values of the state variable and using Black-Scholes theory to price such options. This is the heart of the BMBL theory. We do not have space to discuss it any more here. At any rate, using it, firms can, in principle, at least, get enough information from market data to solve (A5.18) to some degree of accuracy.

Notes

1. This research was supported partially by NSF Grant SOC 74–19692 to the University of Chicago. Part of this paper was written in the summer of 1977, while I was at the Australian National University. The stimulating research environment at the Australian National University was very helpful. The paper was finished at the California Institute of Technology, where I was a Fairchild Scholar.

This work has been presented at the Australian Graduate School of Management, the University of Texas Business School at Austin, the University of Houston, Department of Economics, the University of Wisconsin, Madison Workshop on Economic Theory, and the Graduate School of Industrial Administration, Carnegie-Mellon University. I would like to thank T. Bewley, S. Bhattacharya, R. Lucas, S. Magee, M. Magill, L. McKenzie, M. Miller, E. Prescott, J. Scheinkman, R. Kihlstrom, L. Mirman, S. Richard, and M. Rothschild for helpful comments. Most of all, I would like to thank F. R. Chang for a careful reading of this paper and for finding errors. I also thank Editor McCall and the conference participants for helpful comments.

None of the above are responsible for any errors or shortcomings of this paper. This paper is half of my "An Integration of Stochastic Growth Theory and the Theory of Finance," 9 February 1978. The other half of the 9 February 1978 paper is Brock (1978).

2. A parable may be helpful. There is one good. Call it "shmoos." Imagine that there are N "cottage" industries that consumers operate. Industry i costlessly turns one shmoo into capital of type i with a one-period lag. The consumer, at date t, must commit x_{it} shmoos to cottage technology i before r_t is revealed.

After r_t is revealed by nature the one-period-lag production process of type i emits x_{it} units of capital of type i. Hence, after r_t is revealed this precommitted capital is inelastically supplied. It cannot be changed until period $t+1$.

Now imagine that there are a large number of firms of each type and a large number of consumers of each type so that the price-taking assumption makes sense. The demand for capital services of type i at date t is determined by the marginal physical product of capital. The intersection of demand for capital services of type i with the perfectly inelastic supply x_{it} determines $R_{i,t+1}$. At the beginning of $t+1$ capital becomes "unfrozen." It is reallocated by the consumption side to supply $x_{i,t+1}$ before r_{t+1} is revealed, and so on it goes.

Notice that the fact that capital is frozen into capital of type i is what causes risk to be borne. If capital can be instantly adjusted when r_t is revealed, then there is no risk to be borne. Adjustment costs give rise to risk in our model.

It may be helpful for the reader to think of Z_{it} as units of perfectly divisible "land" and $\pi_{i,t+1}$, given by (3.1), to be the landowner's period earnings. The supply of land of type i is perfectly inelastic at unity. The price P_{it} is just the price of a unit of land of type i at date t.

3. It may be easier for the reader to follow this discussion if we operate in a slightly different space.

Suppose that consumers have read accounting textbooks so that they know (A5.5) in forming their expectations. Let

$$s_{it} = Z_{it}^d / Z_{it}^s$$

denote the percentage of firm i's shares demanded by the consumer. Upper d,s denote demand and supply, respectively. Using (A5.5), rewrite the consumer's budget constraint (A5.6) thus:

$$c_t + \sum_{i=1}^{N} P_{it} Z_{it}^d = c_t + \sum_{i=1}^{N} s_{it} V_{it} = \sum_{i=1}^{N} (d_{i,t-1} + P_{it}) Z_{i,t-1}^d = \sum_{i=1}^{N} s_{i,t-1}(V_{it} + N_{it}).$$

The last equality follows from (A5.5). Hence, view the consumer as choosing $\{c_t, s_{it}\}$ to solve

$$\max E_1\{ \sum_{t=1}^{\infty} \beta^{t-1} u(c_t)\},$$

$$\text{s.t. } c_t + \sum_{i=1}^{N} s_{it} V_{it} \leqq \sum_{i=1}^{N} s_{i,t-1}(V_{it} + N_{it}), t = 1, 2, \ldots,$$

$$s_{it} \geqq 0, i = 1, 2, \ldots N, \qquad t = 1, 2, \ldots,$$

$$s_{i0} = 1, i = 1, 2, \ldots, N.$$

Here the consumer faces $\{N_{it}, V_{it}\}$ parametrically. Notice that MM value invariance is embedded in the consumer's expectation that the value at t plus net cash flow at t (i.e., $V_{it} + N_{it}$) must equal $(d_{i,t-1} + P_{it}) Z_{i,t-1}^s$ via the firm's accounting constraint (A5.5).

We may now define REE as above. The only difference is that the consumer faces $\{\bar{V}_{it}, \bar{N}_{it}\}$ and chooses $\{s_{it}\}$ instead of choosing $\{Z_{it}\}$. In equilibrium we require the optimal choice of the consumer to satisfy

$$\bar{s}_{it} = 1, i = 1, 2, \ldots, N, \qquad t = 1, 2, \ldots$$

It is easy to follow the argument of section 1.3 (i.e., lemma 3.2) and use the necessity of the transversality condition at infinity from the consumer's side to prove

$$V_{it} = E_t \sum_{s=t+1}^{\infty} \Pi_s N_s,$$

where $\{\Pi_s, N_s\}$ are evaluated from the planner's problem (2.1).

Notice that only V_{it} is unique in equilibrium. Any P_{it}, Z_{it} such that

$$P_{it} Z_{it} = V_{it}$$

is equilibrium.

References

Banz, E., and Miller, M. 1978. Prices for state-contingent claims: Some estimates and applications. *Journal of Business* 51: 653–72.

Benveniste, L. M., and Scheinkman, J. A. 1977. Duality theory for dynamic optimization models of economics: The continuous time case. Forthcoming in *Journal of Economic Theory*.

Bewley, T. 1972. Existence of equilibria in economies with infinitely many commodities. *Journal of Economic Theory* 4: 514–40.

———. 1977. The permanent income hypothesis. *Journal of Economic Theory* 16: 252–92.

Breedon, D., and Litzenberger, R. 1978. Prices for state-contingent claims implicit in option prices. *Journal of Business* 51: 621–51.

Brock, W. A. 1974. Discussion of Roy Radner's survey paper. Paper read at Toronto AEA meetings, 1972. In Intriligator, M. D., and Kendrick, D. A., eds., *Frontiers of quantitative economics*, vol. 2, pp. 91–92. New York: North-Holland Publishing Company.

———. 1979. An integration of stochastic growth theory and the theory of finance—part I: The growth model. In Green, J., and Scheinkman, J., eds., *General equilibrium, growth, and trade*. New York: Academic Press.

Brock, W. A., and Gale, D. 1970. Optimal growth under factor augmenting progress. *Journal of Economic Theory* 1: 927–29.

Brock, W. A., and Majumdar, M. 1978. Global asymptotic stability results for multi-sector models of optimal growth under uncertainty when future utilities are discounted. *Journal of Economic Theory* 18: 225–43.

Brock, W. A., and Mirman, L. 1972. Optimal economic growth and uncertainty: The discounted case. *Journal of Economic Theory* 4: 479–513.

———. 1973. Optimal economic growth and uncertainty: The no discounting case. *International Economic Review* 14: 560–73.

Calvo, G. 1979. On models of money and perfect foresight. *International Economic Review* 20: 83–103.

Cass, D.; Okuno, M.; and Zilcha, I. 1979. The role of money in supporting the Pareto optimality of competitive equilibrium in consumption-loan models. *Journal of Economic Theory* 20: 41–80.

Cox, J.; Ingersoll, J.; and Ross, S. 1978. Notes on a theory of the term structure of interest rates. Graduate School of Business Research Paper 468. Stanford University, August 1978.

Fama, E. 1976. *Foundations of finance*. New York: Basic Books.

Gale, D. 1973. Pure exchange equilibrium of dynamic economic models. *Journal of Economic Theory* 6: 12–36.

Hellwig, M. Undated. A note on the intertemporal capital asset pricing model. Department of Economics, Princeton University. Mimeographed.

Johnsen, Thore H. 1978. The risk structure of security prices: Notes on multiperiod asset pricing. Columbia University Working Paper. Columbia University.

Loéve, M. 1963. *Probability theory*. Princeton, New Jersey: D. Van Nostrand Company.

Los, J., and Los, M., eds. 1974. *Mathematical models in economics*. Amsterdam: North-Holland Publishing Company.

Lucas, R. E., Jr. 1978. Asset prices in an exchange economy. *Econometrica* 46: 1429–45.

McFadden, D. 1973. On the existence of optimal development programmes in infinite horizon economics. In Mirrless, J., and Stern, N., eds., *Models of economic growth*. New York: Halsted Press.

Malinvaud, E. 1953. Capital accumulation and efficient allocation of resources. *Econometrica* 21: 233–68. Also, 1962. A corrigendum. *Econometrica* 30: 570–73.

Merton, R. 1973. An intertemporal capital asset pricing model. *Econometrica* 41: 867–87.

Miller, M., and Modigliani, F. 1961. Dividend policy, growth, and the valuation of shares. *Journal of Business* 34: 411–33.

Mirman, L., and Zilcha, I. 1975. On optimal growth under uncertainty. *Journal of Economic Theory* 11: 329–40.

———. 1976. Unbounded shadow prices for optimal stochastic growth models. *International Economic Review* 17: 121–32.

———. 1977. Characterizing optimal policies in a one-sector model of economic growth under uncertainty. *Journal of Economic Theory* 14: 389–401.

Prescott, E., and Mehra, R. 1980. Recursive competitive equilibria: The case of homogeneous households. *Econometrica* 48: 1365–79.

Radner, R. 1974. Market equilibrium and uncertainty: Concepts and problems. In Intriligator, M. D., and Kendrick, D. A., eds., *Frontiers of quantitative economics*, vol. 2, pp. 43–90. New York: North-Holland Publishing Company.

Richard, Scott F. 1978. An arbitrage model of the term structure of interest rates. Carnegie-Mellon University Working Paper 19–76–77. Carnegie Mellon University.

Ross, S. 1976. The arbitrage theory of capital asset pricing. *Journal of Economic Theory* 13: 341–59.

Rubenstein, M. 1976. The valuation of uncertain income streams and the pricing of options. *Bell Journal of Economics* 7: 407–25.

Scheinkman, J. A. 1977. Notes on asset pricing. Department of Economics, University of Chicago. Mimeographed.

Wilson, C. 1978. An infinite horizon model with money. Social Systems Research Institute Working Paper 7814. University of Wisconsin.

Zilcha, I. 1976. On competitive prices in a multi-sector economy with stochastic production and resources. *Review of Economic Studies* 43: 431–38.

Comment   Edward C. Prescott

The last decade has seen a proliferation of empirical studies documenting the stochastic behavior of security prices and returns. Defining a security's risk premium to be its expected return relative to the expected return of some chosen market portfolio, the predominance of evidence is that sizable risk premiums do exist. Some securities have expected returns that are 10 percent or more higher than the expected return of some other securities. These premiums are not associated with the uncertainty in the return per se but are associated with the covariance of the return with the selected market portfolio. Securities with high covariance with the market return have above-average expected returns, and those with small or negative covariance have below-average expected return. These facts have been well-documented by Black, Jensen and Scholes (1972), Fama and MacBeth (1973), and others.

The motivation for examining the relationship between a security's expected returns and its covariance with a market portfolio was provided by the capital asset pricing model developed by Sharpe, Lintner, and Mossin. This theory assumes a distribution of security returns along with some strong assumptions about individual preferences. The problem addressed by the theory was the allocation of this risk among investors and the pricing of the risk. It was not a theory of the source of variations in returns, as it considered only the demand side of the market.

Tests of the capital asset pricing model have found some important empirical anomalies. This motivated Ross (1976) to develop an alternative theory which he called the arbitrage pricing theory. Rather than making strong assumptions on preference, he merely assumed monotonicity and concavity of utility functions and based his theory primarily on an assumed linear return generating process. Recently Roll and Ross (1979) subjected that theory to a number of tests and concluded that the theory performed well under empirical scrutiny. This empirical analysis finds three and possibly four factors affecting returns.

Neither the two-parameter capital asset pricing model nor the arbitrage pricing theory explains why the returns vary. Brock develops a dynamic general equilibrium model which he contends, and I concur, is

Edward C. Prescott is professor of economics at the University of Minnesota.

needed if the source question is to be addressed. His is a simple model with homogeneous, infinitely lived consumers with a time separable utility function, a single capital good, and shocks to technology which are identically and independently distributed over time. His model is very similar to the one of Lucas (1978) except that capital accumulation is permitted. For specification of his technology, a return generating process results which is approximately equal to the linear one assumed by the arbitrage theory.

The single capital good might be thought to be potatoes, which can be either eaten or planted in any one of n fields. The next period's capital is the resulting output of potatoes summed over all fields. The source of risk is that the output of a field depends not only upon the capital invested there but also upon a random shock r_t. Different fields are affected in different ways by the realization of the random variable r_t. For example, if rain is plentiful, fields at the top of hills where drainage is good will have large output while fields in valleys with poor drainage will not. The converse is true if there is little rainfall. The distribution of rainfall, the relative supplies of land types, and the beginning of period capital determine the price of the different types of land jointly with the consumption and investment allocation decision.

The principal point of these comments is that one could obtain three factors if one applied the arbitrage pricing theory, even if there were a single type of field and only a single multiplicative shock to the production function. To see why this is possible, consider the following very simple example of Brock's environment:

$$\text{preference: } \sum_{\tau=0}^{\infty} \beta^t u(c_t),$$

$$\text{technology: } 0 \le c_t \le r_t.$$

We abstract away from capital because it is not needed to establish the point, and one can use Lucas's (1978) analysis to conclude the asset price is

$$P_t = E\{ \sum_{s=t}^{\infty} \beta^{s-t} u'(r_s)/u'(r_t)\}.$$

This security corresponds to ownership of the divided stream r_s for $s \ge t$ at time t. The period return of this equity is

$$\frac{P_{t+1} + r_t - P_t}{P_t},$$

as r_t is the dividend paid in period t. The price P_t is the predividend price. All prices are in terms of potatoes.

If one applies the methods of Arrow and Debreu, one prices units of consumption in period $t+1$ conditional upon the event r_{t+1} with all such securities priced in terms of consumption in period t. These prices are denoted by $\sigma(r_{t+1}; r_t)$. Assuming a finite number m of possible events (that the distribution of r is discrete), any security can be represented as a linear combination of these elementary securities.

In a sense, there are m sources of risk associated with the possible realizations of r_{t+1}. In another sense, there is a single source of shock, namely, the output shock. The latter sense seems more natural and will be implicit in the subsequent discussion.

Three interesting derived securities are as follows: The first is the linear combination of the Arrow elementary securities which correspond to dividend payment r_s in period s with $s \geq t$. This is just the equity share of the firm. The second security pays one unit of consumption in period $t+1$ for all realizations of r_{t+1}. This is a real bill, or if there is no uncertainty in the price level, it corresponds to a period bond or bill. The third security is a consol paying one unit of consumption not only in period $t+1$ but in all future periods. They are three linear independent combinations of the elementary securities.

If different firms correspond to different combinations of these three derived securities, applications of the Ross arbitrage pricing theory will yield three factors and one might incorrectly assume that there are three sources of risk. This illustrates that new securities which are not linear combinations of existing securities can introduce new factors in the returns generating process.

Development of a theory to explain the source or sources of risk is needed if we are to answer the questions posed by Brock at the beginning of his paper. The structures which we can analyze are limited to be of the variety considered by Brock or closely related ones; the next stage is to determine whether such abstractions are consistent with the data. For such a theory to be a good theory, it must not only explain the observed risk premiums but also be consistent with the observed variability of consumption and output over time. Possibly, in order to explain the large risk premiums which characterize security markets, it will be necessary to impose such extreme curvature on the utility function that the resulting equilibrium variability in consumption is less or variability in output greater than is observed.

My conjecture is that the principal source of risk is the business cycle. If this is correct, it surely will be necessary to introduce the labor supply decision, for most fluctuations in output are associated with variation in labor input—not with variation in the capital stock or with variation in the productivity of factors. Another possible generalization of the model (see Prescott and Mehra 1980) is to relax the assumption of a linear production transformation curve between the investment and consumption good and to take into consideration multiplicity of capital-good types. Brock's technology implies a constant relative price of the consumption and investment good, and this is inconsistent with the cyclical variability of this relative price. Such factors would clearly explain the serial correlation properties of the stock market. Possibly assuming persistence in the process governing the technology shock will prove fruitful. All these generalizations are feasible.

To conclude, it is time to determine whether the Brock abstraction or more likely a close cousin of it can be used to develop a theory of the source or sources of nondiversible risk. Rajnish Mehra and I have begun such a search. Such a theory might explain why the risk characteristics of particular securities change over time and might be of use in selecting corporate investment decisions as well.

References

Black, F.; Jensen, M. C.; and Scholes, M. 1972. The capital asset pricing model: Some empirical test. In Jensen, Michael, ed., *Studies in the theory of capital markets*, pp. 79–121. New York: Praeger.

Fama, E. F., and MacBeth, J. D. 1973. Risk, return, and equilibrium: Empirical tests. *Journal of Political Economy* 81: 607–36.

Lucas, R. E., Jr. 1978. Asset prices in an exchange economy. *Econometrica* 46: 1426–46.

Prescott, E. C., and Mehra, R. 1980. Recursive competitive equilibrium: The case of homogeneous households. *Econometrica* 48: 1365–80.

Roll, R., and Ross, S. A. 1979. An empirical investigation of the arbitrage pricing theory. School of Organizations and Management Working Paper. Yale University.

Ross, S. A. 1976. The arbitrage theory of capital asset pricing. *Journal of Economic Theory* 13: 341–59.

2   Planning and Market Structure

Dennis W. Carlton

2.1 Introduction

In many markets, the successful entrepreneur is the one who has the skill to plan his production in advance to take advantage of predicted demand conditions. Production takes time, and the entrepreneur who waits until the last moment to expand or contract production may often earn lower profits than an entrepreneur with better forecasting skills. In fact, a large fraction of many managers' time is spent trying to figure out what demand will be and how best to meet it. It is clear that early revelation of demand has a benefit from society's veiwpoint since it gives suppliers notice to expand or contract production. It is also clear that it may be costly to forecast demand.

How does information get transmitted from demanders to suppliers in a market? We show that a competitive market is not well suited to the efficient transmission of this information. We then show how a firm with some monopoly power will have a greater incentive than competitive firms to cause this transmission of information to occur. The stability of markets over time—measured in terms of price and quantity variance—will differ greatly depending on whether planning takes place or not. We argue that, when planning is possible, a market structure with some monopoly power may emerge. This market will have more quantity variation and less price variation than would the same market if it were competitively organized. To obtain insight into the likely behavior of a

Dennis W. Carlton is professor in the Law School, University of Chicago.

The author thanks the NSF for support and Gary Becker, William Brock, Carl Futia, Milton Harris, Jerry Hausman, Paul Joskow, Edward Lazear, Sam Peltzman, Edward Prescott, and participants in seminars at Northwestern University, Bell Laboratories, and the University of Chicago and at the NBER Conference on the Economics of Information and Uncertainty for helpful comments.

market structure with firms possessing some monopoly power, we analyze the behavior of a market with a dominant firm(s) and competitive fringe. The dominant firm will have an incentive to invest in information while the competitive fringe will not. The size of the competitive fringe will depend on such things as information costs and demand variability. The competitive fringe shrinks when there is a decrease in the marginal cost of information or an increase in the uncertainty of demand. An interesting result is that the dominant firm may choose to produce in some states of demand even though it knows for sure that prices will not cover constant marginal cost. This result occurs because the dominant firm realizes that the size of the competitive fringe responds to the dominant firm's production strategy. The dominant firm keeps prices low in some realizations of demand to make entry of new firms unattractive. This strategy turns out to be profit maximizing since the strategy increases the monopoly power of the dominant firm when demand is high. Such a strategy is closely related to the concepts of "predatory" or "limit" pricing. However, instead of having the undesirable welfare consequences usually associated with "predatory" pricing, in this case the strategy produces a market outcome that is superior to that of both competition and pure monopoly.

2.2 Competitive Case

We want to investigate the case where there are many demanders each of whom has a random demand that makes a negligible contribution to total demand, which will also be random. Initially, we let the random demands of each demander be independent of each other. Both the mean and variance of total demand are finite, even though we have many demanders. At a cost, the realization of random demand for any fraction of the market can be discovered early enough to allow suppliers to adjust their production plans if necessary. (An alternative interpretation is that at a cost the prediction error of forecast can be reduced.)

To formally model this situation we proceed as follows.[1] Let total demand be random and be given by $a - p + \epsilon$, where ϵ is a normal random variable with mean 0 and variance σ^2, a is a constant, and p is price.[2] Imagine a continuum of demanders between $[0,1]$, and let $W(Z)$ be defined as a normal random variable with mean $Z(a-p)$ and variance $Z\sigma^2, Z \in [0,1]$. $W(Z)$ can be interpreted as the random demand for the first fraction Z of the market. Assume that the random demands of any nonoverlapping interval of demanders are independent of each other so that the increment to total demand by agents in the interval $[Z_0, Z_0 + dZ]$ is independent of the level of demand $W(Z_0)$ for the first fraction Z_0 of the market. $W(Z)$ is then a Wiener process with $W(1)$ equaling $a - p + \epsilon$.

Suppose that at a cost it is possible to determine the realization of the random component of demand one period early.[3] Suppose that demanders are ordered in terms of increasing cost of acquiring information so that it costs $C(F)$ to learn in advance the demands of the first F percent[4] of the market with $C'(F) > 0$ and $C''(F) > 0$. If a firm has devoted $C(F)$ resources to information gathering, then it follows from the properties of a Wiener process that the firm knows that the market demand can be written as

$$(1) \qquad a - p + \sqrt{F}\, V_1 + \sqrt{1-F}\, V_2,$$

where V_1 and V_2 are independent normal random variables, with mean 0 and variance σ^2, and where the realization of V_1 becomes known to the firm but that of V_2 remains unknown at the time the firm must make some productive decisions.[5]

Competitive risk neutral suppliers must produce[6] one period before all demand is costlessly revealed. Only if someone has invested resources to predict demand will suppliers know enough to adapt to changes in demand. There are constant returns to production rates, which are required to be finite. Let it cost c to produce one unit of the good. No production can take place once the market opens. For simplicity we assume that the good cannot be stored for more than one period. Therefore, the supply of the good in any period is exactly equal to the previous period's production. A risk neutral supplier will sign a fixed price forward contract to sell at price p^* only if the expected price paid on the spot market $\bar{p}$ is less than or equal to p^*. Hence, a supplier will offer fixed price contracts only if $p^* \geq \bar{p}$.

If no information about the random components of demand is available to any supplier, then ex ante a supply firm's random profit stream is unchanged over time and each supplier will produce a fixed amount. In equilibrium, the total market supply S must be such that expected price equals the cost of production c. For the linear demand curve presented earlier, it is straightforward to show that, in equilibrium with no information about the randomness in demand, $S = a - c$, $p = c + \epsilon$, $E(p) = c$, and var $(p) = \sigma^2$.

It is clear that if it were always possible for suppliers to expand and contract production so that price equaled c, then society would be operating efficiently. Exactly the amount demanded would be produced at a price equal to the marginal cost. If information acquisition and transmission are costless, we can imagine demanders costlessly announcing their demands in advance and the market responding efficiently.

What happens when information acquisition is not costless? Clearly, for sufficiently small information costs it will still be efficient for investment in information to occur to enable the planning of next period's supply. However, in this situation each demander will have no incentive to spend resources to figure out his demand and a supplier will have no incentive to purchase information from an individual demander. Although society would be made better off by information investment and transmission, individual agents do not invest in information because they do not perceive the general equilibrium effects of their (collective) noninvestment in information since each agent by assumption is infinitesimal and thus correctly ignores the effect of his actions on the price distribution.

To illustrate the lack of incentives for information transmission, first consider a demander. A demander has two choices. He can choose not to invest in information and next period pay random price p, or he can spend some amount δ to figure out his next period's demand.[7] If he has invested in information, he can sell his information to a supplier (only one for now) for some amount I and then buy on the spot market paying random price p. Because the demander is small, his information has no effect on the distribution of p. Alternatively, instead of the demander separately selling his information and then buying on the spot market, we can imagine the demander being offered a fixed price forward contract at some p^* in return for his information. A demander prefers to face a variable price distribution rather than a price stabilized at the mean of the price distribution. Under variable prices the demander could consume the fixed amount he finds optimal under the fixed mean price. However, substitution possibilities enable the demander to take advantage of the variable price by consuming more of the product when its price is low and less of the product when its price is high. In this way demanders can achieve higher utility or profits. Stated in another way, since the expenditure function (if the demander is a consumer) and the cost function (if the demander is a firm) are concave in price, Jensen's inequality ensures that demanders have a preference for a variable price instead of a price stabilized at the mean.[8] For the buyer to accept a contract with fixed price p^*, p^* would have to be below $\bar{p}$, where $\bar{p}$ is the expected spot price; otherwise, it follows from the above discussion that there is no expected gain to the demander from investing in the information.

Now consider suppliers. How much would any one supplier pay for information from an individual demander? An individual demander has no influence on price, and since each supplier can sell all he wants at the (unknown) market price next period, no supplier has an incentive to buy (valueless) information from one demander. This means that the amount I a supplier would pay for information from one demander is zero.[9] The same reasoning shows that a risk neutral supplier would never sign a fixed price contract at p^*, if $p^* < \bar{p}$, in return for knowing an individual's demand. Since the demander invests in information only if he can either sell the information for $I > \delta$ or sign a fixed price contract at p^*, with $p^* <$

$\bar{p}$, we see that under the stated assumptions in a competitive market no incentive for information transmission between individual buyers and sellers will arise if it is costly to acquire information.

In the above discussion we only considered information transmission between one demander and one seller. A demander was not allowed to resell his information. Information from one demander (of measure zero) is valueless to a firm. However, it is true that information from a number of demanders (of positive measure) is valuable since their demand will influence price. Could one imagine a market in which each supplying firm pays an infinitesimal amount to a group of demanders and thus each supplier knows something about the entire demand? The special problems associated with information suggest that such an information market may not be feasible. Since these problems have been extensively discussed in the literature (see, e.g., Arrow 1971; Green 1973; Grossman 1976, 1977; Grossman and Stiglitz 1976, 1980), we give only a brief discussion here.

First, consider the monitoring problem. Is each supplier expected to keep track of the accuracy of each of the infinite number of demanders' response? (Notice that an exchange of information between a demander and a supplier automatically does this if the demander reveals his information to a supplier by signing a purchase contract specifying a quantity and if the demander does not break the contract.) Second and more important, whenever a group of suppliers obtain information about demand, the only possible equilibrium consistent with competitive assumptions is one in which the suppliers adjust production until expected price equals the constant marginal cost c. When this happens, the incentives of supplying firms to invest resources to learn total demand in order to predict price totally vanish.[10]

Could there be a competitive equilibrium in which supplying firms have different information sets purchased from different groups of demanders? The answer again is no because the supplying firms would then have incentives to merge their information sets to improve the accuracy of their demand forecasts and then we would return to the situation just discussed where expected price would fall to constant marginal cost c, or else to a situation where the firms would collectively try to earn a return on the information by cartelizing and behaving monopolistically. Could a trade association form, assess fees on supplying firms, and provide incentives for some demanders to figure out and reveal their future demands? For the reasons just discussed it would be difficult to enforce participation in the association.[11] But even if a trade association did organize, it is plausible that the trade association would not only coordinate information flows but also serve as a vehicle toward cartelization of the industry. In fact, any time the information is provided by one central source, the possessor of the information can become a producer and behave monopolistically to take advantage of the information. In short, purely competitive behavior and information transmission do not seem compatible in the model under examination.

The same exact problems persist in the case where individual demands are correlated. Any time firms have spent resources to acquire the same information set, they have an incentive to merge to avoid the duplicative costs of acquiring the same information. Any time firms have different information sets, they have an incentive to merge to pool information to more accurately predict demand. Any time a group of competitive firms obtain information about demand, the only possible equilibrium consistent with competitive behavior requires production to be adjusted until expected price equals constant marginal costs.[12]

The conclusion of this analysis is that under competition there is no mechanism to ensure that investment in information occurs to the degree that society finds optimal. In the special case just examined here, no investment occurs. This does *not* mean that there can never be situations in which competitive supplying firms have an incentive to discover demand by offering a lower price to those who order in advance, only that it is unlikely that a competitive environment will provide the correct investment incentives. For example, if those who order in advance are less costly to serve, if supply curves are upward sloping, or if firms can lower operating costs by reducing the variability of their cash flow, then we can expect some forward contracts to emerge which will as a by-product transmit information from suppliers to demanders. (See Carlton 1978, 1979a, 1979b, for incentives for forward contracting.) The point is that although forward contracts may come into existence even when it is costly to obtain information on demand, the correct incentives to transmit information will not necessarily be provided.

We have argued that for the market conditions under examination there may be incentives for mergers. In an industry where information considerations, and not other issues like probability of obtaining delivery, are important, it is plausible to expect that the industry may evolve until one large firm (or a few) emerges which has some market power. It is only by the acquisition of market power that a firm in the model acquires an incentive to invest in information. Information is valuable only if the recipients of the information have the power to prevent industry production from expanding to the point where expected price equals constant marginal cost.[13] Before we examine the stability and consequences of this market power, let us investigate and compare the behavior of a monopolist and a social planner.

2.3   The Monopoly Case

How would a monopolist operate—would he have an incentive to invest in information, and would he invest an optimal amount? Let us use the simple example of the previous section to illustrate the monopolist's incentives to invest in information. Suppose as before that there is a continuum of demanders between 0 and 1, that demanders are ordered in terms of the increasing cost of eliciting information, and that the demands of agents in nonoverlapping intervals are independent. Let F be the number between 0 and 1 such that all information about demanders between 0 and F is collected while information about all demanders between F and 1 is not.[14] By the argument given in the previous section, the demand curve the monopolist sees after his collection of information can be written as

$$D(P) = a - p + \sqrt{F} V_1 + \sqrt{1-F} V_2,$$

where V_1 and V_2 are independent normal variables with mean 0 and variance σ^2, and where the realization of V_1 is observed by the monopolist before production occurs.

Conditional on knowing V_1 and F, the monopolist must decide how much to produce and offer on the market next period. The price will be random and will equate supply to demand. Production S occurs before total demand is observed, and it costs c to produce a unit of the good.

The monopolist sets S to maximize expected profits,[15] which are given by

$$E(\pi(S)/V_1, F) = E[p-c]S.$$

Price p is given by equating demand $D(p)$ to supply S. Therefore,

$$p = a - S + \sqrt{F} V_1 + \sqrt{(1-F)} V_2,$$

and

$$E(\pi(S)|V_1, F) = E[a - S + \sqrt{F} V_1 + \sqrt{(1-F)} V_2 - c]S,$$

or

$$E(\pi(S)|V_1, F) = S(a - S + \sqrt{F} V_1 - c).$$

Hence, in the profit maximizing solution,

$$S = \frac{a+c+\sqrt{F} V_1}{2}, \quad p = \frac{a+c}{2} + \frac{\sqrt{F}}{2} V_1 + \sqrt{1-F} V_2,$$

and

$$E(\pi/V_1, F) = \left(\frac{a - c + \sqrt{F} V_1}{2}\right)^2.$$

Since F must be chosen before V_1 is observed, the expected value H from observing the fraction F of the population is[16]

$$H(F) = E(\pi \mid V_1, F) = E\left(\frac{a - c + \sqrt{F}\,V_1}{2}\right)^2 = \frac{(a - c)^2 + F\sigma^2}{4}.$$

Expected profits are increasing in F and σ^2. Marginal expected profits are increasing in σ^2. If $C(F)$ is the cost of acquiring information on fraction F of the population, then the optimal (interior) F satisfies

$$H'(F) = C'(F) \text{ or } \frac{\sigma^2}{4} = C'(F) \text{ and } C''(F) > 0.$$

Three solutions are possible. Either $(a)\,F = 0$ and $C'(0) \geq H'(0)$, $(b)\,0 < F < 1$ and $C(F)$ rises faster than $H(F)$, or $(c)\,F = 1$ and $C'(1) \leq H'(1)$. It immediately follows that investment in information will be higher the higher is σ^2 and the lower is the marginal cost of information schedule.

The monopolist has an incentive to invest in information because by learning about demand next period he is better able to plan production this period and thereby more fully exploit his monopoly power next period. The expected monopoly price is $(a + c)/2$, which exceeds the expected competitive price c derived in the previous section; the variance of the monopoly price is $\sigma^2(1 - (3F/4))$, which is lower than the variance of the competitive price σ^2; while the variance of the quantity is $(F/4)\sigma^2$, which of course exceeds the zero variance in quantity supplied under competition. As one would expect, planning reduces price variance but increases quantity variance.

2.4 Social Planner

How would a social planner invest in information to maximize expected consumer surplus?[17] Using the same production and demand example as before, we have that, conditional on observing V_1 for fraction F of the population, consumer surplus equals

$$\text{SUR}(S, F, V_1) = \int_0^S [a + \sqrt{F}\,V_1 + \sqrt{(1 - F)}\,V_2 - q]\,dq - cS.$$

Expected surplus[18] conditional on V_1 and F is therefore

$$\text{SUR}(S, F, V_2) = [a + \sqrt{F}\,V_1 - c]S - \frac{S^2}{2}.$$

The optimal values satisfy $S = (a + \sqrt{F}\,V_1 - c)$, $p = c + \sqrt{1 - F}\,V_2$, variance $(p) = (1 - F)\sigma^2$, variance $(S) = F\sigma^2$, and $\text{SUR} = (a + \sqrt{F}\,V_1 - c)^2/2$. To choose F optimally, the social planner must maximize

$$E(\text{SUR}) - C(F),$$

or

$$\frac{(a-c)^2}{2} + \frac{F\sigma^2}{2} - C(F).$$

Hence $\qquad\qquad \sigma^2/2 = C'(F).$

The marginal benefits of increasing F are greater for the social planner than for the monopolist ($\sigma^2/2$ versus $\sigma^2/4$); therefore, the monopolist underinvests in information. The intuitive reason for the discrepancy in incentives is the usual one that explains why a monopolist's conduct is not efficient. The benefit to the social planner of finding out and satisfying some increase in demand is related to the area bounded by the initial expected demand curve, the new demand curve, and the marginal cost curve. In contrast, the corresponding benefit to the monopolist is related to the area bounded by the initial expected marginal revenue curve, the new marginal revenue curve, and the marginal cost curve. For the linear example, this latter area is always smaller than the former.

The optimal solution involves a higher value to information than the monopolist calculates. The monopolist underinvests in information relative to the social optimum, but overinvests relative to the competitive outcome. This is a general result that will tend to occur so long as the marginal revenue curve shifts less than the demand curve in response to each new piece of information.[19] The variance of price in the socially optimal solution is lower than in the monopoly solution (whose price variance is lower than in the competitive solution). The variance of quantity in the socially optimal solution is higher than in the monopoly solution (whose quantity variance is higher than in the competitive solution).

2.5 Comparison of Monopoly and Competition

Which is worse, having a monopolist who does some information processing or having competitors who do none? To obtain some insight into this question, let us compare the competitive solution with no planning to the monopoly solution under the extreme assumption that the monopolist plans perfectly and that we ignore the costs of information gathering. This comparison will provide us with the most favorable case[20] to monopoly and will allow us to draw conclusions about the maximum trade-off between planning efficiency and deadweight loss.

If the demand curve is $q = a - p + \epsilon$ with ϵ a normal random variable with mean 0 and variance σ^2, and constant marginal production costs are c, then (from section 2.2) in equilibrium under competition no planning occurs and the amount supplied will equal $a - c$, the expected price will equal c, the actual price will equal $c + \epsilon$, and the variance of price will equal σ^2. In comparison to the ideal world of perfect planning, we can calculate the expected deadweight loss that comes from not planning. For each realization of ϵ, we can regard the competitive equilibrium as resulting from an imposition of a (random) tax equal to the discrepancy between actual price and the constant marginal cost c. This discrepancy equals ϵ. Since the demand curve has slope -1, the expected value of the resulting deadweight loss equals $\frac{1}{2}\sigma^2$, where σ^2 is the variance of ϵ.

If we calculate the deadweight loss of a monopolist who plans relative to the ideal world of marginal cost pricing and planning, we see from section 2.3 that the discrepancy between price and marginal cost for any realization ϵ equals $((a-c)/2) + (\epsilon/2)$ so that the expected deadweight loss equals $((a-c)^2/8) + (\sigma^2/8)$. The deadweight loss of monopoly that results from nonmarginal cost pricing rises slower as σ^2 increases than does the deadweight loss from (unplanned) competition (that also results in [ex post] nonmarginal cost pricing). For very large values of σ^2, the deadweight loss from monopoly power is swamped by the deadweight loss that results from not planning, while exactly the opposite is the case for small values of σ^2.

How large does σ^2 have to be before monopoly is better than competition? The answer is when $\sigma = (a-c)/\sqrt{3}$. The average level of demand at the competitive price equals $a-c$. Therefore, the implied coefficient of variation necessary for monopoly to be preferred to competition is about .58. This strikes me as a fairly high value. For example, in many manufacturing markets a conservative estimate (95 percent confidence interval) of demand would be, say, ± 20 percent of the previous year's level (correcting for trend). Using the normal distribution as an approximation, this would approximately imply a coefficient of variation of only .1. Only if one felt that an interval slightly larger than 0 to twice the level of average demand represented a 95 percent confidence interval would the coefficient of variation rise to .58.

In order to see whether the above results were robust to a different specification of demand, I redid the calculations for demand curves of the form $A_0 v/p^\eta$, where A_0 is a constant, η is the price elasticity, and v is assumed to be lognormally distributed with mean 0 and variance σ^2. Table 2.1 reports the threshold value for σ beyond which monopoly with planning is superior to unplanned competition.

The standard deviation σ gives an idea of the proportional variation in demand. For example, a $\sigma = \ln 2$ (.69) would imply that a 95 percent confidence interval would include demands that were approximately between ¼ and 4 times the average level. Even the lowest threshold value of .82 in table 2.1 suggests that a 95 percent confidence region would have to be larger than ¼ to 4 times the average demand level. Again, the levels of demand variation that are required before monopoly deadweight

Table 2.1   **Threshold Values of σ beyond Which Monopoly Dominates Competition**

Elasticity η	Threshold Values of σ
1.5	1.25
2	1.07
3	.95
4	.91
10	.82

losses are exceeded by planning losses seems so high as not to be applicable to most industries.

The above numerical calculations suggest that it is unlikely that the planning benefit that accompanies monopoly will exceed the deadweight inefficiency loss that also accompanies monopoly. However, there are two very good reasons to believe that the above (standard) framework for calculating deadweight losses may be inappropriate in this instance. Unfortunately, the quantitative significance of these effects are difficult to assess.

The first qualification relates to a point made by Stigler (1939) in regard to a cost function and adjustment costs. If the output of a firm must vary, then the cost of producing might well depend on how adaptable the technology is. If adjustment costs are an increasing convex function of the adjustment (e.g., Lucas 1967), then the implied variability of output in the social optimum will be lower than that implied by the above framework, where constant returns to scale are postulated. This suggests that the difference between the socially optimal output and the competitive output will diminish relative to that between the socially optimal output and the monopoly output. The position of competition relative to monopoly would then improve from that portrayed in table 2.1.

A second qualification is that it is inappropriate to use the same demand curve to calculate the monopoly deadweight loss and the competitive price fluctuations that will prevail in response to demand shifts. Demand curves, like supply curves, have a time dimension associated with them that depends on adjustment costs. In the very short run most demand curves are probably very inelastic because it takes consumers time to adapt to any price change. Although it would take us too far afield to discuss how the formation of expectations of future prices is affected by current price, it seems clear that the monopoly price markup is based not on the "short-run" elasticity of demand but on a "long-run" elasticity of demand, provided the firm wishes to continue in business.[21] However, when calculating how price will fluctuate in the unplanned competitive world, the short-run demand curve is the appropriate one to use since no one firm has an incentive to concern itself with the effect of its actions on future price expectations. Although applying Stigler's (1939) reasoning to input price fluctuations leads us to expect the short-run demand curve to be more elastic the more variable prices are (i.e., demander firms pay to have a technology with lots of substitutability),[22] it still seems plausible to expect that the relevant short-run demand elasticity determining price fluctuations under (unplanned) competition could be lower than the elasticity determining the monopoly markup. When this is the case, the results of table 2.1 will understate the deadweight losses under competition that arise from not planning relative to those that arise from monopoly power with planning.

2.6 Dominant Firm and Competitive Fringe

In this section the behavior of an industry structure with a dominant firm and a competitive fringe is examined. There are at least two reasons to justify such a market structure in the model being examined. First, suppose that only one firm (or a few firms which decide to collude) has access to an *information acquisition* technology. Then this firm would become a dominant firm which would use information on demand to determine its output, which the firm realizes affects price. Free entry and access to the *production* technology would ensure that a nonplanning competitive fringe would continue to enter as long as expected price exceeded constant marginal production costs.

The second reason justifying a market structure with a dominant firm that plans and a competitive fringe that does not plan is based on the earlier discussion where we argued that firms would have an incentive to merge for information reasons.[23] The merged firm would have to acquire some market power if it were to continue to have an incentive to acquire information. But how, with free entry, could the merged firm maintain its market power? There are at least two possible answers. Once the merged firm is created and it collects information and earns above-normal profits, it would be necessary for another firm to enter and do whatever the merged firm was doing in order to erode the monopoly profits. The second firm to enter realizes that its profitability will depend on the initial firm's behavior in response to its entry. When such interdependence arrangements are necessary to determine the profitability of entry, entry is thought to be more difficult than when entry can occur on a small scale with market conditions taken as given. In *Barriers to New Competition*, Bain (1956) labeled such a condition an economy-of-scale barrier to entry. A second possible explanation of why the large merged firm with market power can persist utilizes Stigler's (1964) theory of oligopoly. Suppose that all firms which acquire information collude but that there is a cost to enforcing the collusive agreements.[24] These costs rise as the number of firms taking part in the collusive arrangement increases.[25] Equilibrium will require that firms be indifferent between joining the collusive arrangement or remaining outside the arrangement and not collecting information. In terms of the assumptions of the model, this would require that the competitive fringe (which does not plan) earn zero profits and that the number of firms which belong to the cartel be such that enforcement costs dissipate the profits of the cartel. The cartel would have market power in the sense that they take into account their effect on price.

Regardless of which reason is responsible for the existence of a market structure with a dominant firm (or colluding firms) and a competitive fringe, the interesting feature of this market structure is that the dominant firm will take into account how its production strategy influences the size of the competitive fringe. The competitive fringe will affect but not eliminate the market power of the dominant firm. The reason is that, as before, production decisions must be made before demand is observed. The competitive fringe which does not invest in information will therefore base its output decisions on expected price, which in equilibrium must equal the constant marginal production cost. The dominant firm, on the other hand, is in the position of having invested in information to obtain an advance reading on demand before it produces. The dominant firm will produce little in low realizations of demand and a lot in high realizations of demand. The competitive fringe remains finite despite constant returns to scale precisely because of its inability to forecast demand as accurately as the dominant firm. The size of the competitive fringe will be endogenously determined by the price distribution, which itself is endogenously influenced by the dominant firm's production strategy.[26]

Let us now examine the equilibrium conditions in the industry. Let $\tilde{Q}(p)$ be the random distribution of demand at price p. Let $C(F)$ be the cost of learning for certain the demands of F percent of the population, with $C'(F) > 0$. Let S be the amount that is supplied by the fringe. The value of S will be unchanged over time because ex ante the world always looks the same to the competitive fringe (i.e., the dominant firm is able to keep secret its future production plans from the competitive fringe). Because of the assumption of constant returns to scale, the expected price must equal the constant cost of production c in equilibrium. The dominant firm will use the residual demand curve to determine its optimal investment in information and its production response to that information. Let $m(\gamma, F)$ be the amount the dominant firm supplies when it observes random state of demand γ after it has sampled F percent of total demand.[27] Price will be determined by the condition

(2) $$\tilde{Q}(p) = m(\gamma, F) + S.$$

For a fixed F, S, and strategy $\{m(\gamma, F)\}$ and for a random γ and $\tilde{Q}$, (2) induces a distribution on price p. Call this distribution $f_1(p; F, S, m(\gamma, F))$, which we abbreviate as $f_1(p)$. It is this distribution that will determine whether there is an incentive for the competitive fringe to expand or contract. In equilibrium it must be the case that the size of the competitive fringe S is such that the expected value of price equals c, the constant marginal production cost, or

(3) $\int p f_1(p)dp = c.$

The dominant firm will realize how S is determined and will take (3) into account in determining its optimal supply strategy. We can think of (3) as establishing a relation between S and the strategy $\{m(\gamma, F)\}$ of the dominant firm. In other words, since the dominant firm's supply strategy affects the price distribution, which affects the size of the competitive fringe, the dominant firm will act like a Stackelberg competitor taking (3) as determining the competitive fringe's response to his *strategy*.

How is $m(\gamma, F)$ determined? For the moment let us hold F constant and ignore information acquisition costs $C(F)$. For *fixed* S, F, γ, and $m(\gamma, F)$, (2) induces a distribution on p. Call this distribution $f_2(p)$.[28] (If $F = 1$, no residual randomness is left after the information acquisition takes place and $f_2(p)$ is degenerate. Remember that the dominant firm only observes the random demand of F percent of the market. The observed γ refers only to the first F percent of the market.) Expected profits, π_1, conditional on S, F, γ, and $m(\gamma, F)$ equal

$$\pi_1(m(\gamma, F)) = \int \pi_0(m(\gamma, F), p) f_2(p)dp,$$

where

$$\pi_0(m(\gamma, F), p) = [p - c] m(\gamma, F).$$

The monopolist wants to choose a strategy that maximizes the expectation of $\pi_1(m(\gamma, F))$ when γ is regarded as random. The monopolist therefore maximizes $\pi(F) = E(\pi_1(m(\gamma, F)))$ with expectations taken with respect to γ. Finally, the monopolist chooses the optimal amount of investment in information by maximizing $\pi(F) - C(F)$ or equivalently by choosing F such that

(4) $\pi'(F) = C'(F).$

Throughout the maximization, the relation between S and $m(\gamma, F)$ as summarized in (3) is taken into account.

The above formulation can be used to determine the optimal F, optimal strategy, $m(\gamma, F)$, and resulting S that characterize equilibrium in the model. One interesting feature of this model is that the dominant firm will find it optimal to produce positive output even when the expected price is below the constant costs of production. In other words, even if the dominant firm knows in advance that demand is so low relative to the amount supplied by the competitive fringe that price will be below the constant production costs, the dominant firm may still choose to produce. This strategy is profit maximizing for the firm because although the firm loses money when it produces when price is below constant production costs, if it did not produce in those demand states then the price distribution would be affected in such a way as to encourage entry. This resulting entry would reduce profits of the dominant firm in all states of demand. The dominant firm follows a conscious policy of trying to keep price low in some states to discourage entry so that when demand is high, the dominant firm can reap high monopoly profits.

There is one inessential indeterminacy in the problem that becomes obvious on reflection. Suppose that the monopolist's optimal output m as a function of the observed state of nature γ is $m(\gamma)$.[29] Let

$$\min_{\gamma} m(\gamma) > 0.$$

Suppose the competitive output is S. Notice that the price distribution, output produced, and monopoly profits are unchanged if we consider the equilibrium monopoly output $m^*(\gamma) = m(\gamma) + \Delta$, and equilibrium competitive supply $S^* = S - \Delta$ for

$$0 < \Delta < \min_{\gamma} m(\gamma).$$

Since on any fixed amount of output Δ expected profits are zero, we see that the relevant issue is not the size of the monopolist's output relative to the competitive fringe, but rather the variation in the monopolist's output above some fixed level. As long as a firm produces a fixed amount of output, it makes no difference whether we regard the firm as part of the competitive fringe or as a division of the dominant firm. For expositional ease, in the example to follow I will make S as large as possible so that

$$\min_{\gamma} m(\gamma) = 0.$$

However, the reader should bear in mind that this assumption has no effect on the market equilibrium.

A simple example is the easiest way to illustrate the above points and show how the dominant firm can solve for its optimal strategy. In the example, we will for simplicity initially suppress the decision of the firm to optimally acquire information.

Assume that some dominant firm either has perfect information about demand or has determined that it is optimal for it to be perfectly informed. Let the market demand curve be

$$D(p) = a - p + \epsilon,$$

where ϵ is a random variable with mean 0 and variance σ^2, p is price, and a is a constant. (For purposes of this section, the probability distribution of ϵ need not be specified.) Let S stand for the output of the competitive fringe. Production by the competitive fringe must occur before price is observed. Competitive entry will occur until expected price equals constant production cost c. Since ex ante the world always looks the same to the competition fringe, S will be a constant. The residual demand curve facing the dominant firm is

$$D^R(p) = a - p - S + \epsilon.$$

By assumption, the dominant firm has invested in information and knows ϵ before production decisions are made. Let $m(\epsilon)$ represent the optimal output of the dominant firm when ϵ is observed. Then price is a random variable that varies as ϵ varies. Price is determined by the condition (analogous to (2)) that supply equals demand or

$$S + m(\epsilon) = a - p + \epsilon$$

or

(5) $$p = a - S - m(\epsilon) + \epsilon.$$

The above equation determines the distribution of price. In particular, the expected value of price is

$$E(p) = a - S - E[m(\epsilon)].$$

Expansion of the competitive fringe will continue until $E(p) = c$ or until

$$c = a - S - E(m(\epsilon)),$$

so

(6) $$S = a - c - E(m(\epsilon)).$$

This last condition determines S as a function of the entire output strategy of the dominant firm. The dominant firm recognizes this interdependence and takes it into account in determining its optimal strategy. We can now write down the dominant firm's optimization problem.[30] The dominant firm wishes to choose the function $m(\epsilon)$ to maximize the expected value of profits with price being determined by (5) and the size of the competitive fringe being determined by (6).

Mathematically, the dominant firm wants to

$$\max_{m(\epsilon)} \int [p(\epsilon) - c] m(\epsilon) \, dG(\epsilon)$$

subject to $p(\epsilon) = a - S - m(\epsilon) + \epsilon$, and $S = a - c - \int m(\epsilon) \, dG(\epsilon)$, where $G(\epsilon)$ is the cumulative density of the random variable ϵ.

Substituting $p(\epsilon)$ and S into the profit expression, we obtain the following calculus of variations problem:

$$\max_{m(\epsilon)} \int [\bar{m} - m(\epsilon) + \epsilon] m(\epsilon) \, dG(\epsilon),$$

where $\bar{m} = E(m(\epsilon))$.

Consider the variation $\delta s(\epsilon)$ around the optimal policy $m(\epsilon)$. Let $m^*(\epsilon)$ $= m(\epsilon) + \delta s(\epsilon)$, and therefore $\bar{m}^*(\epsilon) = \bar{m}(\epsilon) + \delta \bar{s}(\epsilon)$, where a bar stands for expected value. Substitute $m^*(\epsilon)$ into the objective function and set the derivative with respect to δ equal to 0 when δ is zero. This derivative with respect to δ must[31] equal 0 if $m(\epsilon)$ is the optimal policy. Performing these calculations, one finds that the solution is

$$m(\epsilon) = \frac{\epsilon}{2} + K, \quad S = a - c - K,$$

(7) $\qquad m(\epsilon) + S = a - c + \epsilon/2, \quad \text{and} \quad p = c + \epsilon/2,$

where K is a constant.

To avoid the indeterminacy of K and in view of the previous discussion, we let $\epsilon_{min} = \min \epsilon$ and set $K_{min} = \epsilon_{min}/2$. Setting $K = K_{min}$ in (7) ensures that

$$\min_{\epsilon} m(\epsilon) = 0$$

so that $m(\epsilon) \geq 0$ for all ϵ.[32]

Notice that when $\epsilon < 0$, $p(\epsilon) - c < 0$, yet the dominant firm still produces a positive quantity. Price being below marginal cost does not imply that marginal revenue is below marginal cost for the dominant firm. As discussed earlier, the feedback of the output strategy on the size of the competitive fringe explains this result. The dominant firm's strategy then is to produce in all states—but to produce the most when demand and price are the highest. This profit maximizing behavior can be viewed as a sophisticated form of "predatory" or "limit" pricing in which the dominant firm occasionally chooses to produce and sell at prices below marginal cost in an effort to control the size of the competitive fringe.

The expected profits of the optimally behaving dominant firm equal

$$\int [\bar{p} - c] m(\epsilon) \, dG(\epsilon) = \int (\bar{m} - m(\epsilon) + \epsilon) m(\epsilon) \, dG(\epsilon) = \int \left(\frac{\epsilon}{2}\right)^2 dG(\epsilon) = \frac{1}{4}\sigma^2,$$

where σ^2 is the var ϵ. This result is intuitively appealing. The advantage of the dominant firm is its ability to detect changes in demand. The level of demand will only influence the size of the competitive fringe. Therefore, profits of the dominant firm will depend on the changes (variability) in demand and not on the average level of demand.

The deviation of price from marginal cost equals $\epsilon/2$ so that the expected deadweight loss to society from the dominant firm equals $\frac{1}{8}\sigma^2$.

Even though the competitive output derived in section 2.2 and the *expected* market output in this case[33] are identical, because output of the dominant firm varies in response to ϵ, the deadweight loss is *lower* in a market structure with a dominant firm and competitive fringe than in a purely competitive market.[34] The intuitive reason for this result is that the competitive fringe removes any persistent expected distortions between price and marginal cost, while the dominant firm, even though it follows a "predatory" policy, makes sure that industry output responds to shifts in demand. Any laws limiting the ability of the dominant firm to respond to demand fluctuations (such as one prohibiting production if price is below c) will tend to increase deadweight loss.

In the preceding example, the optimal choice of information investment was suppressed and for expositional simplicity was taken to be complete (the fraction $F = 1$ of the population was surveyed by the dominant firm). The level of F will of course determine the type of uncertainty in demand that the dominant firm and competitive fringe face. The marginal cost of information will influence the optimal F, which will in turn influence the size of the competitive fringe. If no information is collected by the monopolist, then all market power vanishes and we approach the (unplanned) competitive equilibrium discussed in section 2.2. If complete investment ($F = 1$) takes place, then we approach the market equilibrium just presented.

To examine these points more concretely, consider the more general demand curve used earlier:

$$D(p) = a - p + \sqrt{F}\, V_1 + \sqrt{1-F}\, V_2,$$

where $0 < F < 1$, V_1 and V_2 are independent random variables with mean 0 and variance σ^2 (for purposes of this section, the probability distributions of V_1 and V_2 need not be specified), the realization of $\sqrt{F}\, V_1$ can be observed at cost $C(F)$, and $\sqrt{1-F}\, V_2$ is unobservable at the time production must occur. Following the steps presented earlier in this section for determining the optimal policy, it follows that, for fixed F, the optimal strategy of the dominant firm as a function of the observed V_1 and the resulting equilibrium are given by

$$m(V_1) = \sqrt{F}\,\frac{V_1}{2} + K, \quad S = a - c - K, \quad S + m(V_1) = a - c + \frac{\sqrt{F}}{2}V_1,$$

$$p(V_1, V_2) = c + \frac{\sqrt{F}}{2}V_1 + \sqrt{1-F}\,V_2$$

$$\pi(F) = F\frac{\sigma^2}{4} \text{ (ignoring information acquisition costs),}$$

where K is the arbitrary constant discussed earlier. If $C(F)$ is the cost of finding out about F percent of the population, the optimal F (assuming an interior solution) satisfies $\pi'(F) = \sigma^2/4 = C'(F)$. Recalling the results of section 2.3, we see that although the profits of the dominant firm are lower than those of the monopolist, the incentives to invest in information are unchanged. This result is not of course general. The differences in information investment will in general depend on the differences in behavior of the marginal revenue schedule to new information in the regions of the monopoly and dominant firm output (see the discussion in the appendix).

If we measure the size of the competitive fringe by the minimum output that is always produced,[35] then it is clear from the solution just presented that the size of the competitive fringe shrinks as investment in information (i.e., F) increases. The optimal F increases as the variance of demand increases and as the marginal cost of information falls. Therefore, it follows that the larger the variance of demand and the lower the marginal cost of information, the smaller the size of the competitive fringe. It also follows that under the same conditions, the profits of the dominant firm rise.[36]

2.7 Summary and Conclusions

We have examined market structure in markets where knowledge of the next period's demand is socially beneficial to suppliers since it enables suppliers to better plan their production. When demand is random, the purely competitive market does not generate the correct incentives for collection of the information about the demand uncertainty. Although private institutions might develop to collect such information, because of the usual problems with appropriability of information, there is no reason to believe that the socially optimal amount of information will be collected. Examination of the monopoly case showed that although the monopoly firm does have an incentive to invest resources in planning and thereby does adjust its output to demand fluctuations, the deadweight losses from the monopoly are likely to swamp any losses that arise from not planning in the purely competitive case.

We next examined a market structure with a dominant firm(s) and competitive fringe. This market structure could arise if one or a few colluding firms had sole access to information acquisition or if, as a result of the natural incentives to merge, one or a few colluding firms emerge that are able to maintain and exercise market power. Analysis of this market structure showed that the size of the competitive fringe would be positively related to the marginal cost of information and negatively related to the variance of demand. The profits of the dominant firm would be positively related to the variability in demand and negatively related to the total and marginal cost of information. The dominant firm follows a "predatory" policy designed to limit the size of the competitive fringe. The dominant firm produces even when price is below marginal cost in order to keep the competitive fringe small and thereby increase its monopoly returns when demand is high. The dominant firm has an incentive to vary its output in response to demand fluctuations. The presence of the competitive fringe removes any persistent distortion between price and marginal cost. As a result, the deadweight loss to society from a market structure consisting of a dominant firm with a competitive fringe is lower than the deadweight loss from a market structure of either pure competition (with no planning) or pure monopoly (with planning).

The links between information, planning market structure, and behavior seem to be sufficiently strong to warrant further research. Understanding these links could improve our understanding of differences in market behavior. For example, in markets with little planning the variation of prices should be greater than in markets with much planning, while just the reverse should be true for quantity variation. In markets with planning, contracts may be the mechanism by which demanders convey information to suppliers and which suppliers use to make sure that what demanders predict for their demands turns out to be their demands. A contract[37] specifying a quantity to be bought at tomorrow's prevailing price plus a discount equal to the demander's information cost of predicting demand could emerge as the most efficient mechanism for suppliers to acquire information.

Knowledge of the link between market behavior and structure and planning and information could also be useful in the formulation of a coherent public policy toward market structure. When the purely competitive outcome is not the socially desirable one, one must treat proposals to break up industries into atomistic competitors very cautiously. On the one hand, if entry barriers in *production* exist, then the analysis of the pure monopoly case in section 2.5 suggests that in most instances the argument that planning would be harmed by deconcentration should not be considered a valid defense. On the other hand, if no production advantages are present and a competitive fringe exists, then the analysis of section 2.6 suggests that the planning argument, if true, should indeed be considered a reasonable defense.

Appendix: Investment in Information: Monopolist versus Social Planner

In this appendix we discuss the conditions under which a monopolist will tend to underinvest in information relative to the social optimum. The conditions required seem sufficiently plausible to make the underinvestment result the most likely case. However, to dispel any notion that the underinvestment result must occur, we offer the following counterexample.

Suppose that there are only two possible states of demand as represented by the two demand curves shown in figure 2.1.
Let marginal cost equal $5. The social planner will maximize expected consumer surplus by producing any quantity in excess of 200. The social planner has absolutely no incentive to invest in information to find out which state of demand will prevail. The monopolist, on the other hand, has an incentive to invest in information to determine whether he should produce slightly less than 100 units and earn profits of about $500 or whether he should produce slightly less than 200 and earn profits of about $1,000. The fact that the change in revenue for the monopolist can be

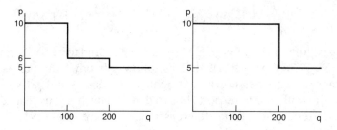

Fig. 2.1

much greater than the change in demand price is what generates the incentive for the monopolist to overinvest.

If we rule out very different behavior in the response of the marginal revenue (MR) and inverse demand (P) function to new information in the region of the monopoly solution and social optimum, respectively, then we will tend to see the monopolist underinvesting in information. The reason is simple—and is easiest to explain when (using the notation of section 2.3) the effect of the random demand component V_1 is symmetric on $\partial P/\partial F$ and $\partial MR/\partial F$ (i.e., $(\partial P/\partial F)(-V_1) = -(\partial P/\partial F)(V_1)$) and the error distribution V_1 is symmetric. Assume that $\partial P/\partial F$ and $\partial MR/\partial F$ are approximately equal on the relevant ranges so that new information does not shift the MR curve by more than it shifts the P curve.[38]

Using the notation of section 2.4, we have

$$\text{SUR}(F) = \int d\psi_1 \int d\psi_2 \left[\int_0^{S(V_1, F)} P(q, V_1, V_2, F) dq - c S(V_1, F) \right],$$

where ψ_i is the cumulative density of V_i and $S(V_1, F)$ has been chosen optimally (i.e., $S(V_1, F)$ maximizes $\int d\psi_2 \int_0^S P(q, V_1, V_2, F) dq - cS$). By the envelope theorem,

$$(A1) \qquad \frac{\partial \text{SUR}(F)}{\partial F} = \int d\psi_1 \int d\psi_2 \int_0^{S(V_1, F)} \frac{\partial P}{\partial F}(q, V_1, V_2, F) dq.$$

The monopolist's profits equal

$$\pi(F) = \int d\psi_1 \int d\psi_2 \int_0^{S^*(V_1, F)} [\text{MR}(q) - c] dq,$$

where $\text{MR}(q)$ is marginal revenue at output q and S^* is chosen optimally (i.e., $S^*(V_1, F)$ maximizes $\int d\psi_2 \int_0^S [\text{MR}(q, V_1, V_2, F) - c] dq$). The envelope theorem allows us to calculate $\pi'(F)$ as

$$(A2) \qquad \pi'(F) = \int d\psi_1 \int d\psi_2 S^* \frac{\partial P}{\partial F} = \int d\psi_1 \int d\psi_2 \int_0^{S^*(V_1, F)} \frac{\partial \text{MR}}{\partial F} dq.$$

From the symmetry assumption, it follows that $\text{SUR}'(F) > \pi'(F)$, provided that

$$\int_{S(-V_1,F)}^{S(V_1,F)} \left|\frac{\partial P}{\partial F}\right| dq \text{ exceeds } \int_{S^*(-V_1,F)}^{S^*(V_1,F)} \left|\frac{\partial MR}{\partial F}\right| dq.$$

In general, the range $[S(V_1, F), S(-V_1, F)]$ will tend to be wider than the range $[S^*(V_1, F), S^*(-V_1, F)]$. This follows directly from our assumptions since it can be shown that $\partial S^*/\partial V_1$ exceeds $\partial S/\partial V_1$,[39] so that a monopolist will tend to respond less to demand fluctuations than a social planner. Hence, under the stated assumptions, the quantity

$$\int_{S(-V_1,F)}^{S(V_1,F)} \left|\frac{\partial P}{\partial F}\right| dq$$

will tend to exceed

$$\int_{S^*(-V_1,F)}^{S(V_1,F)} \left|\frac{\partial MR}{\partial F}\right| dq.$$

We expect then that provided the behavior of MR and P to new information in the relevant ranges is not too dissimilar, the monopolist will tend to underinvest in information.

Notes

1. This paragraph makes rigorous the ideas of the previous paragraph. This paragraph can be omitted if the reader is willing to accept that a demand curve like equation (1) is consistent with the ideas of the previous paragraph.

2. For simplicity, throughout this paper we ignore the nonnegativity constraint on price and quantity. The probability of negative values can be made arbitrarily small by appropriate choice of a and σ^2.

3. Alternatively, at a cost, it is possible to reduce the prediction error of total demand below σ^2.

4. F will be a number between 0 and 1. However, for expositional simplicity we will talk about the first F percent of the market, rather than the first $100 F$ percent of the market.

5. Alternatively, the information investment of $C(F)$ has lowered the prediction error of demand from σ^2 to $(1 - F)\sigma^2$.

An alternative, perhaps more readable and less rigorous, derivation goes as follows: Imagine that there are N demanders each of whom has a demand curve $f(p) + \epsilon_i$, $i = 1,\ldots,N$, where ϵ_i are independent normal random variables with mean 0 and variance σ^2. Total mean demand is $Nf(p)$, while the variance of demand is $N\sigma^2$. We want to let the number of demanders become large and the demand curve change so that (a) each demander becomes an infinitesimally small part of the market and (b) the mean and variance of total industry demand remain bounded and approach some finite values. One way to do this is to let N approach ∞ at the same rate that expected demand per agent approaches zero and at the same rate that the variance of ϵ_i goes to zero. For example, if agents in any interval $[Z_0 + dZ, Z_0]$ demand $(a - p)dZ + \eta\sqrt{dZ}$, where η has mean zero and variance σ^2, then the total demand of agents in $[Z_0 + dZ, Z_0]$ is going to zero as is the variance. However, the total demand in the interval $Z \in [0,1]$ can be written as $a - p$ plus a normal random variable with mean 0 and variance σ^2. If demands of agents in the interval

[0,*F*] are added to the (independent) demands of agents in the interval [*F*,1], we obtain total demand; hence, total demand can be written as

$$a - p + W_1(F) + W_2(1 - F),$$

where $W_1(F)$ and $W_2(1 - F)$ are independent normal random variables with mean 0 and variances $F\sigma^2$ and $(1 - F)\sigma^2$, respectively. (See Cox and Miller 1970 for a more detailed discussion.)

6. Similar results emerge as long as suppliers must make some commitment to production before demand is known.

7. It is, of course, irrelevant whether the demander hires someone else to figure out his future demand or whether he does it himself.

8. Restrictions on the ability to borrow and to save to smooth income over time as well as ignorance of the relevant price distributions can sometimes alter the preference of demanders for variable versus fixed prices (see Hanoch 1974). These conditions seem unlikely to apply to firms. We ignore these conditions in the remainder of the paper.

9. The arguments in this paragraph can be restated precisely as follows: It can be shown that in competitive equilibrium with expected price equal to c, the marginal gain in a supplier's profits from knowing an agent's demand is of order dZ^2 while the marginal cost of acquiring the information is of order dZ. Therefore, no (infinitesimal) supplier has an incentive to acquire information. Only if suppliers are of finite measure and thereby have some market power to prevent expected price from equaling c can there be an incentive for a supplier to purchase information from a demander.

10. This point is similar to the one Arrow (1971) makes about incentives for discovery of new production techniques that will be widely copied immediately after their introduction. It is also related to the point that Green (1973), Grossman (1976, 1977), and Grossman and Stiglitz (1976, 1980) analyze in the context of efficient markets.

11. A trade association of demanders that reveals information to suppliers runs into the same problem.

12. With correlated demands and costs to information acquisition, a futures market among demanders cannot exist if price accurately aggregates demand information (Green 1973; Grossman and Stiglitz 1976). A "noisy" futures market (i.e., one where price does not reveal completely the knowledge of the informed traders [Grossman and Stiglitz 1980]) could provide an incentive for demanders to acquire information, earn a return on it, and thereby transmit "noisy" information to suppliers. Suppliers would then have an incentive to contact the knowledgeable demanders to get rid of the "noise" in the signal, and then would be back to the situation discussed above where firms have incentives to merge and where competitive firms adjust production until expected price equals marginal cost at which point incentives for information transmission vanish.

Ostroy's comments which criticize me for never having considered the case of correlated demands completely baffle me in light of the paragraph in the text above. Correlated demands do not eliminate the externality problem, contrary to Ostroy's comments. The externality problem persists under competition regardless of the stochastic demand structure.

Incidentally, Ostroy's criticism of the independent stochastic setup of demand is unfounded. Ostroy criticizes the assumption of the independence of individual demands because it implies that the fraction of individual demand that is explained by price becomes vanishingly small relative to the fraction of aggregate demand explained by price—and Ostroy knows of no justification for this result. Ostroy's "criticism" is equivalent to the "criticism" that the R^2 of an equation based on aggregate data is higher than the R^2 of an equation based on less aggregate data, and that the R^2 falls as the data become more disaggregated. Contrary to Ostroy's implication, such behavior of R^2 is indeed common (see, e.g., p. 181 of Theil 1971). This behavior provides an empirical confirmation of the applicability of the independent stochastic specification.

13. This expectation is with respect to the price distribution conditioned on the information.

14. An alternative interpretation is that investment can be undertaken to reduce the prediction error of demand next period by F percent.

15. Expectation is taken with respect to V_2.

16. Expectation is taken with respect to V_1.

17. The analysis assumes that expected consumer surplus is the appropriate indicator of welfare. See Carlton (1978) for an examination of this issue.

18. Expectation is taken with respect to V_2.

19. See appendix for more detailed discussion.

20. This comparison favors monopoly because it follows from the model that the deadweight loss of a monopolist falls as information acquisition costs decline to zero, and he acquires more information about demand to improve his planning.

21. In a continuous time model of demand with cost of adjustment, "long" and "short" run are not precise terms. The basic point is that in equilibrium, monopoly price can be a constant. Although raising price above this constant might initially lead to high profits, eventually, after demand has adjusted, total profits will fall. A monopolist may operate in the inelastic portion of his (very) "short-run" demand curve.

22. The fact that price variability can affect demand by influencing preferences for technologies with lots of substitution possibilities would also have to be taken into account in comparing monopoly to competition. Since the price variability of monopoly is closer to that of the social optimum than is the price variability of competition, we expect this effect to improve the position of monopoly relative to competition.

23. Earlier, we also briefly discussed incentives to merge among buyers. We henceforth ignore this possibility by making the implicit assumption that it is very costly to organize buyers, though not sellers. However, the reader should realize that the subsequent analysis could easily be redone with a dominant buyer (not seller) who gathers information, a non–information gathering group of buyers, and competitive sellers.

24. Recall that if firms which acquire information do not collude to restrict output, then it is impossible for there to exist an equilibrium that provides incentives for information acquisition in the model under examination.

25. This cost could be in the form of a price lower than the monopoly one. The point is that a useful theory of oligopoly may be one that postulates similar patterns of behavior to the oligopoly as a monopolist would exhibit but that allows the returns to the oligopoly to be below those of the monopoly because of the difficulty of colluding.

26. The reader who is not interested in the general solution to this problem can skip to the paragraph after equation (4).

27. The monopolist observes that γ is the value of a random parameter (a sufficient statistic) for the first F percent of total market demand. If no sufficient statistic exists, then γ can be regarded as the vector of random components for the first F percent of the market.

28. Recall that $f_1(p)$ was based on the assumption that F, S, $m(\gamma, p)$ were fixed but γ was random.

29. For notational simplicity, we henceforth will suppress F in writing $m(\gamma, F)$ and simply use $m(\gamma)$ to stand for the firm's optimal strategy.

30. Several nonnegativity constraints are being ignored for simplicity. We later give an example to show that there is a solution with these constraints satisfied.

31. Since the objective function is concave, this condition is necessary and sufficient for a maximum.

32. We must also require that $S \geq 0$ and $p(\epsilon) \geq 0$ for all ϵ. A numerical example satisfying all required nonnegativity constraints is $c = 2$, $a = 10$, and ϵ uniform on $[-1, 1]$. The optimal strategy is $m(\epsilon) = \epsilon/2 + \frac{1}{2}$, the competitive fringe output is $S = 7\frac{1}{2}$, and the price is $p(\epsilon) = 2 + \epsilon/2$.

33. Recall that market output $S + m(\epsilon_1) = a - c + \frac{1}{2}\epsilon$.

34. Even if we assume the profits are dissipated by cartel enforcement costs and therefore include profits as part of the deadweight loss, the conclusion stated in the text is valid.

35. Whether the constant amount is produced by the dominant firm or a competitive firm is irrelevant. No monopoly profits can be made on this output.

36. More precisely, if we perturb the initial optimal solution by lowering the marginal cost of information and by not increasing the total cost of information at the initial optimum, then profits rise in the new optimal solution.

37. See Carlton (1979b) for further discussion about the information role of contracts.

38. If the (inverse) demand relation can be written as $P = g(q) + \sqrt{F} V_1 + \sqrt{1-F} V_2$ for some $g(\cdot)$ with V_1, V_2 independent, then these assumptions will be satisfied exactly.

39. If $\partial MR/\partial V_1 = \partial P/\partial V_1$ as assumed (this is the same assumption as $\partial MR/\partial F = \partial P/\partial F$), then the condition required for $\partial S/\partial V_1 > \partial S^*/\partial V_1$ is simply that the slope of the MR curve exceeds that of the P curve in the relevant ranges. This follows since by comparative statics we have

$$\frac{\partial S}{\partial V_1} = -\int d\psi_2 \frac{\partial P}{\partial V_1} \div \int d\psi_2 \frac{\partial P}{\partial S}.$$

and

$$\frac{\partial S^*}{\partial V_1} = -\int d\psi_2 \frac{\partial MR}{\partial V_1} \div \int d\psi_2 \frac{\partial MR}{\partial S^*}.$$

Again, we see that the underinvestment result depends on how different the behavior of MR and P are over different ranges of output.

References

Arrow, Kenneth. 1971. Economic welfare and the allocation of resources for invention. In *Essays in the theory of risk bearing*. Chicago: Markham.

Bain, Joseph. 1956. *Barriers to new competition*. Cambridge, Mass.: Harvard University Press.

Carlton, Dennis. 1978. Market behavior with demand uncertainty and price inflexibility. *American Economic Review* 68 (September): 571–87.

———. 1979a. Vertical integration in competitive markets under uncertainty. *Journal of Industrial Economics* 28 (March): 189–209.

———. 1979b. Contracts, price rigidity, and market equilibrium. *Journal of Political Economy* 87 (October): 1034–62.

Cox, D. R., and Miller, H. D. 1970. *A theory of stochastic processes*. London: Methuen.

Green, Jerry. 1973. Information, efficiency, and equilibrium. Discussion Paper 284, Harvard Institute of Economic Research. Harvard University.

Grossman, Sanford. 1976. On the efficiency of competitive stock markets where traders have diverse information. *Journal of Finance* 31, no. 2: 573–85.

———. 1977. The existence of futures markets, noisy rational expectations, and informational externalities. *Review of Economic Studies* 64, no. 3 (October): 431–49.

Grossman, Sanford, and Stiglitz, Joseph. 1976. Information and competitive price systems. *American Economic Review* 66: 246–53.

———. 1980. On the impossibility of informationally efficient markets. *American Economic Review* 70 (June): 393–408.

Hanoch, Giora. 1974. Desirability of price stabilization or destabilization. Discussion Paper 351, Harvard Institute of Economic Research. Harvard University.

Lucas, Robert E., Jr. 1967. Adjustment costs and the theory of supply. *Journal of Political Economy* 75 (August): 321–24.

Stigler, George J. 1939. Production and distribution in the short run. *Journal of Political Economy* 47: 312–22.

———. 1964. A theory of oligopoly. *Journal of Political Economy* 72, no. 1 (February): 44–61.

Theil, Henri. 1971. *Principles of econometrics*, New York: Wiley.

Comment   Jean-Jacques Laffont

The message that Dennis Carlton wants to transmit is clear and interesting, but I will argue that he does not provide a totally convincing model and that he ignores a number of alternatives relevant for his problem.

Information about future demand conditions of a given commodity is in a world of a large number of buyers and sellers, a public good. There is a free rider problem in the financing of this public good from the point of view of sellers of the commodity, and demanders prefer random prices, that is to say, no production of public good. Consequently, it is argued that in a competitive situation no information will be bought and therefore that the outcome will be inefficient. Information here is some sort of public input for sellers. Hence, when the seller is a monopoly, it is in his interest to finance information gathering; indeed, the free rider problem disappears since he is the only one to use that information.

The author then compares the two inefficiencies, that associated with monopolistic behavior on one hand and that associated with the free rider problem on the other. The numerical values given in this comparison are not to be taken seriously, I think, but illustrate the trade-off.

Jean-Jacques Laffont is professor, Université des Sciences Sociales de Toulouse.

The basic assumption, which is implied by the use of a continuum, is that the search cost of information is, for an individual, infinitely larger than the use he can make out of it. It is not clear to me that in this problem such is necessarily the case.

First, if the seller faces a large number of stochastically independent buyers, a small random sample may be of great value in predicting the future demand conditions, suggesting that the modelization of the aggregate demand function is rather special (see also J. Ostroy's comment).

Second, it is implicitly assumed that the market will be unable to react to the inefficiency created by the lack of forecasting. Why does not a (competitive) industry appear in the production of this information? The success of DRI on the stock market suggests that selling information to a large number of users is not so difficult despite a real public good aspect to it.

Third, recent literature on incentives has shown that there are many ways in which the state can intervene to mitigate the free rider problem.

Therefore, the simple comparison between monopoly and competition is not really policy relevant.

In the last section the author suggests that the "most likely" market structure will be a monopoly with a fringe of competitors, but the reasons why this should be the case remain mysterious.

Comment   Joseph M. Ostroy

The author asks, "How [well] does information get transmitted from demanders to suppliers in a competitive market?" The answer is, "We show that a competitive market is uniquely unsuited to the efficient transmission of this information." After examination of the competitive case, Carlton addresses the equilibrium and efficiency properties of monopoly and dominant firm models. I shall confine my remarks to the competitive market. My conclusion will be that the author's results can be attributed to a rather extreme assumption on the stochastic properties of individual demands. Once these assumptions are denied, the usual efficiency properties of competitive equilibrium reemerge and, unless there are scale economies in production (ruled out by the author), monopoly would not arise.

I shall focus on the demand side of the market which the author requires to have the following three properties:

(I) a large number of buyers,   •

Joseph M. Ostroy is associate professor of economics at the University of California, Los Angeles.

(II) random disturbances to individual demands are independently distributed, and

(III) aggregate demand, the average of individual demands, has a nonvanishing variance.

Condition (I) would be required for a competitive market even without stochastic elements. Coupled with (II) no buyer/seller has much of an incentive to reveal/discover the value of anyone's random component of demand because this will have little influence on market price, the medium through which rewards for such communication are obtained. For example, if price will not change as a result of its discoveries, why should a firm want to know the value of some one or a few individuals' random components of demand. Without (III), the market-clearing price will not fluctuate and the market will behave as if individual demands were perfectly certain.

An appeal to Laws of Large Numbers would appear to contradict the existence of (I), (II), and (III). We may have (I) and (III) if, for example, the random components of individual demands are perfectly correlated. We may have (II) and (III) if the number of buyers is small. And (I) and (II) are compatible if we rule out (III). How then can we achieve (I)–(III)? The answer is that we must require the variance of each individual's demand to overwhelm the price-determined, or nonrandom, component.

Let $\omega_n = (X_1^n, \ldots, X_n^n)$, where for each $i = 1, \ldots, n$, $X_i^n \in \{\sigma_n, -\sigma_n\}$, and let $\Omega_n = \{\omega_n\}$. It will also be convenient to define $\omega_n^0 = \Sigma_{i=1}^{i=n} X_i^n$.

The demand side of a market with n agents is denoted M_n and is defined by the n demand functions $d_i: R \times \Omega_n \rightarrow R$, $i = 1, \ldots, n$, where

$$d_i(p, \omega_n) = f(p) + X_i^n.$$

We are assuming that each agent's demand is composed of the sum of a deterministic term $f(p)$ that does not vary with the particular agent in M_n or the size of the market, and a random term X_i^n that varies with i and n.

Condition (II), independence, is obtained by assuming each $\omega_n \in \Omega_n$ has probability $(2^n)^{-1}$. Therefore, $E(X_i^n) = 0$ and var $(X_i^n) = \sigma_n^2$. Note that while the mean of individual random variables is independent of i and n, the variance of individual demand may depend on the number of agents in the market.

Because n will vary, normalize quantities so that aggregate demand $D_n(p, \omega_n)$ is average demand—i.e.,

$$D_n(p, \omega_n) = n^{-1} \Sigma d_i(p, \omega_n) = f(p) + n^{-1} \omega_n^0.$$

(This is in line with the author's analysis.)

The following result is a corollary of the Kolmogorov version of the Strong Law of Large Numbers (W. Feller, *Introduction to Probability Theory and Its Applications*, vol. 1, 2d ed. [New York: Wiley], pp.

243–44): If $(\sqrt{n})^{-1}\sigma_n \to 0$, then for any $\epsilon > 0$ and $\delta > 0$, there is an N such that for $n > N$,

$$\text{prob}\{|D_n(p,\omega_n) - f(p)| > \epsilon\} < \delta.$$

Therefore, if the standard deviation of individual demands σ_n is uniformly bounded, the stochastic component of aggregate demand vanishes. (This follows from the standard version of the Strong Law.) Further, even if $\sigma_n \to \infty$ but not as rapidly as $\sqrt{n}$, the same conclusion holds. Thus, the only possibility for achieving (I)–(III) is to add

(IV) $\lim(\sqrt{n})^{-1}\sigma_n \neq 0.$

The objection may be made that (IV) is needed simply because the definition of aggregate demand is average demand. This is certainly true, but as far as the implications for competitive analysis are concerned division by n is warranted. Let p^* be the competitive equilibrium price when there is no randomness ($\sigma_n = 0$)—i.e., p^* equals the constant marginal cost assumed in the paper. Assume for convenience that $f(p^*) = 1$. Now suppose sellers supply $nf(p^*) = n$ units each period and that the realized market-clearing price p fluctuates around p^* to compensate for the realized value of ω_n^0.

Realized price will be a function of ω_n^0 that solves the demand = supply equation

$$nf(p) + \omega_n^0 = nf(p^*) = n.$$

Dividing by n, p varies with ω_n^0 to satisfy

$$f(p) + n^{-1}\omega_n^0 = 1.$$

Again, we reach the conclusion that the distribution of realized prices collapses on p^*, unless we admit (IV).

These results indicate that if σ_n is uniformly bounded and n is large, the randomness can be ignored. However, there is a small difficulty. Let Φ_n be the distribution of prices in M_n when sellers supply $nf(p^*)$, and let $v(\Phi_n)$ be the value of the loss attributed by a typical buyer to Φ_n as compared with a distribution which has all its mass on p^*. The latter distribution might be achieved by permitting buyers to communicate the realizations of their random variables before supply decisions are made. There does not seem to be any guarantee that what might be called here the value of perfect information $nv(\Phi_n)$ goes to zero as n increases. However, such losses appear to be unavoidable.

Presumably, there is some cost c of communication of the realization of any buyer's random variable. By *independence*, total costs of communication vary directly with the number of buyers in the market, e.g., nc. When σ_n is uniformly bounded above, we may conclude that since Φ_n collapses to p^*, $v(\Phi_n) \to 0$. Therefore, the net benefits of communication to completely stable prices are

$$n[v(\Phi_n) - c],$$

which are negative when n is sufficiently large.

If the error terms were *dependent*, all of the above would change. Take the extreme case where the error terms are perfectly correlated: $X_i^n = \sigma_n$ implies $X_j^n = \sigma_n$ with probability one. Clearly, since ω_n^0 would take only the values $n\sigma_n$ or $-n\sigma_n$ with equal probability, the variance of individual and average demand would be identical and there would be no need to consider increasing σ_n. Now the question of communication becomes more interesting. Knowledge of one buyer's error term tells you everything. It would be redundant for all suppliers individually to discover the value of the random variable or for all buyers to communicate their identical information. But which buyer will reveal it, or how many sellers will try to discover it? Because he assumes independence, these problems cannot arise in the author's formulation of the problem.

Returning to the model under discussion, we have shown that (I)–(III) implies (IV). This means that *the proportion of an individual's demand that is explained by price becomes vanishingly small*—i.e.,

$$\lim_n \frac{f(p)}{f(p) + \sigma_n} = 0.$$

I know of no precedent, empirical or theoretical, to justify (IV). Perhaps it might be used as a mathematical expression of the idea that in some markets individual demands are simply not very much influenced by price even though aggregate demand appears to be! But this would be the starting point for a very different paper.

3 Statistical Decision Theory Requiring Incentives for Information Transfer

Jerry R. Green

A model of decision making under uncertainty is presented in which one agent receives information and transmits it to another who makes a decision that affects them both. Because their utilities differ, the former will not necessarily transmit the observation accurately to the latter.

We study the problem faced by the decision maker. He must balance the potentially conflicting goals of efficient actions versus accurate information transmission. Some characteristics of optimal action plans are derived.

We also study the effect of improving the information structure on the value of the problem. Better information may be harmful, in general; but a sufficient condition for it to be beneficial is that there are only two possible observations.

3.1 Introduction

In organizations, large and small, the locus of decision making is often separate from that of information gathering. When all agents within such a system have common values, there is no incentive for the information gatherers to distort their observations. But this is often not the case. The design of the decision making procedures for the organization must balance the feasibility of eliciting accurate information transmission against the efficiency of the decisions taken.

In this paper a simple model of this type is presented.[1] Optimal decision rules are analyzed, and properties of these rules are derived in some

Jerry R. Green is professor of economics at Harvard University.

This research was conducted while the author was an Overseas Fellow of Churchill College, Cambridge. It was supported by NSF Grants SOC 71-03803 and APR 77-06999 to Harvard University.

special cases. We also study the impact of improving the information structure used by the information gatherer on the decision maker's welfare.

The following results are demonstrated:

1. If there are only two possible actions and two possible observations, either a first-best can be attained or else there is no value to the information at all.

2. If there are more than two possible actions, it may be the case that a randomized decision rule is required to attain the optimum. Moreover, such a rule may place a positive probability on selecting actions that are dominated.

3. If there are more than two observations, the optimum may involve a situation where the decision maker knows that the information gatherer is transmitting the observations imperfectly. Thus, information may be of some value, but not as much as it would have been had it been received by the decision maker directly.

4. The value of improved information may be negative.

5. However, if we are comparing information structures both of which involve only two possible observations (but an arbitrary number of states and actions), then the criterion of "more informativeness" used in statistical decision theory always agrees with the ordering relevant to the decentralized problem we have posed.

There are three strands of literature with a good deal of similarity to the model studied herein: team theory, principal-agent problems, and incentive compatibility (with preferences unknown). Before proceeding to the main part of the paper, a brief comparison of our model with each of these is probably worthwhile.

In team theory the actions of each individual are taken separately, perhaps after some communication,[2] whereas in this model there is a central decision maker who chooses a single action affecting both his welfare and that of the information gatherer. Those papers in team theory that do address issues of partially conflicting goals have retained this feature of decentralized actions. They also have tended to allow monetary transfers that, in conjunction with the team's decision rules, affect the members' incentives. Nevertheless, at least in a formal sense, this model lies close to team theory in spirit.

Principal-agent problems share the feature of partially conflicting goals.[3] However, the locus of information gathering and action is coincident rather than separate. Their interesting features arise, rather, from the imperfect way in which risks can be shared and in the conflict between such risk sharing and the appropriate motivation of the agent. In the present model there is no explicit risk sharing possible, although considerations of this sort do indirectly affect the dependence of optimal actions on the observations transmitted.

Incentive compatibility has primarily concentrated on the imperfect, or more explicitly, dispersed, knowledge about the preferences of the individuals composing the economy.[4] In this paper such information is perfect. The element of gamesmanship that is present is that the decision maker must bind himself in advance to a course of action that depends on the information transmitted to him. The information gatherer will optimize his transmission against this background—and the decision maker must take this into account ex ante. By using this "Stakelberg" format, the problem becomes trivial from a game-theory point of view. This approach has been chosen for its simplicity and also because we believe it more closely characterizes the reality of such situations than do other possibilities.

There is a further difference between most of the papers in incentive compatibility and this one. These papers concentrate on the possibility or impossibility of attaining true Pareto optima, that is, allocations compatible with feasibility in the physical sense but unconstrained by informational imperfections. When Pareto optima are attainable, it is necessary to elicit all of the relevant information about the environment. Therefore, all attention in this literature has been centered on designing mechanisms where truth-telling, or its essential equivalents, has been required.[5] In this paper the potential for full optimality is present only in some very special cases. The second-best nature of the optimum imposed by the necessity for incentives in the information transmission process is explicitly recognized. It is not the case, therefore, that we have imposed truth-telling as an absolute constraint. Rather, we let the problem itself dictate the (constrained) optimal accuracy of the information that is to be elicited.

The remainder of the paper is organized as follows: Section 3.2 describes the model and defines the constrained optimization of the decision maker. In section 3.3 several results concerning the nature of the constrained optimum are proved. Examples of various types of phenomena possible in such a second-best situation are given and discussed. Section 3.4 concerns the value of improving the information structure. A brief conclusion follows.

3.2 Description of the Model

We consider an individual who must choose from among a collection $A = \{a_1, \ldots, a_K\}$ of *actions*. The result of these actions is uncertain at the date at which the choice must be made. It depends on which *state of nature* from among those in $\Theta = \{\theta_1, \ldots, \theta_M\}$ will arise. We assume that this individual is a von Neumann–Morgenstern expected utility maximizer and that his *utility* is given by the entries in the $K \times M$ matrix

$$U = (u_{km}),$$

where u_{km} is the utility if a_k is chosen and θ_m occurs.

Before the action must be chosen, some information relevant to the prediction of the state of nature can be obtained. This is modeled by introducing a set of *observations* $Y = \{y_1, \ldots, y_N\}$ and for each $\theta_m \in \Theta$ a probability vector $(\lambda_{m1}, \ldots, \lambda_{mN})$, where λ_{mn} is to be interpreted as the conditional probability of observing y_n given that the true state is θ_m. One writes the $M \times N$ *likelihood matrix*

$$\Lambda = (\lambda_{mn}).$$

An *information structure* is described completely by its likelihood matrix (the set Y being relevant only through the number of points it contains, which is given implicitly in the dimensionality of Λ). One nevertheless speaks of the information structure (Y, Λ), or simply Λ, without fear of confusion.

The individual has a *prior probability* distribution $\pi = (\pi_1, \ldots, \pi_M)$ over Θ, where π_m is the probability of θ_m.

In the absence of information the act a_{m^*} for which $U\pi$ has its maximal component would be selected.

If the individual could observe $y \in Y$ before choosing an act, he would compute the optimal act by forming his posterior probability according to Bayes's rule:

$$p(\theta_m | y_n) = \frac{\lambda_{mn} \pi_m}{\sum_{m'=1}^{M} \lambda_{m'n} \pi_{m'}}.$$

Writing

$$P = (p(\theta_m | y_n))_{\substack{m=1,\ldots,M \\ n=1,\ldots,N}}$$

as the $M \times N$ *matrix of posteriors*, the matrix product UP determines his optimal action plan according to the location of the maximal elements within each column.

This is the standard problem of statistical decision theory. This paper addresses a problem of essentially the same nature. It differs in that the observation $y \in Y$ is not received directly by the individual who chooses actions but rather by someone else. To distinguish them clearly, we will call this other person the *agent* and the individual we have been discussing above, the *planner*.

The agent may have a different utility function from the planner. The agent's utility depends on the planner's action and on the realized state. Call his utility matrix $U' = (u'_{km})$.

The model works roughly as follows: The planner announces the way in which his action will depend on the observation transmitted to him.

The agent sees y_n and forms his posterior. Since we will assume that the agent and planner share the same prior distribution, this is just the nth column of the matrix P. The agent then transmits some element $y' \in Y$ which may or may not be the truth y_n. Thus, there are three factors influencing the choice of y': the true value of the observation y_n, the agent's utility U', and the courses of action to which the planner has committed himself.

We will be considering this system from the planner's point of view, under the assumption that both the information structure (Y, Λ) and the agent's utility (U') are known to him. It is clear that if $U = U'$, then there is no barrier to the policy of announcing the optimal action plan, which will induce the agent to transmit the true observation in every instance. But if $U \neq U'$, then announcing the optimal action plan may induce the agent to lie, and therefore may produce suboptimal results.

Because of these considerations, it may be the case that an announced action plan that is stochastic is necessary to achieve the best results.[6] We define the planner's *random action plan* denoted by an $N \times K$ Markov matrix

$$Z = (z_{nk}),$$

where z_{nk} is the probability that the planner will choose a_k given that the agent responds with y_n. It is in the spirit of the literature on incentive compatibility and optimal taxation that the planner actually will make his choices according to Z rather than choose either the unconstrained best action at that stage or the best action from among those k' for which $z_{nk'} > 0$ (and which he therefore could claim to have produced as the result of the promised randomization).

The responses of the agent are thus determined by the maximal elements from within each column of the $N \times N$ matrix:

$$ZU'P.$$

We will define the *response pattern* R induced by Z as follows: Let R be an $N \times N$ matrix in which every column is a probability vector concentrated on the maximal elements of $ZU'P$ within that column. Since U' and P are fixed and are known to the planner, we are interested in the correspondence that sends Z into the set of all matrices R generated in this way. Letting $\mathcal{M}$ and $\mathcal{M}^T$ be the set of all Markov matrices and their transpositions, then

$$\phi : \mathcal{M} \overrightarrow{\rightarrow} \mathcal{M}^T,$$

$$\phi(Z) = \{R \mid R \text{ is a response pattern induced by } Z\},$$

is this correspondence.

Typically, the maximal elements in all of the columns of $ZU'P$ will be unique, in which case of course $\phi(Z)$ consists of a single matrix of zeros and ones.

The planner tries to choose Z to his own best advantage. If Z induces the response pattern $R \in \phi(Z)$, the actual actions that the planner will be taking as they depend on the true observation of the agent are given by $R^T Z$, where R^T denotes the transpose of R.

We can now calculate the planner's expected utility attained when he announces the action plan Z. Let the probability vector $q = (q_1, \ldots, q_N)^T$ be the probabilities of observing the various points in Y when the information structure is (Y, Λ) and the prior is π. We have $q = \Lambda^T \pi$. Let the symbol $\hat{}$ over a vector denote the diagonal matrix with that vector on the diagonal. The planner's expected utility when R is the agent's response pattern is given by

$$\text{trace } R^T Z U P \hat{q},$$

or, admitting the possibility that the agent will choose the best response pattern from among those to which he is indifferent, we have

(1) $$\max_{R \in \phi(Z)} \text{trace } R^T Z U P \hat{q}.$$

The *planner's problem* is to maximize (1) over $Z \in \mathcal{M}$, knowing the correspondence ϕ.

The second-best nature of this problem is clear from the fact that a single decision maker would maximize trace $Z U P \hat{q}$, with Z unconstrained, but here, the range of the correspondence that sends Z into $\{Z' \in \mathcal{M} \mid Z' = R^T Z, \text{ for } R \in \phi(Z)\}$ may be much smaller than $\mathcal{M}$.

The fact that ϕ is an upper semicontinuous correspondence, but not a continuous one, means that the objective function (1) will not necessarily be continuous in Z. It will be upper semicontinuous (as a function), so a maximum will surely exist. In this section we show that it can be solved by converting it into a linear programming problem.

Nonstochastic response patterns give rise to mappings of the set of observations into itself. We will say that ρ is a *response rule* associated with a response pattern $R_\rho \in \mathcal{M}^T$ whenever

$$r_{\rho(y_n) y_n} = 1,$$

$$r_{y_{n'} y_n} = 0 \quad \text{for all } y_{n'} \neq \rho(y_n).$$

Our search for the (second-best) optimum for the planner's problem involves a comparison of the optimal action plans inducing all the N^2 possible response rules. For each fixed ρ we are therefore limited to the action plans $Z \in \phi^{-1}(R_\rho)$. These are defined by a system of linear inequalities as follows: let $ZU'P = V$ be an $N \times N$ matrix, whose typical element is $v_{y_{n'} y_n}$. We need to have[7]

(2) $v_{\rho(y_n)y_n} \geqq v_{y_{n'}y_n}$ for every n, n'.

One can then express the planner's problem for each fixed ρ as

(3) $\max_{Z \in \mathcal{M}}$ trace $R_\rho ZUP\hat{q}$

subject to (2). This is a linear programming problem. The overall optimum is found by comparing the values of these problems over all possible response rules.

Although these remarks seem to imply that we will have to look at N^2 separate problems, we will now argue that *it suffices to solve the one for which ρ is fixed at the identity.*

Theorem 1

The optimum in the planner's problem can be found by solving

(4) $\max_{Z \in \mathcal{M}}$ trace $ZUP\hat{q}$

subject to

(5) $v_{y_ny_n} \geqq v_{y_{n'}y_n}$ for every n, n',

where

$$ZU'P = V = (v_{y_{n'}y_n}).$$

Proof

Suppose the optimum of (3) subject to (2) exceeded the optimum of (4) subject to (5) for some response rule ρ other than the identity. Let the optimal action plan be Z. We will show that a trivial modification of Z leads to another action plan $\hat{Z}$ for which (5) is satisfied and such that the value of (4) is the same as the value of (3).

This construction is done in a very simple way: Let $\hat{Z} = R_\rho^T Z$. The nth row of $\hat{Z}$ is the $\rho(n$th) row of Z. Since there are no rows of $\hat{Z}$ which were not rows in Z, the effective choices open to the agent are, if anything, more limited. But since he chose the random action corresponding to the $\rho(n$th) row of Z in response to y_n, he will now choose (or at least be indifferent to the choice of) the nth row of $\hat{Z}$. This proves that (5) is satisfied.

Since the random actions chosen in response to the observations are $R^T Z$ under Z and R as well as under $\hat{Z}$ and the truthful response rule, (4) and (3) have the same value. QED.

It will often be the case that the solution to (4) subject to (5) will involve a Z matrix with several rows identical.[8] That means that "truthful" responses are elicited in a situation with fixed alternatives. The essential response pattern is distorted by the necessity to use the same actions in several cases—which means that these observations are really not being distinguished in any genuine sense. Nevertheless, theorem 1 is a useful computational tool since it reduces an apparently complex situation to a single linear program.

3.3 Optima in the Planner's Problem

In order to develop some further intuition about the nature of this problem we will now examine several special cases.

The first develops the general proposition that with two actions and two possible observations the problem of the planner exhibits a type of degeneracy.

Theorem 2

If $K = N = 2$, the planner's problem has an optimum of one of the following two forms: (i) A first best is attainable. (ii) The agent's information is valueless in that the action plan is independent of the observation transmitted.

Proof

Let $\bar{U}' = U'P$ be any 2×2 matrix. Consider $ZU'P$ given by

$$\begin{pmatrix} z_1 & 1-z_1 \\ z_2 & 1-z_2 \end{pmatrix} \begin{pmatrix} \bar{u}'_{11} & \bar{u}'_{12} \\ \bar{u}'_{21} & \bar{u}'_{22} \end{pmatrix} = \begin{pmatrix} z_1(\bar{u}'_{11}-\bar{u}'_{21})+\bar{u}'_{21} & z_1(\bar{u}'_{12}-\bar{u}'_{22})+\bar{u}'_{22} \\ z_2(\bar{u}'_{11}-\bar{u}'_{21})+\bar{u}'_{21} & z_2(\bar{u}'_{12}-\bar{u}'_{22})+\bar{u}'_{22} \end{pmatrix}.$$

If $\phi(Z)$ contains the truthful response pattern $R_\rho = I$, then we must have

(6)
$$z_1(\bar{u}'_{11} - \bar{u}'_{21}) \geq z_2(\bar{u}'_{11} - \bar{u}'_{21}),$$
$$z_2(\bar{u}'_{12} - \bar{u}'_{22}) \geq z_1(\bar{u}'_{12} - \bar{u}'_{22}), \quad z_1,z_2 \in [0,1].$$

There are obviously two cases according to the sign of $(\bar{u}'_{11} - \bar{u}'_{21})(\bar{u}'_{12} - \bar{u}'_{22})$. If this is positive, the agent prefers one of the acts to the other independent of his observation; in that case, clearly, he will always respond with whichever element of Y associates a higher probability to the act he prefers. Only the action plan inducing his indifference, $z_1 = z_2$, remains within the truth-telling domain. The planner has thus chosen to act independently of the information reported, so that the best action is simply

$$\arg \max_{a \in A} U\pi.$$

In the more interesting case of $(\bar{u}'_{11} - \bar{u}'_{21})(\bar{u}'_{12} - \bar{u}'_{22}) < 0$ we have from (6) that either $z_1 \geq z_2$ (when $\bar{u}'_{11} - \bar{u}'_{21} > 0$) or $z_2 \geq z_1$ (when $\bar{u}'_{12} - \bar{u}'_{22} > 0$).

Consider the problem that the planner would face if he had perfect information:

$$\max_{Z^* \in \mathcal{M}} \text{trace } Z^*UP\hat{q}.$$

If the information is at all relevant to the planner, the nature of this optimum involves either $z_1{}^* = 1$, $z_2{}^* = 0$, or $z_2{}^* = 1$, $z_1{}^* = 0$. Therefore, when the truth-telling constraint is $z_1 \geq z_2$, either the first-best can be implemented (when $z_1{}^* = 1$, $z_2{}^* = 0$) or else the best policy is to set $z_1 = z_2 = 1$ if

$$\arg \max_{a \in A} U\pi = a_1$$

or $z_1 = z_2 = 0$ if

$$\arg \max_{a \in A} U\pi = a_2.$$

Other cases are completely symmetric. QED..

In the case of two states and two acts ($K = M = 2$, but N arbitrary), similar restrictions on the form of the optimum can be established. Here, however, it is the agent's optimum which might be implemented.

Theorem 3

If $K = M = 2$, the solution to the planner's problem must be one of the following two types: (i) a choice of action independent of the information transmitted; (ii) an action plan that implements the first-best solution for the agent.

Note that the second-best nature of the problem from the planner's point of view is in full force here. The agent's optimal action plan may be quite different from the planner's.

Proof

Let P be the posterior matrix in which the observations have been reordered (if necessary), so that

(7) $p_{11} > p_{12} \ldots > p_{1N}$,

and thus

$$p_{21} < p_{22} \ldots < p_{2N}, \text{ as } p_{1n} + p_{2n} = 1 \qquad \text{for all } n.$$

Consider $u_{11} - u_{21}$ and $u_{12} - u_{22}$. If these are of the same sign, the optimal action plan is obviously of type (i). Therefore, we assume without loss of generality that $(u_{11} - u_{21}) > 0$ and $(u_{12} - u_{22}) < 0$.

If $u'_{11} - u'_{21}$ and $u'_{12} - u'_{22}$ have the same sign, then the agent will always respond with the same $y_n \in Y$, namely, that one for which z_{n1} is maximal (minimal) if they are both positive (negative). This would also lead to a solution of type (i).

Let us therefore take the case of $u'_{11} - u'_{21} > 0$, $u'_{12} - u'_{22} < 0$.

Let $\mathcal{N}_p = \{n \mid u_{11}p_{1n} + u_{12}p_{2n} > u_{21}p_{1n} + u_{22}p_{2n}\}$,

$\mathcal{N}_A = \{n \mid u'_{11}p_{1n} + u'_{12}p_{2n} > u_{21}p_{1n} + u_{22}p_{2n}\}$.

These are the sets of observations that would lead the planner and the agent, respectively, to choose a_1 if they were to have perfect information about that observation.

Because of (7) we see that $\mathcal{N}_p$ and $\mathcal{N}_A$ can be described by two "cutoff" indices n^*_p and n^*_A:

$$\mathcal{N}_p = \{n \mid 1 \leq n \leq n^*_p\},$$
$$\mathcal{N}_A = \{n \mid 1 \leq n \leq n^*_A\}.$$

Again, we can assume without loss of generality that $n^*_p < n^*_A$, for if $n^*_p = n^*_A$, then the first-best for the planner and the agent coincide and this action plan can be implemented with truthful responses.

We know that the first-best action plan for the agent, where $z_{n1} = 1$ if $n \in \mathcal{N}_A$, and $z_{n1} = 0$ otherwise, induces honest responses and can thus be implemented. Suppose that another action plan Z^* is the true optimum in the planner's problem. Let n_{max} and n_{min} be indices of the observations such that

$$z^*_{n_{max}1} \geq z^*_{n1} \geq z^*_{n_{min}1} \qquad \text{for all } n.$$

The agent's response pattern will then be of the form

$$\rho(y_n) = y_{n_{max}} \qquad \text{if } n \in \mathcal{N}_A,$$
$$\rho(y_n) = y_{n_{min}} \qquad \text{if } n \notin \mathcal{N}_A.$$

Therefore, the planner's expected utility level is

$$[u_{11}z^*_{n_{max}1} + u_{21}(1 - z^*_{n_{max}1})](\sum_{\mathcal{N}_A} p_{1n}q_n)$$

$$+ [u_{12}z^*_{n_{max}1} + u_{22}(1 - z^*_{n_{max}1})](\sum_{\mathcal{N}_A} p_{2n}q_n)$$

$$+ [u_{11}z^*_{n_{min}1} + u_{21}(1 - z^*_{n_{min}1})](\sum_{n \notin \mathcal{N}_A} p_{1n}q_n)$$

$$+ [u_{12}z^*_{n_{min}1} + u_{22}(1 - z^*_{n_{min}1})](\sum_{n \notin \mathcal{N}_A} p_{2n}q_n).$$

Because $n \notin \mathcal{N}_A \rightarrow n \notin \mathcal{N}_p$, the planner can increase his expected utility by decreasing $z^*_{n_{min}1}$ to zero. Thus, $z^*_{n_{min}1} = 0$.

Suppose that $z^*_{n_{max}1} < 1$. Let us take the difference between the optimal expected utility of the planner and that obtained at the agent's first-best, which is implemented by $z^*_{n_{max}1} = 1$:

$$(8) \qquad u_{11}(z^*_{n_{max}1} - 1) + u_{21}(-z^*_{n_{max}1})(\sum_{\mathcal{N}_A} p_{1n}q_n)$$

$$+ u_{12}(z^*_{n_{max}1} - 1) + u_{22}(-z^*_{n_{max}1})(\sum_{\mathcal{N}_A} p_{2n}q_n).$$

Note that the derivative of (8) in $z^*_{n_{max}1}$ is

(9) $(u_{11} - u_{21}) (\sum_{\mathcal{N}_A} p_{1n}q_n) + (u_{12} - u_{22}) (\sum_{\mathcal{N}_A} (1 - p_{1n})q_n).$

Thus, if (9) is positive, then $z^*_{n_{max}1}$ should be increased to one, implementing the agent's first-best. If (9) is negative, then $z^*_{n_{max}1}$ should be zero. It follows that $z^*_{n1} = 0$ for all n and that the solution is of type (i).

Finally, we must take the case where the planner and the agent have diametrically opposed goals: $u'_{11} - u'_{21} < 0$ and $u'_{12} - u'_{22} > 0$, in addition to our maintained hypotheses $u_{11} - u_{21} > 0$, $u_{12} - u_{22} < 0$. The set $\mathcal{N}_A$ can then be characterized as

$$\mathcal{N}_A = \{n | N \geq n \geq n^{**}_A\}.$$

There are two possibilities according to whether or not $n^{**}_A \leq n^*_p$. If so, then, the decision to choose a_1 independent of the observation transmitted dominates anything that can be sustained by a nontrivial response function (i.e., anything obtained by $z^*_{n_{max}1} > z^*_{n_{min}1}$). If not, then a_2 dominates. QED.

The simple types of optima observed when either $K = M = 2$ or $K = N = 2$ do not persist in more complex cases. There are essentially two phenomena at issue. They highlight the second-best nature of the problem we have posed and contrast it with those that have been studied in the earlier literature on incentive compatibility.

The planner's expected utility would improve if he could obtain more accurate answers. But to do so he may have to commit himself to an action plan that deviates from his own (unconstrained) choice, given the information that he will eventually possess. A potential tension is thus established between the nonoptimality of actions and the inaccuracy of responses.

When there are more than two actions, some positive probability may even have to be placed on an action that is *dominated* from the planner's point of view, in order to induce truthful responses by the agent. The cost of this nonoptimality may be outweighed by the value of the information so obtained. This is the content of the next example.

When there are more than two possible observations, the information may be of some value but may be imperfectly elicited in that truth-telling is obtained in an action plan Z with some identical rows. Observations corresponding to identical rows of Z are being lumped together in the information transmission process for all practical purposes. Note that, by theorem 3, such a situation must involve either more than two acts or more than two states; otherwise, either the information would be valueless or a genuine truth-telling situation would exist.

Example 1

Let $N = 2$, $M = 2$, $K = 3$, and

$$P = \begin{pmatrix} 3/4 & 1/4 \\ 1/4 & 3/4 \end{pmatrix} \quad q = \begin{pmatrix} 1/2 \\ 1/2 \end{pmatrix},$$

$$U' = \begin{pmatrix} 0 & -1 \\ 2 & 0 \\ 0 & -4 \end{pmatrix} \quad U = \begin{pmatrix} -2 & 3 \\ 0 & 0 \\ -1 & -1 \end{pmatrix}.$$

Let

$$Z = \begin{pmatrix} z_{11} & z_{12} & 1 - z_{11} - z_{12} \\ z_{21} & z_{22} & 1 - z_{21} - z_{22} \end{pmatrix},$$

incorporating the Markovian nature of Z in the notation.

To induce truth-telling we must choose Z so that the matrix ZUP has the larger element of each column on the diagonal. Writing

$$ZUP = \begin{bmatrix} (3/4)z_{11} + (10/4)z_{12} - 1 & (9/4)z_{11} + (14/4)z_{12} - 3 \\ (3/4)z_{21} + (10/4)z_{22} - 1 & (9/4)z_{21} + (14/4)z_{22} - 3 \end{bmatrix},$$

we see that the necessary and sufficient conditions for truth-telling are

(10) $(10/3)(z_{22} - z_{12}) < (z_{11} - z_{21}) < (14/9)(z_{22} - z_{12}).$

In addition, we require

(11) $z_{ij} \geq 0$ for $i,j = 1,2$, $z_{11} + z_{12} \leq 1$, $z_{21} + z_{22} \leq 1$.

Note that from the planner's point of view, act a_3 is dominated by random acts assigning weight to a_1 and a_2 with at least half the probability on the latter. In an unconstrained statistical decision problem, a_3 would never be selected. But we will now observe that a_3 is part of the optimal action plan because of its role in inducing the agent to tell the truth.

Following the solution method outlined in section 3.2, we compute the optimum assuming the planner is constrained to choose $Z \in \phi^{-1}(I)$; that is,

$$\max 1/2 \text{ trace } ZUP$$

subject to (10) and (11). This optimum is given by

$$Z = \begin{pmatrix} 0 & .643 & .357 \\ 1 & 0 & 0 \end{pmatrix},$$

and the value of the objective function[9] is 0.696.

Note that this value is in between what can be achieved in the first-best ($z_{21} = z_{12} = 1$ and all other z's zero), which gives an expected utility of 0.875, and what can be achieved independent of information ($z_{11} = z_{21} = 1$ and all other z's zero), which yields 0.5.

Example 2

In this example we show how a situation of truth-telling can actually transmit information imperfectly in that the optimal Z matrix has some, but not all, rows identical. By theorem 1 we will obtain "truth-telling" as a response rule, but the planner will not be able to utilize the distinctions between certain observations.

Let

$$U'P = \begin{pmatrix} 1 & 3/2 & 0 \\ 0 & 1 & 0 \\ 0 & 0 & 1 \end{pmatrix},$$

$$UP = \begin{pmatrix} 5 & -1 & -1 \\ 0 & 0 & 0 \\ 0 & 0 & 0 \end{pmatrix},$$

$$q = (1/3,\ 1/3,\ 1/3)^{\mathrm{T}}.$$

Solving the problem by writing the single linear program (4) subject to (5) yields the solution

$$Z = \begin{pmatrix} 1 & 0 & 0 \\ 1 & 0 & 0 \\ 0 & 1 & 0 \end{pmatrix}$$

in which the value to the planner is 4/3. Note that observations y_1 and y_2 are not being distinguished here. The first-best is 5/3, and the best unconditional action (a_1) would yield 1.

Although truthful responses are elicited, the agent is indifferent between this and the response pattern

$$R = \begin{pmatrix} 1 & 1 & 0 \\ 0 & 0 & 0 \\ 0 & 0 & 1 \end{pmatrix}.$$

3.4 The Value of Improving the Agent's Information

We now turn to the second theme of this paper: is it true that planners would necessarily want to improve the information structures of their agents? To investigate this issue it is necessary to have a criterion through which the superiority of one information structure over another can be asserted.

In statistical decision theory, the following definition of *more informativeness*, or superiority, is standard: (Y, Λ) is said to be more informative than (Y', Λ') if, for any U and any π, the maximal expected utility attainable with (Y, Λ) is at least as large as that attainable under (Y', Λ').

Blackwell (1951) has given a criterion equivalent to the fact that (Y, Λ) is more informative than (Y', Λ'): there exists a Markov matrix B such that $\Lambda' = \Lambda B$.

The elements of B can be interpreted[10] as if they were the conditional probabilities of $y' \in Y'$ given $y \in Y$. But actually the *joint* distribution of y and y' may not be like this, and in any event it is not specified. The theorem simply says that if one information structure is better than another, one can imagine that the poorer one is a garbled version of the better one; for this reason it is called quasi garbling.[11]

When (Y, Λ) is more informative than (Y', Λ') and when a prior π is fixed so that $q = \Lambda^T \pi$ and $q' = \Lambda'^T \pi$ can be computed, there exists another matrix C, which relates the two posterior matrices according to[12]

(12)   i) $P' = PC$,

      ii) $q = Cq'$,

      iii) C is the transpose of a Markov matrix, $C \in \mathcal{M}^T$.

Moreover, the existence of such a matrix C implies that the matrix B whose elements are given by

(13) $$b_{nn'} = \frac{c_{nn'} q'_{n'}}{q_n}$$

will satisfy $B \in \mathcal{M}, \Lambda' = \Lambda B$; hence, the existence of such a C is equivalent to the more informativeness criterion.

When the agent's information structure changes, there are two effects on the planner's problem. First, there is a new function ϕ describing the response rule. The observation sets Y and Y' may be entirely different. But even if Y and Y' have equal numbers of elements, the new information will generally alter the accuracy of the responses made for any action plan. Second, there is a direct beneficial impact on the utility attainable for the planner under any fixed response function. The trouble is, of course, that taking advantage of this superior information may entail using an action plan at which the requisite pattern of information transfer will not be forthcoming from the agent.

By presenting a counterexample, we now proceed to establish that an improvement in information may be harmful. The analysis of the counterexample will rely heavily on the properties of optimal action plans derived in theorem 3 for the case $K = M = 2$.

Example 3

Let $K = M = 2$ and

$$\pi = (1/2, 1/2),$$

$$P = \begin{pmatrix} 3/4 & 1/2 & 0 \\ 1/4 & 1/2 & 1 \end{pmatrix},$$

$$q = (1/2, 1/4, 1/4)^T,$$

$$P' = \begin{pmatrix} 3/4 & 1/4 \\ 1/4 & 3/4 \end{pmatrix},$$

$$q' = (1/2, 1/2)^T.$$

One can compute directly that the matrix C given by

$$C = \begin{pmatrix} 1 & 0 \\ 0 & 1/2 \\ 0 & 1/2 \end{pmatrix}$$

satisfies (12) and hence establishes that the information structure for which P is the posterior is superior to that for which P' is the posterior.

Take the utility matrices for the planner and the agent given by

$$U = \begin{pmatrix} 2 & 0 \\ 0 & 4 \end{pmatrix}$$

and

$$U' = \begin{pmatrix} 4 & 0 \\ 0 & 2 \end{pmatrix}.$$

By theorem 3, we know that the optimum for the planner's problem in either case is either a situation in which the information is not being used at all or one in which the agent is attaining his own first-best. The value of the planner's problem without information is the maximal element of $U\pi$, which is 2, and occurs when a_2 is chosen with certainty.

The agent's problem with the poorer information structure is optimized with the action plan

$$Z' = \begin{pmatrix} 1 & 0 \\ 0 & 1 \end{pmatrix},$$

which is also the action plan for the planner's first-best and generates an expected utility of 9/4 ($= \text{trace } Z'UP'\hat{q}'$) for the planner. As this is above 2, the action plan Z' is the overall optimum for the information structure P'.

With the better information structure the action plan that implements the first-best for the agent is

$$Z = \begin{pmatrix} 1 & 0 \\ 1 & 0 \\ 0 & 1 \end{pmatrix}.$$

But this lowers the planner's expected utility to 2 ($= \text{trace } ZUP\hat{q}$). Thus, the planner can get at most an expected utility of 2 under the better information structure, by theorem 3, and he will prefer to give the agent the worse information structure.

Despite the rather negative conclusion of the previous example there is one case in which it can be proved that superior information is necessarily beneficial. This is in the comparison of information structures each of which has only two possible observations. Such systems are called *binomial channels* in the information theory literature.

Theorem 4

The value of the planner's problem under (Y, Λ) is necessarily at least as high as that under (Y', Λ') if (Y, Λ) is more informative than (Y', Λ') and both are binomial channels.

This theorem will be proved in two steps. First, we will establish that if Z is an action plan compatible with truth-telling under (Y', Λ'), then Z will also elicit truth-telling under (Y, Λ). Second, we prove that if an action plan Z that induces truth-telling is optimal under (Y', Λ') and continues to induce truth-telling under (Y, Λ), then the planner's expected utility improves. Since the optimum is always attained by truth-telling, by theorem 1, this would suffice.

By rearranging the labeling of y'_1, $y'_2 \in Y'$ we can, without loss of generality, establish that the Markov matrix B (defined by (13)) has its maximal element in each row on the diagonal.

Lemma

If C and B are 2×2 matrices related by (13) and B has its maximal element in each row on the diagonal, then C satisfies the same property.

Proof

Straightforward.

Lemma

Let C have its largest element in each row on the diagonal. Let $ZU'PC$ have its maximal element in each column on the diagonal; then $ZU'P$ has the same property.

Proof

Denote $ZU'P = \bar{Z}$ and

$$C = \begin{pmatrix} c_{11} & c_{12} \\ 1 - c_{11} & 1 - c_{12} \end{pmatrix}.$$

We need to establish that

(14) $$c_{11}(\bar{z}_{11} - \bar{z}_{12}) + \bar{z}_{12} > c_{11}(\bar{z}_{21} - \bar{z}_{22}) + \bar{z}_{22},$$

(15) $$c_{12}(\bar{z}_{21} - \bar{z}_{22}) + \bar{z}_{22} > c_{12}(\bar{z}_{11} - \bar{z}_{12}) + \bar{z}_{12},$$

(16) $$c_{11} > c_{12}$$

together imply

(17) $$\bar{z}_{11} > \bar{z}_{21} \text{ and } \bar{z}_{22} > \bar{z}_{12}.$$

Another way of writing (14) and (15) is

(18) $$c_{11}(\bar{z}_{11} - \bar{z}_{21}) > (1 - c_{11})(\bar{z}_{22} - \bar{z}_{12}),$$

(19) $$c_{12}(\bar{z}_{11} - \bar{z}_{21}) < (1 - c_{12})(\bar{z}_{22} - \bar{z}_{12}).$$

So we want to show that (16), (18), and (19) imply (17). From (18) and (19) and because $c_{11}, c_{12} \in [0,1]$ we have the implications

$$\bar{z}_{22} - \bar{z}_{12} > 0 \text{ implies } \bar{z}_{11} - \bar{z}_{21} > 0,$$

$$\bar{z}_{11} - \bar{z}_{21} > 0 \text{ implies } \bar{z}_{22} - \bar{z}_{12} > 0.$$

Therefore, $\bar{z}_{11} - \bar{z}_{21}$ and $\bar{z}_{22} - \bar{z}_{12}$ must have the same sign. If they are both negative, then we have

$$\frac{c_{11}}{1 - c_{11}} < \frac{z_{22} - z_{12}}{z_{11} - z_{21}} < \frac{c_{12}}{1 - c_{12}},$$

contradicting (16). Therefore, (14), (15), and (16) imply $\bar{z}_{11} - \bar{z}_{21}$ and $\bar{z}_{22} - \bar{z}_{12}$ are both positive, which is (17). QED.

Recall that $q = Cq'$ is the distribution of the $y \in Y$ when q' is the distribution of $y' \in Y$. Since Z elicits truth-telling behavior under either information structure, we want to prove

Lemma

$$\text{Trace } \bar{Z}C\hat{q}' < \text{trace } \bar{Z}(\hat{C}q').$$

Proof

Straightforward computations lead to

$$\text{trace } \bar{Z}C\hat{q}' = (\bar{z}_{11}c_{11} + \bar{z}_{12}(1 - c_{11}))q'_1 + (\bar{z}_{21}c_{12} + \bar{z}_{22}(1 - c_{12}))q'_2$$

and

$$\text{trace } \bar{Z}(\hat{C}q') = \bar{z}_{11}(c_{11}q'_1 + c_{12}q'_2) + \bar{z}_{22}((1 - c_{11})q'_1 + (1 - c_{12})q'_2).$$

Therefore, we want to show that

(20) $$(\bar{z}_{22} - \bar{z}_{12})(1 - c_{11})q'_1 + (\bar{z}_{11} - \bar{z}_{21})c_{12}q'_2 \geqq 0.$$

By the previous lemma, $\bar{z}_{22} - \bar{z}_{12} > 0$ and $(\bar{z}_{11} - \bar{z}_{21}) > 0$. Thus, (20) follows from the nonnegativity of C. QED.

Combining these three lemmas, we see that the action plan Z satisfies the truth-telling constraints for the better information structure and induces a higher expected utility, which proves theorem 4.

3.5 Conclusions

A simple model of decision making in a two-person organization has been presented that attempts to capture the separation between information gathering and action. The problem has been shown to be equivalent to a linear program. Special situations in which a first-best could be attained have been analyzed.

In general, the optimal action plan may be random and may place some weight on dominated strategies. It may elicit truthful responses, but not in a way that allows effective use of this information.

Then we studied the behavior of the value of the problem when there is an improvement in the agent's information structure. This value may respond perversely in general. However, when the information structures being compared involve only two possible observations, the two criteria must agree.

Notes

1. We do not present any explicit models in which the structure developed here could be applied. Some possible examples are stockbroker-client or physician-patient relations; relations between superiors and subordinates within a firm, or between central management of a firm and that of a subdivision. More general models in which there are several players but emphasis on a separation between decision making and information gathering will be studied in later work. This would extend the range of applicability to situations in which there is some gamesmanship required among the information gatherers, as, for example, among several divisions of the same firm which are to be allocated resources for investment.

2. The basic reference is Marschak and Radner (1972). The problem of incentives in team theory has been treated by Groves (1973), retaining the feature of decentralized actions in the hands of the direct receivers of information.

3. See Ross (1973), Wilson (1969), Shavell (1979), and Holmström (1979).

4. A partial summary of the work in this area is given in Green and Laffont (1979). Dasgupta, Hammond, and Maskin (1979) have been particularly concerned with the Nash and Stakelberg equilibrium approaches. Gibbard (1977) and Zeckhauser (1969) use random decision devices, but in a different spirit than we will do here.

Most closely related to the present paper is Myerson (1979). Although formally concerned with unknown preferences, his analysis is similar in spirit to ours. He allows for random decision. He shows that using the space of possible utilities as a strategy space is adequate for the implementation of constrained optima as Bayesian equilibria (Nash equilibria in the game of incomplete information). However, the example he presents has only two possible utilities, and therefore cannot display some of the phenomena we look at in section 3.3 of this paper.

Rosenthal (1978) proves that full information Pareto optimality is generally unattainable in such games, and he provides a sufficient condition under which a Bayesian equilibrium can implement such optima.

5. Groves and Ledyard (1977) have a strategy space much smaller than the space of unknown parameters, but the domain over which its equilibria exist is hard to delineate. Myerson (1979) and Rosenthal (1978) impose truth-telling as a constraint in their definition of equilibrium. The actual constrained Pareto optima we obtain in this paper do involve

truth-telling. However, it is not imposed in the solution concept, but rather emerges as a characteristic of the second-best. See theorem 1.

6. See example 1.

7. We will always follow the practice of writing the constraints on responses of the agent as weak inequalities, expressing the fact that if he is indifferent between response patterns, we can assume that he will make the indicated choice.

8. See example 2.

9. The true optimum differs slightly because of rounding error. This calculation was performed on an electronic computer.

10. See Marschak and Miyasawa (1968) or McGuire (1972).

11. Another advantage of having this theorem is that it provides a constructive method to check this relationship between information structures. The existence of such a matrix can be determined by solving a system of linear inequalities, whereas the definition requires, in principle, that a comparison be made over all U, π.

12. See Marschak and Miyasawa (1968, p. 154). Our equation (13) is their (8.23).

References

Blackwell, D. 1951. Comparison of experiments. In J. Neyman, ed., *Proceedings of the Second Berkeley Symposium on Mathematical Statistics and Probability*, pp. 93–102. Berkeley and Los Angeles: University of California Press.

Dasgupta, P.; Hammond, P.; and Maskin, E. 1979. The implementation of social choice rules. *Review of Economic Studies* 66 (no. 2): 185–216.

Gibbard, A. 1977. Manipulation of schemes that mix voting with chance. *Econometrica* 45 (no. 3): 665–82.

Green, J., and Laffont, J.-J. 1979. *Incentives in public decision-making.* Amsterdam: North-Holland.

Groves, T. 1973. Incentives in teams. *Econometrica* 41 (no. 4): 617–32.

Groves, T., and Ledyard, J. 1977. Optimal allocation of public goods: A solution to the 'free-rider' problem. *Econometrica* 45 (no. 4): 783–809.

Holmström, B. 1979. Moral hazard and observability. *Bell Journal of Economics* 10 (no. 1): 74–91.

McGuire, C. B. 1972. Comparison of information structures. In Radner, R., and McGuire, C. B., eds., *Decision and organization*, chap. 5. Amsterdam: North-Holland.

Marschak, J., and Miyasawa, K. 1968. Economic comparability of information systems. *International Economic Review* 9 (no. 2): 137–74.

Marschak, J., and Radner, R. 1972. *Economic theory of teams.* Cowles Foundation Monograph 22. New Haven: Yale University Press.

Myerson, R. 1979. Incentive compatibility and the bargaining problem. *Econometrica* 47 (no. 1): 61–74.

Rosenthal, R. 1978. Arbitration of two-party disputes under uncertainty. *Review of Economic Studies* 45 (no. 3): 595–604.

Ross, S. 1973. The economic theory of agency: The principal's problem. *American Economic Review* 63 (no. 2): 134–39.

Shavell, S. 1979. Risk sharing and incentives in the principal and agent relationship. *Bell Journal of Economics* 10 (no. 1): 55–73.

Wilson, R. 1969. The structure of incentives for decentralization under uncertainty. In *La décision*, pp. 287–308. Paris: CNRS.

Zeckhauser, R. 1969. Majority rule with lotteries on alternatives. *Quarterly Journal of Economics* 83: 696–703.

Comment   Andrew Postlewaite

Green presents a model of decision making under uncertainty in which one agent receives information and transmits it to a principal. The principal then makes a decision (chooses an act) on the basis of the information received. Both the principal and the agent then receive a payoff which depends on both the state of the world and the action chosen by the principal. It is assumed that the principal must commit himself to an action plan which determines which action (possibly a probability distribution over several actions) he will take given any information signal transmitted by the agent. Thus, the principal is faced with a possible incentive problem. If the principal commits himself to taking the action which is best for him given any information signal, this may be harmful to the agent. In this case it could be in the agent's interest to transmit incorrect signals. Hence, the principal, recognizing the incentives he creates for the agent, assumes that the agent will behave in a purely self-interested manner and will transmit whatever (possibly false) information signal which according to the principal's action plan gives the agent his highest payoff.

It is assumed that both the principal and the agent know the probabilities of the states, the probabilities of the signals the agent could receive in each state, and the payoffs each will receive given the state and action taken by the principal. Thus, for any action plan the principal contemplates, he can precisely calculate what signal the agent will transmit given the information signal that the agent has observed (received). This, with the probabilities of the states and information signals, is sufficient for the principal to determine his own expected payoff for any action plan. He chooses the action plan which maximizes his expected payoff.

Through a series of examples we will examine the possible effects of improved information on both the principal and the agent. In each of the examples, the set of actions the principal can take are $A = \{a_1, a_2, a_3, a_4\}$

Andrew Postlewaite is associated with the Wharton School of the University of Pennsylvania, Philadelphia.

and the states of the world are $Y = \{y_1, y_2, y_3, y_4\}$; the payoffs to the principal and the agent for each action and state of the world are given in the matrices in figure C3.1.

For all of the examples we assume probability $(y_i) = \frac{1}{4}, i = 1, 2, 3, 4$. For each of the examples we will consider two information structures. In the first structure, W, the agent will observe s_1 if either y_1 or y_2 is the true state and s_2 if either y_3 or y_4 is the true state. In each example we will compare the information structure W with an improved structure I where the agent observes the state precisely; i.e., he observes s_i if y_i is the true state, $i = 1, 2, 3, 4$.

Before beginning the examples it will be helpful to write down the matrices of expected payoffs for the action and information signals for the worse information structure W. These are given in figure C3.2.

If action a_1 is taken when the signal s_1 is observed by the agent, the principal's payoff is either $2b$ or 0 depending upon whether y_1 or y_2 is the true state. Since each has probability $\frac{1}{2}$ given s_1, the principal's expected payoff is b in this case. The other numbers for the principal and the agent are calculated in this manner.

The first case we will examine is that where the improved information structure I yields higher expected payoffs for both the principal and the agent.

Case I. Suppose

$$e > d > b > c > 0$$

and

$$j > h > f > g > 0.$$

Consider an action plan for the principal given as follows: $a_4 = f(s_1), a_3 = f(s_2)$; i.e., the principal takes a_4 when s_1 is transmitted and a_3 when s_2 is transmitted. Notice that this guarantees the agent (expected) payoff j

Principal

A \ Y	1	2	3	4
1	2b	0	2c	0
2	0	2c	0	2b
3	2d	0	2e	0
4	0	2e	0	2d

Agent

A \ Y	1	2	3	4
1	0	2f	0	2g
2	2g	0	2f	0
3	2h	0	2j	0
4	0	2j	0	2h

Fig. C3.1

	Principal			Agent	
A \ S	S_1	S_2	A \ S	S_1	S_2
1	b	c	1	f	g
2	c	b	2	g	f
3	d	e	3	h	j
4	e	d	4	j	h

Fig. C3.2

regardless of the signal if he transmits the information correctly. Since we assumed j was larger than any payoff in his matrix for information structure W, it is in his best interests to transmit the signal correctly. This yields the principal a payoff of e, which is the best he can get for the structure; thus, this is the "solution" for the structure W.

Now consider the improved structure I and the action plan

$$a_3 = f(s_1) = f(s_3),$$
$$a_4 = f(s_2) = f(s_4).$$

This gives the agent h in states 1 and 4 and j in states 2 and 3 if he transmits the signals correctly. These by assumption are the largest payoffs he can get in the respective states. They similarly yield the principal either d or e, which are his highest possible payoffs given the states. Hence, this action plan is the solution for information structure I.

Note that here the expected payoffs for the principal and the agent are $d + e$ and $h + j$, respectively, as compared with e and j for information structure W.

The fact that the improved information structure I is better for both the principal and the agent in this example is not surprising. Given the assumed inequalities, the interests of the two agents coincide for the relevant actions a_3 and a_4. The common interests yield "truth-telling" on the agent's part for that action plan which gives the principal his highest payoff for any observed signal. In this case we should expect improved information to yield higher payoffs for both principal and agent than the worse information structure.

The next example shows how the improved information structure can hurt both principal and agent.

Case II. Suppose

$$b > d + e > \tfrac{1}{2}(b + c) > c > 0 \qquad d, e > 0$$

and

$$f > h + j > \tfrac{1}{2}(f + g) > g > 0 \qquad h, j > 0.$$

For information structure W consider the action rule

$$a_1 = f(s_1),$$

$$a_2 = f(s_2),$$

The agent receives f if he reports the signal truthfully. Since, by assumption, f is the largest payoff possible, he will do so. Since this yields the principal b, his highest possible payoff, this action plan is optimal.

While in information structure W the agent's and principal's interests essentially coincide, this dramatically changes when we go to the improved information structure I. Here there is absolute conflict between the agent and principal for actions a_1 and a_2: if one gets a positive payoff, the other receives nothing. Clearly the information the agent transmits is worthless to the principal if he takes only actions a_1 and a_2. Any use he makes of the signals the agent sends can be exploited by the agent. The best the principal can do if he is to use only actions a_1 and a_2 is to ignore the signals received, e.g., use an action plan such as

$$a_1 = f(s_i) \qquad i = 1, 2, 3, 4$$

which would yield the principal $\tfrac{1}{2}(b + c)$. If, however, he chooses action plan

$$a_3 = \hat{f}(s_1) = \hat{f}(s_3),$$

$$a_4 = \hat{f}(s_2) = \hat{f}(s_4),$$

the agent will find it in his best interest to transmit the correct signals. This gives $d + e$ to the principal, which by assumption is better than he can do using only a_1 and a_2. But this yields both the agent and the principal less than their respective payoffs under the worse information structure W.

So far, we have only shown that the action plan $\hat{f}$ for information structure I leaves the players worse off than in the worse information structure W. But $\hat{f}$ is not in fact the optimal information structure for I. Since the agent has a strict incentive to transmit signals truthfully (i.e., this yields him strictly higher payoff than any other response pattern), the principal could use a stochastic action plan which would put a small positive probability on a_1 and a_2 for the appropriate signals without destroying the agent's incentives. This would leave the principal slightly better off and the agent slightly worse off than under $\hat{f}$. The probability that can be placed on a_1 and a_2 without destroying the incentives (and thus making the information worthless here) becomes arbitrarily small as h gets arbitrarily close to j. Thus, we see that if the assumed inequalities hold and also if h is sufficiently close to j, the improved information structure I leaves both agent and principal worse off than they are in structure W.

A few words about this example. Green makes the point that the principal's optimal action plan may involve positive probabilities on dominated actions. If $c > e$ and $g > j$, that is precisely what is happening here. Action a_1 dominates a_3 and a_2 dominates a_4, yet the optimal action plan involves placing most of the probability on a_3 and a_4. This example shows clearly how the problem of the agent's incentives makes this necessary.

A second aspect to point out is how the better information structure makes both players worse off. Actions a_1 and a_2 are the best actions to take from a joint point of view so long as states $\{y_1, y_2\}$ can be distinguished from $\{y_3, y_4\}$. The worse information structure allows an action plan to distinguish them because the interests of the two coincide. The better information structure gives enough information to put the players in conflict with each other as to which of the actions a_1 or a_2 is best. Given the framework of this model, both agents would theoretically agree to use information structure W rather than the improved structure I.

This raises a question which is essentially outside of this model. How is the information structure determined, and what is the "information about the information"? Although both principal and agent do better under W than I, this is because the optimal action plan under W picks only a_1 and a_2. Given this fact, the agent has an incentive to secretly "get the better information" in I. Thus, even the availability of the better information structure I would prevent the principal from using only actions a_1 and a_2 unless he could ensure that the agent would not observe the more precise information signals in I. We will say a bit more below about the questions of who chooses the information structure and the degree of common knowledge about the information structure being used.

So far we have provided examples of an improved information structure either benefiting both principal and agent or hurting both. It is also possible that the improved information structure I can help the agent and hurt the principal.

Case III. Suppose

$$b > c > d > e > 0 \qquad b > d + e$$

and

$$f > g > j > h > 0 \qquad f < j + h.$$

This example is similar to Case II. For structure W, the optimal action rule is $a_1 = f(s_1)$, $a_2 = f(s_2)$. This induces truthful responses from the agent and yields payoffs of b and f to the principal and agent, respectively.

If the information structure is I and h is very close to j, the optimal action rule puts nearly all probability on a_3 and a_4, yielding approximately $d + e$ to the principal and $j + h$ to the agent; from the assumed inequalities we see that the agent is better off and the principal worse off.

Each of the three cases above was explicitly or implicitly mentioned in Green's paper. The last case—that in which the agent is worse off and the principal better off under the improved information structure—was not. At first glance one might think this case particularly paradoxical. Cannot the agent simply "ignore" the better information? Yet as Case II illustrated, the structure of the model essentially prevents an agent from ignoring information. The principal commits himself to an action rule, and if he knows that information is available he can design his action rule so that an agent would be even worse off if he did ignore the information. It is this Stackelberg-like feature which has the principal but not the agent commit himself which gives rise to these phenomena.

In fact a simple transformation of Case III gives rise to an example where the agent is worse off and the principal better off under the improved information structure.

Case IV. Suppose

$$b > c > d > e > 0 \qquad b < d + e$$

and

$$f > g > j > h > 0 \qquad f > j + h.$$

An argument as in Case III shows that if h is close to j, the payoffs to the principal and agent are b and f, respectively, under W and approximately $d + e$ and $h + j$, respectively, under I. That the principal is better off and the agent worse off follows from the assumed inequalities.

As we mentioned above, the question of how the information structure is determined becomes important. Does the agent or the principal decide on the structure? Is the structure itself a matter of negotiation? In the examples in both Case II and Case IV, if the agent had the ability to commit himself to the worse information structure, he would *if* he could also convince the principal that he had done so.

It also should be pointed out that the results of the examples would be drastically changed even if we left aside the question of determination of the information structure, but only reversed the roles of leader and follower in the model. Consider a situation where the agent commits himself to a response rule and the principal then chooses an action. It is straightforward to construct examples where both principal and agent are better off with the roles of leader-follower reversed. In such cases we might expect the reversed roles "institutionalized." The model examined in the paper is but one of a class of similar models. Which model is operative for a particular application would perhaps be endogenously determined in an expanded setting.

Comment   John G. Riley

In the basic model of information acquisition as developed by Blackwell (1951) and Marschak and Miyasawa (1968), an individual may be viewed as paying a predetermined fee to an information service. The latter then delivers one of a set of messages which have the effect of updating the individual's beliefs as to the likelihood of the various states of nature. Swept into the background is the issue of how the purchaser of information (hereafter referred to as the "principal") verifies the accuracy of the information.

Even if the "agent" operating the information service simply collects and processes data, verification of computations, etc., is a costly process. However, more commonly the principal relies at least in part on the expertise of the agent. Verification is then only indirect. The principal either develops a long-term relationship with the agent or, alternatively, relies on the reputation the latter has developed.

Green's starting point is to consider what sort of contracts between principal and agent might be negotiated when such indirect verification is not available. For the problem to be interesting it is necessary that both the purchaser and gatherer of information have an interest in the final outcome. In general these interests will not coincide and, as a result, the agent may have an incentive to reveal false information. When such is the case, Green examines the potential benefits to the principal if he precommits himself, for every feasible message, to a particular action (or, more generally, to probability weights on different actions).

The first result is that the principal can do no better than induce truthful information transfer. Appropriately interpreted this is essentially definitional. Let there be n possible messages from agent to principal. The latter announces that if he receives message m_i, he will take probabilistic action $z_i = (z_{i1}, \ldots, z_{in})$, where z_{ij} is the probability assigned to action j. Effectively the agent then freely chooses from the set of probabilistic actions $Z = \{z_1, z_2, \ldots, z_n\}$. Thus, without loss of generality we may relabel the elements of this set so that z_i^* is the action chosen by the agent when the *truth* is message i.

Using this result, it is then shown that if there are only two states of nature and either two actions or two possible messages, the principal's optimal response is (i) to not make use of the information, or (ii) to accept

John G. Riley is professor of economics, University of California, Los Angeles.

the message without any precommitment strategy. In more complex environments it is shown that probabilistic precommitments can increase the expected utility of the principal. An example is provided in which the principal finds it desirable to introduce an action that is strictly dominated by another action. To understand this result, I find figure C3.3 helpful. On the horizontal axis is the possibility p of state 1, and on the vertical axis expected utility of the principal, which we may write as

$$U(p;a_i) = pu_1(a_i) + (1-p)u_2(a_i),$$

where $u_s(a_i)$ is the utility of the principal in state s if he takes action a_i. Without the services of the information gathering agent the principal, with prior probability $p_0 = .5$, chooses action a_1. Suppose that the agent receives one of the following two messages with equal probability:

$$m_1: p = .8, \qquad m_2: p = .2.$$

If the agent always tells the truth, the principal has an expected utility of AB when $m = m_1$ and CD when $m = m_2$. Since each message is received with equal probability the ex ante expected utility is EG and the net value of the information is FG.

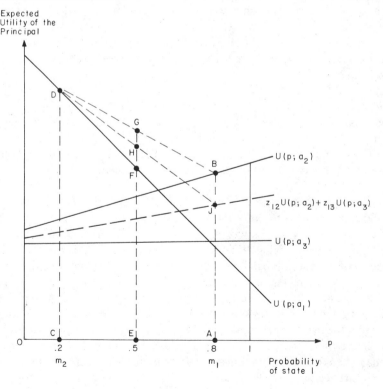

Fig. C3.3   The value to the principal of receiving information.

Suppose next that action a_2 is the dominant action from the viewpoint of the agent. Then rather than reveal the truth he will always pass on the message $m = m_1$. Obviously this is valueless to the principal. To combat this problem, the principal announces that if the message received is $m = m_1$ he will adopt action a_2 with probability z_{12} and action a_3 with probability z_{13}. The expected utility of the principal is then the weighted average

$$z_{12}U(p;a_2) + z_{13}U(p;a_3).$$

As long as action a_3 is sufficiently worse for the agent than a_1 when the truth is $m = m_2$, and better than a_1 when the truth is $m = m_1$, his optimal response is to reveal the truth. As a result the expected utility of the principal is AJ if $m = m_1$ and CD if $m = m_2$, and the information service has an expected value of FH.

In the final section of his paper Green asks whether a more informative agent is necessarily more valuable to the principal. Except in a very special case he finds that the opposite may be true: even after an optimal revision of his precommitment strategy the principal may be worse off. Again I find a diagram helpful in understanding this conclusion. The top part of figure C3.4 once again depicts the choices open to the principal for the case of two states and two actions. The bottom part illustrates the expected utility of the agent. With only the two messages $m = m_1, m = m_2$ the interests of agent and principal always coincide. However, suppose that message m_2 is really a "garbled" version of the following two messages;

$$m_{2\alpha}: p = 0, \qquad m_{2\beta}: p = 0.4,$$

that is, the agent receives a message but is not sure whether it is $m_{2\alpha}$ or $m_{2\beta}$. If he assigns equal probabilities to the two alternatives, his information is summarized by the message m_2. Clearly an agent who is able to unscramble such a message is sensibly described as being better informed.

As depicted in figure C3.4 revelation of the unscrambled truth is of no additional benefit to the principal since his optimal action is a_1 for $m = m_{2\alpha}$ and $m = m_{2\beta}$. However, the interests of principal and agent no longer always coincide. If $m = m_{2\beta}$, the optimal action from the viewpoint of the agent is a_2. Therefore, the agent has an incentive to conceal the fact that he has unscrambled message m_2 and to reveal the false message m_1. But suppose the principal were to learn that the agent had become better informed. With only two actions Green's theorem 3 tells us that the best the principal can do is either to ignore the agent entirely or to accept his message as if it were the truth. If he does the latter, he knows that when the agent announces m_1 there is one chance in three that $p = .4$ and two chances in three that $p = .8$. The principal then assigns a probability of $\frac{1}{3}(.4) + \frac{2}{3}(.8) = .66$ to state 1, and his expected utility falls

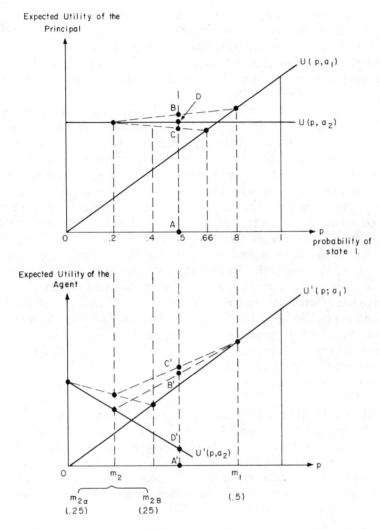

Fig. C3.4   More informative information leaving both principal and agent worse off.

from AB to AC. A similar argument for the bottom part of figure C3.4 establishes that the agent's expected utility rises from $A'B'$ to $A'C'$. Of course this is also the outcome when the principal is unaware that the agent has become better informed.

The other alternative open to the principal is to ignore the agent and use only his prior probability of state 1 (.5). Clearly this is preferred since it yields an expected utility of AD while lowering the expected utility of the agent to $A'D'$. Therefore, if the information contained in message m_2

becomes unscrambled, the expected utility of the principal drops from AB to AD and the expected utility of the agent drops from $A'B'$ to $A'D'$. This is another simple example of the phenomenon first noted by Andrew Postlewaite: additional information can hurt both parties. Indeed, in this example the coarser information benefits both principal and agent while the finer information is valueless!

I shall conclude with some more general remarks. The main inference that I draw from Green's paper is that we cannot expect to obtain more than a multitude of special cases unless the model is refined in some way. One line of attack would be to focus more closely on the way in which the agent is compensated by the principal. Implicitly compensation takes the form of a fixed fee paid in advance. However, by contracting to pay a fee contingent upon the eventual state of nature the principal might be able to eliminate, or at least reduce, the extent to which his interests conflict with those of the agent. A second approach would be to take explicit account of the repetitive nature of informational exchanges. In each of the applications suggested by the author (stockbroker-client, physician-patient, manager-worker) it is hardly surprising that the information purchaser is usually observed in a long-term relationship with the information gathering agent. If precommitment strategies of the sort described above have practical relevance, surely they are only likely in situations which are sufficiently repetitive to allow the principal to learn the interests of the agent and vice versa.

References

Blackwell, D. 1951. Comparison of experiments. In Neyman, J., ed., *Proceedings of the Second Berkeley Symposium on Mathematical Statistics and Probability*, pp. 93–102. Berkeley and Los Angeles: University of California Press.

Marschak, J., and Miyasawa, K. 1968. Economic comparability of information systems. *International Economic Review* 9, no. 2: 137–74.

4 Corporate Financial Structure and Managerial Incentives

Sanford J. Grossman and Oliver D. Hart

4.1 Introduction

In this paper we study the incentive effects of the threat of bankruptcy on the quality of management in a widely held corporation. In so doing we develop an equilibrium concept which may be useful in studying a wide class of other problems. The equilibrium concept is relevant whenever there is moral hazard in principal-agent relationships. We model the idea that the agent can engage in precommitment or bonding behavior which will indicate to the principal that he will act in the principal's interest.

The starting point of our analysis is the idea that in a corporation owned by many small shareholders there is an "incentive problem"; i.e., the managers (or directors) have goals of their own, such as the enjoyment of perquisites or the maximization of their own income, which are at variance with the goals of shareholders, which we assume to be profit or market value maximization. There are a number of ways to overcome this incentive problem. First, managers can be given salary incentive schemes (e.g., profit sharing arrangements or stock options) to get their interests to move toward those of shareholders. Second, shareholders can write a corporate charter which permits and to some extent encourages takeover bids. As a result, if the corporation is badly run, a raider can make a profit by buying the company at a low price, reorganizing it, and reselling it at a high price. The threat of such a takeover bid will in general lead current management to achieve higher profits.[1]

Sanford J. Grossman is professor of economics, University of Chicago. Oliver D. Hart is professor of economics, London School of Economics.

The authors would like to thank David Champernowne and David Kreps for helpful suggestions.

Although both salary incentive schemes and takeover bids can reduce the seriousness of the "incentive problem," they will not in general eliminate it completely. In this paper we study a third factor which may be important in encouraging managers to pursue the profit motive: the possibility of bankruptcy. If managers do not seek high profits, the probability that the corporation will go bankrupt increases. If the benefits managers receive from the firm are lost in the event of bankruptcy, managers may prefer to maximize profits or come close to it rather than to risk sacrificing their perquisites.

Clearly the efficacy of bankruptcy as a source of discipline for management will depend on the firm's financial structure—in particular, its debt-equity ratio. As an illustration of this, ignore takeover bids and consider the old argument that, in a perfectly competitive world with free entry, firms must profit maximize if they are not to go out of business. Suppose that the profit maximizing production plan involves an investment outlay of $100 which gives a return stream whose present value is $100 (so that net present value is zero—this is the free entry condition). Then if a firm raises the $100 investment cost by issuing *equity*, the firm is under no pressure to maximize profit at all. In particular, once having raised the $100, there is nothing to stop the firm's managers from canceling the investment project and spending the money on themselves! All that will happen is that the value of the equity will fall to zero; i.e., those who purchased the firm's shares will lose $100. (Of course, if this is anticipated by shareholders, they will not purchase the firm's shares and management will not be able to raise the $100.) Note, however, how the story changes if the $100 investment outlay is raised by *debt*. Then any choice other than the profit maximizing plan will lead to bankruptcy with certainty. Thus, whether competition leads to profit maximization depends crucially on the firm's financial structure.[2]

It is clear from the above arguments that it will generally be in the shareholders' interest for a firm to issue debt as well as equity since this raises profit. In a mature corporation, however, the power to determine the firm's financial structure usually rests in the hands of *management*, not the shareholders. Furthermore, since debt increases the probability of bankruptcy, it would seem never to be in management's interest for there to be debt. In this paper we will develop a model to explain the existence of debt even under the assumption that management controls the firm's financial structure.[3]

The reason that debt may be beneficial to management is the following. If management issues no debt, then it is safe from bankruptcy. Among other things this means that it is in a relatively unconstrained position and therefore has less reason to profit maximize. As a result, the market will put a low valuation on the firm and its cost of capital will be high. Conversely, if management issues debt, then shareholders know that it is personally costly to management not to profit maximize (because managers lose the perquisites of their position when the firm goes bankrupt). Hence, in this case, the market will recognize that profits will be higher and so the firm will have a high market value. Thus, there is a positive relationship between a firm's market value—i.e., the value of debt *plus* equity—and its level of debt. Therefore, to the extent that management would like its firm to have a high market value, it may wish to issue debt.

There are at least three reasons managers may want to increase the firm's market value V. (1) Their salaries may depend on V (through a salary incentive scheme). (2) The probability of a takeover bid will be smaller the higher the price a raider has to pay for the firm, and this price will in general be positively related to V. (3) If managers are issuing *new* debt and equity, then the higher V is, the more capital the managers will be able to raise. Furthermore, the more capital the managers can raise, the more they can in general increase their perquisites. In sections 4.2–4.4 we analyze a model where the third reason is central to the managers' desire to increase V (this model can be easily modified to analyze the first reason too, however). Section 4.5 shows that the second reason can also be incorporated into our model.

An alternative interpretation can also be given to the model of sections 4.2–4.4. It applies to the case of an entrepreneur who wishes to set up a firm but does not have sufficient funds to finance it. Other things equal, the entrepreneur would like to finance the firm by issuing equity since he does not then risk bankruptcy. However, in order to achieve a high market value for his project, he may have to issue some debt in order to convince the market that he will pursue profits rather than perquisites. The trade-offs faced by the entrepreneur are the same as those faced by corporate management in the model of this paper.

We think of the issuing of debt as being an example of *precommitment* or *bonding* behavior. Consider the shareholders and management as in a principal-agent relationship where shareholders are the principal and management is the agent. Then, by issuing debt, management (the agent) deliberately changes its incentives in such a way as to bring them in line with those of shareholders (the principal)—because of the resulting effect on market value. In other words, it is as if, by issuing debt, the management bonds itself to act in the shareholders' interest.[4] This relates closely to another example of a bonding equilibrium. Consider the use of bail bonds in criminal proceedings. The accused person offers to put up a sufficiently large bail bond, so that the judge knows that it would be extremely costly (and thus unlikely) for the accused not to return to the court for his trial.

The above example will help to distinguish a bonding equilibrium from a signaling equilibrium. The bail bond is useful for the judge even if he knows the characteristics of the accused person. This is to be distinguished from a signaling or screening situation, where the judge does not know the accused's characteristics and bail is a screening device. In particular, suppose that there are two types of accused persons, with one type having an exogenously higher probability of jumping bail (i.e., leaving the country) than the other type. Further, suppose that the type with the high probability of jumping bail is less wealthy (or has higher borrowing costs) than the other type. In this case the size of the bail bond is a screening device and the amount of bail the accused offers to "put up" is a *signal* about what type of person he is. It will be clear from the formal analysis which follows that a bonding equilibrium is not related to a signaling equilibrium: the former involves agents communicating their endogenous intentions, while the latter involves agents communicating their exogenous characteristics.[5]

The paper is organized as follows. In sections 4.2–4.4 we present the basic model and develop the notion of precommitment or bonding for the case where management wishes to increase V in order to have more funds at its disposal. In section 4.5 we generalize the analysis to the case where increases in V are desired in order to reduce the probability of a takeover bid. Finally, in section 4.6 we discuss how our explanation of the role of debt differs from others that have been proposed in the literature.

4.2   The Model

Consider a corporation whose manager (or management) has discovered a new investment opportunity. We assume that the firm must raise all of the funds required for the investment by borrowing or issuing shares in the enterprise.[6] For simplicity, ignore all the old investments and the old claims on the corporation. Let the investment opportunity be described by the stochastic production function

$$(1) \qquad\qquad q = g(I) + s,$$

where I is the level of investment undertaken by the firm, $g(I)$ is the expected profit from this investment, and s is a random variable with mean zero. We will assume that investors in the firm—be they creditors or shareholders—are risk neutral and that the expected return per dollar which can be obtained on investments elsewhere in the economy is given by $R > 0$ (R should be interpreted as one plus the interest rate).[7]

The model is a two-period one. The level of investment I is chosen "today," and profit q is realized "tomorrow." If traders know the investment level I and they are risk neutral, then the market value of the firm, i.e., the value of its debt and equity, is given by

$$(2) \qquad\qquad V = \frac{g(I)}{R}.$$

Note that this is true whatever debt-equity ratio is chosen by the manager. This suggests that the firm's market value will be independent of its debt-equity ratio, i.e., that the Modigliani-Miller theorem will apply. However, this is the case only if the manager's choice of I is independent of the debt-equity ratio. In the model presented below, I will depend crucially on the level of debt and so V will not be independent of the debt-equity ratio.

Consider first the case where the manager's investment decision is observable to the market. By (2), if the manager chooses the level of investment I, then the net market value of the firm is

$$(3) \qquad V - I = \frac{g(I)}{R} - I.$$

If the manager's salary and perquisites are an increasing function of $V - I$, then I will be chosen to maximize the expression in (3). This is of course the classical solution—the firm's financial decision is irrelevant and the production plan is chosen to maximize net market value.

The assumption that the market observes I is a strong one. In general, monitoring the firm's activities is a costly operation. If a firm's shares and bonds are widely dispersed, it will not be in the interest of individual bondholders and shareholders to incur these costs. In this paper we investigate the consequences of dropping the assumption that I is observed. We will assume that the market has no direct information about I. However, the market will be assumed to be able to make inferences about I from actions taken by the manager—in particular his choice of the debt-equity ratio. These inferences are possible because bankruptcy is assumed to be costly for the manager—this is another difference between the present model and the classical one.

Suppose that the firm raises outside funds equal to V dollars. Let this amount be divided between debt and equity in such a way that the total amount owing to the firm's creditors when "tomorrow" arrives is D dollars. We assume that the firm will go bankrupt if and only if the firm's profits are less than D, i.e., if and only if

$$(4) \qquad g(I) + s < D.$$

Note that bankruptcy can occur even if $D = 0$ if s is large and negative (we allow profit to be negative).

Let the manager have a concave von Neumann–Morgenstern utility function $U(C)$ defined over nonnegative consumption C. We assume that, if V dollars are raised and I dollars are invested, the manager will have $V - I$ left for consumption and so his utility is $U(V - I)$.[8] It will be assumed, however, that this utility is realized only if the firm does not go bankrupt. If the firm does go bankrupt, we suppose that a receiver is able to recover the $V - I$ and so the manager's utility is $U(0)$. Since U is defined only up to positive linear transformation, we will assume without loss of generality that $U(0) = 0$.

In the remainder of this section we analyze the optimal choice of I for the manager, for given values of V and D. We assume that the manager chooses I before s is known. Thus, given (V,D), he maximizes expected utility; i.e.,

(5) $U(V - I)$ prob[no bankruptcy] $= U(V - I)$ prob$[s \geq D - g(I)]$.

We will assume that s is a random variable with distribution function F and density function f. Then we can rewrite the manager's maximization problem as

(6) $\max_{I} U(V - I)(1 - F(D - g(I)))$ subject to $0 \leq I \leq V$.

Since $V - I$ is decreasing in I and $(1 - F(D - g(I)))$ is increasing in I, the trade-off for the manager, given V and D, is between choosing investment levels which give high consumption but a high probability of bankruptcy, and those which give low consumption and a low probability of bankruptcy.

In order to proceed, we will make some further assumptions about U, F, and g. We will assume that (1) U is thrice differentiable with $U'(0) = \infty$, $U' > 0$, $U'' \leq 0$; (2) F is thrice differentiable with $f(x) > 0$ for all x; (3) g is thrice differentiable with $g(0) = 0$, $g' > 0$, $g'' < 0$ and $g'(0) = \infty$, $\lim_{x \to \infty} g'(x) = 0$. Let

(7) $h(I,V,D) = U(V - I)(1 - F(D - g(I)))$.

Then

(8) $h_I \equiv \dfrac{\partial h}{\partial I} = -U'(V - I)(1 - F(D - g(I)))$
                          $+ U(V - I)f(D - g(I))g'(I)$.

Therefore, for I to be a solution to (6), it is necessary that

(9a) $\begin{cases} h_I \leq 0 \text{ if } I = 0, \\[4pt]$
(9b) $h_I = 0 \text{ if } 0 < I < V, \\[4pt]$
(9c) $h_I \geq 0 \text{ if } I = V. \end{cases}$

However, since $U'(0) = \infty$ and $F(x) < 1$ for all finite x (this follows from the fact that $f(x) > 0$ for all x), $h_I < 0$ if $I = V > 0$. On the other hand, if $I = 0$ and $V > 0$, $h_I > 0$ since $g'(0) = \infty$. Therefore, if $V > 0$, (9a) and (9c) are impossible and

(10) $h_I = 0$

must hold at the optimal I; i.e.,

(11)
$$\frac{U'(V-I)}{U(V-I)} = \left(\frac{f(D-g(I))}{1-F(D-g(I))}\right)g'(I).$$

On the other hand, if $V = 0$, then the constraint $0 \le I \le V$ implies that $I = 0$ is optimal for the manager.

Let us concentrate on the case $V > 0$. Equation (11) is then a necessary condition for an optimum, but not in general a sufficient one. One case where sufficiency is guaranteed is if $f(x)/(1 - F(x))$ is everywhere an increasing function of x.[9] Let

$$r(x) = \frac{f(x)}{1-F(x)}.$$

Lemma 1. If $r(x)$ is an increasing function of x, then (11) is a sufficient as well as a necessary condition for I to be an optimal choice for the manager, given (V,D).

Proof. The left-hand side (LHS) of (11) is strictly increasing in I, while, if $r(x)$ is increasing in x, the right-hand side (RHS) of (11) is decreasing in I. Therefore, (11) can hold for at most one value of I. Since (11) is a necessary condition for optimality and since an optimum certainly exists by Weierstrass's theorem, this proves that (11) holds if and only if we are at the optimum. QED.

For most of what follows we will confine our attention to distribution functions $F(\cdot)$ for which $r(x)$ is strictly increasing in x. In reliability theory, $r(x)$ is called the "hazard rate." Our assumption of an increasing hazard rate is satisfied for many well-known distributions such as the exponential, the gamma and Weibull with degrees of freedom parameter larger than 1, and the normal distribution, Laplace, and uniform (Barlow and Proschan 1975, p. 79). In our context the hazard rate has the following interpretation. If net liabilities $D - g(I) = y$, then bankruptcy occurs when $s \le y$. Suppose the manager decreases $g(I)$ by t. Then this increases net liabilities to $y + t$. In the event that $s \le y$, it does not matter that net liabilities are increased to $y + t$ since bankruptcy would have occurred in any case. Therefore, the increase in the conditional probability of bankruptcy in going from y to $y + t$, given no bankruptcy at y, is $(F(y + t) - F(y))/(1 - F(y))$. Thus, $r(y)$ is the

$$\lim_{t \to 0} (1/t)(F(y+t) - F(y))/(1 - F(y)),$$

which is the increase per dollar of net liabilities in the conditional probability of bankruptcy given $s \ge y$. So $r(y)$ is like the marginal cost in the probability of bankruptcy. Thus, $r'(y) > 0$ is like an increasing marginal cost condition.

Assumption 1. $r'(x) > 0$ for all x.

We have seen that, if assumption 1 is satisfied, (11) has a unique solution and so there is a unique optimal choice of I for the entrepreneur. We write the optimal I as $I(V,D)$ (if $V = 0$, $I(V,D) = 0$). It is easy to show by standard arguments that $I(V,D)$ is a continuous function of (V,D). In fact, more can be established.

Lemma 2. If $V > 0$, $I_V \equiv \partial I/\partial V$ and $I_D \equiv \partial I/\partial D$ exist. Furthermore, $0 < I_V < 1$ and $0 \le I_D < [g'(I(V,D))]^{-1}$

Proof. Differentiating (8), we obtain

(12) $$I_V = -\frac{h_{IV}}{h_{II}} \text{ and } I_D = -\frac{h_{ID}}{h_{II}} \text{ if } h_{II} \ne 0.$$

Now

(13) $$h_{II} = U''(1 - F) - U'fg' - U'fg' + Ufg'' - Uf'g'^2$$

$$= U''(1 - F) - U'fg' + Ufg'' - (U'fg' + Uf'g'^2)$$

(14) $$= U''(1 - F) - U'fg' + Ufg'' - Ug'^2(f^2/(1 - F) + f'),$$

where we are using (11). Therefore,

(15) $$h_{II} = U''(1 - F) - U'fg' + Ufg'' - Ug'^2(1 - F)r' < 0$$

by assumption 1. On the other hand,

(16) $$h_{IV} = -U''(1 - F) + U'fg'.$$

Putting (12), (15), and (16) together, we get $0 < I_V < 1$. Also,

(17) $$h_{ID} = U'f + Uf'g' = Ug'\left(\frac{f^2}{1 - F} + f'\right) = Ug'(1 - F)r',$$

where we use (11) again. Putting (12), (15), and (17) together, we obtain $0 \le I_D < [g'(I(V,D))]^{-1}$. QED.

We see from lemma 2 that I is increasing in both V and D; i.e., if the manager obtains more funds he will use some of them (but not all) on additional investment, while if the volume of funds stays the same but a greater fraction is in the form of debt this will also lead him to invest more.[10] Further, $0 \le I_D < (g')^{-1}$ means that the level of debt is chosen such that an increase of a dollar in the amount to be paid back next period calls forth less investment than is actually required to increase the expected value of output by a dollar.

4.3   The Determination of Equilibrium

In the last section we showed how the manager's choice of I depends on V and D. In this section we study how V depends on I. We also analyze the optimal choice of D for the manager.

If I was observable to the market, then as we have noted before V would be given simply by

(18) $$V = \frac{g(I)}{R}.$$

However, I is not observable. Therefore, (18) must be replaced by

(19)
$$V = \frac{g(I^P)}{R},$$

where I^P is the market's perceived value of I. We will assume that the market's perceptions are "rational" in the sense that investors in the market know the utility function U and the distribution function F and so can calculate how much the manager will invest for each value of V and D; i.e., we assume that the market knows the function $I(V,D)$. Hence, we may rewrite (19) as

(20)
$$V = \frac{g(I(V,D))}{R}.$$

We see then that, given D, the equilibrium V and I are solutions of equation (20). For each value of V, there is an optimal choice of I for the manager, $I(V,D)$. However, for an arbitrary V, say V_a, $I(V_a,D)$ will not satisfy (20). If $V_a > g(I(V_a,D))/R$ the firm will be overvalued, while if $V_a < g(I(V_a,D))/R$ it will be undervalued. Only if (20) holds will investors be prepared to pay exactly V_a for the firm, and so only in this case will the system be in equilibrium.

Definition. Given D, a bonding or precommitment equilibrium is a nonnegative pair $(I(D),V(D))$ such that

$$(A) \quad U(V(D) - I(D))(1 - F(D - g(I(D))))$$

$$\geq U(V(D) - I)(1 - F(D - g(I))) \text{ for all } V \geq I \geq 0;$$

$$(B) \quad V(D) = g(I(D))/R.$$

It is useful to rewrite (20) as

(21)
$$g^{-1}(RV) = I(V,D).$$

The LHS of (21) is a strictly increasing, convex function of V with slope zero at $V = 0$. The RHS of (21), on the other hand, is, by lemma 2, a strictly increasing function of V with slope between zero and one, satisfying $0 \leq I(V,D) \leq V$. The two functions are drawn in figure 4.1. It is clear from figure 4.1 that $V = 0$ is a solution to (21) and that there is always at least one other solution $V > 0$, since $g'(0) = \infty$, and $I_V > 0$. Note that the $V = 0$ equilibrium arises because if the market thinks the firm is worthless, then it *will* be worthless because it will be impossible to raise any capital.

Proposition 1. For each D, $V = 0$ is a solution of (21) and there is at least one other solution $V > 0$.

It is worthwhile to consider at this point the role of bankruptcy in the model. In the absence of bankruptcy, the manager's utility would be just

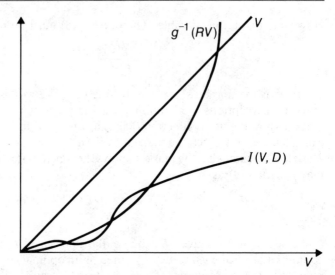

Fig. 4.1

$U(V - I)$. Given V, this is maximized by setting $I = 0$. But since, for each V, the manager's optimal response is to set $I = 0$, this means that the only solution of (21) is $I = V = 0$, and thus no capital can be raised. With bankruptcy, however, other equilibria also exist. The reason is that, since bankruptcy is undesirable, the manager, by taking on debt, can convince the market that he will invest precisely in order to avoid this undesirable outcome. Thus, although bankruptcy is unpleasant for the manager, it permits him to achieve equilibrium situations which make him better off than the no-bankruptcy situation $I = V = 0$.

We will assume that the manager selects D and, if there are multiple equilibria resulting, can choose among them. Given D, if there are just two equilibria $V = 0$ and $V > 0$, then it is clear that the manager is better off at the $V > 0$ equilibrium. This is because $I < V$ when $V > 0$ and so $U(V - I)(1 - F(D - g(I))) > 0$. However, if there are two or more equilibria with $V > 0$, then it is not clear which of them is optimal for the manager. If $V_A > V_B > 0$ are two equilibria for some D, then $I_A = g^{-1}(RV_A) > g^{-1}(RV_B) = I_B$ and so the risk of bankruptcy $F(D - g(I))$ is lower at I_A than at I_B; however, $V_A - I_A$ may be less than $V_B - I_B$, in which case consumption benefits are higher at I_B.

For each D, let $V(D)$ denote an optimal equilibrium for the manager; i.e., $V(D)$ maximizes $U(V - I(V,D))(1 - F(D - g(I(V,D))))$ over all V satisfying

(22) $$V = \frac{g(I(V,D))}{R}.$$

Then, it is optimal for the manager to choose the level of debt D so as to maximize

(23) $U(V(D) - I(V(D),D))(1 - F(D - g(I(V(D),D))))$.

An analysis of the maximization of (23) is somewhat complicated. First, $V(D)$ may not be uniquely defined for some D; i.e., there may be multiple optima given D. Second, even if $V(D)$ is uniquely defined, it may not be continuous in D. Suppose that A is the best equilibrium in figure 4.2 for the manager at a particular level of D. Then it is clear that a small change in D can result in the equilibrium A disappearing, with a resulting discontinuous shift in the manager's optimal equilibrium.

Of course, if V is discontinuous in D, we can certainly not apply a calculus argument (at least directly) to determine the optimal D.

It turns out, however, that things become much easier if we regard I rather than D as the manager's choice variable. Let $\hat{I}$ satisfy $g(\hat{I})/R = \hat{I}$. For each $0 < I < \hat{I}$, consider the following equation:

(24)
$$\left| \frac{U'\left(\frac{g(I)}{R} - I\right)}{U\left(\frac{g(I)}{R} - I\right)} \right| \frac{1}{g'(I)} = r(D - g(I)) .$$

Equation (24) is simply the first-order condition for the manager's problem, equation (11), with V set equal to $g(I)/R$. Let us try to solve (24) for D. By assumption 1, the RHS is strictly increasing in D. Therefore, if there is a solution at all to (24), it is unique. However, there may be no solution to (24)—this will be the case if

$$U'\left(\frac{g(I)}{R} - I\right) \bigg/ U\left(\frac{g(I)}{R} - I\right) g'(I) \geq \lim_{x \to \infty} r(x) .$$

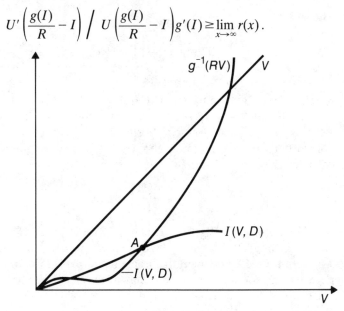

Fig. 4.2

If there is a solution to (24), denote it by $D(I)$ (we allow $D(I)$ to be negative—see below). What is the interpretation of $D(I)$? It is simply the level of debt which sustains the equilibrium (V,I), where $V = g(I)/R$; i.e.,

$$I\left(\frac{g(I)}{R}, D(I)\right) = I.$$

The reason is that if we set $V = g(I)/R$, we see from (24) that (11) is satisfied when $D = D(I)$. But by lemma 1, this means that $I = I(V,D)$; i.e., I is an optimal choice for the manager given V and D. (If $D < 0$, then the equilibrium (V,I) is sustained by the manager's lending rather than borrowing.)

Suppose that $D(I)$ is well defined at $I = I^0 > 0$, i.e., that (24) can be solved at $I = I^0$. Then, since $r(x)$ is strictly increasing, it is clear that (24) can also be solved in a neighborhood of I^0. Furthermore, since the LHS and RHS of (24) are continuous functions, $D(I)$ must be continuous at I^0. We will now show that $D(I)$ is also differentiable at I^0.

Lemma 3. If $D(I)$ is defined at $I = I^0 > 0$, then it is also defined in a neighborhood of I^0. Furthermore, it is continuous and differentiable at $I = I^0$.

Proof. Only differentiability remains to be established. However, this follows from differentiating (24) with respect to I:

$$\left[Ug'U''\left(\frac{g'}{R} - 1\right) - U'(Ug'' + U'\left(\frac{g'}{R} - 1\right)g')\right] \Big/ (Ug')^2 = r'(x)(D' - g').$$

Therefore,

$$(25) \quad D' = g' + \left[\frac{g'UU''\left(\frac{g'}{R} - 1\right) - U'Ug'' - U'^2g'\left(\frac{g'}{R} - 1\right)}{(Ug')^2 r'(x)}\right],$$

which is finite by assumption 1. QED.

Note that at $I = 0$, $D(I)$ is completely arbitrary; i.e., any value of D sustains the $I = 0$, $V = 0$ equilibrium.

In order to say something about the sign and magnitude of $D'(I)$, consider (25). Let I^* satisfy

$$(26) \quad \frac{g'(I^*)}{R} = 1;$$

i.e., I^* maximizes $(1/R)g(I) - I$. Then $g'(I)/R \gtrless 1$ as $I \lessgtr I^*$. Therefore, if $I \geq I^*$, the bracketed term in (25) is positive, from which it follows that $D' > g' > 0$. If $I < I^*$, however, the bracketed term in (25) may be positive or negative and so, in particular, we may have $D' < 0$. We have established

Lemma 4. Suppose that $D(I)$ is defined at $I > 0$. If $I \geq I^*$, $D' > g' > 0$. If $I < I^*$, $D' \gtrless g'$ according to whether

$$\frac{d}{dI}\left\{\left(\frac{U'\left(\frac{g(I)}{R}-1\right)}{U\left(\frac{g(I)}{R}-1\right)}\right)\frac{1}{g'(I)}\right\} \gtreqless 0.$$

It should be noted that there are some utility functions and production functions for which

(27)
$$\frac{d}{dI}\left\{\left(\frac{U'\left(\frac{g(I)}{R}-1\right)}{U\left(\frac{g(I)}{R}-1\right)}\right)\frac{1}{g'(I)}\right\} > 0$$

for all I. An example is $U = c^b$, $0 < b < 1$, and $g(I) = I^{1/2}$, in which case the LHS of (27) is

$$\frac{d}{dI}\left(\frac{2b}{\frac{1}{R} - I^{1/2}}\right) > 0.$$

In such cases, lemma 4 tells us that $D'(I) > 0$ everywhere that $D(I)$ is defined. Thus, the graph of D against I is as in figure 4.3. Since $V = g(I)/R$, D will also be an increasing function of V in such cases.

However, if (27) does not hold everywhere, then the graph of D against I is as in figure 4.4. Again, the graph of D against V will have a similar shape.

If we invert $D(I)$ to get I as a function at D, we can see again why problems arise when D is regarded as the manager's independent variable. There is no difficulty, of course, in the case of figure 4.3, but in the case of figure 4.4, I is multivalued for some values of D and can also be discontinuous.

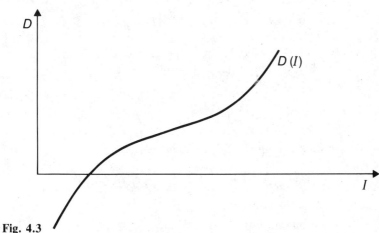

Fig. 4.3

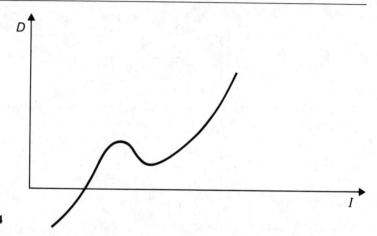

Fig. 4.4

Lemma 4 gives us information not only about D' but also about $D' - g'$. If $D' > g'$ (resp. $D' < g'$), this tells us that an increase in I leads to an increase (resp. decrease) in $D(I) - g(I)$ and hence to a higher (resp. lower) chance of bankruptcy. Note also that if we think of D as a function of V rather than I, then

$$\frac{dD}{dV} = \frac{dD}{dI} \frac{dI}{d\left(\frac{g(I)}{R}\right)} = \frac{RD'}{g'},$$

and so $D' > g'$ implies that $dD/dV > R$; i.e., an increase in debt repayment of one dollar leads the firm's market value to increase by less than $1/R$ dollars.

Having analyzed the relationship between D and I, let us return to the manager's choice of optimal debt level D. Regarding I as the independent variable, we may write the manager's problem as follows:

(28)
$$\max_{I} U\left(\frac{g(I)}{R} - I\right)(1 - F(D(I) - g(I))),$$

where I is restricted to those values for which $D(I)$ is defined.

Lemma 5. The problem in (28) has at least one solution.

Proof. Let $A = \{I \mid D(I) \text{ is defined}\}$. Let

$$\sup_{I \in A} U\left(\frac{g(I)}{R} - I\right)(1 - F(D(I) - g(I))) = \alpha > 0.$$

Then we can find a sequence $I_r \in A$ such that

(29a)
$$U\left(\frac{g(I_r)}{R} - I_r\right)[1 - F(D(I_r) - g(I_r))] \to \alpha$$

as $r \to \infty$. Clearly $0 \le I_r \le \hat{I}$, where $g(\hat{I})/R = \hat{I}$. Therefore, we may assume without loss of generality that $I_r \to I'$. Furthermore, $0 < I' < \hat{I}$ since otherwise the LHS of (29a) → 0. Clearly I' is a solution to (28) as long as $I' \in A$. But $I' \notin A$ implies that (24) cannot be satisfied, which in turn implies that

(29b)
$$\left| \frac{U'\left(\frac{g(I')}{R} - I'\right)}{U\left(\frac{g(I')}{R} - I'\right)} \right| \frac{1}{g'(I')} \geq \lim_{x \to \infty} \frac{f(x)}{1 - F(x)}.$$

In fact, we can say more than this. Since $I_r \in A$ for all r and $I_r \to I'$, (29b) must hold with equality and $(D(I_r) - g(I_r)) \to \infty$ as $r \to \infty$. But this is impossible since then the LHS of (29a) tends to zero. QED.

Let I be a solution to the manager's overall maximization problem. It is clear from the proof of lemma 5 that $0 < I < \hat{I}$. Furthermore, we know that $D(I)$ is defined at I and hence, by lemma 3, that it is differentiable at I. Therefore, we may differentiate the expression in (28) to get the following necessary condition for optimality:

(30)
$$U'\left(\frac{g(I)}{R} - I\right)\left(\frac{g'(I)}{R} - 1\right)(1 - F(D(I) - g(I)))$$

$$- U\left(\frac{g(I)}{R} - I\right)f(D(I) - g(I))(D'(I) - g'(I)) = 0.$$

Rewriting (30), we obtain

(31)
$$\left| \frac{U'\left(\frac{g(I)}{R} - I\right)}{U\left(\frac{g(I)}{R} - I\right)} \right| \frac{1}{g'(I)} = \left(r(D(I) - g(I))\right) \frac{(D'(I) - g'(I))}{\left(\frac{g'(I)}{R} - 1\right)g'(I)}.$$

But we know that (24) must hold at $D = D(I)$. Therefore, putting (24) and (31) together, we get

(32)
$$\frac{D' - g'}{\left(\frac{g'}{R} - 1\right)g'} = 1;$$

that is,

(33)
$$D'(I) = \frac{(g'(I))^2}{R}.$$

Proposition 2. A necessary condition for I to be an optimal level of investment for the manager is that (33) holds.

It follows immediately from proposition 2 that the optimal level of $I <$ I^*, where

(34)
$$\frac{g'(I^*)}{R} = 1.$$

For $I \geq I^* \Rightarrow g'(I)/R \leq 1 \Rightarrow D' = g'^2/R \leq g'$, which contradicts lemma 4.

Proposition 3. If I is an optimal level of investment for the manager, then $I < I^*$, where I^* maximizes $g(I)/R - I$. In other words, there is underinvestment relative to the "classical" situation where I is observable.

If fact, proposition 3 is obvious even without appealing to (33). For if $g'/R \leq 1$, then by reducing I the manager increases $U(g(I)/R - I)$. However, by lemma 4, $(D - g(I))$ goes down and so the probability of bankruptcy is reduced. Hence, the manager is made unambiguously better off.

The relationship between $D'(I)$ and $(g'(I))^2/R$ is graphed in figure 4.5. In general, there may be more than one I satisfying (33). Thus, (33) is not a sufficient condition for optimality.

At this stage, the role of assumption 1 may become clearer. It enables us to solve for D uniquely in terms of I and hence, by regarding I rather than D as the manager's independent variable, to obtain (33) as a necessary condition for optimality. If assumption 1 does not hold, then there may be several D's corresponding to a particular I. Furthermore, even if there is a unique optimal choice of D for each I for the manager, the function $D(I)$ may not be continuous. Thus, the same problems arise when we regard I as the independent variable as do when we regard D as the independent variable. It would be interesting to know whether some other argument can be used to derive (33) as a necessary condition if assumption 1 fails.

4.4 Comparative Statics Results

In the last section, we showed how the optimal (I,V,D) combination is chosen by the manager. We now consider how the manager's choice varies with changes in F and U.

Comparative statics results are particularly difficult in this problem because there are many opposing effects. From (8) it is clear that for a given D, the relevant marginal threat of bankruptcy rises when the hazard rate r rises, and I will increase in response to a rise in r. This can be interpreted as an attempt by the manager to increase investment to lower the threat of bankruptcy. Unfortunately, the situation is far more complex because D will not stay constant. Recall that $D(I)$ is the level of debt necessary to convince the market that I will be the chosen investment level. For a given I, when the threat of bankruptcy changes, the size of debt necessary to convince traders that the manager will invest I changes. From (24) it can be seen that for a *given I*, an increase in the hazard rate

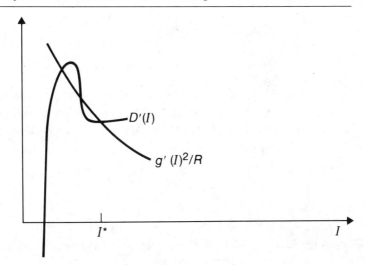

Fig. 4.5

will cause the manager to reduce D at I. This has a further effect on I which may go in the opposite direction to the initial effect.

To analyze the above, let t be a real-valued parameter which represents some aspect of F or U. We want to know how I changes and how $D(\cdot)$ changes as t changes. In what follows we will assume that at the initial value of t there is a unique optimal I for the manager, denoted by $I(t)$. We will sometimes write $D_t(I)$ to emphasize that the function $D(I)$ depends on t. From the analysis of the previous section we know that

$$D'_t = \frac{g'^2}{R}$$

at $I(t)$. In fact, we know more: from the second-order conditions we have
   Lemma 6. $D''_t - (2g'g''/R) \geq 0$ at $I = I(t)$.[11]
   Proof. Suppose that $D''_t - (2g'g''/R) < 0$ at $I(t)$. Then for $I > I(t)$ and I close to $I(t)$, $D'_t < g'^2/R$. Therefore, by (24),

$$\frac{U'}{Ug'} = r_t > r_t \left(\frac{D'_t - g'}{\left(\dfrac{g'}{R} - 1 \right) g'} \right),$$

where r'_t is the derivative of the hazard rate for the distribution indexed by t. Hence,

$$U'\left(\frac{g'}{R} - 1 \right)(1 - F) - Uf(D'_t - g') > 0.$$

But from the second-order conditions for the problem in (28), we know that the LHS of (30) cannot be positive for all $I > I(t)$, I close to $I(t)$. This is a contradiction. QED.

Definition. We will say that $I(t)$ is a *regular* maximum if $D_t'' - (2g'g''/R) > 0$ at $I = I(t)$.

From now on we concentrate on regular maxima. The following proposition is obvious in view of lemma 6.

Proposition 4. Suppose that at $t = t_0$, $I(t_0)$ is a unique optimal investment level for the manager. Suppose also that $I(t)$ is a regular maximum. Then a sufficient condition for $I(t)$ to be increasing (resp. decreasing) in t in the neighborhood of t_0 is that

$$\frac{\partial}{\partial t}(D_t' - \frac{g'^2}{R}) < 0 \,(\text{resp.} > 0)$$

at $I = I(t)$.

Of course, if I is increasing in t, then so is $V = g(I)/R$.

Let us use proposition 4 to calculate how I varies as the distribution F changes. We know from (25) that

$$(35) \qquad D_t' = g' + \left[\frac{g'UU''\left(\frac{g'}{R} - 1\right) - U'Ug'' - U'^2g'\left(\frac{g'}{R} - 1\right)}{U^2g'^2r_t'}\right].$$

Furthermore, at the optimum, since $I(t) < I^*$,

$$D_t' = \frac{g'^2}{R} > g'.$$

Therefore, the bracketed term in (35) is positive. It follows that any change in F which causes $r_t'(D_t(I) - g(I))$ to increase will reduce D_t' and hence $(D_t' - (g'^2/R))$. We have therefore

Proposition 5. Suppose that at $t = t_0$, $I(t_0)$ is a unique optimal investment level for the manager. Suppose also that $I(t)$ is a regular maximum. Then if only the hazard rate $r_t(x) \equiv f_t(x)/(1 - F_t(x))$ depends on t, a sufficient condition for $I(t)$ to be increasing (resp. decreasing) in t in a neighborhood of t_0 is that $(d/dt)\, r_t'[D_t(I(t_0)) - g(I(t_0))] > 0\,(\text{resp.} < 0)$ at $t = t_0$.

In order to understand the above condition, write $r_t'[D_t(I(t_0)) - g(I(t_0))]$ as $r_t'(x_t)$, where $x_t = D_t(I(t_0)) - g(I(t_0))$. Note that $D_t(I(t_0))$ is just the level of debt the manager must take on in order to sustain $I = I(t_0)$ when t_0 changes to t. Therefore, by (24),

$$\left|\frac{U'\left(\frac{g'(I(t_0))}{R} - I\right)}{U\left(\frac{g(I(t_0))}{R} - I\right)}\right| \frac{1}{g'(I(t_0))} = r_{t_0}(x_{t_0}) = r_t(x_t).$$

Hence, the condition $(d/dt)\, r_t'(x_t) > 0$ means than an increase in t leads to an increase in r_t', where r_t' is evaluated at x_t and x_t satisfies $r_t(x_t) = r_{t_0}(x_{t_0})$.

To see how this condition works, consider the uniform distribution which ranges from $-t \leq s \leq t$ (this distribution satisfies assumption 1 only for $-t < s < t$). The hazard rate is

$$r_t(x) = \frac{1}{t - x}, \text{ and } r_t' = \frac{1}{(t - x)^2} = [r_t(x)]^2.$$

Assume that $-t < D_t(I(t_0)) - g(I(t_0)) < t$. Then

$$\frac{dr_t'}{dt}(D_t(I(t_0))) - g(I(t_0)))) = 2r_t\frac{dr_t}{dt} = 0,$$

where the latter equality follows from the fact that $D_t(I(t_0))$ must change in such a way that r_t is constant. Thus, in the uniform case, if $I(t)$ is differentiable, then $(dI(t)/dt) = 0$. A complete analysis of the uniform case appears in the appendix.

As another application of the proposition, consider the double exponential distribution (this distribution satisfies assumption 1 only for $x < 0$). The double exponential distribution function with mean zero and variance $2t^2$ is given by

$$F_t(x) = \begin{cases} \frac{1}{2}\exp{(x/t)} & \text{for } x < 0 \\ 1 - \frac{1}{2}\exp{(-x/t)} & \text{for } x \geq 0. \end{cases}$$

The hazard function is thus given by

$$r_t(x) = \frac{f_t(x)}{1 - F_t(x)} = \begin{cases} \dfrac{1/2t(\exp{(x/t)})}{1 - \frac{1}{2}\exp{(x/t)}} & \text{for } x < 0 \\ 1/t & \text{for } x \geq 0 \end{cases}.$$

Consider (24). It is clear from this equation that $D_{t_0}(I(t_0)) - g(I(t_0)) \leq 0$. For if $D_{t_0}(I(t_0)) - g(I(t_0)) > 0$, then, by reducing D, the manager can keep (24) satisfied and at the same time decrease the probability of bankruptcy, hence making himself better off. Suppose that $x = D_{t_0}(I(t_0)) - g(I(t_0)) < 0$. Then

$$r_t'(x) = \frac{\dfrac{1}{2t^2}\exp{(x/t)}}{[1 - \frac{1}{2}\exp{(x/t)}]^2} = \frac{1}{t^2}\frac{z}{(1 - z)^2} = \frac{r_t(x)}{t(1 - z)},$$

where $z \equiv \frac{1}{2}\exp{(x/t)}$. Consider now a change in t and x which keeps $r_t(x)$ constant. Since $r_t = (z/t(1 - z))$ stays constant when t increases, it follows that z rises when t rises and hence $t(1-z)$ rises when t rises. Therefore, an increase in t lowers $r'_t(D_t(I(t_0)) - g(I(t_0)))$. Thus proposition 5 implies that an increase in t (i.e., an increase in the variance of s) lowers I.

The above results can be used to explain the role of debt and equity in our model. Consider the market value of the firm's equity V_e, which in this risk neutral world with limited liability is given by

$$(36) \qquad V_e \equiv E \max(0, g(I) - D_t + s).$$

Recall that distribution functions are indexed by t.

Proposition 6. Suppose that the distribution function of s changes in such a way that (a) s becomes more risky (i.e., a mean-preserving spread occurs) *and* (b) (dr'_t/dt) $(D_t(I(t_0)) - g(I(t_0))) < 0$ *and* (c) the hazard rate increases: $\partial r_t/\partial t > 0$. Then this increases the value of equity V_e and decreases the value of debt.

Proof. Note that the LHS of (24) must be increasing at an optimal I; if it were not, then the manager could reduce D and raise I, and still satisfy the first-order conditions for a maximum and be better off. From proposition 5, assumption (b) implies that I falls. Thus, the LHS of (24) falls. However, assumption (c) implies that the RHS of (24) rises. Hence, equilibrium can be maintained only if $D_t(I) - g(I)$ falls. Thus, (b) and (c) imply that $g(I) - D_t(I)$ rises and this tends to raise V_e. Assumption (a) raises V_e for a given $g(I) - D_t$ because $\max(0,s)$ is a convex function of s. Hence, all the effects together raise V_e. Finally, since I falls $V = g(I)/R$ falls and hence the value of debt $= V - V_e$ falls. QED.

Note that conditions (a)–(c) are quite strong. For the double exponential distribution, a rise in t satisfies (a) and (b) but only satisfies (c) for some values of t. For the uniform distribution, an increase in t always lowers the hazard rate so (c) and (a) can never both be satisfied.

Let us turn now to comparative statics involving changes in U. Suppose that U is replaced by $V = U^\alpha$, where $\alpha < 1$. Consider the effect on D' in (35). Now

$$(37) \qquad V' = \alpha U^{\alpha-1} U',$$

$$V'' = \alpha(\alpha - 1)U^{\alpha-2}U'^2 + \alpha U^{\alpha-1}U''.$$

Therefore,

$$(38) \qquad g'VV''\left(\frac{g'}{R} - 1\right) - V'Vg'' - V'^2 g'\left(\frac{g'}{R} - 1\right)$$

$$= g'\left(\frac{g'}{R} - 1\right)[\alpha(\alpha - 1)U^{2\alpha-2}U'^2 + \alpha U^{2\alpha-1}U'']$$

$$- \alpha U^{2\alpha-1}U'g'' - g'\left(\frac{g'}{R} - 1\right)\alpha^2 U^{2\alpha-2}U'^2$$

$$= \alpha U^{2\alpha - 2}[g'UU''\left(\frac{g'}{R} - 1\right) - U'Ug'' - U'^2 g'\left(\frac{g'}{R} - 1\right)].$$

It follows that

$$D' = g' + \left[\frac{\left[\alpha U^{2\alpha - 2}[g'UU''\left(\frac{g'}{R} - 1\right) - U'Ug'' - U'^2 g'\left(\frac{g'}{R} - 1\right)]\right]}{V^2 g'^2 r'}\right]$$

$$= g' + \alpha \left[\frac{\left[g'UU''\left(\frac{g'}{R} - 1\right) - U'Ug'' - U'^2 g'\left(\frac{g'}{R} - 1\right)\right]}{U^2 g'^2 r'}\right].$$

Hence, an increase in α raises D' and hence $(D' - (g'^2/R))$. An application of proposition 4 therefore yields

Proposition 7. If U is replaced by $V = U^\alpha$, where $\alpha < 1$, then I will decrease.

Replacing U by U^α, $\alpha < 1$, means, of course, that the manager becomes more risk averse. It might be wondered whether a more general increase in risk aversion—represented by replacing U by $H(U)$, where H is an arbitrary increasing concave function—leads to a decrease in I. The answer appears to be no in general.

Comparative statics results can also be obtained for changes in R and $g(\cdot)$. These must be interpreted carefully however, since changes in R and g will also affect the classical solution I^*. We will not consider such comparative statics in this paper.

4.5 Comments and Extensions

The previous section examined the relationship between the risk of bankruptcy faced by a manager and his incentive to maximize the value of the firm. To see one implication of the theory, consider the case of no uncertainty. Then the manager loses all his benefits (i.e., goes bankrupt) whenever $g(I) < D$. Thus, he will always choose I such that $g(I) = D$; i.e., $I(D) = g^{-1}(D)$. Thus,

$$(39) \qquad V(D) = \frac{g(I(D))}{R} = \frac{D}{R}.$$

The manager maximizes his expected utility by maximizing $U(V(D) - I(D)) = U((D/R) - g^{-1}(D))$ from which it is clear that $g'(I(D)) = R$. Recall that $g'(I^*) = R$, where I^* is the profit maximizing level of investment. Hence, the manager maximizes the net market value of the firm.

It is clear that the equity of the above firm is worthless. In particular, the above firm is financed totally by debt. The firm borrows $g(I^*)/R$ and pays back $D = g(I^*)$. The manager consumes $V(I^*) - I^* = g(I^*)/R - I^*$. Because there is no randomness in production, the manager is able to adjust his investment so that he just pays back the debt with nothing left over for the shareholders. Of course, shareholders take this into account initially, and so it is impossible and unnecessary for the manager to raise capital with equity. Thus, we are led to the conclusion that a firm with no randomness in production will be owned essentially by the manager who receives the residual income $V(I^*) - I^*$ and finances his investment totally by debt!![12]

If s becomes random, however, then equity will in general have a positive value given by $\max(0, g(I) + s - D)$. Thus, randomness in production will cause the manager to reduce debt levels to the point where equity finance becomes possible and useful. Equity will have value as long as there are realizations of s where $g(I) + s > D$. When s is random, the only way the manager can reduce his probability of bankruptcy is to create more events where $g(I) + s > D$.

Note that the model can be interpreted as a model of an entrepreneur who wants to raise capital rather than as a model of corporate directors. In particular, it is a model of an entrepreneur with an investment opportunity but no capital of his own. Suppose that if the entrepreneur raises V dollars by the sale of debt and equity, then he spends $V - I$ on capital equipment useful only for his own consumption and invests I in the firm. If the entrepreneur goes bankrupt, assume that the consumption equipment $V - I$ is taken away from him. (For simplicity, suppose that it is worthless to the creditors who can only get $\min(D, g(I) + s)$.) Under these assumptions, the model applies directly to an entrepreneur who wants to raise capital from investors who cannot monitor how much he invests directly.

In the model we have presented, the only reason the manager wants to increase V is that he can thereby increase his consumption benefits $V - I$. However, there is another important reason that the manager may desire increases in V: to reduce the probability of a takeover bid. In Grossman and Hart (1980) we analyzed the probability of takeover bids occurring as a function of the differential between the potential worth of the firm to the raider (i.e., the party making the takeover bid) and the price he has to pay to get shareholders to tender their shares. It was argued that, if a corporation is badly managed because it is widely held and thus each shareholder is too small for it to be in his interest to monitor management, then a raider can become a large shareholder and to some extent internalize externalities which exist across small shareholders. That is, the raider, because he becomes a large shareholder, has an incentive to monitor management.

The model of section 4.2–4.4 can easily be modified to take into account the possibility of takeover bids. In order to concentrate on the implications of the takeover threat, let us drop the assumption that the manager's consumption benefits depend directly on the firm's market value V. Instead, assume that the manager has a fixed amount of capital K at his disposal which he can spend on either investment I or consumption $K - I$ (we imagine that K was raised sometime in the past). Thus, the manager's utility is given by $U(K - I)$. We assume, however, that this utility is realized only if the firm is not taken over and does not go bankrupt. As in Grossman and Hart (1980), we assume that the probability of a takeover bid is a decreasing function of the market value of the firm V: $\bar{q}(V)$, where $0 \leq \bar{q}(V) < 1$.[13]

Stiglitz (1972) has emphasized the fact that raiders, by purchasing equity, can often change production plans to hurt bondholders. Bondholders can write restrictive covenants to try to prevent this from occurring. To avoid analyzing this issue, we assume that the bondholders are perfectly protected, in that we require the raider to buy up the equity plus the bonds of the firm. It is for this reason that we take the probability of a takeover bid to be a function $\bar{q}(V)$ of the firm's total market value.

It is straightforward to compute the optimal action for the manager under the threat of a takeover bid. Given V and D, the manager chooses I to maximize

(40) $$U(K - I)(1 - F(D - g(I)))q(V),$$

where $q(V) = 1 - \bar{q}(V)$. It is clear from (40) that V has no effect on the manager's choice of I since $q(V)$ appears multiplicatively. This occurs because we have assumed that the investment policy of current management is reversible by the raider, so that the probability of a raid depends on the price the raider must pay for the firm, which is V, and the potential worth of the firm—which is independent of what current management is doing.

Note that V is the value of the firm under current management in the event that there is no raid. Thus, as in sections 4.2–4.4, V is just the discounted expected output of current management.

Although V does not affect the manager's choice of I, it does affect his utility. Let $I(D)$ be the solution to (40). Then the manager's expected utility is

(41) $$U(K - I(D))(1 - F(D - g(I(D))))q(g(I(D))/R),$$

and the manager will choose D to maximize this expression. An analysis of this problem can be carried out along the same lines as in sections 4.2–4.4. Although there are some mathematical differences, the basic conclusions are the same. In particular, it will be in the interest of management to issue debt because this increases I (through the $I(D)$ function) and hence $V = g(I)/R$, and therefore reduces the probability of a takeover bid. Note that, as in the case of the analysis of sections 4.2–4.4, the existence of bankruptcy penalties is crucial to this argument. In the absence of such penalties, I does not depend on D and hence issuing debt will affect neither V nor the probability of a takeover.

4.6 Conclusions

In this paper we have developed a theory to explain the use of debt as a financial instrument. The theory is based on the idea that the managers of a firm which is mainly equity-financed do not have a strong incentive to maximize profit—in particular, since without debt, bankruptcy does not occur, bad managers are not penalized in the event of low profit. Thus, such a firm will have a low value on the stock market. We have argued that management can use debt to precommit itself in such a way that managers can avoid losing their positions only by being more productive. Thus, debt increases the firm's market value. We have also analyzed the determinants of the optimal level of debt for management.

It is interesting to compare our theory of the role of debt with other theories. The most celebrated result on a firm's financial structure is the Modigliani-Miller theorem, which states that the owners of a firm will be indifferent about its debt-equity ratio—in particular, the firm's market value will be independent of the debt-equity ratio. Since this result was established, numerous efforts have been made to relax the assumptions underlying the theorem in order to find a role for debt. Early attempts focused on the assumptions of no bankruptcy and/or no taxes. It was argued that if the probability of bankruptcy is positive, then, as long as investors cannot borrow on the same terms as the firm, i.e., go bankrupt in the same states of the world, then, by issuing debt, the firm is issuing a new security, and this will increase its market value. Also, if debt payments are tax deductible—as they are in the United States or the United Kingdom, for example—then the debt-equity ratio will again affect market value.

More recent attempts to explain the importance of debt have focused on a different assumption of the Modigliani-Miller theorem: that the firm's production plan is independent of its financial structure. Stiglitz (1974) and Jensen and Meckling (1976) consider the situation of an entrepreneur who has access to an investment project, but does not have the funds to finance it. If the entrepreneur raises the funds by issuing equity, then since he will have a less than 100 percent interest in the project, he will not manage it as carefully as he should from the point of view of all the owners; i.e., in the language of this paper, he will take too many perquisites. If, on the other hand, the entrepreneur issues debt, then his incentive to work will be reduced much less since, except in bankrupt states, he gets the full benefit of any increase in profits. Thus, to Stiglitz and to Jensen and Meckling, debt is a way of permitting expansion without sacrificing incentives. The trade-off for the entrepreneur is between issuing equity, which permits the sharing of risks, and issuing debt, which leads to a high market value for the project through the incentive effect.

The model developed in this paper also relies on the idea that, for incentive reasons, a firm's production plan will depend on the firm's financial structure. However, we have assumed that management has a zero (or close to zero) shareholding in the firm. As a result, a switch from debt finance to equity finance does not change management's marginal benefit from an increase in profit directly. Rather, the incentive effect comes from the desire to avoid bankruptcy. Thus, in particular, whereas a change in bankruptcy penalties would not have a significant effect in the Jensen-Meckling, Stiglitz analysis, it is of crucial importance in our model.

In recent papers Ross (1977, 1978) develops a signaling model to explain the debt-equity ratio. He considers a situation in which there are firms of exogenously given different qualities, where these qualities are known to management but not to the market. Ross shows that under these circumstances debt can be a signal of firm quality. In particular, in equilibrium there will be a positive relationship between a firm's debt-equity ratio and its market value. The point is that it will not pay a firm of low quality to try to signal that it is of high quality by issuing a lot of debt since the costs to management—in the form of a high probability of bankruptcy—are too high.

We have already noted in section 4.1 the difference between a signaling equilibrium and the bonding or precommitment equilibrium developed in this paper. As another illustration of the difference, note that, in contrast to Ross's analysis, our analysis, without further assumptions, says nothing about the cross-section relationship between market value and the debt-equity ratio. This is because we explain the equilibrium level of debt of a firm as a function of the firm's stochastic production function, the rate of interest, and managerial tastes. The cross-section relationship will therefore depend entirely on how these parameters are distributed in the population of firms. For example, if different firms are identical except with respect to the riskiness of s, then proposition 6 gives sufficient conditions for the debt-equity ratio to be an increasing function of market value. However, if the conditions of proposition 6 are not satisfied or if firms differ in other ways, then the debt-equity ratio could easily be a decreasing function of market value.

The manager's potential loss of his benefits under the threat of bankruptcy is one of the many possible incentive schemes which can induce good managerial performance. In complex corporations, information relevant to the optimal managerial incentives can only be acquired with control. An important benefit of both the bankruptcy and the takeover incentive schemes (which is not possessed by a salary incentive scheme) is that control over information automatically passes out of the hands of current management.

Appendix

In this appendix, we give a complete analysis of the case where s is uniformly distributed on $[-\bar{s},\bar{s}]$ and (U,g) take the following special forms:

$$U = c^b, 0 < b < 1,$$

$$g = I^{1/2}.$$

To simplify matters, we will assume that $R = 1$. Note that $I^* = \frac{1}{4}$ in this example.

Note that the uniform distribution satisfies assumption 1 only for $-\bar{s} < x < \bar{s}$. For this reason we must modify slightly the analysis of previous sections.

Suppose that the manager chooses the investment level I, where $\hat{I} > I > 0$. (Recall that $g(\hat{I})/R = \hat{I}$.) Then in equilibrium $V = g(I) = I^{1/2}$. As in section 4.3, we can ask what is the smallest level of debt which will sustain this equilibrium. Let $D(I)$ represent this. Then, if $-\bar{s} < D - I^{1/2} < \bar{s}$, we know that (24) must hold; i.e.,

(A1)
$$\left(\frac{b}{(I^{1/2} - I)} \right) \frac{2}{I^{-1/2}} = \frac{1/2\bar{s}}{1 - \left(\dfrac{D - I^{1/2} + \bar{s}}{2\bar{s}} \right)} = \frac{1}{\bar{s} - D + I^{1/2}}.$$

Hence,

(A2)
$$I^{1/2} = \frac{1 - 2b\bar{s} + 2bD}{2b + 1}$$

or

(A3)
$$D = \frac{(2b + 1)I^{1/2} - 1 + 2b\bar{s}}{2b}.$$

However, it is also possible that $D - I^{1/2} = \bar{s}$ or $D - I^{1/2} = -\bar{s}$ (it is easy to see that $D > I^{1/2} + \bar{s}$ or $D < I^{1/2} - \bar{s}$ cannot be solutions since small reductions in D leave the manager's optimum unchanged and increase his utility). The first case is impossible since the manager goes bankrupt for sure. He can always do better by raising I slightly. Hence, we need only consider the second case, $D - I^{1/2} = -\bar{s}$. Since $f(x)/(1 - F(x))$ is differentiable to the right at $x = -\bar{s}$, a necessary condition for this case is

(A4)
$$\left(\frac{b}{(I^{1/2} - I)} \right) \frac{2}{I^{-1/2}} \leq \frac{1}{\bar{s} - D + I^{1/2}},$$

which gives

(A5)
$$I^{1/2} \le \frac{1 - 2b\bar{s} + 2bD}{2b + 1}$$

or

(A6)
$$D \ge \frac{(2b + 1)I^{1/2} - 1 + 2b\bar{s}}{2b}.$$

We are now in a position to establish the following:

Result. $D(I) = \max\{[((2b + 1)I^{1/2} - 1 + 2b\bar{s})/2b], I^{1/2} - \bar{s}\}$.
The proof of this is simple. We have already established that $D(I)$ equals either $[((2b + 1)I^{1/2} - 1 + 2b\bar{s})/2b]$ or $I^{1/2} - \bar{s}$. Suppose that

(A7)
$$\frac{(2b + 1)I^{1/2} - 1 + 2b\bar{s}}{2b} > I^{1/2} - \bar{s}.$$

Then D cannot equal $I^{1/2} - \bar{s}$ since (A6) is contradicted. On the other hand, if

(A8)
$$\frac{(2b + 1)I^{1/2} - 1 + 2b\bar{s}}{2b} < I^{1/2} - \bar{s},$$

then setting $D(I) = [((2b + 1)I^{1/2} - 1 + 2b\bar{s})/2b]$, we get from (A8) that

(A9)
$$D(I) - I^{1/2} < -\bar{s},$$

which, as we have argued previously, cannot be a solution (a small reduction in D leaves the manager's optimum unchanged and increases his utility).

We illustrate the above result in figure 4.A.1. The heavy black line gives D as a function of $I^{1/2}$. Note that if

(A10)
$$\frac{-1 + 2b\bar{s}}{2b} > -\bar{s},$$

then $[((2b + 1)I^{1/2} - 1 + 2b\bar{s})/2b]$ and $I^{1/2} - \bar{s}$ do not intersect at any $I > 0$ and $D(I)$ is given by $[((2b + 1)I^{1/2} - 1 + 2b\bar{s})/2b]$ for all I.

Define I_0 to be the positive value of I at which the two lines intersect, if such an I exists, and to be zero otherwise. By simple calculation,

(A11)
$$I_0^{1/2} = \max(1 - 4b\bar{s}, 0).$$

We consider now the manager's choice of the optimal I. The manager maximizes

$$U(g(I) - I)(1 - F(D(I) - g(I))).$$

Three cases can be distinguished: (1) The optimal $I > I_0$. Then D is differentiable at I, and so, by proposition 2,

$$D'(I) = g'(I)^2.$$

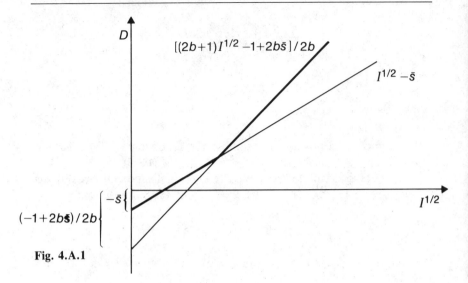

Fig. 4.A.1

Hence,

$$\left[1/2\left(\frac{(2b+1)}{2b}\right)I^{-1/2}\right] = \frac{1}{4I},$$

which yields

$$I = \left(\frac{b}{2b+1}\right)^2.$$

(2) The optimal $I < I_0$. Again D is differentiable and so

$$D'(I) = g'(I)^2.$$

This time we get

$$(1/2)I^{-1/2} = \frac{1}{4I};$$

i.e.,

$$I = 1/4.$$

(3) The optimal $I = I_0$. Now D is no longer differentiable, but it is differentiable to the right and to the left. Since I_0 is optimal, we know therefore that the expression in (30) is nonpositive if $D'(I)$ is evaluated according to (A3) and is nonnegative if $D'(I)$ is evaluated according to $D = I^{1/2} - \bar{s}$. This yields a modified version of (33):

$$D'(I) \quad \begin{matrix} \geq g'(I)^2 \text{ if } D'(I) \text{ is evaluated according to (A3),} \\ \leq g'(I)^2 \text{ if } D'(I) \text{ is evaluated according to } D = I^{1/2} - \bar{s}. \end{matrix}$$

Hence, we get

$$\left(\frac{b}{2b+1}\right)^2 \leq I_0 \leq 1/4.$$

Cases (1)–(3) establish the following result.

Result. If $I_0 > 1/4$, then it is optimal to set $I = 1/4$. If

$$\left(\frac{b}{2b+1}\right)^2 \leq I_0 \leq 1/4,$$

it is optimal to set $I = I_0$. Finally, if

$$I_0 < \left(\frac{b}{2b+1}\right)^2,$$

it is optimal to set

$$I = \left(\frac{b}{2b+1}\right)^2.$$

The optimal debt levels can also be easily computed. If $I = 1/4$, $D = I^{1/2} - \bar{s} = 1/2 - \bar{s}$. If $I = I_0$, $D = I_0^{1/2} - \bar{s}$. Finally, if

$$I = \left(\frac{b}{2b+1}\right)^2,$$

$D = 1/2 - 1/2b + \bar{s}$. Using (A11), we may graph the optimal I and D as functions of $\bar{s}$, as in figure 4.A.2. We see that I decreases as the variance of s rises. Further, $I \rightarrow I^*$, $D \rightarrow D^* = g(I^*)$ as variance $s \rightarrow 0$. It is also worth noting that D is not monotonic in $\bar{s}$.

Notes

1. See Grossman and Hart (1980). In that paper it is shown that the takeover threat will be effective only if free riders are excluded to some extent from sharing in the improvements in the firm brought about by the raider.

2. See Winter (1971) for a discussion of other factors concerning the impact of competition on profit maximization.

3. Note that the initial shareholders may want to write a corporate charter which constrains the debt-equity ratio to be at the level which maximizes managerial effort. However, suppose that the best ratio depends on variables which are not known at the time the charter is written, and may only be observable at great cost in the future. It may then be preferable for the initial shareholders to give management some flexibility in the choice of financial structure because this will allow management to base its actions on private information. We will consider the extreme case where management has complete freedom about the choice of financial structure.

4. Jensen and Meckling (1976) have studied another example of precommitment or bonding behavior. They consider a situation where an entrepreneur must decide what share to retain in his firm. If the entrepreneur runs the firm, his share in the firm will determine to what extent he pursues profits rather than perquisites. Therefore, his shareholding (assumed to be publicly known) is an example of *precommitment* in the same way that debt is in our model.

5. The work by Ross (1977) and Leland and Pyle (1977) derives signaling equilibrium debt-equity ratios. In both cases, the debt-equity ratio is a signal to the financial market about the exogenous quality of the firm. The assumption that bankruptcy costs are correlated with the exogenous quality of firms drives their signaling equilibrium.

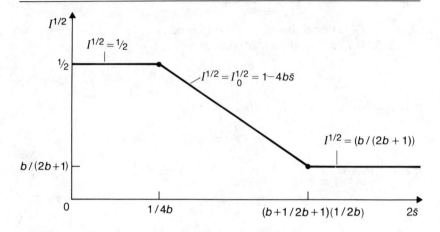

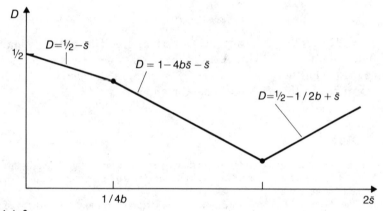

Fig. 4.A.2

6. This assumption is made for simplicity only. The analysis can easily be generalized to the case where the corporation has some initial capital and needs to raise only a fraction of the required funds from outside sources.

7. The assumption of risk neutrality is justified if investors hold well-diversified portfolios and the firm's return is uncorrelated with the returns of other firms in the economy.

8. In order to concentrate on the role of debt, we are ignoring any incentive schemes which are designed to raise the value of equity when a new investment project is undertaken. That is, for simplicity we assume that the manager gets all the surplus $(V - I)$ from the firm's investment opportunity and that none of it accrues to initial shareholders. It is easy, however, to generalize our analysis to the case where the manager gets only some part of an increase in V; i.e., the manager's utility is $U(\phi(V) - I)$, where $0 \leq \phi(V) \leq V$. Note that it is essential that the manager get some surplus from working for the firm for the threat of bankruptcy to be an effective incentive scheme. See Calvo (1978) on a related topic.

9. We say that $h(x)$ is increasing if $x' > x \Rightarrow h(x') \geq h(x)$. If $x' > x \Rightarrow h(x') > h(x)$, we say that h is strictly increasing.

10. A "revealed preference" proof can be used to show that assumption 1 is unnecessary for the result that I is increasing in V.

11. Note that D_I'' is well-defined—simply differentiate (25) in the proof of lemma 3.

12. This result should be treated with some caution. In this paper we have ignored incentive schemes which make the manager's remuneration a function of ex post profit, $g(I)$ + s. If such schemes are possible, then in the case $s \equiv 0$, the investment level $I = I^*$ can also be sustained by having 100 percent equity and an incentive scheme of the form: the manager is fired unless ex post profit = $g(I^*)$. Clearly in the case of certainty this accomplishes exactly what debt does in our model; namely, the manager is removed if his profit falls below some critical level.

13. For example, if the corporate charter is such that the raider can buy the firm for V, then the raider's profit is $g(K)/R - V$ since once he takes over he can set $I = K$, if the actions of the previous manager are reversible.

References

Barlow, Richard, and Proschan, Frank. 1975. *Statistical theory of reliability and life testing.* New York: Holt, Rinehart, & Winston.

Calvo, G. A. 1978. Supervision, and utility, and wage differentials across firms. Department of Economics, Columbia University. Mimeographed.

Grossman, Sanford, and Hart, Oliver. 1980. Takeover bids, the free-rider problem, and the theory of the corporation. *Bell Journal of Economics* 11, no. 1: 42–63.

Jensen, M., and Meckling, W. 1976. Theory of the firm: Managerial behavior, agency costs, and capital structure. *Journal of Financial Economics* 3: 305–60.

Leland, Hayne, and Pyle, D. 1977. Informational asymmetrics, financial structure, and financial intermediation. *Journal of Finance* 32, no. 2: 371–88.

Ross, Steven. 1977. The determination of financial structure: The incentive-signaling approach. *Bell Journal of Economics* 8, no. 1: 23–40.

———. 1978. Some notes on financial incentive-signaling models, activity choice, and risk preference. *Journal of Finance* 33, no. 3: 777–91.

Stiglitz, Joseph. 1972. Some aspects of the pure theory of corporate finance, bankruptcies, and takeovers. *Bell Journal of Economics* 3, no. 2: 458–82.

———. 1974. Incentives and risk sharing in sharecropping. *Review of Economic Studies* 41(2), no. 126: 219–57.

Winter, S. 1971. Satisficing, selection, and the innovating remnant. *Quarterly Journal of Economics* 85, no. 2: 237–61.

Comment   Hayne E. Leland

Bonding or prepositioning behavior is modern terminology for an age-old phenomenon. Recall the story of Odysseus wishing to hear the Sirens, those scantily clad beauties whose provocative cries inevitably drew sailors to their deaths upon the rocks. By agreeing to have himself tied to the mast, Odysseus convinced his crew to sail within earshot. By this bonding bind, or binding bond, Odysseus was able to avoid an immoral hazard.

Contemporary examples of prepositioning in financial contracts include bond covenants, in which equity holders voluntarily agree to forego certain actions in order to issue debt at favorable rates. More exactly, they agree to accept heavy penalties if they undertake such actions, thereby convincing bondholders they will forego them.

The reason agents may agree to such restrictions of choice is straightforward. In the absence of restrictions, agents may be motivated to make decisions detrimental to the other party, the "principal." Recognizing this, the principal will reward the agent less than he would if the agent were willing to forego these actions. The "moral hazard" of the situation can be reduced or eliminated, and both sides can gain, if the agent restricts his actions, or agrees to penalties which induce him to do so.

The nature of optimal principal/agent contracts has been examined in several recent papers. Theoretical foundations were laid by Wilson (1968), Spence and Zeckhauser (1971), and Ross (1973). Subsequent extensions include those by Harris and Raviv (1979), Holmstrom (1979), Leland (1978), and Townsend (1979). In general, these studies show that Pareto optimal contracts should depend upon the action of the agent if the true state of nature is not observable. If the action itself cannot be directly observed but there exists some monitor whose value is correlated with the action, then agents' rewards should depend upon this monitor.[1]

The Grossman-Hart (GH) contribution fits neatly into the general framework of the principal/agent problem. In GH, a potential moral hazard exists because the stockholders cannot directly observe the investment decisions of the manager. The problem can be reduced, to the ultimate benefit of the manager/entrepreneur, if the manager is willing to make his reward conditional on the true future value of the firm, represented by $g(I) + s$. GH consider a simple, dichotomous form of contingent reward, with

$$\text{Reward} = V(D) - I \quad \text{if } g(I) + s \geqq D$$
$$= 0 \qquad\qquad \text{if } g(I) + s < D,$$

Hayne E. Leland is professor of business administration, University of California, Berkeley.

where D is the amount promised to debtholders and must be chosen optimally by the manager–entrepreneur. High levels of D induce the manager to restrict his choice to high levels of I; thus, the choice of $D > 0$ can be viewed as "prepositioning behavior." The analysis is complicated by the fact that V depends upon D in a manner consistent with "rational expectations." A major contribution by GH is to deal fully with this aspect of the problem.[2]

It should be understood that the GH model *does* require the true future value of the firm to be observable (in the future) by at least one party, since bankruptcy depends upon whether this value falls short of or exceeds D. A critical modeling assumption is whether all participants, or just the manager, will observe this future value.

Most financial models assume that the true future value is in fact the future market value, which will be observable by all parties. If this is the case, a dichotomous contract similar to GH's could be implemented even if the firm has no debt: the manager would announce that he would forego all reward ("resign in disgrace") if the firm's future market value did not meet a specified minimum level. Such a contract presumably would motivate the manager in a manner identical to the case with debt, and might be preferable since it would avoid possible costs associated with bankruptcy.

More complex reward schedules will most likely be preferred to the simple dichotomous schedule considered by GH, if all parties observe the future firm value. Stock options, for example, are regularly granted to managers. The principal/agent literature offers suggestions as to the nature of the optimal contract, although the rational expectations feedback is likely to make the problem discouragingly complex.

The GH analysis is more compelling, I feel, when it is presumed that the "true" future value of the firm can be observed only by the firm's manager and does not coincide with the future market value which can be observed by all participants. While not consistent with most literature on "efficient markets," such a view does seem to be expressed by the authors in their conclusion.

In this case, stockholders can observe only whether the manager repays D or not. Clearly, this event is (coarsely) correlated with the future true value of the firm, and thereby both parties can gain by basing managerial reward on whether D is repaid. Note that the previously suggested scheme, that the manager agree to resign in disgrace if future firm value did not exceed a minimum level, would not work here: the manager could always maintain that firm value exceeded this minimum without fear of contradiction.

However, if the observable future market value were correlated with the unobservable (to stockholders) true future value, received theory suggests that improvements could be obtained by basing compensation on this imperfect monitor. If both the repayment of debt and the future market value provided nonidentical information about true future value, then the optimal contract would involve both the use of bankruptcy penalties and the use of stock-related rewards. Casual observation of real-world managerial compensation suggests that this is indeed the case.

The GH paper represents an important step in applying the theory of agency to managerial rewards and financial structure. As such, it extends the work of Jensen and Meckling (1976), and suggests that many other interesting questions in financial structure can be addressed with these techniques.

Notes

1. For a clear exposition of these results, see Holmstrom (1979). If the utility of the agent depends only on his reward, and not independently upon his choice of action, Leland (1978) shows that Pareto optimality does not require observation of the agent's actions when both principal and agent have utility functions exhibiting linear risk tolerance with equal slopes. In this case, the optimal reward schedule for the agent is a linear function of the value resulting from his services.

2. It should be noted that the use of debt to motivate managers does not eliminate its role as a potential signal of the quality of a firm's future prospects. While all managers may want some debt in their structure to signal their honest intentions, managers in firms with better prospects will be willing to incur greater debt.

References

Harris, M., and Raviv, A. 1979. Optimal incentive contracts with imperfect information. *Journal of Economic Theory* 20: 231–59.

Holmstrom, B. 1979. Moral hazard and observability. *Bell Journal of Economics* 10 (Spring): 74–92.

Jensen, M., and Meckling, W. 1976. Theory of the firm: Managerial behavior, agency costs, and ownership structure. *Journal of Financial Economics* 3 (October): 305–60.

Leland, H. 1978. Optimal risk sharing and the leasing of natural resources. *Quarterly Journal of Economics*, August:

Ross, S. 1973. The economic theory of agency: The principal's problem. *American Economic Review* 63: 134–39.

Spence, M., and Zeckhauser, R. 1971. Insurance, information, and individual action. *American Economic Review* 61: 380–87.

Townsend, R. 1979. Optimal contracts and competitive markets with costly state verification. *Journal of Economic Theory* 21: 265–93.

Wilson, R. 1968. The theory of syndicates. *Econometrica* 36: 119–32.

5 A Competitive Entrepreneurial Model of a Stock Market

Richard E. Kihlström and Jean-Jacques Laffont

5.1 Introduction

In the study of the stock market's role in the economy, two closely related questions arise. First, is the allocation of risk and capital that results from competitive trading in firm shares and debt efficient in some appropriate sense? Second, what is or should be the objective of the firm?

The second question arises because the traditional profit maximization hypothesis cannot be implemented when profits are uncertain as they will be when contingent claims markets are incomplete. Incompleteness of these markets is, in general, a feature of economies in which the only institution for the exchange of risks is a stock market for firm shares. The question of what a firm maximizes is not merely of intrinsic interest. In fact, the study of stock market efficiency requires a model of firm behavior. If, in particular, we are interested in the efficiency of competitive stock markets, the firm's behavior must be competitive in an appropriate sense.

The present paper is intended as a contribution to the recent literature which focuses on the above-mentioned questions. Section 5.9 contains a brief survey of this literature. A more complete survey is provided by Baron (1979).

The initial work on the efficiency of a stock market is that of Arrow (1953), which was subsequently elaborated by Debreu (1959). Arrow

Richard E. Kihlstrom is professor of economics and finance at the University of Pennsylvania, Philadelphia. Jean-Jacques Laffont is professor, Université des Sciences Sociales de Toulouse.

Financial support from the National Science Foundation is gratefully acknowledged. The authors would also like to thank Jacques Drèze, Sanford Grossman, Oliver Hart, Krishna Ramaswamy, Hugo Sonnenschein, and participants at the 1978 Stanford Summer Workshop on Mathematical Economics for helpful comments.

assumed that contingent claims markets were complete and showed that the stock market allocation of risk was efficient in a first-best sense. Debreu's extension of Arrow's work incorporated production. Because he retained Arrow's assumption of complete contingent claims markets, Debreu could assume that firms maximized profits. Like Arrow, Debreu was able to show that the competitive equilibrium was efficient.

The first paper to study stock market economies with production in which the implied contingent claims markets were incomplete was by Diamond (1967). Diamond suggested a concept of second-best efficiency which he showed to be appropriate for use in judging the optimality of a stock market. Using this concept, he demonstrated the second-best efficiency of the stock market allocation of risk and productive resources. By restricting the technology to satisfy a condition that he called *stochastic constant returns to scale*, Diamond was able, in an incomplete market setting, to formalize the hypothesis of stock market value maximization as an extension of profit maximization. He therefore solved the problem of specifying a criterion for a firm maximization by limiting the technologies under consideration. A subsequent paper by Leland (1974) showed that under Diamond's assumption of stochastic constant returns to scale, stockholders unanimously agree that stock market value maximization should be the firm's objective.

For our paper, as for virtually all of the "post-Diamond" literature, Diamond's paper serves as the point of departure. We adopt his concept of restricted efficiency and attempt to obtain analogues of his results in situations characterized by technologies which do not exhibit stochastic constant returns to scale. We assume that firms are created and run by expected utility maximizing entrepreneurs who simultaneously make portfolio decisions on their own account and operating and financial decisions on their firm's account. This hypothesis of firm behavior is the basis for our extension of Diamond's concept of equilibrium. In assuming that entrepreneurs maximize expected utility we are following Kihlstrom and Laffont (1979). In fact, the economy studied in this paper differs from that of Kihlstrom and Laffont (1979) in only one respect: the presence of a stock market which permits entrepreneurs to share the risks associated with their firms.

In our theory the firm is competitive in the sense that entrepreneurs take all prices as given. They are able to obtain capital, the only productive resource in our model, in a competitive bond market or by issuing firm shares in a competitive stock market. Bond market competition implies that the price of debt is treated as given. Competition in the stock market is reflected in the fact that the relationship between a firm's operating and financial decisions and its share value is treated parametrically by all entrepreneurs.

In order to ensure that the model is competitive, we assume the existence of a large number of individuals each of whom can create a firm and become an entrepreneur. Following Aumann (1964), we introduce the large numbers assumption formally by assuming a continuum of individuals. The technology required by entrepreneurs is assumed to be available to all, at a cost. Thus, entry is unlimited but not costless.

Other conditions appear to be necessary to ensure competition. Specifically, each entrepreneur who chooses a specific operating and financial decision for his firm should face stock market competition for investor capital. This will be true if there is a large number of entrepreneurs who make the same choices and whose outputs are, in some sense, statistically dependent. If outputs of two identical firms are independent, shares in these firms are not perfect substitutes, and this tends to reduce competition. To ensure competition in the stock market, we assume that the returns across firms are statistically dependent. We also assume that individuals are divided into types and that there is a large number of individuals of each type.

The formal structure of the model is presented in section 5.2.

The third section describes the roles played in our theory by two classical results and by the arguments traditionally employed to establish these results. One of these results is the Modigliani and Miller (1958) theorem, which asserts that, in equilibrium, financial decisions are irrelevant. The other well-known result is that the equilibrium value of an existing firm is the market value of the productive resources invested in its creation and operation. These results arise as necessary conditions for the equilibrium defined in section 5.2. They imply that, in equilibrium, all individuals are indifferent between becoming entrepreneurs or remaining nonentrepreneurs (capitalists, in our terminology). The proof given in section 5.3 that these classical results are necessary for equilibrium is an adaptation to our formal structure of the traditional arguments normally used to obtain them. The fundamental idea is that, in equilibrium, any possibility of arbitrage profits must be eliminated. The Modigliani-Miller theorem is necessary to prevent profitable arbitrage between debt and equity. When the stock market value of a firm equals the value of the resources it employs, arbitrage strategies involving firm entry or exit will, of necessity, fail to earn profits.

The third section also discusses the role of price expectations in the model. Since the shares of firms which are actually observed in equilibrium are traded, their expected price can be assumed to equal their actual price. There will, however, be many operating and financial decisions which could have been chosen but are not. These are identified with potential firms about which individuals are assumed to have share price expectations. For these potential (as opposed to existing) firms, the possibility of free entry determines only upper bounds on the expectations. The expectations at which these upper bounds are attained even for potential firms will be referred to as *classical expectations*. They will play a crucial role in the analysis which follows section 5.3.

For the case of classical expectations, section 5.4 establishes the existence of an equilibrium and describes its structure. The existence proof is simplified by the fact that the model exhibits several special properties. These are described in the propositions and lemmas of section 5.4, which precede the existence theorem. In order to prove the existence theorem, the special properties of the model are used to show that an equilibrium can be identified with the equilibrium of a simple two-good pure trade competitive economy.

The first result in section 5.4 is proposition 3, which asserts that optimal portfolios of all individuals have an extremely simple form. Specifically, it asserts that any entrepreneur's portfolio contains only shares in his own firm or in firms operated in the same way as his firm. Nonentrepreneurs, i.e., capitalists, are shown to hold shares in only those firms which are operated in the same way that they themselves would operate a firm if they were to become entrepreneurs. The optimality of nondiversification established in proposition 3 depends crucially on two assumptions: the concavity of the production function in the variable or operating inputs, and the statistical dependence of the outputs of all firms.

The next important result in section 5.4 is lemma 2, which implies that the entrepreneur's maximization problem has a unique solution. This is important for the proof of existence. The proof of lemma 2 is slightly complicated because of a nonconvexity introduced by the fact that the entrepreneur makes a portfolio decision for his own account as well as a production decision on his firm's account. A related nonconvexity was first observed by Drèze (1974).

The simplified structure of an equilibrium implied by proposition 3 is described in proposition 4. In the equilibrium, there are as many types of firms as there are types of individuals. There is, in essence, a type of firm created for each type of investor. Each type of individual holds shares in only the firms created by entrepreneurs of his type. This clientele effect results in unanimity among the shareholders of every firm about the goals the firm should pursue. This effect was discussed earlier by Smith (1970).

The remainder of section 5.4 transforms the equilibria with the simple structure described in proposition 4 into equivalent equilibria of a two-good pure trade competitive economy. Theorem 1 of this section uses this transformation to obtain an equilibrium. This transformation is also the basis for the efficiency theorem of section 5.5. In theorem 2 of that section it is shown that the equilibrium is efficient in the second-best sense defined by Diamond (1967). The marginal conditions for Arrow-Debreu first-best efficiency are stated in proposition 7 of section 5.5. These conditions are used to explain why, in general, the equilibrium is inefficient in the Arrow-Debreu sense. Proposition 8 uses the marginal conditions to prove that an equilibrium is first-best efficient if there are sufficiently many risk neutral individuals or if all individuals are alike.

Section 5.6 argues that the equilibrium studied in this paper is an appropriate generalization of Diamond's model to the case in which there may not be stochastic constant returns to scale. To support this assertion, it is shown that the equilibrium studied here coincides with Diamond's when the technology exhibits stochastic constant returns to scale. Section 5.6 also interprets our equilibrium as a generalization to the case of uncertainty of the classical model of perfect competition in which firms produce at the point of minimum average cost. Our model is shown to reduce to the perfectly competitive equilibrium when there is no uncertainty.

Section 5.7 is the only section to consider equilibria with nonclassical expectations. It conjectures that such equilibria exist and are, in general, inefficient.

Section 5.8 observes that our results can be interpreted as a demonstration that the need for a stock market only arises when there are fixed costs to entry, uncertainty, and risk aversion on the part of a large number of investors. It is shown that if one of these features is absent, the market in firm shares is unnecessary since the economy can achieve the same allocation without a stock market. In a closely related sharecropping context in which there are no fixed costs, the irrelevance of a market for output shares has been demonstrated by Stiglitz (1974) and Newbery (1977).

Section 5.9 contains a brief survey of recent literature and describes where our work fits within this literature. This survey includes a discussion of an externality which arises in stock market economies because, as Smith (1970) and Drèze (1974) pointed out, the firm's production decision is a public good for the shareholders.

5.2 Introduction to the Entrepreneurial Stock Market Model

There is a continuum of individuals each of whom is associated with a point in the interval [0,1]. There are two goods: "capital," an input; and a consumption good, "income." Each person begins with an endowment of $A > 0$ units of income and one unit of capital. These endowments of capital and income are received without uncertainty. The fact that capital is purely an input and not a consumption good is reflected in the fact that income is the only argument in the individual utility functions. Each individual α is assumed to have a twice differentiable von Neumann–Morgenstern utility function $u(I,\alpha)$ defined on $[0,\infty)$ with positive and nonincreasing marginal utility of income at all nonnegative income levels;

i.e., $u' > 0$ and $u'' \leq 0$. At times, we will find it convenient to assume that u is strictly concave or even that $u'' < 0$.

We will also make frequent use of the following assumption.

A1. *There are n types of individuals, where n is a finite integer. For all individuals of type i, there is a common utility function $u(\cdot,i)$. Thus, if α is of type i, we will let $i(\alpha) = i$ denote his type and his utility function will be*

$$u(\cdot,\alpha) = u(\cdot,i(\alpha)).$$

The measure of the set of individuals of type i is denoted by μ_i. For each $i = 1,\ldots,n$, $\mu_i > 0$.

Note that our assumptions imply that

$$\sum_{i=1}^{n} \mu_i = 1.$$

Each individual can choose to be an entrepreneur or a capitalist. If he becomes an entrepreneur, his capital endowment is expended on entrepreneurial activities. By investing his capital in this way, the entrepreneur obtains the income producing technology described by the production function $g(K,\tilde{x})$. The first argument K in this function represents the operating or variable capital employed by the entrepreneur in his firm. It does not include the one unit of entrepreneurial capital which is the fixed or set up cost of the firm. Thus, the total capital employed by the firm is $K + 1$, the operating capital plus the entrepreneurial capital. The second argument $\tilde{x}$ is a random variable which influences the output of all firms.

A number of assumptions will now be made about g and $\tilde{x}$. First, to avoid technicalities associated with differentiation under the integral, we hypothesize that $\tilde{x}$ takes value in a finite subset $X = \{x_1,\ldots,x_S\}$ of some finite dimensional subspace. Next, we assume that regardless of the level of operating capital K, the worst that can happen is that there is no output. Thus, for all x in X and all $K \geq 0$, $g(K,x) \geq 0$. If $K = 0$, output must be zero for all possible x values; i.e., $g(0,x) = 0$ for all $x \in X$. In addition, there is assumed to be some $x \in X$, say, $x = \underline{x}$, for which $g(K,\underline{x}) = 0$ for all $K \geq 0$. The assumption of existence of such an $\underline{x}$ is not essential to the analysis. It is used primarily to simplify the discussion. We also assume that for all $K \geq 0$ and all $x \neq \underline{x}$ the marginal product is positive and decreasing; i.e., $g_K(K,x) > 0$ and $g_{KK}(K,x) < 0$, if $K \geq 0$ and $x \neq \underline{x}$. It will be necessary to assume that for each $x \neq \underline{x}$, there exists a capital level $K(x)$ at which

(1) $$g(K(x),x) = g_K(K(x),x)[K(x) + 1].$$

For a specific x, $K(x)$ is as shown in figure 5.1. Note that $K(x)$ maximizes

$$\frac{g(K,x)}{(1 + K)},$$

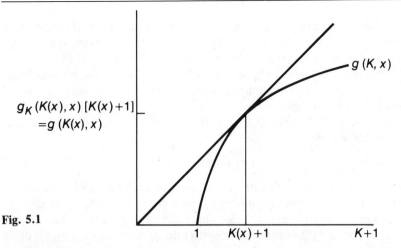

Fig. 5.1

which is output per unit of capital. Similarly for any capital price r, $K(x)$ minimizes

$$\frac{r(1 + K)}{g(K,x)} \, ,$$

which is the firm's average cost. Thus, by assuming that $K(x)$ exists we are in effect assuming that for each x, there exists an output level, specifically $g(K(x),x)$, at which average cost is minimized.

The random variable $\tilde{x}$ is assumed to be the same for all firms. It is furthermore hypothesized that all individuals agree about the distribution of $\tilde{x}$. This distribution is denoted by ρ. (In fact, this assumption can be weakened somewhat when assumption A1 holds. Specifically, it is possible to assume only that all individuals of each type i agree about the distribution of $\tilde{x}$.)

The expenditure of entrepreneurial capital is, in essence, the payment of a set up cost which transfers to the entrepreneur the technology described by the production function. The entrepreneur thus becomes the sole owner of the firm and is free to make all productive and financial decisions associated with his firm's operation. Specifically, he can choose the firm's investment level K as well as the debt-equity level. In addition to making decisions on the firm's account, the entrepreneur will also be faced with financial decisions to be made on his own account. He can, for instance, sell some or all of the shares in his firm. The proceeds from this sale can then either be held as what is essentially a safe asset or be used to purchase shares in firms operated by other entrepreneurs. Because the entrepreneur is initially the sole owner of the firm, he can make all of these decisions, whether for his own account or the firm's, so as to further his own personal interests, i.e., so as to maximize his own expected utility.

Since our aim is to construct a competitive model of the stock and capital markets, we assume that the prices in these markets are fixed by supply and demand and taken as given by all traders. Thus, a typical entrepreneur α can either purchase all of the capital $K(\alpha)$ he decides to employ at a price r (denominated in income terms), or obtain all or part of this capital by the sale of his firm's shares in the competitive market for these shares. If all of the firm's capital is purchased, its debt is $rK(\alpha)$ and its profits will be

$$g(K(\alpha),\tilde{x}) - rK(\alpha).$$

If, in addition, all of the shares to the firm are retained by the initial owner, i.e., the entrepreneur, then he will receive all of these profits. If, however, the entrepreneur decides to retain only $\gamma(\alpha)$ of the shares in his firm, he can sell the remaining $1 - \gamma(\alpha)$ shares for $M(\alpha)[1 - \gamma(\alpha)]$ units of capital, where $M(\alpha)$ is the competitively determined market price for a share in the firm. (Notice that we have assumed that the price of shares is denominated in capital terms.) The capital proceeds from this sale either can be retained for the firm's account and used in production or can be sold for the entrepreneur's private account. If it is sold for private account, the entrepreneur may receive payment in different forms. On the one hand, he can sell the capital directly in the capital market and receive the price r. On the other hand, he can sell it in the markets for shares to firms operated by other entrepreneurs. For example, he can buy a share in the firm run by β at a cost of $M(\beta)$ capital units, where $M(\beta)$ is the competitive price of a share in β's firm.

If $S(\alpha)$ units are retained for production on the firm's account, the firm's debt is reduced from $rK(\alpha)$ to $r[K(\alpha) - S(\alpha)]$. The amount $K(\alpha) - S(\alpha)$, which will usually be denoted by $B(\alpha)$, is the amount of capital the firm raises by incurring debt. The firm's profits will then be

(2) $$\tilde{\pi}(K(\alpha), B(\alpha)) = g(K(\alpha),\tilde{x}) - rB(\alpha)$$

of which entrepreneur α will receive

(3) $$\gamma(\alpha)\tilde{\pi}(K(\alpha), B(\alpha)).$$

Equation (2) makes it clear that two firms run by different entrepreneurs, say, α and β, will generate identical profit distributions if $K(\alpha) = K(\beta)$ and $B(\alpha) = B(\beta)$. For this reason, we will assume that in an equilibrium there is a function N,

$$N : [0, +\infty) \times (-\infty, +\infty) \rightarrow (-\infty, +\infty),$$

which relates a firm's capital input and debt capital levels to the price of the firm. Thus, if a firm employs K units of capital and raises B capital units by issuing debt, its price will be $N(K,B)$. We are explicitly assuming that N is the same for all entrepreneurs. Thus, $M(\alpha)$ depends on α only through $K(\alpha)$ and $B(\alpha)$; i.e.,

(4) $$M(\alpha) = N\big(K(\alpha), B(\alpha)\big).$$

In the remainder of the paper $M(\alpha)$ will always be given by (4).

Suppose then that α employs $K(\alpha)$ units of capital and sells $[1 - \gamma(\alpha)]$ shares to the firm to obtain $M(\alpha)[1 - \gamma(\alpha)]$ units of capital. Also, suppose that he finances $B(\alpha)$ units of capital purchase by issuing debt at a cost of $rB(\alpha)$ to the firm. He must then retain $K(\alpha) - B(\alpha)$ of the capital obtained by the sale of shares for use in production by the firm. If the remaining

$$M(\alpha)[1 - \gamma(\alpha)] - [K(\alpha) - B(\alpha)]$$

units of capital are then sold on his personal account for income at the price r, the entrepreneur's income is

(5) $A + r\{M(\alpha)[1 - \gamma(\alpha)] - [K(\alpha) - B(\alpha)]\} + \gamma(\alpha)\widetilde{\pi}[K(\alpha), B(\alpha)]$.

Note that this expression (5) for entrepreneur α's final wealth will also hold if $B(\alpha)$ exceeds $K(\alpha)$, i.e., if the entrepreneur issues debt on the firm's account which exceeds that required to finance the firm's operating capital. If the excess capital $[B(\alpha) - K(\alpha)]$ thereby obtained is then sold on private account, the entrepreneur's final wealth is increased by $r[B(\alpha) - K(\alpha)]$ so that, as stated, (5) does represent final wealth. It should be clear that the entrepreneur could use this procedure to increase his wealth indefinitely unless either he is explicitly prohibited from using it or the market responds to it by revaluing the firm when $B(\alpha)$ is increased. Modigliani and Miller have argued that the latter will happen, and we will return to discuss how their arguments imply a relationship between $M(\alpha)$ and $B(\alpha)$ which permits an equilibrium to exist.

We now want to assume that the entrepreneur buys shares in other firms. In the discussion of this case, α's holding of his own firm is treated symmetrically with his holding of other firms. For the purpose of representing α's portfolio problem, let E be the (Lebesgue measurable) set of entrepreneurs. If E' is a Lebesgue measurable subset of E, $\Gamma(\alpha, E')$ will denote the (nonnegative) number of shares of firms in E' held by α. The portfolio held by α is therefore represented by the nonnegative measure $\Gamma(\alpha)$ defined on E and its Lebesgue measurable subsets.

In the discussion which follows, we will find it convenient to omit the adjective "Lebesgue measurable" when referring to subsets of E and functions with domain E. The reader should keep in mind, however, that *all* such subsets and functions are assumed to be Lebesgue measurable. In particular, for every Lebesgue measurable $E' \subseteq E$, the function $\Gamma(\cdot, E') : E \rightarrow [0, \infty)$ is assumed to be Lebesgue measurable.

In the terminology just introduced, the entrepreneur's portfolio problem is to choose a nonnegative measure $\Gamma(\alpha)$. The restriction to nonnegative measures is an embodiment of the assumption that short sales are impossible. This restriction is imposed to avoid the possibility that infinite profits can be obtained by using strategies which involve short sales. This problem is known to arise in models similar to that being described here if short sales are not ruled out or at least limited.

For the purpose of further interpreting $\Gamma(\alpha)$, suppose that α chose to invest in only two firms: his own and that run by β. Then $\Gamma(\alpha,\{\alpha\}) = \gamma(\alpha)$ > 0 would be the number of shares α holds in his own firm and $\Gamma(\alpha,\{\beta\}) >$ 0 would be the number of shares he holds in firm β. Since he holds only these firms, $\Gamma(\alpha, E \sim \{\alpha,\beta\}) = 0$. A second example arises if α holds shares in all firms and there exists a "density function" $\gamma(\alpha,\beta) > 0$ such that $\Gamma(\alpha,E') = \int_{E'}\gamma(\alpha,\beta)d\mu(\beta)$, where μ is the Lebesgue measure. Then $\gamma(\alpha,\beta)$ can be interpreted as α's holding in firm β.

Using the notation just introduced, the entrepreneur's random income is

(6)
$$\widetilde{W}_E(K(\alpha), B(\alpha), \Gamma(\alpha)) = A + r\{[M(\alpha)$$
$$- \int_E M(\beta)\Gamma(\alpha,d\beta)] - [K(\alpha) - B(\alpha)]\} + \int_E \widetilde{\pi}(K(\beta), B(\beta))\Gamma(\alpha, d\beta),$$

where, for each β, including α, $\widetilde{\pi}(K(\beta, B(\beta))$ is defined by (2) and $M(\beta)$ $= N(K(\beta), B(\beta))$. If one recalls that our notation treats α's holding of shares in his own firm symmetrically with his holding of shares in other firms, it will be clear that (5) is the special case of (6) in which the entrepreneur retains only shares in his own firm.

Entrepreneur α's problem then is to choose $K(\alpha)$, $B(\alpha)$, and $\Gamma(\alpha)$ so as to maximize

(7)
$$Eu(\widetilde{W}_E(K(\alpha), B(\alpha), \Gamma(\alpha)), \alpha).$$

In order to avoid the problems associated with bankruptcy, this choice is assumed to be made subject to the constraint that (6) be nonnegative with probability one. Since $g(K,\underline{x}) \equiv 0$, this will be true if and only if $(K(\alpha), B(\alpha), \Gamma(\alpha))$ satisfies

(8) $A + r\{M(\alpha) - \int_E [M(\beta) + B(\beta)]\Gamma(\alpha, d\beta) - [K(\alpha) - B(\alpha)]\} \geq 0$.

Note that in solving this problem, α is assumed to recognize that the price $M(\alpha)$ of his firm will be related to its capital input and debt level by (4). He also takes the share price $M(\beta)$ and the decisions $(K(\beta), B(\beta))$ of all other entrepreneurs $\beta \in E$ as given.

Capitalists face a decision problem which is analogous to the entrepreneurs'. Specifically, either capitalists can sell their capital for income, receiving r income units for each capital unit sold, or capital can be exchanged for shares in firms at the competitive prices $M(\beta) =$

$N(K(\beta), B(\beta))$. When the portfolio $\Gamma(\alpha)$ is chosen, capitalist α's random income is

(9) $\quad \tilde{W}_C(\Gamma(\alpha)) = A + r[1 - \int_E M(\beta)\Gamma(\alpha, d\beta)] + \int_E \tilde{\pi}(K(\beta), B(\beta))\Gamma(\alpha, d\beta)$

and he chooses $\Gamma(\alpha)$ to maximize

(10) $\qquad\qquad Eu(\tilde{W}_C(\Gamma(\alpha)), \alpha)$.

For capitalists, the problem of bankruptcy is avoided by assuming that $\Gamma(\alpha)$ is chosen subject to the constraint that (9) be nonnegative with probability one. This is true if and only if

(11) $\qquad\qquad A + r[1 - \int_E [M(\beta) + B(\beta)]\Gamma(\alpha, d\beta)] \geq 0$.

Note that in (9) and (10) α is *not* included in E; thus, he must take as given the profit variables $\tilde{\pi}[K(\beta), B(\beta)]$ of *every* firm in which he may invest. This situation is to be contrasted with that represented by (6) and (7) in which $\alpha \in E$ and can make a simultaneous choice of $\tilde{\pi}(K(\alpha), B(\alpha))$ and $\Gamma(\alpha)$.

Individual α will be an entrepreneur if and only if

(12) $\displaystyle \max_{\substack{K(\alpha)\geq 0 \\ B(\alpha) \\ \Gamma(\alpha)\geq 0}} Eu(\tilde{W}_E(K(\alpha), B(\alpha), \Gamma(\alpha)), \alpha) \geq \max_{\Gamma(\alpha)\geq 0} Eu(\tilde{W}_C(\Gamma(\alpha)), \alpha)$;

he will be a capitalist if and only if the inequality in (12) is reversed. Having defined E as the set of entrepreneurs, we will let C be the set of capitalists.

Definition 1. A competitive stock market entrepreneurial equilibrium (CSMEE) *is a partition $\{E, C\}$ of $[0,1]$, a capital price $r \in [0, +\infty)$, and functions $N: [0, +\infty) \times (-\infty, +\infty) \to (-\infty, +\infty)$, $K: E \to [0, +\infty)$, $B: E \to (-\infty, +\infty)$, $\Gamma: [0,1] \to$ the set of nonnegative measures on the Lebesgue measurable subsets of E, such that (i) (12) holds for each $\alpha \in E$ and (12) is reversed for each $\alpha \in C$, (ii) $(K(\alpha), B(\alpha), \Gamma(\alpha))$ maximizes (7) subject to (8) for each $\alpha \in E$, (iii) $\Gamma(\alpha)$ maximizes (10) subject to (11) for each $\alpha \in C$, (iv) $\int_0^1 \Gamma(\alpha, E')\mu(d\alpha) = \mu(E')$ for each subset E' of E, and (v) $\int_E K(\beta)\mu(d\beta) = \mu(C)$.*

In this definition, condition (iv) expresses the equality of supply and demand in the market for shares for firms. If, for example, there is a density function $\gamma(\alpha,\beta)$ such that, for each α and E',

$$\Gamma(\alpha, E') = \int_{E'} \gamma(\alpha,\beta)\mu(d\beta),$$

then, the supply equals demand condition

$$\int_0^1 \gamma(\alpha,\beta)\mu(d\alpha) = 1, \qquad \text{for each } \beta,$$

implies that

$$\int_0^1 \int_{E'} \gamma(\alpha,\beta)\mu(d\beta) = \mu(E')$$

as required by (iv).

Condition (v) in definition 1 asserts that capital supply equals capital demand.

5.3 The Function N and the Modigliani-Miller Theorem

In this section we will use adaptations of familiar arguments to obtain restrictions on the function N which are necessary for the existence of an equilibrium. These conditions will on the one hand facilitate the interpretation of the function N and on the other hand simplify the following discussion of existence of equilibrium. In this discussion, there is one particular N function which will play a crucial and classical role. This function will be denoted by N_C and is defined by

$$N_C(K,B) = 1 + K - B.$$

When this function describes the market valuation of firms employing any operating capital level K of which any amount B is raised as debt, the equilibrium exhibits two classical properties. First, it is impossible to earn arbitrage profits by setting up a firm and then selling all of the shares at the market price. In fact, this type of arbitrage will be unprofitable when and only when $N(K,B) \leq N_C(K,B)$. For if a firm is set up which employs K units of operating capital and issues debt to raise B of these capital units, the entrepreneur will have invested $1 + K - B$ units of equity capital. If $N(K,B) \leq N_C(K,B)$, the market value (in capital terms) of the firm created with this investment is no larger than $1 + K - B$. Thus, an investment of $1 + K - B$ units of equity capital has resulted in the creation of an asset with a capital value smaller than or equal to the investment. The result is no profits. Profits are possible, however, if $N(K,B)$ exceeds $N_C(K,B)$. For in this case an investment of $1 + K - B$ units of equity capital creates a firm with a market value in excess of $1 + K - B$.

The second well-known result implied by the fact that $N(K,B) = N_C(K,B)$ for all (K,B) is the Modigliani-Miller theorem, which has two important consequences. The first is that $N(K,B) + B$, the value of the firm (in capital terms), is constant for all firms employing the same level of operating capital K. In fact,

$$N_C(K,B) + B = 1 + K.$$

This equality asserts that the capital value of the firm equals the total capital invested in it, a simple restatement of the no arbitrage profits condition just discussed. The second consequence of Modigliani and Miller's theorem is that all individuals—the entrepreneur as well as all potential and actual investors—are indifferent about B, the debt financed capital level. Since B is the sole financial decision made by the entrepreneur on the firm's account, the firm's financial policy is irrelevant to all individuals. This universal indifference to B is a simple consequence of the expressions for W_C and W_E which emerge when $1 + K - B$ is substituted in (6) and (9). In particular, when $N(K,B) = N_C(K,B)$ for all (K,B), then

$$(13) \quad \tilde{W}_E(K,B,\Gamma) = \tilde{W}_C(\Gamma) = A + r[1 - \int_E \Gamma(d\beta)] + \int_E [g(K(\beta),\tilde{x})$$

$$- rK(\beta)]\Gamma(d\beta) = A + r[1 - \int_E [1 + K(\beta)]\Gamma(d\beta)] + \int_E g(K(\beta),\tilde{x})\Gamma(d\beta)$$

for all (K,B,Γ). Notice that for no firm β does $B(\beta)$ appear in the expressions given for $\tilde{W}_E(K,B,\Gamma)$ and $\tilde{W}_C(\Gamma)$.

Another important consequence of $N(K,B) = N_C(K,B)$ is the equality of $\tilde{W}_E(K,B,\Gamma)$ and $\tilde{W}_C(\Gamma)$ expressed in (13). In writing this equality, it was implicitly assumed that $K \in \{K(\beta): \beta \in E\}$, which means, in effect, that the set $\{K(\beta): \beta \in E\}$, and therefore the availability of investment opportunities, is the same for both entrepreneurs and capitalists. This equality implies that once $\{K(\beta): \beta \in E\}$ is determined, all individuals are indifferent between being entrepreneurs and capitalists. Of course entrepreneurs are able to choose K and B for their own firms and thereby influence $\{K(\beta): \beta \in E\}$, the set of investment opportunities. Furthermore, the (K,B) choice is made simultaneously with the choice of a portfolio. This is a choice not available to capitalists as long as they remain capitalists. Because entrepreneurs have an option not open to capitalists, it appears that, in spite of (13), some individuals may strictly prefer the former role to the latter. But capitalists who are not satisfied with the investment opportunities available from existing firms can always choose to become entrepreneurs and thereby create new firms in which to invest. Thus, not only are K, B, and Γ chosen simultaneously by entrepreneurs, but all individuals choose Γ at the same time that they decide whether to be entrepreneurs or capitalists. Any individual who is a capitalist in equilibrium has chosen not to exercise the option to become an entrepreneur. This choice indicates satisfaction with the investment opportunities made available by other entrepreneurs. Thus, in an equilibrium characterized by $N(K,B) = N_C(K,B)$, the entrepreneur's ability to make a (K,B) choice not available from other entrepreneurs is superfluous, and all individuals are indifferent between being entrepreneurs and capitalists.

The equilibria on which this paper focuses are those in which $N(K,B) = N_C(K,B)$ for all possible (K,B) choices. There are, however, other equilibria in which this equality may fail to hold at some (K,B) choices. But even in these other equilibria N and N_C are closely related. This relationship will be described by two propositions which are stated and proved in the remainder of the present section. The first proposition asserts that N_C serves as an upper bound above which the equilibrium N can *never* rise. This proposition is proved by demonstrating that if N rises above N_C for any (K,B) choice, then every individual will, in preference to remaining a capitalist, create a firm employing K units of operating capital and raising B of these capital units with debt. As noted above, this type of arbitrage operation is profitable if and only if $N(K,B)$ exceeds $N_C(K,B)$. When all individuals attempt to exploit these profitable arbitrage possibilities, all capital is used as entrepreneurial capital; none remains to satisfy the demand for operating capital. Thus, equilibrium in the capital market is inconsistent with $N(K,B) > N_C(K,B)$ at any possible (K,B) choice.

The second proposition is somewhat weaker. It asserts that at the equilibrium (K,B) levels, $N(K,B)$, in fact, equals $N_C(K,B)$. To be perfectly correct, it can only be said that for almost all entrepreneurs α, $N(K(\alpha),B(\alpha)) = N_C(K(\alpha),B(\alpha))$. We will now state and prove these results and then return to a discussion of the difficulties created by the fact that, in some equilibria, N may differ from N_C.

Proposition 1 (Modigliani-Miller). In a CSMEE,

(14) $$N(K,B) \leq 1 + K - B$$

for all possible (K,B) choices (not just the equilibrium choice).

Proof. If (14) fails because at some (K,B)

(15) $$N(K,B) > 1 + K - B,$$

then (15), (6), and (9) imply that, for any $\Gamma(\alpha)$,

$$\tilde{W}_C(\Gamma(\alpha)) = A + r[1 - \int_E M(\beta)\Gamma(\alpha,d\beta)] + \int_E \tilde{\pi}(K(\beta),B(\beta))\Gamma(\alpha,d\beta)$$

(16) $$< A + r\{[N(K,B) - \int_E M(\beta)\Gamma(\alpha,d\beta)] - [K - B]\}$$

$$+ \int_E \tilde{\pi}(K(\beta),B(\beta))\Gamma(\alpha,d\beta) = \tilde{W}_E(K,B,\Gamma(\alpha)).$$

Thus, the random income achievable by becoming an entrepreneur is sure to exceed the random income obtainable as a capitalist for every choice of $\Gamma(\alpha)$. In making this statement, it was assumed that α chose the same portfolio after he became an entrepreneur that he chose before becoming an entrepreneur. This is clearly possible for an entrepreneur even though the existence of his own firm creates a new investment opportunity, i.e., one which was not available when he was a capitalist. It is possible because both as an entrepreneur and as a capitalist, α takes the capital input choices of other firms as given and because the entrepreneur can always sell the one share in his own firm for $N(K,B)$ to obtain the portfolio. Inequality (16) asserts that α will be sure to have more income after becoming an entrepreneur, employing K, issuing rB as debt on the firm's account, and then selling the firm to buy $\Gamma(\alpha)$. Because of this, *every* individual will prefer to be an entrepreneur rather than to remain a capitalist, but then $\mu(C) = 0$ and condition (v) in the definition of an equilibrium must fail to hold. Thus, N could not be an equilibrium price if (15) holds for some (K,B). QED.

As remarked earlier, proposition 1 implies that, for all (K,B),

$$N(K,B) \leq N_C(K,B).$$

We can now show that for those (K,B) which appear in the equilibrium the upper bound becomes effective. The proof proceeds by demonstrating that no entrepreneur will ever choose a (K,B) at which $N(K,B)$ is actually less than $N_C(K,B)$. He will always prefer to be a capitalist instead. A complication arises here which did not appear in the proof of proposition 1. The problem occurs because an individual α who would choose $(K(\alpha), B(\alpha))$ if he were an entrepreneur may be unique in preferring that choice. If he chooses to be a capitalist, he eliminates an important investment opportunity. This problem is avoided if assumption A1 holds. Under this assumption, no individual α is ever unique in his preference for a specific $(K(\alpha), B(\alpha))$. Thus, no individual who chooses to be a capitalist eliminates an investment opportunity which other entrepreneurs will not provide for him.

Since $N(K(\alpha), B(\alpha)) = N_C(K(\alpha), B(\alpha))$ for almost all entrepreneurs α, (13) holds and almost all individuals are indifferent between being workers and capitalists.

Proposition 2 (Modigliani-Miller). Suppose that Assumption A1 holds. In a CSMEE,

$$(17) \qquad N(K(\alpha), B(\alpha)) = 1 + K(\alpha) - B(\alpha)$$

for almost all (Lebesgue measure) $\alpha \in E$. Furthermore, in equilibrium almost all individuals of the same type have the same expected utility; i.e., if $u(\cdot, \alpha) = u(\cdot, \alpha')$ and $\alpha \in E$ while $\alpha' \in C$, then

$$(18) \quad \max_{\Gamma(\alpha')} Eu(\widetilde{W}_C(\Gamma(\alpha')), \alpha') = \max_{\substack{\Gamma(\alpha) \\ K(\alpha) \\ B(\alpha)}} Eu(\widetilde{W}_E(K(\alpha), B(\alpha), \Gamma(\alpha)), \alpha)$$

or if $u(\cdot, \alpha) = u(\cdot, \alpha')$ and α and α' are in E, then

$$(19) \qquad \max_{\substack{\Gamma(\alpha) \\ K(\alpha) \\ B(\alpha)}} Eu(\widetilde{W}_E(K(\alpha), B(\alpha), \Gamma(\alpha)), \alpha)$$

$$= \max_{\substack{\Gamma(\alpha') \\ K(\alpha') \\ B(\alpha')}} Eu(\widetilde{W}_E(K(\alpha'), B(\alpha'), \Gamma(\alpha')), \alpha').$$

Thus, condition (12) *must hold with an equality for all individuals who will therefore be indifferent between being entrepreneurs and capitalists.*

The proof of this proposition is contained in appendix 1.

Because $N = N_C$ only at equilibrium choices for (K,B), it is not always true that investors are indifferent about a firm's B choice. If a significant number of firms employ $K(\alpha)$ units of operating capital and choose to raise $B(\alpha)$ capital units through debt, then

$$N(K(\alpha), B(\alpha)) = 1 + K(\alpha) - B(\alpha).$$

But there may be some other B level at which

$$N(K(\alpha), B) < 1 + K(\alpha) - B.$$

In that case, $B(\alpha)$ is definitely preferred to B. If, however, there is also a significant number of firms which choose (K', B') with $K' = K(\alpha)$, then

$$N(K(\alpha), B(\alpha)) + B(\alpha) = N(K(\alpha), B') + B' = 1 + K(\alpha)$$

and all individuals are indifferent between the financial decisions $B(\alpha)$ and B'.

As mentioned above, the analysis to follow will concentrate on the case in which

(20) $$N(K, B) = N_C(K, B)$$

for all (K,B). We will demonstrate the existence of such equilibria. We will also show in section 5.5 that the equilibria in which (20) always holds are efficient in the restricted sense of the term introduced by Diamond (1967). It will furthermore be seen in section 5.7 that there may exist many other equilibria in which (20) does not always hold and that many of these equilibria may be inefficient. These facts underline the central role of the function N_C as well as the importance of providing a satisfactory interpretation for the function N_C to justify the assumption that $N = N_C$.

For (K,B) levels which are observed in a particular equilibrium, $N(K,B)$ is easily interpreted as the observed price of shares of firms employing K operating capital units and raising B of these units as debt. If, in equilibrium, no firm chooses (K,B), then $N(K,B)$ must be interpreted as the price individuals expect to prevail if such firms are introduced. It might be thought that if the expectations N are to be "rational" or self-fulfilling, then N must equal N_C everywhere. Whether this is true depends on the sense in which the expectations are rational. Suppose, first, that N is rational in the sense that if $N(K,B)$ is expected to be the price of shares in a firm which chooses (K,B) and if a significant number of entrepreneurs (a set of positive Lebesgue measure) do, in fact, choose (K,B), then the actual equilibrium price of their firms is $N(K,B)$. This is a rather weak form of the rational expectations hypothesis, since it only requires actual fulfillment of expectations at (K,B) levels observed in equilibrium. For (K,B) pairs not chosen by a significant number of firms, the expectation $N(K,B)$ is never confirmed by observation because shares of firms choosing (K,B) are never exchanged at $N(K,B)$. But the expectation $N(K,B)$ is never refuted either, since shares of these firms are never exchanged at prices other than $N(K,B)$.

Using this rational expectation interpretation of N, proposition 1 asserts that an expectation of $N(K,B) > N_C(K,B)$ can never be fulfilled. Proposition 2 asserts that for (K,B) choices observed in equilibrium, the only N which is rational is $N(K,B) = N_C(K,B)$. In view of these propositions, an expectation $N(K,B) < N_C(K,B)$ can be rational in the sense just described if no significant number of firms choose to employ K units of operating capital and raise B of these units with debt. And, in fact, an equilibrium in which (20) fails to hold at some (K,B) can be interpreted as a case in which this situation arises. Thus, the rational expectations interpretation just presented is not sufficient to justify the assumption that (20) holds everywhere.

There is a stronger form of the rational expectations hypothesis which can be used to justify the assumption that (20) holds everywhere. In particular, we could interpret rationality to require that the equilibrium expectation $N(K,B)$ actually be confirmed, or at least confirmable in some sense, at all (K,B) levels. We could, for example, argue that individuals who understand the economy and its operation will, in essence, know proposition 2; i.e., they will know that if a (K,B) is going to be observed in any equilibrium, it must be true that (20) holds at (K,B). Sophisticated individuals will thus know that the only price expectations $N(K,B)$ that can ever be confirmed by observation are $N(K,B) = N_C(K,B)$ and that for other expectations the most that can be said is that they can never be refuted by observation. If we ask that rational expectations have this potential for confirmation, then $N(K,B) = N_C(K,B)$ is the unique rational price expectations function.

5.4 Properties of the Equilibria

The purpose of this section is to describe the properties of the entrepreneurial stock market equilibria and show that such equilibria exist. As mentioned above, this is done under the assumption that (20) holds at all (K,B) levels. In this case, (13) implies that any entrepreneur α can be regarded as maximizing the special case of (7) in which $M(\beta) = 1$ and $K(\beta) = B(\beta)$ for all β, including α, in E. When (20) holds for all (K,B), (13) also implies that capitalists maximize the special case of (10) which is also obtained by setting $M(\beta) = 1$ and $K(\beta) = B(\beta)$ for all $\beta \in E$. Thus, entrepreneur α chooses $K(\alpha) \geq 0$ and $\Gamma(\alpha) \geq 0$ subject to (8) (with $B(\beta) = K(\beta)$ for all $\beta \in E$) so as to maximize

(21) $Eu\left(A + r[1 - \int_E [1 + K(\beta)]\Gamma(\alpha, d\beta)] + \int_E g(K(\beta), \tilde{x})\Gamma(\alpha, d\beta), \alpha\right).$

If α is a capitalist, he takes $K(\beta)$ as given for all $\beta \in E$ and chooses $\Gamma(\alpha) \geq 0$ to maximize (21) subject to (11) (with $B(\beta) = K(\beta)$ for all $\beta \in E$).

Using this simplification, we first show that the decision problems of capitalists and entrepreneurs can be substantially simplified. Specifically we show that no entrepreneur α will ever hold shares in a firm which employs capital in an amount which differs from his own optimal capital demand $K(\alpha)$. Furthermore, because the x's are the same for all firms, each entrepreneur considers a partial share in his own firm as a perfect substitute for a partial share in any other firm which employs capital at the level which is optimal for him. As a consequence of these results, we will be able to assume that the entrepreneur's problem is to choose $K(\alpha)$ and $\gamma(\alpha)$ to maximize the expected utility of his income which is related to these decisions by the special case of (5) in which $B(\alpha) = K(\alpha)$. Formally, entrepreneur α's problem is then to choose $K(\alpha) \geq 0$ and $\gamma(\alpha) \geq 0$ so as to maximize

(22) $$H^\alpha(K(\alpha), \gamma(\alpha)) = Eu(A + r[1 - \gamma(\alpha)]$$
$$+ \gamma(\alpha)[g(K(\alpha), \tilde{x}) - rK(\alpha)], \alpha).$$

The special case of (8) which restricts the entrepreneur's $(K(\alpha), \gamma(\alpha))$ choice is

(23) $$A + r[1 - \gamma(\alpha)(1 + K(\alpha))] \geq 0.$$

We will denote the solution to this problem by $[\hat{K}(\alpha), \hat{\gamma}(\alpha)]$.

By similar arguments, analogous results can be established for the capitalist. That is, we can show that if there is an existing firm which is operated in the same way that a particular capitalist α would run it—i.e., which chooses to employ the same amount of capital α would employ if he were to become an entrepreneur—then α will hold shares only in that firm and others run the same way. Furthermore, for α, shares in all firms operated in this way are perfect substitutes. Because of these results, we will be able to assume that the capitalist's problem is to choose $\gamma(\alpha)$ so as to maximize his expected utility when his income is related to this decision by the special case of (5) in which $B(\alpha) = K(\alpha)$ and $K(\alpha)$ is the capital level which he would choose if he were an entrepreneur. Formally, then, the capitalist chooses $\gamma(\alpha) \geq 0$ to maximize (22) where $K(\alpha) = \hat{K}(\alpha)$, and this choice is made subject to the constraint (23).

Lemma 1. Assume that N satisfies (20). If $K(\alpha) = K(\alpha')$, then any investor β, whether he is an entrepreneur or a capitalist, is indifferent when choosing between portfolios $\Gamma(\beta)$ for which $\Gamma(\beta, \{\alpha'\}) + \Gamma(\beta, \{\alpha\}) = \delta$, where δ is some positive constant.

Proof. When $K(\alpha) = K(\alpha') = K$ and $\Gamma(\beta, \{\alpha'\}) + \Gamma(\beta, \{\alpha\}) = \delta$,

$$\Gamma(\beta,\{\alpha\})[g(K(\alpha),\tilde{x}) - rK(\alpha)] + \Gamma(\beta,\{\alpha'\})[g(K(\alpha'),\tilde{x}) - rK(\alpha')]$$
$$= \delta(g(K,\tilde{x}) - rK].$$

Thus, each portfolio satisfying the hypothesis of the proposition yields a distribution of returns which is the same as the distribution of returns obtained by holding δ shares in either firm α or firm α'. QED.

Proposition 3. Assume that N satisfies (20), and that A.1 holds. Let $(\hat{K}(\alpha),\hat{\Gamma}(\alpha))$ maximize (7) subject to $K(\alpha) \geq 0$, $\Gamma(\alpha) \geq 0$, and (8). Let $I_\alpha = \{\alpha' : K(\alpha') = \hat{K}(\alpha)\}$. Then $\hat{K}(\alpha) = \hat{K}(\alpha)$, $\hat{\Gamma}(\alpha,I_\alpha) = \hat{\gamma}(\alpha)$, and $\hat{\Gamma}(\alpha, E \sim I_\alpha) = 0$ where $(\hat{K}(\alpha),\hat{\gamma}(\alpha))$ maximizes (22) subject to $K(\alpha) \geq 0$, $\gamma(\alpha) \geq 0$, and (23). Thus, an entrepreneur invests only in firms which are run as he runs his own firm and he chooses $\gamma(\alpha) \geqq 0$ and $K(\alpha) \geqq 0$ subject to (23) to maximize (22). (If in equilibrium $\hat{\gamma}(\alpha) > 1$, he must be interpreted as investing in at least one other firm which employs $\hat{K}(\alpha)$.)

For any $\alpha \in C$, let $I_\alpha = \{\alpha' \in E: K(\alpha') = \hat{K}(\alpha)\}$, where $\hat{K}(\alpha)$ and $\hat{\gamma}(\alpha)$ are assumed to maximize (22) subject to (23) and the nonnegativity constraints. In equilibrium, I_α is not empty; i.e., there is some entrepreneur who runs his firm as α would if α were an entrepreneur; $\Gamma(\alpha,I_\alpha) = \hat{\gamma}(\alpha)$ and $\Gamma(\alpha, E \sim I_\alpha) = 0$.

Remarks. Proposition 3 can be interpreted as asserting that the assumption of a concave production function and the assumption that $\tilde{x}$ is the same for all firms together imply that all of the possibilities for diversification available in the stock market are dominated by the investment opportunities available through the production function. However, in order to exploit these opportunities, it may be necessary to retain only a partial share of the output from the production function or, if γ exceeds one, to receive a multiple of the output from the production function. The latter can be achieved by replication of a firm.

The mathematical result which is given a stock market interpretation in proposition 3 was obtained earlier and given a closely related sharecropping interpretation by Newbery (1977).

We are indebted to Sanford Grossman for suggesting the idea of the simple proof which appears below. Note that this proof does not require differentiability of u or g. Our original proof was substantially longer and did use arguments which depended on differentiability.

It should also be emphasized that the assumption that $\tilde{x}$ is the same for every firm is crucial to the proof of this result. If $\tilde{x}$ were a different random variable for each firm, individual investors would find it advantageous to hold diversified portfolios; i.e., the stock market would augment the diversification possibilities available with the production function.

Proof. Jensen's inequality and the strict concavity of g for each $x \neq \underline{x}$ imply that for any portfolio $\Gamma(\alpha)$ and for each $x \neq \underline{x}$,

$$(24) \quad \Gamma(\alpha, E) \left[g \left(\frac{\int_E K(\beta)\Gamma(\alpha, d\beta)}{\Gamma(\alpha, E)}, x \right) - r \left(\frac{\int_E K(\beta)\Gamma(\alpha, d\beta)}{\Gamma(\alpha, E)} \right) \right]$$

$$> \int_E [g(K(\beta), x) - rK(\beta)]\Gamma(\alpha, d\beta).$$

Thus, any entrepreneur or capitalist can obtain higher returns in each state x by becoming an entrepreneur employing

$$\frac{\int_E K(\beta)\Gamma(\alpha, d\beta)}{\Gamma(\alpha, E)}$$

units of operating capital and holding only $\Gamma(\alpha, E)$ shares in his own firm than he can by holding any diversified portfolio $\Gamma(\alpha)$. Note that the cost of $\Gamma(\alpha, E)$ shares in his own firm is the same as the cost of the portfolio $\Gamma(\alpha)$. QED.

Proposition 3 reduced the entrepreneur's problem to one of maximizing, by his $(K(\alpha), \gamma(\alpha))$ choice, (22). It also showed that the capitalist is faced with a simple choice of $\gamma(\alpha)$ for a fixed $K(\alpha)$ level. The next lemma shows that if solutions to both of these problems exist, they are unique.

Lemma 2. Assume that N satisfies (20) *and that u is strictly concave. If there exists a* $(\hat{K}(\alpha), \hat{\gamma}(\alpha))$ *choice which maximizes* (22) *and for which $\hat{K}(\alpha) > 0$, it is unique.*

Remark. In standard proofs, uniqueness follows from strict concavity of the criterion function. In the present context, this approach is inapplicable because H^α is not concave in $(K(\alpha), \gamma(\alpha))$. It is, however, strictly concave in $K(\alpha)$ and in $\gamma(\alpha)$. These facts can be easily verified by differentiation when u and g are twice differentiable and when u is strictly concave. If $u'' < 0$, the uniqueness of $(\hat{K}(\alpha), \hat{\gamma}(\alpha))$ can nevertheless be demonstrated by showing that, in spite of the nonconcavity of H^α, the second-order sufficient conditions for a maximum are satisfied at any $(\hat{K}(\alpha), \hat{\gamma}(\alpha))$ which satisfy the first-order conditions. Functions which have this property are referred to as strictly pseudoconcave and have unique maxima. The proof of pseudoconcavity of H^α requires that H^α be twice differentiable. It is, however, possible, using the proof which follows, to prove uniqueness of $(\hat{K}(\alpha), \hat{\gamma}(\alpha))$ directly and simply without assuming differentiability.

When u is concave but not necessarily strictly concave, a similar argument implies that $\hat{K}(\alpha)$ is unique. In this case, $\hat{\gamma}(\alpha)$ is not necessarily unique.

Proof. Suppose that there exist two maximizing choices $(\hat{K}_1(\alpha), \hat{\gamma}_1(\alpha))$ and $(\hat{K}_2(\alpha), \hat{\gamma}_2(\alpha))$ with, say, $\hat{K}_1(\alpha) > 0$. Then, as in the proof of proposition 2, the strict concavity of g for each $x \neq \underline{x}$, implies that for any $t \in (0, 1)$ and for any $x \neq \underline{x}$,

$$\gamma_t(\alpha)\left[g(K_t(\alpha), x) - rK_t(\alpha) \right] > t\hat{\gamma}_1(\alpha)[g(\hat{K}_1(\alpha), x) - r\hat{K}_1(\alpha)]$$

$$+ (1 - t)\hat{\gamma}_2(\alpha)[g(\hat{K}_2(\alpha), x) - r\hat{K}_2(\alpha)],$$

where

$$\gamma_t(\alpha) = t\hat{\gamma}_1(\alpha) + (1 - t)\hat{\gamma}_2(\alpha)$$

and

$$K_t(\alpha) = \frac{t\hat{\gamma}_1(\alpha)\hat{K}_1(\alpha) + (1 - t)\hat{\gamma}_2(\alpha)\hat{K}_2(\alpha)}{t\hat{\gamma}_1(\alpha) + (1 - t)\hat{\gamma}_2(\alpha)}.$$

Thus,

$$Eu\big(A + r[1 - \gamma_t(\alpha)] + \gamma_t(\alpha)[g(K_t(\alpha),\tilde{x}) - rK_t(\alpha)],\alpha\big)$$

(25)
$$> Eu\big(A + r[1 - t\hat{\gamma}_1(\alpha) - (1 - t)\hat{\gamma}_2(\alpha)]$$

$$+ t\hat{\gamma}_1(\alpha)[g(\hat{K}_1(\alpha),\tilde{x}) - r\hat{K}_1(\alpha)] + (1 - t)\hat{\gamma}_2(\alpha)[g(\hat{K}_2(\alpha),\tilde{x}) - r\hat{K}_2(\alpha)],\alpha\big)$$

because of the monotonicity of u. Now the strict concavity of u implies that

$$Eu\big(A + r[1 - t\hat{\gamma}_1(\alpha) - (1 - t)\hat{\gamma}_2(\alpha)] + t\hat{\gamma}_1(\alpha)[g(\hat{K}_1(\alpha),\tilde{x}) - r\hat{K}_1(\alpha)]$$

$$+ (1 - t)\hat{\gamma}_2(\alpha)[g(\hat{K}_2(\alpha),\tilde{x}) - r\hat{K}_2(\alpha)],\alpha\big)$$

(26)
$$> tEu\big(A + r[1 - \hat{\gamma}_1(\alpha)] + \hat{\gamma}_1(\alpha)[g(\hat{K}_1(\alpha),\tilde{x}) - r\hat{K}_1(\alpha)],\alpha\big)$$

$$+ (1 - t)Eu\big(A + r[1 - \hat{\gamma}_2(\alpha)] + \hat{\gamma}_2(\alpha)[g(\hat{K}_2(\alpha),\tilde{x}) - r\hat{K}_2(\alpha)],\alpha\big)$$

$$= H^\alpha(\hat{K}_1(\alpha),\hat{\gamma}_1(\alpha)) = H^\alpha(\hat{K}_2(\alpha),\hat{\gamma}_2(\alpha)).$$

Combining (25) and (26) implies that

$$H^\alpha(K_t(\alpha),\gamma_t(\alpha)) > H^\alpha(\hat{K}_1(\alpha),\hat{\gamma}_1(\alpha)) = H^\alpha(\hat{K}_2(\alpha),\hat{\gamma}_2(\alpha)).$$

Thus, neither $(\hat{K}_1(\alpha),\hat{\gamma}_1(\alpha))$ nor $(\hat{K}_2(\alpha),\hat{\gamma}_2(\alpha))$ can maximize H^α, a contradiction. QED.

Lemmas 1 and 2 and propositions 1–3 can now be used with assumption A1 and the assumption that u is concave to simplify substantially the structure of a CSMEE. The simplifications are described in proposition 4, which follows. Before stating the proposition, it is useful to recall that μ_i represents the measure of the set of individuals of type i who have the common utility function $u(\bullet,i)$. If $i = i(\alpha)$, we define $H^i = H^\alpha$.

Proposition 4. Suppose that (20) holds at all (K,B) and that assumption A1 holds. Then in a CSMEE there are

(27)
$$v_i = \gamma_i\mu_i$$

entrepreneurs who operate firms which employ K_i units of capital, where K_i is the capital demand which together with γ_i maximizes the function H^i defined by (22) for type i individuals. Since γ_i is the demand for shares by each of the μ_i type i individuals, (27) expresses the equality of supply and demand as required by (iv) of definition 1. If $\gamma_i < 1$, then $v_i < \mu_i$ and there are fewer firms of type i than individuals of type i. All individuals of type i

are indifferent between being capitalists and entrepreneurs. Thus, any v_i of the μ_i type i individuals will be entrepreneurs. The remaining $\mu_i - v_i$ type i individuals will be capitalists. If $\gamma_i > 1$, then $v_i > \mu_i$ and there must be more firms of type i than there are individuals of type i. The entrepreneurs for $v_i - \mu_i$ of these firms can be of some type $j \neq i$. These individuals of type j can become entrepreneurs, choose K_i as the capital level for their firm, and sell their one unit share in the firm. If they set $B_i = K_i$, then they will receive 1 capital unit for the firm and they will be in the same position as a capitalist of type j. They will then hold γ_j shares in a firm run by some entrepreneur of type j.

The condition that capital supply equals capital demand is

$$(28) \qquad \sum_{i=1}^{n} v_i K_i = 1 - \sum_{i=1}^{n} v_i$$

or

$$(29) \qquad \sum_{i=1}^{n} v_i(1 + K_i) = 1,$$

which becomes

$$(30) \qquad \sum_{i=1}^{n} \mu_i \gamma_i (1 + K_i) = 1$$

when (27) is substituted. Because of (30), γ_i cannot exceed one for all i.

The proposition follows immediately from lemmas 1 and 2 and propositions 1–3. The following corollary is also immediate.

Corollary to proposition 4. If (20) holds at all (K,B) and assumption A1 holds with $n = 1$, then in a CSMEE,

$$(31) \qquad v_1 = \hat{\gamma}_1 = \frac{1}{\hat{K}_1 + 1}.$$

Because of proposition 4, a vector $\langle \{(\hat{K}_i, \hat{\gamma}_i)\}_{i=1}^{n}, r \rangle$ can be identified with a CSMEE if, for each i, $(\hat{K}_i, \hat{\gamma}_i)$ maximizes H^i and if $\hat{\gamma}_i$ and $\hat{K}_i$ satisfy (30).

This simplification will prove to be essential in the demonstration that an equilibrium exists. Another essential step in this demonstration is a transformation of each individual's maximization problem. This transformation serves two purposes. On one hand, it reduces the individual maximization problem to a form in which the existence of a solution is more easily obtained. On the other, it makes it possible to reduce the problem of finding a CSMEE to one of finding a competitive equilibrium in a simple two-good pure trade economy. These reductions in turn permit the application of familiar arguments to obtain an equilibrium.

An appealing feature of the transformation of the individual maximization problem and of the equilibrium is the alternative interpretation of the CSMEE which results. In the present paper we will pause only briefly to discuss this alternative interpretation. An extended discussion is contained in a subsequent paper (Kihlstrom and Laffont 1980).

The first part of the transformation referred to is accomplished by letting

(32) $$C_i = \gamma_i[1 + K_i]$$

and defining a function F^i by

(33) $$F^i(K_i, C_i) \equiv Eu\left(A + r[1 - C_i] + C_i \frac{g(K_i, \tilde{x})}{[1 + K_i]}, i\right).$$

It is easily shown that if $(\hat{K}_i, \hat{\gamma}_i)$ maximizes H^i subject to $K_i \geq 0$, $\gamma_i \geq 0$, and (23), then $\hat{K}_i$ and

(34) $$\hat{C}_i = \hat{\gamma}_i[1 + \hat{K}_i]$$

maximize F^i subject to $K_i \geq 0$, $C_i \geq 0$, and

(35) $$A + r[1 - C_i] \geq 0.$$

Similarly, if $(\hat{K}_i, \hat{C}_i)$ maximize F^i subject to $K_i \geq 0$, $C_i \geq 0$, and (35), then $\hat{K}_i$ and

(36) $$\hat{\gamma}_i = \frac{\hat{C}_i}{[1 + \hat{K}_i]}$$

maximize H^i subject to $K_i \geq 0$, $\gamma_i \geq 0$, and (23). It is also easily shown that the uniqueness of $(\hat{K}_i, \hat{C}_i)$ is equivalent to the uniqueness of $(\hat{K}_i, \hat{\gamma}_i)$.

The function F^i and the variable C_i can be interpreted by assuming that $B_i = 0$, i.e., by assuming that all capital is equity capital and that equity capital can be supplied by either the entrepreneur or others. In that case, all of the firm's capital, $[1 + K_i]$, is obtained in return for equity. The amount C_i can be interpreted as the equity capital supplied by each individual of type i to firms of type i, i.e., those employing K_i. When C_i is related to γ_i and K_i by (32), i will receive a share of $g(K_i, \tilde{x})$ which equals

(37) $$\gamma_i = \frac{C_i}{1 + K_i}.$$

Thus, the income i receives from firms of type i in state x is

(38) $$C_i \frac{g(K_i, x)}{[1 + K_i]}.$$

Now if individuals of type i decide to supply an amount C_i of equity capital which is less than the one unit of capital with which they are endowed, they will have $(1 - C_i)r$ capital units that can be sold at the price r to individuals of other types. If C_i is chosen to exceed the one-unit capital endowment, then $(C_i - 1)$ capital units will have to be purchased at the price r from individuals of other types. In either case, $(1 - C_i)r$ units of income will be added to the share (38) received from firms of type i. Of course, when C_i exceeds one, this addition results in a reduction of $r(C_i - 1)$ in the income consumed.

Notice that when (32) is substituted in (30), the result is

$$(39) \qquad \sum_{i=1}^{n} \mu_i C_i = 1,$$

which asserts that the total equity capital supplied is equal to the economy's total supply of capital. Equation (38) can also be written as

$$(40) \qquad \sum_{i=1}^{n} \mu_i(1 - C_i) = 0.$$

Note also that (32) and (27) imply

$$(41) \qquad v_i(1 + K_i) = \mu_i C_i.$$

Since $v_i(1 + K_i)$ is the total capital demand by all firms of type i and $\mu_i C_i$ is the total equity capital supplied by type i individuals, (41) expresses the equality of supply and demand for equity capital to type i firms.

The transformation just described permits us to interpret a CSMEE as the equilibrium of an economy in which capital can be either sold or supplied to firms for equity. The share of output received from a firm is proportional to the share of equity capital supplied to that firm. For each type i there are firms which employ the K_i desired by type i individuals. Specifically, the type i firm employs K_i, which together with C_i maximizes F^i defined by (33). The number of firms of type i is v_i. Since v_i satisfies (41), there is an equality of the supply of and the demand for equity capital for type i firms. Because of (40), or equivalently (39), there is also an equality of supply of and demand for capital across types. Note in fact that (39) can, using (41), be written as (29), which asserts that total firm demand for capital equals supply.

Note that if there were no uncertainty, each firm would maximize output per unit of capital in order to maximize F^i. This criterion is analogous to the criterion employed in models of labor management. In that literature, labor managed firms are assumed to maximize output per worker. Because of this analogy, we use the term *capital management equilibrium* (CME) to refer to a vector $\langle\{(\hat{K}_i, \hat{C}_i)\}_{i=1}^{n}, r\rangle$ if, for each i, $(\hat{K}_i, \hat{C}_i)$ maximizes F^i and if (39) holds.

Having defined F^i, C^i and a CME, we have only completed the first step in the transformation used to obtain the existence of $(\hat{K}_i, \hat{\gamma}_i)$ and of a CSMEE. The second step is to solve the problem of maximizing F^i sequentially. We first demonstrate in lemma 3 below that for each C_i there exists a $\bar{K}(C_i)$ which maximizes $F^i(K_i, C_i)$. It is then shown in lemma

4 that for certain values of r, there exists a $\bar{C}_i$ which maximizes $F^i(\bar{K}_i(\bullet),\bullet)$. This accomplished, it is easily seen that $\hat{C}_i = \bar{C}_i$ and $\hat{K}_i = \bar{K}_i(\bar{C}_i)$.

Before stating these lemmas, we describe the third and final step in the process by which the problem of proving the existence of a CSMEE is reduced to one of finding a competitive equilibrium. In this step we demonstrate how the CME can be reinterpreted as a competitive equilibrium in a two-good pure trade economy. In order to define this simple economy, we first define a new "good" and let G_i denote the quantity of this good consumed by individuals of type i. The quantity G_i is assumed to be related to the quantity C_i by the budget constraint

$$(42) \qquad G_i = A + r(1 - C_i).$$

Note that when (35) holds, the consumption of G_i will always be nonnegative. Individual i's preferences for alternative (G_i, C_i) bundles are represented by the "utility function"

$$(43) \qquad V^i(G_i, C_i) \equiv \max_{K_i} Eu\left(G_i + C_i \frac{g(K_i,\tilde{x})}{[1 + K_i]}, i\right).$$

This utility function is well defined when G_i satisfies (42) because of the existence (yet to be demonstrated in lemma 3) of $\bar{K}_i(C_i)$ for each C_i. In this two-good economy r will be the price of "good" C while the price of good G will be one. Each individual will begin with an endowment vector

$$(44) \qquad \omega_i = (\omega_{G_i}, \omega_{C_i}) = (A, 1)$$

of these two goods. Note that with this endowment vector and with prices so defined, equation (42) becomes the budget constraint faced by all individuals. A vector $\langle \{(\hat{G}_i, \hat{C}_i)\}_{i=1}^n, r \rangle$ is a competitive equilibrium for this economy if, for each i, $(\hat{G}_i, \hat{C}_i)$ maximizes $V^i(G_i, C_i)$ subject to (42) and the nonnegativity constraints $G_i \geq 0$ and $C_i \geq 0$, and if supply equals demand in both markets, i.e., if

$$(45) \qquad \sum_{i=1}^n \mu_i \hat{C}_i = 1$$

and

$$(46) \qquad \sum_{i=1}^n \mu_i \hat{G}_i = A.$$

Note that (45) is the same as (39) and that, as usual, (46) is implied by Walras's law and by (45). Walras's law is also true for the usual reason; i.e., it follows from the budget constraint (42).

It is now a simple matter to use the observation just made to establish in proposition 5 the relationship between a CSMEE and the competitive equilibrium just defined.

Proposition 5. Assume that (20) *holds for all* (K, B), *and that assumption* A1 *holds. Then* $\langle\{(\hat{\gamma}_i, \hat{K}_i)\}_{i=1}^n, r\rangle$ *is a CSMEE if and only if* (i) *the allocation* $\langle\{(\hat{G}_i, \hat{C}_i)\}_{i=1}^n, r\rangle$ *is a competitive equilibrium of the economy in which there are* μ_i *consumers with utility functions* V^i *defined by* (43) *and every consumer has the initial endowment* ω *defined by* (44) *and* (ii) $\hat{K}_i = \bar{K}_i(\hat{C}_i)$; *i.e.,* $\hat{K}_i$ *maximizes*

$$Eu\left(\hat{G}_i + \hat{C}_i \frac{g(K_i, \tilde{x})}{[1 + K_i]}, i\right)$$

Proposition 5 will make it possible for us to prove in theorem 1 below that a CSMEE exists. This will be done by demonstrating the existence of a competitive equilibrium in the economy just described. This demonstration can be accomplished with standard arguments if the choice $(\hat{C}_i, \hat{G}_i)$ that maximizes V^i subject to (42) can be shown to be unique for each r and to vary continuously with r. The uniqueness has already been established by lemma 2 for the case in which $u(\cdot, i)$ is strictly concave. But the existence and continuity in r of an optimizing choice have yet to be demonstrated. The proof of existence is implied by lemmas 3 and 4, which we now state. As mentioned earlier, lemma 3 asserts that for each C in the interval $(0, (A/r) + 1]$, there exists a $\bar{K}_i(C)$ which maximizes $F^i(K, C)$. Lemma 4 demonstrates the existence of $\hat{C}_i$ as the C value which maximizes $F^i(\bar{K}_i(C), C) = V^i(A + r(1 - C), C)$.

The proofs of these lemmas, which are given in appendix 2, use the second differentiability of u and g. This is, in fact, the first point at which differentiability has been used. It will be noted, however, that in stating and proving these lemmas, u is not assumed to be *strictly* concave.

Lemma 3. For each $r \geq 0$ *and* $C_i \in (0, (A/r) + 1]$, F^i *is a strictly pseudoconcave function of* K_i *and there exists a unique* $\bar{K}_i(C_i)$ *which maximizes* $F^i(K_i, C_i)$ *subject to* $K_i \geq 0$. *Furthermore, when* $C_i \in (0, (A/r) + 1]$, $\bar{K}_i(C_i)$ *is a differentiable function of* C_i *and of* r. *If the individuals of type i are risk neutral, i.e., if* $u(\cdot, i)$ *is linear, or if* $g(K, x)$ *satisfies Diamond's assumption of stochastic constant returns to scale, i.e., if X is a subset of real numbers and*

(47) $$g(K, x) = h(K)x,$$

then for all $C_i \in (0, (A/r) + 1]$, $\bar{K}_i(C_i) = K^*$, *where* K^* *is the unique K which maximizes expected output per capital unit,*

(48) $$\frac{Eg(K, \tilde{x})}{[1 + K]},$$

and which is the unique solution to

(49) $$\frac{Eg(K, \tilde{x})}{[1 + K]} = Eg_K(K, \tilde{x}).$$

Finally, when the investors in i are risk averse,

(50) $$\lim_{C_i \to 0} \bar{K}_i(C_i) = K^*.$$

Figure 5.2 uses equation (49) to describe K^*. Also note that when g satisfies (47), (49) is equivalent to

(51) $$h(K) - h'(K)(1 + K) = 0.$$

In this case figure 5.2 can be reinterpreted to obtain figure 5.3.

Lemma 4. First suppose that

(52) $$r = \frac{Eg(K^*, \tilde{x})}{[1 + K^*]}.$$

If i is a risk neutral type, then $\hat{K}_i = K^*$ and $\hat{C}_i$ can be chosen arbitrarily. If, however, i is a risk averse type, then $\hat{K}_i = 0 = \hat{C}_i$.

Next, suppose that

(53) $$r < \frac{Eg(K^*, \tilde{x})}{[1 + K^*]}.$$

If, in this case, i is a risk neutral type, then $(\hat{K}_i, \hat{C}_i) = (K^*, (A/r) + 1)$. If type i individuals are risk averse, then $\hat{K}_i > 0$ and $\hat{C}_i > 0$.

Finally, assume that

(54) $$r > \frac{Eg(K^*, \tilde{x})}{[1 + K^*]}.$$

In this case $\hat{K}_i = \hat{C}_i = 0$ for risk averse as well as for risk neutral types.

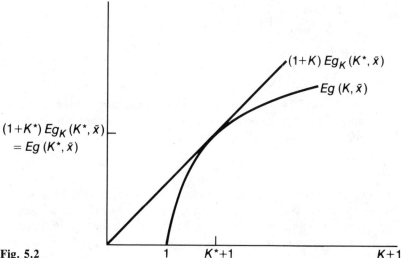

Fig. 5.2

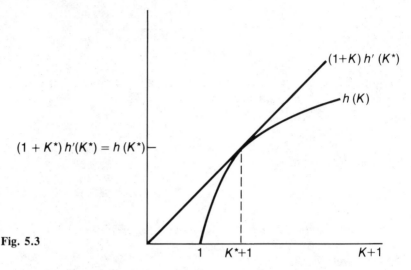

Fig. 5.3

In interpreting (52), (53), and (54) and subsequent references to these equations and inequalities, it should be recalled that K^* is the unique operating capital level at which (49) holds.

These lemmas can now be used to prove that a competitive equilibrium exists in the two-commodity pure trade economy. As noted, this implies the existence of a CSMEE.

Proposition 6. If assumption A1 is satisfied, then there exists a competitive equilibrium $\langle \{(\hat{G}_i, \hat{C}_i)\}^n_{i=1}, r \rangle$ *such that, for each i,* $(\hat{G}_i, \hat{C}_i)$ *maximizes* $V^i(G_i, C_i)$ *subject to (42) and the nonnegativity constraints are such that (45) and (46) hold. If individuals of one type, say, type 1, are risk neutral and if*

(55)
$$\mu_1 \geq \frac{1}{[A/Eg_K(K^*, \tilde{x})] + 1},$$

then (52) holds,

$$\hat{C}_1 = \frac{1}{\mu_1},$$

and $\hat{C}_i = 0$ *for* $i = 2, \ldots, n$. *If all individuals are risk averse or if individuals of some type, say, type 1, are risk neutral but (55) fails, then (53) holds. In the second of these two cases*

(56)
$$\hat{C}_1 = \frac{A}{r} + 1.$$

Proof. The assumptions made about u and g imply that V^i is a continuous function. When no individuals are risk neutral, this continuity together with the uniqueness of $\hat{C}_i$ implies that $\hat{C}_i$ is a continuous function of r. Using this continuity, standard proofs of existence yield an equilibrium.

If individuals of some type, say, type 1, are risk neutral, the choice $(\hat{K}_1, \hat{C}_1)$ may not be unique. In particular, if (52) holds, then $\hat{K}_1 = K^*$ and $\hat{C}_1$ can be chosen arbitrarily. This nonuniqueness causes no problem in the risk neutral case since the linearity of u and the fact that $K_1(C_1) = K^*$ for all C_1 imply that V^1 is linear; i.e.,

$$(57) \qquad V^1(G_1, C_1) = G_1 + C_1 \frac{Eg(K^*, \tilde{x})}{[1 + K^*]}.$$

Thus, for risk neutral individuals, preferences are convex and the resulting demand correspondence is upper semicontinuous. Again, standard existence proofs are applicable.

If μ_1, the measure of the set of risk neutral types, is sufficiently large in the sense that (55) holds, then the equilibrium is easily exhibited. In this case r can be equated to

$$Eg_K(K^*, \tilde{x}) = \frac{Eg(K^*, \tilde{x})}{[1 + K^*]}.$$

Lemma 4 then implies that for the risk averse types, i.e., for $i = 2, \ldots, n$, $\hat{C}_i = 0$. Thus, the equilibrium condition (45) reduces to

$$(58) \qquad \hat{C}_1 = \frac{1}{\mu_1}.$$

When (55) holds, $\hat{C}_1 = (1/\mu_1)$ will be less than $(A/r) + 1$, the bound imposed on C_1 by the condition (35). Lemma 4 implies that $\hat{C}_1$ solves the maximization problem of the type 1 individuals when r satisfies (52). Taken together, these remarks imply that when type 1 individuals are risk neutral and (55) holds,

$$\langle (A + r(1 - \frac{1}{\mu_1}), \frac{1}{\mu_1}), (A + r, 0) \ldots (A + r, 0), r \rangle$$

is an equilibrium if r is given by (52).

Suppose now that type 1 individuals are risk neutral but that (55) fails or that all individuals are risk averse. We want to show first that (53) holds, i.e., that neither (52) nor (54) holds. Lemma 4 implies immediately that (54) is inconsistent with equilibrium, since in that case

$$(59) \qquad \sum_{i=1}^{n} \mu_i \hat{C}_i = 0,$$

so that supply cannot equal demand in the C market. The same situation occurs (i.e., (59) also holds) if r satisfies (52) and if all individuals are risk averse. When individuals of type 1 are the only risk neutral individuals but (55) fails, lemma 4 implies

$$(60) \qquad \sum_{i=1}^{n} \mu_i \hat{C}_i = \mu_1 \hat{C}_1 \leq \mu_1 \left[\frac{A}{Eg_K(K^*, \tilde{x})} + 1 \right].$$

if r satisfies (52). If (55) fails, then (60) implies that equation (45) must also fail and again (52) is inconsistent with equilibrium.

When r satisfies (53), (56) follows from lemma 4. QED.

The existence of a CSMEE when (20) holds is established in the theorem which follows. The theorem also describes the influence of attitudes toward risk and of certain important technological assumptions on the equilibrium allocations and on the price of capital. The theorem follows immediately from the results obtained above. Together with the interpretative remarks that follow, it can be viewed as a summary of the results established up to this point.

Theorem 1. Suppose that assumption A1 is satisfied and that (20) holds for all (K, B). Then there exists a CSMEE $\langle \{(\hat{\gamma}_i, \hat{K}_i)\}_{i=1}^{n}, r \rangle$. If all individuals are risk averse or if one type of individual, say, type 1, is risk neutral but the number of risk neutral individuals is small in the sense that (55) fails, then $\hat{\gamma}_i > 0$, $\hat{K}_i > 0$, $v_i = \hat{\gamma}_i \mu_i > 0$, r satisfies (53) and for any $i > 1$,

$$
(61) \quad
\begin{aligned}
r &= \frac{Eu'(A + r[1-\hat{\gamma}_i] + \hat{\gamma}_i[g(\hat{K}_i,\tilde{x}) - r\hat{K}_i], i) g_K(\hat{K}_i,\tilde{x})}{Eu'(A + r[1-\hat{\gamma}_i] + \hat{\gamma}_i[g(\hat{K}_i,\tilde{x}) - r\hat{K}_i], i)} \\[2mm]
&= \frac{Eu'(A + r[1-\hat{\gamma}_i] + \hat{\gamma}_i[g(\hat{K}_i,\tilde{x}) - r\hat{K}_i], i)\dfrac{g(\hat{K}_i,\tilde{x})}{[1 + \hat{K}_i]}}{Eu'(A + r[1-\hat{\gamma}_i] + \hat{\gamma}_i[g(\hat{K}_i,\tilde{x}) - r\hat{K}_i], i)} \\[2mm]
&< \frac{Eg(\hat{K}_i,\tilde{x})}{[1 + \hat{K}_i]} < \frac{Eg(K^*,\tilde{x})}{[1 + K^*]}
\end{aligned}
$$

In the latter of these two cases, we will have, in addition, $K_1 = K^*$ and

$$
(62) \quad \hat{\gamma}_1 = \frac{(A/r) + 1}{[1 + K^*]}.
$$

If type 1 individuals are risk neutral and there are enough individuals of this type, in the sense that (55) holds, then r satisfies (52), $\hat{\gamma}_i = 0$, $\hat{K}_i = 0$, and $v_i = \hat{\gamma}_i \mu_i = 0$ for $i = 2, \ldots, n$ while $\hat{K}_1 = K^*$,

$$
\hat{\gamma}_1 = \frac{1}{\mu_1[1 + K^*]},
$$

and

$$
v_1 = \hat{\gamma}_1 \mu_1 = \frac{1}{[1 + K^*]}.
$$

Thus, if there are enough risk neutral individuals, all firms maximize expected profits and are held only by risk neutral individuals. The price of capital is the expected marginal product of capital in this case.

If g satisfies Diamond's assumption of stochastic constant returns to scale (i.e., if (47) holds), then $\hat{K}_i = K^*$ for all types i, even those which are risk averse. In this case, (29), which expresses the equality of capital supply and demand, can be reinterpreted to obtain the expression

(63)
$$\sum_{i=1}^{n} \hat{v}_i = \frac{1}{1 + K^*}$$

for the number of firms.

If $n = 1$ (i.e., if all individuals are the same), then

$$v_1 = \hat{\gamma}_1 = \frac{1}{\hat{K}_1 + 1}$$

and $\hat{K}_1$ will be determined by

(64)
$$Eu'(A + \left[\frac{1}{\hat{K}_1 + 1}\right] g(\hat{K}_1, \tilde{x}), 1) g_K(\hat{K}_1, \tilde{x})$$

$$= Eu'(A + \left[\frac{1}{\hat{K}_1 + 1}\right] g(\hat{K}_1, \tilde{x}), 1) \frac{g(\hat{K}_1, \tilde{x})}{[1 + \hat{K}_1]}.$$

In this case

$$r = \frac{Eu'\left(A + \left[\frac{1}{\hat{K}_1 + 1}\right] g(\hat{K}_1, \tilde{x}), 1\right) g_K(\hat{K}_1, \tilde{x})}{Eu'\left(A + \left[\frac{1}{\hat{K}_1 + 1}\right] g(\hat{K}_1, \tilde{x}), 1\right)}.$$

Remarks. We are able to achieve an equilibrium because of a large-number hypothesis. Specifically, an equilibrium exists because there are many individuals of each type. To understand why this large-number hypothesis is necessary for equilibrium, note that in our model any individual will exercise his option to become an entrepreneur if the market fails to supply him with the investment opportunity, i.e., the firm, that he would find it optimal to create for himself as an entrepreneur. As a result, an equilibrium must supply the optimal investment opportunity for essentially every individual. However, because of the fixed costs, not all individuals will be able to be entrepreneurs; some will have to be satisfied with the investment opportunities provided for them by other entrepreneurs. Now capitalists of type i will of course be willing to invest in shares of firms created by type i entrepreneurs. In order to achieve an equilibrium in the market for shares to firms of type i, it must be possible to adjust the number of type i firms continuously until the supply of shares of these firms equals the demand, i.e., until equation (27) holds. If the supply of type i shares provided by an entering or exiting firm is a significant part of the total, variations in the number of firms do not result in continuous variations in the supply of type i shares. When, as we assume, there is a large number (continuum) of possible firms of any type, each firm's supply of shares is insignificant and (27) can always be obtained by continuous variations in the number of firms.

The contrast between the case in which (55) holds and the case when it fails should be emphasized. When (55) holds, there is a relatively large number of risk neutral individuals. In equilibrium, this group holds all shares to all firms. Because all final owners of firms are risk neutral, the firms are operated at the K level which maximizes expected profits when r, the price of capital, equals its expected marginal product. In order to guarantee that risk neutral investors are indifferent between capital sales for the fixed return r and the purchase of equity shares, the price of capital must also equal expected output per unit of capital. When this is true, all *risk averse* individuals actually prefer capital sales at r to the purchase of equity shares. The condition (55) guarantees that when r equals expected output per capital unit, risk neutral individuals possess enough initial wealth to avoid a positive probability of bankruptcy when they buy all shares to the $1/(1 + K^*)$ firms. To understand why this is so, suppose that these firms have no debt, so that the value of their shares is $1 + K^*$. At this price the capital value of all $1/(1 + K^*)$ shares is 1. When r equals both the expected output per capital unit and the expected marginal product of capital, the capital value of the initial endowment (A,1) is

$$[A/Eg_K(K^*,\tilde{x})] + 1.$$

Thus, the total capital value of the endowment of the entire set of risk neutral individuals is

(65) $$\mu_1\{[A/Eg_K(K^*,\tilde{x})] + 1\}.$$

When this exceeds or equals 1, the capital value of all shares, the probability of bankruptcy is zero if all $1/(1 + K^*)$ debtless firms are held by the μ_1 risk neutral individuals. As asserted, the case in which the expression in (65) exceeds or equals one is exactly the case in which (55) holds.

When (55) fails, risk neutral investors do not possess enough resources to buy all $1/(1 + K^*)$ firms. In this case, risk averse buyers must be induced to hold shares in firms. The inducement is provided for *all* types when r falls below expected output per capital unit. Thus, individuals of all types hold shares to firms. The firms held by these risk averse individuals will not, in general, maximize expected profits unless there is stochastic constant returns to scale. And, in fact, there will in general be a different type of firm, i.e., a firm with a different K level, for each type of individual.

When r is exceeded by expected output per capital unit, risk neutral individuals have a real preference for equity shares over capital sales at r

and this preference is never eliminated until the maximum number of shares are purchased. This, of course, occurs when (62) holds.

Note that the extreme case in which there are no risk neutral individuals can also be interpreted as a case in which (55) fails because $\mu_1 = 0$. In the other extreme case which occurs when all individuals are risk neutral, (55) must hold because $\mu_1 = 1$ and

$$[A/Eg_K(K^*,\bar{x})] + 1 > 1.$$

When there are stochastic constant returns to scale, all firms choose to operate at the output level which maximizes expected profits if r equals the expected marginal product of capital. In this case r will actually equal the marginal product of capital if and only if (55) holds. In other cases, r will be lower than the expected marginal product of capital since, in these cases, r satisfies (61).

The fact that (47) implies that individuals of all types choose to operate their firms at K^* is a manifestation of the results obtained by Ekern and Wilson (1974), Leland (1974), and Radner (1974). They showed that such unanimity would be achieved when a condition they called *spanning* was satisfied. Stochastic constant returns to scale are a special case of spanning.

Proof. Using (36) and (42), the equilibrium $\langle\{(\hat{G}_i,\hat{C}_i)\}_{i=1}^n, r\rangle$ which was shown to exist in proposition 6 can be translated into a CSMEE. For the cases in which (55) does and does not hold when type 1 individuals are risk neutral and for the case in which no individuals are risk neutral, the same equations can be used to translate, in an obvious way, the descriptions of $\langle\{(\hat{G}_i,\hat{C}_1)\}_{i=1}^n, r\rangle$ obtained in proposition 6 into descriptions of the CSMEE.

The results for the case in which (47) holds follow from the results obtained for this case in lemma 3.

Finally, the expressions for r provided by the first two equalities in (61) are obtained from the first-order conditions for $\hat{K}_i$ and $\hat{\gamma}_i$, respectively. The first inequality in (61) follows from the fact that $u'' < 0$, while the second inequality follows from the definition of K^*.

The results for the case $n = 1$ also follow immediately from the first-order conditions. QED.

5.5 Efficiency

The present section asks whether and in what sense a CSMEE is efficient. Again, the discussion is limited to the case in which expectations are classical in the sense that $N = N_C$. The well-known theorem that a competitive equilibrium is efficient and the fact that a CSMEE is such an equilibrium in a suitably defined two-good pure trade economy combine to imply that a CSMEE is efficient relative to the class of basic allocations which are representable as allocations of the two goods in this pure trade economy. This fact will make it possible to establish that a CSMEE is efficient in the restricted sense of the term employed by Diamond (1967).

The proof is not immediate only because there are some allocations that are feasible in the restricted sense of Diamond which are not representable as feasible allocations in the two-good pure trade economy. Unrepresentable Diamond restricted feasible allocations are those in which individuals hold diversified portfolios not satisfying $\Gamma(\alpha, E \sim I_\alpha) = 0$. It is easily seen, however, that, for reasons identical to those underlying proposition 3, allocations involving diversified portfolios can be Pareto dominated by undiversified portfolios which are representable in the two-good pure trade economy. The formalization of this argument is the proof of theorem 2 below.

In the unrestricted sense of the term associated with Arrow and Debreu, a CSMEE is not in general efficient. This situation can occur because there are allocations of the basic economy which are not achievable as Diamond feasible allocations in the stock market economy and are also not representable in the above described two-good pure trade economy. Indeed, some of these unrepresentable allocations can be shown to Pareto dominate the CSMEE. This will be done after theorem 2. At that point we will also give conditions under which the CSMEE is unrestricted efficient. Briefly, this occurs when all individuals are alike or if the set of risk neutral individuals, which we again identify with type 1 individuals, is sufficiently large to imply that (55) holds. These results will follow from an application of the marginal conditions for unrestricted efficiency, obtained in Kihlstrom and Laffont (1979). These marginal conditions can also be applied to demonstrate that when Diamond's assumption of stochastic constant returns to scale is satisfied, all but one of the manifestations of "first-best" inefficiency disappear. Specifically, in this case all firms' production decisions are at efficient levels and the number of firms is efficient. The allocation of risk remains inefficient because the opportunities for exchanging risks in the market for firm shares are not sufficiently rich.

Before stating theorem 2, it is necessary to describe the set of allocations which are feasible in the restricted sense of Diamond. Diamond efficient allocations can then be formally discussed as the set of Diamond feasible allocations which are not Pareto dominated by other Diamond feasible allocations. The discussion of Diamond restricted feasible and Diamond efficient allocations is naturally preceded by some consideration of unrestricted feasibility and efficiency. Thus, we begin by defining the set of unrestricted efficient allocations. The definitions of unrestricted feasibility and unrestricted or "first-best" efficiency are adaptations to the present context of the familiar definitions of feasibility and efficiency applied in the Arrow-Debreu analysis of markets for contingent claims.

Definition 2. A contingent claims allocation *is a specification of a partition* $\{E, C\}$ *of* $[0, 1]$ *and of two Lebesgue measurable functions*

$$K: E \rightarrow [0, \infty)$$

and

$$y: [0, 1] \times X \rightarrow [0, \infty)$$

such that

(66) $$\int_E K(\alpha)\mu(d\alpha) = \mu(C)$$

and for each $x \in X$

(67) $$\int_0^1 y(\alpha, x)d\alpha = \int_E g(K(\alpha), x)d\alpha + A.$$

As usual, the set of feasible allocations satisfying definition 2 can be interpreted as the set of choices available to a central planner. Such a planner can, by assigning individuals to their respective roles in the economy, choose the set E of entrepreneurs and C, the set of capitalists. He can also assign a capital allocation $K(\alpha)$ to each entrepreneur α in the chosen set E. Finally, he can distribute to each individual α in $[0, 1]$ a contingent claims vector $\langle y(\alpha, x) \rangle_{x \in X}$. Of course, the allocation he chooses is necessarily restricted by the limited availability of income in each state x and of capital. He does, however, have some control over the availability of income in state x. This control is exercised when he chooses E, C, and $K(\bullet)$. His choice of E and C determines the number of firms. The amount produced by each of these firms is determined by the capital allocation $K(\bullet)$. Once these choices have been made, the availability restriction imposed on the allocation of contingent claims to wealth in state x is the supply equal demand condition (67). The choice of E, C, and $K(\bullet)$ is constrained by the availability of capital. This constraint is imposed in the capital supply equal capital demand equation (66).

In making choices, a planner is assumed to be guided by the usual principle of efficiency which is embodied in the following definition.

Definition 3. A contingent claims allocation is efficient if (i) it is feasible in the sense that it satisfies definition 2 and (ii) there is no other feasible allocation which Pareto dominates it, i.e., which makes a significant subset of individuals better off while making almost no one worse off.

The concept of efficiency introduced by Diamond demands less than definition 3. Specifically, it imposes restrictions, beyond those imposed in (66) and (67) by availability, on the set of permissible contingent claims allocations against which a potentially Diamond efficient allocation is compared. Of course, any Diamond efficient allocation must also satisfy these added restrictions. These new restrictions take the form of additional constraints imposed on the relationship between $y(\alpha,x)$, individual α's claim to consumption in state x, and x, the state on which $y(\alpha,x)$ is contingent. In particular, individuals are permitted to receive income in two forms. First, they can be paid or pay fixed amounts not contingent on the random variable $\tilde{x}$. Second, they can receive a proportional share, fixed in advance, of the output of any existing firm. The share is fixed in the sense that the proportion received from any firm is independent of x, the outcome of $\tilde{x}$. The contingent claims allocations obtainable are the same as those achievable when the only institution for the exchange of risk is a stock market in which firm shares are traded for fixed payments. The imposition of these restrictions on $y(\alpha,x)$ has the effect of constraining the planner to use the same risk trading institutions as those used by the market. If a planner cannot, using only the market institutions, Pareto dominate a market allocation, then that allocation is Diamond efficient.

The following definition describes the set of Diamond feasible allocations.

Definition 4. A contingent claims allocation is feasible in the sense of Diamond *if there exist two functions*

$$\Gamma: [0,1] \rightarrow \textit{the set of nonnegative measures on the Lebesgue measurable subsets of E}$$

and

$$f: [0,1] \rightarrow (-\infty, +\infty)$$

such that (i) *for each* x $\in$ X *and* $\alpha \in [0,1]$

(68) $$y(\alpha,x) = \int_E g(K(\beta),x)\Gamma(\alpha,d\beta) + f(\alpha),$$

(ii) *for each* $E' \subseteq E$

(69) $$\int_0^1 \Gamma(\alpha, E')\mu(d\alpha) = \mu(E'),$$

and (iii)

(70) $$\int_0^1 f(\alpha)d\alpha = A.$$

A specification of $\{E, C\}$, K, y, Γ, *and f satisfying (66), (68), (69), and (70) will be referred to as a* Diamond feasible allocation.

Definition 4 describes the set of contingent claims allocations achievable when the institutional constraints imposed by the presence of a stock market in firm shares are added to the availability constraints of definition 2. The added restrictions on $y(\alpha,x)$ are imposed by equation (68) in which the fixed payment received or made by α is $f(\alpha)$ and his noncontingent portfolio of shares to firm output is $\Gamma(\alpha)$. The income availability restriction (67) imposed in definition 2 is replaced, in definition 4, by the availability constraint (69) of shares to firms' output and by the constraint (70) on fixed payments. The number of available shares to firms operated by entrepreneurs in some subset E' of E is $\mu(E')$. When $\Gamma(\cdot)$ is the allocation of firm share portfolios, the number of outstanding shares to the firms of the entrepreneurs in E' is the left side of (69). As (69) asserts, these must be equal in any feasible allocation. When $f(\cdot)$ is the allocation of noncontingent payments, the left side of (70) represents the total of these payments. The amount A represents the economy's total initial allocation of nonrandom income. As (70) asserts, this is the amount available for the purpose of making nonrandom payments. Note that (68)–(70) imply (67) so that this condition does not have to be explicitly introduced when $y(\alpha,x)$ satisfies (68) for each α and when $\Gamma(\cdot)$ and $f(\cdot)$ satisfy (69) and (70), respectively.

A planner who is restricted to the choice of a contingent claims allocation which satisfies the stock market institutional constraints added in definition 4 can apply the usual Pareto criteria in the modified or second-best sense introduced by Diamond.

Definition 5. A contingent claims allocation is Diamond efficient if (i) *it is Diamond feasible and* (ii) *there is no other Diamond feasible allocation which Pareto dominates it, i.e., which makes a significant subset of individuals better off while making almost no one worse off.*

It can now be shown that a planner with Diamond efficiency as his goal cannot make better use of market institutions than the market does on its own, if individual price expectations are rational in the sense that $N = N_C$. In interpreting the rationality of the expectations, the reader should recall the discussion of rational expectations in section 5.3.

Theorem 2. Assume that N satisfies (20) *and that assumption* A1 *holds. Then a competitive stock market entrepreneurial equilibrium is Diamond efficient.*

Proof. Suppose that $A^* = \langle\{E^*,C^*\}, K^*, y^*, \Gamma^*, f^*\rangle$ is a Diamond feasible allocation which Pareto dominates an equilibrium $\hat{A} = \langle\{\hat{E},\hat{C}\}, \hat{K}, \hat{\Gamma}\rangle$. By what we have shown, for each individual α of type i who is in $\hat{E}$, $\hat{K}(\alpha) = \hat{K}_i, \hat{\Gamma}(\alpha,I_\alpha) = \hat{\gamma}_i$, and $\hat{\Gamma}(\alpha,E \sim I_\alpha) = 0$. Similarly, each individual of type i would also demand $\hat{\gamma}_i$ shares in firms employing $\hat{K}_i$ and would also demand no shares in other firms. Thus, in particular, for every i

$$(71) \qquad Eu\big(A + \hat{r}(1 - \hat{\gamma}_i) + \hat{\gamma}_i[g(\hat{K}_i,\tilde{x}) - \hat{r}\hat{K}_i], i\big)$$
$$\geq Eu\big(A + \hat{r}[1 - \int_{E^*}\Gamma^*(\alpha,d\beta)] + \int_{E^*}[g(K^*(\beta),\tilde{x}) - \hat{r}K^*(\beta)]\Gamma^*(\alpha,d\beta), i\big).$$

In (71), $\hat{r}$ is the equilibrium price of capital. This inequality holds because of proposition 3. (Strictly speaking, proposition 3 implies (71) when E^* is replaced by $\hat{E}$ and Γ^* is replaced by some portfolio of firms which exist in equilibrium. But the same argument as that used to establish proposition

3 applies for any set of entrepreneurs and any portfolio. In particular, it holds for E^* and Γ^*.)

Now if A^* Pareto dominates $\hat{A}$, then for all α

$$(72) \qquad Eu\left(\int_{E^*}g(K^*(\beta),\tilde{x})\Gamma^*(\alpha,d\beta) + f^*(\alpha),i(\alpha)\right)$$

$$\geq Eu\left(A + \hat{r}(1-\hat{\gamma}_{i(\alpha)}) + \hat{\gamma}_{i(\alpha)}[g(K_{i(\alpha)},\tilde{x}) - \hat{r}\hat{K}_{i(\alpha)}],i(\alpha)\right),$$

and the strict inequality must hold for a set of α's of positive μ-measure. In (72), $i(\alpha)$ is α's type. By combining (71) and (72), we can conclude that, for all α,

$$(73) \qquad Eu\left(\int_{E^*}g(K^*(\beta),\tilde{x})\Gamma^*(\alpha,d\beta) + f^*(\alpha),i(\alpha)\right)$$

$$\geq Eu\left(A + \hat{r}[1-\int_{E^*}\Gamma^*(\alpha,d\beta)] + \int_{E^*}[g(K^*(\beta),\tilde{x}) - \hat{r}K^*(\beta)]\Gamma^*(\alpha,d\beta),i(\alpha)\right)$$

and that (73) holds with a strict inequality for a set of α's of positive measure. Now (73) implies that, for all α,

$$(74) \qquad f^*(\alpha) \geq A + \hat{r}[1 - \int_{E^*}(1 + K^*(\beta))\Gamma^*(\alpha,d\beta)]$$

and that (74) holds with a strict inequality for a set of α of positive μ-measure. Thus, integrating (74) over $[0,1]$, we get

$$(75) \qquad \int_0^1 f^*(\alpha)\mu(d\alpha) > A + r[1 - \int_0^1\int_{E^*}\Gamma(\alpha,d\beta)\mu(d\alpha)$$

$$- \int_0^1\int_{E^*}K^*(\beta)\Gamma(\alpha,d\beta)\mu(d\alpha)].$$

Because (69) holds for all $E' \subseteq E$, we can interchange the order of integration in (75) to obtain

$$(76) \qquad \int_0^1\int_{E^*}\Gamma(\alpha,d\beta)\mu(d\alpha) = \Gamma(E^*)$$

and

$$(77) \qquad \int_0^1\int_{E^*}K^*(\beta)\Gamma(\alpha,d\beta)\mu(d\alpha) = \int_{E^*}K(\beta)\mu(d\alpha).$$

Substituting (76) and (77) in (75) and using condition (66) that supply equals demand in the capital market, we obtain

$$(78) \qquad \int_0^1 f^*(\alpha)\mu(d\alpha) > A.$$

Thus, (70) and (66) cannot hold simultaneously for A^*, the allocation which Pareto dominates the equilibrium $\hat{A}$. Thus, $\hat{A}$ must be efficient in the sense of Diamond. QED.

Theorem 2 asserts that a planner who is restricted to using the same institutions as the market cannot Pareto dominate the market allocation. In this appropriate second-best sense, the market is efficient. Suppose, however, that the planner is liberated from the constraints imposed by market institutions and required only to satisfy the availability constraints imposed in definition 2. In that case, he can choose allocations which are not obtainable in a market restricted by the institutional constraints (68)–(70) of definition 4. With these additional choices available the planner can indeed improve on a market allocation chosen subject to the institutional constraints. Thus, as will be shown below, the market allocation is, in general, inefficient in the first-best sense of Arrow-Debreu. We will also show, however, that there are important special cases in which the allocation achieved in a stock market for firm shares is efficient in the "first-best" sense. In these cases, the stock market institutional constraints are not binding. Their relaxation is therefore of no value to a planner. In this case, the enlarged class of feasible allocations satisfying only the availability constraints of definition 2 cannot improve on a market allocation satisfying the more stringent institutional constraints of definition 4.

As an introduction to the discussion of "first-best" efficiency, we recall, in the following proposition, the results obtained in Kihlstrom and Laffont (1979).

Proposition 7. If $\langle\{E,C\},K(\cdot),y(\cdot,\cdot)\rangle$ is efficient in the sense of definition 3, then

$$(79)\qquad \frac{u'(y(\alpha,x),\alpha)}{u'(y(\alpha,x'),\alpha)} = \frac{u'(y(\beta,x),\beta)}{u'(y(\beta,x'),\beta)}$$

for almost all α and β in $[0,1]$ and for all x and x' in X. Furthermore, for almost all α and β in E,

$$(80)\qquad\qquad K(\alpha) = K(\beta) = K^0,$$

where K^0 is determined by

$$(81)\quad Eu'(y(\alpha,\tilde{x}),\alpha)g_K(K^0,\tilde{x})[K^0+1] = Eu'(y(\alpha,\tilde{x}),\alpha)g(K^0,\tilde{x})$$

for almost any α. Conversely, if an allocation satisfies (79), (80), and (81), it is efficient in the sense of definition 3.

The proof of this proposition is contained in Kihlstrom and Laffont (1979). It will not be reproduced here. We will, however, discuss the intuition underlying these results as well as their interpretation. The derivation of these conditions clearly requires the differentiability assumed throughout this paper. For the proof that (79)–(81) are sufficient for efficiency, the assumptions that u and g are concave are also required.

It is well known that in any "first-best" efficient allocation of contingent claims, individual marginal rates of substitution must be equated. Condition (79) is simply an expression of this familiar condition.

The equality of the capital allocation received by each firm expressed in (80) is a less familiar condition. It is closely related to the individual nondiversification result obtained in proposition 3. It asserts that, for the economy, as for any individual, there are no gains to diversification. Economy-wide and individual nondiversification are optimal for the same two reasons: the concavity of the production function in K and the fact that $\tilde{x}$ is the same random variable for all firms. When these two conditions hold, all of the vectors of state-contingent output achievable through diversification across a number of firms can be dominated by some state-contingent output vector obtained by having these same firms produce at a common level. In effect, the possibility of replicating the concave technology makes diversification unnecessary. Suppose, for example, that two firms α and β did receive different capital allocations $K(\alpha) \neq K(\beta)$. The total output of the two firms could be increased in all states x if they each received $\frac{1}{2}[K(\alpha) + K(\beta)]$. This is possible because the strict concavity of g implies that, for all x,

$$2g(\frac{1}{2}[K(\alpha) + K(\beta)],x) > g(K(\alpha),x) + g(K(\beta),x).$$

This improvement would not be possible, however, if the x value in α's production function were ever different from the x value in β's production function.

It should be remarked that the K^0 which solves (81) is independent of α because (79) holds for all α and β. It is this independence which permits economy-wide nondiversification to be optimal, i.e., which permits all firms to produce at the same capital level in an efficient allocation.

Since each firm is operated at K^0, the capital supply equal capital demand condition implies that the total number of firms created when each employs $[1 + K^0]$ total capital units is

$$(82) \qquad v^0 = \left[\frac{1}{1 + K_0}\right].$$

Thus, (82) can be interpreted as an equation which determines v^0, the number of firms. In fact, (82) can be inverted to obtain

$$(83) \qquad K^0 = \frac{1}{v^0} - 1.$$

When (83) is substituted in (81), the result is

$$(84) \quad Eu'(y(\alpha,\tilde{x}),\alpha)g_K(\frac{1}{v^0} - 1,\tilde{x})\frac{1}{v^0} = Eu'(y(\alpha,\tilde{x}),\alpha)g(\frac{1}{v^0} - 1,\tilde{x}),$$

which is the same as equation (39) in Kihlstrom and Laffont (1979). Equation (84) directly determines v^0.

For the purpose of interpreting (81) and (84), we can follow common practice and use $g_K(K^0,x) = g_k((1/v^0)-1,x)$ to measure the income value of capital in state x. The term $g_K(K^0,x)[K^0+1] = (1/v^0) g_K((1/v^0)$ $- 1,x)$ then becomes the income value, in state x, of the $[1 + K^0] = 1/v^0$

total capital units required to operate a firm at K^0. The left sides of (81) and (84) can therefore be interpreted as the expected marginal utility of these $[1 + K^0] = 1/v^0$ capital units. The right sides of (81) and (84) represent the expected marginal utility of the output produced by a firm operated at K^0. Thus, (81) and (84) assert that new firms are created up to the point at which the expected marginal utility of the income value of the capital used to create a new firm and operate it at K^0 is just equated to the expected marginal utility of output produced by the firm.

Equation (81) can also be rewritten to obtain the equation

$$(85) \qquad Eu'(y(\alpha,\tilde{x}),\alpha)g_K(K^0,\tilde{x}) = Eu'(y(\alpha,\tilde{x}),\alpha)\frac{g(K^0,\tilde{x})}{[1 + K^0]},$$

which, using (82) and (83), is, in turn, equivalent to

$$(86) \quad Eu'(y(\alpha,\tilde{x}),\alpha)g_K(\frac{1}{v^0} - 1,\tilde{x}) = Eu'(y(\alpha,\tilde{x}),\alpha)g(\frac{1}{v^0} - 1,\tilde{x})v^0.$$

The expressions in (85) and (86) assert that capital is efficiently divided between its alternative uses as an operating and entrepreneurial input when the expected marginal utility of the marginal product of capital equals the expected marginal utility of the output per unit of capital. The left sides of (85) and (86) clearly measure the marginal utility of an additional unit of operating capital. It will now be argued that the right sides of (85) and (86) measure the marginal utility of an additional unit of entrepreneurial capital. Then (85) and (86) can be interpreted as expressions of a conventional wisdom; viz., an input, in this case capital, is efficiently allocated when it yields the same marginal utility in all alternative uses, in this case as entrepreneurial and as operating capital. To interpret the right sides of (85) and (86), note that when one new firm operating at K^0 is created, it produces $g(K^0,x)$ income units in state x. The proportion of entrepreneurial to total capital used to obtain this output is $1/(1 + K^0)$. Thus,

$$\left[\frac{1}{1 + K^0}\right]g(K^0,x)$$

is the share of additional output attributable to the one unit of entrepreneurial capital used to create the firm. As a consequence, the right sides of (85) and (86) measure the expected marginal utility of an additional unit of entrepreneurial capital.

From proposition 7 it is clear why a CSMEE is inefficient in the unrestricted Arrow-Debreu sense. First, there is no mechanism to guarantee that risk is efficiently allocated. Thus, in general, (79) fails to hold. In addition, there is, in the general case, a misallocation of capital to firms. This occurs because entrepreneurs of different types choose to operate their firms at different K levels. Since $\hat{K}_i$ is, except in special circumstances, different from $\hat{K}_j$ when $i \neq j$, the equality required by (80) fails to hold.

Note that in spite of the fact that (79) and (80) fail to hold in a CSMEE, equation (61) implies that (81) does hold for all i. As noted, however, the $\hat{K}_i$ at which (81) is satisfied is different for each i. This can happen because risk is misallocated and (79) fails. The fact that $\hat{K}_i$ is different for different types makes it impossible to relate the number of firms to the firms' capital demand by a simple equation such as (83). Thus, the efficient number of firms can no longer be deduced from (84), which was obtained from (81) and (83).

Although a CSMEE is not, in general, efficient in the first-best sense, there are special circumstances of some importance in which first-best efficiency is achieved. The proposition which follows describes these cases.

Proposition 8. Assume that $N = N_C$. If individuals of one type, say, type 1, are risk neutral and their number is sufficiently large to imply that (55) holds, then the equilibrium is efficient in the sense of definition 3. The equilibrium is also efficient in this sense if all individuals are alike.

Proof. When type 1 individuals are risk neutral and (55) holds, theorem 1 asserts that all firms are completely owned by risk neutral individuals. Risk averse individuals receive the sure return r for their capital. Thus, all risks are borne by the risk neutral individuals, as they must be if (79) is to hold in this case. Since all firms are operated at K^*, the K level which maximizes expected profits, (80) holds and capital is efficiently allocated across firms. With risk neutral individuals, (81) reduces to (49), which is the equation defining K^*. Thus, the equilibrium K, K^*, is the efficient level at which to operate each firm and the equilibrium number of firms $1/(1 + K^*)$ is also the efficient number.

The proof that the equilibrium is efficient when there is only one type also follows from the marginal conditions derived in proposition 7 and from the properties of the equilibrium established for this case in theorem 1. Again, the important fact is that all firms are operated at the same level $\hat{K}_i$. Because of (61), this is the K level which satisfies (81). The equality of marginal rates of substitution required in (79) is a consequence of the fact that all individuals are identical and hold identical portfolios. QED.

5.6   Relationship of a CSMEE to the Diamond Equilibrium and Long-Run Competitive Equilibrium without Uncertainty

The objective of this brief section is to argue that the equilibrium concept proposed in this paper can be viewed as a generalization of two important concepts of economic equilibrium.

The first of these concepts is Diamond's stock market equilibrium. The second is the classical long-run competitive equilibrium in which production takes place at minimum average cost.

The present model can be related to Diamond's from either of two points of view which differ in their interpretation of the production technology and of Diamond's assumption of stochastic constant returns to scale. The first of these alternative interpretations to be considered is the one implicitly adopted throughout our exposition. Thus, we first identify the technology with the production function g and interpret stochastic constant returns to scale to mean that $g(K,x) = h(K)x$. Using this interpretation and making appropriate adjustments for the fact that we do, but Diamond did not, consider the case of free entry and exit, we will now argue that the stock market equilibrium considered here is the same as that considered by Diamond. Diamond's discussion of this equilibrium concept is limited to the case in which the technology satisfied the assumption of stochastic constant returns to scale. This restriction was necessary to simplify the study of the firm's maximization problem. As Leland (1974), Ekern and Wilson (1974), and Radner (1974) have shown, this assumption implies that stockholders unanimously agree on the choice criterion to be used by the firm. In fact, all stockholders agree that the firm should maximize its stock market value. We replace this criterion for firm maximization by the assumption of entrepreneurial expected utility maximization. Because of the unanimity results just mentioned, expected utility maximization implies stock market value maximization when there are stochastic constant returns to scale. In the present paper, unanimity is manifested in the observation made in the statement of theorem 1 that, when there are stochastic constant returns to scale, all firms produce at K^*, where K^* satisfies (51). Thus, the capital level chosen by all firms in a CSMEE is the same as that chosen in a Diamond equilibrium, whenever Diamond's firm maximization criterion is applicable, i.e., whenever there are stochastic constant returns to scale. Diamond showed that his equilibrium was efficient in a sense consistent with definition 5. His concept of efficiency differed from definition 5 because he did not explicitly consider firm entry and exit or the efficient number of firms. Theorem 2 generalizes this efficiency result of Diamond to the class of technologies g not satisfying stochastic constant returns to scale but in which free entry is permitted. In the case of stochastic constant returns to scale, we obtain a somewhat stronger result than simply efficiency in the sense of definition 5. Specifically, the observation that all firms produce at K^* implies that the CSMEE *allocation of capital* is the same in all respects as the first-best efficient allocation of capital. Since all firms produce at the same K level, the equality (80) required for first-best efficiency is satisfied. This implies that the distribution of capital across firms is efficient. In order to prove that the efficient K level at which all firms should produce is K^* and that the efficient number of firms is $1/(1 + K^*)$, we note that (81) implies (51) when g satisfies (47). In spite of the fact that capital is efficiently allocated, the allocation of risk remains inefficient in the Arrow-Debreu sense because (79) fails to hold.

By interpreting the technology differently, we can reveal the features of our model which permit the generalization of Diamond's result. Specifically, there is a sense in which the technology studied here exhibits not only stochastic constant returns to scale, but constant returns to scale. This property is introduced by our assumption that the technology described by g can be replicated without limit at a cost of one unit of capital per replication. From this point of view, the technology is more accurately represented by the production set

$$(87) \quad \{(y_1,\ldots,y_S,Z) = \left(\int_0^\infty g(K,x_1)\eta(dK),\ldots,\int_0^\infty g(K,x_S)\eta(dK), \right.$$

$$\left. \int_0^\infty [1 + K]\eta(dK) \right) : \eta \text{ is a nonnegative measure on the}$$

Lebesgue measurable subsets of $[0,\infty)$ with

$$\int_0^\infty [1 + K]\eta(dK) < \infty \}.$$

Since this production set is a cone, it exhibits constant returns to scale and *a fortiori* stochastic constant returns to scale in a sense which is slightly more general than that considered by Diamond. The added generality arises because Diamond's production sets are one-dimensional cones.

It should be emphasized that it is precisely the replication possibilities embodied in the free entry assumption which imply the linearity of the production set and thereby lead to the fulfillment of the stochastic constant returns to scale hypothesis.

From this point of view, theorem 2 could be viewed as an extension of Diamond's results to the more general linear technology sets described by (87).

When there is no uncertainty, a CSMEE is the same as a long-run perfectly competitive equilibrium in which entry forces price to equal minimum average cost. To see this, we can view the case of no uncertainty as a special case in which (47) holds with $x = 1$. In this case, a CSMEE is again characterized by the fact that $K = K^*$ for all firms. As before, K^* is determined by (51) and is as shown in figure 5.3. Furthermore, for any r, K^* is the K level which minimizes the average cost $(r(1 + K)/h(K))$.

5.7   CSMEE When $N \neq N_C$

As mentioned earlier, there may exist CSMEE for expectation functions N different from N_C. If so, there should, in fact, be a profusion of such equilibria. Suppose, for example, that we choose an arbitrary $\bar{K}$. Assume now that, for any $B, N(\bar{K}B) = N_C(\bar{K},B)$ but that $N(K,B) <$ $N_C(K,B)$ if $K \neq \bar{K}$. We can then find an $\bar{r}$ and $(\hat{\gamma}_1,\ldots,\hat{\gamma}_n)$ such that, for every i, $\hat{\gamma}_i$ maximizes

$$Eu\left(A + \bar{r}[1 - \hat{\gamma}_i(1 + \bar{K})] + \hat{\gamma}_i g(\bar{K}\tilde{x}), i\right)$$

and such that

$$v = \sum_{i=1}^{n} \mu_i\hat{\gamma}_i = \frac{1}{1 + \bar{K}}.$$

The problem of finding such an equilibrium is simply one of finding a competitive market equilibrium when there is one sure asset and one risky asset with return vector $(g(\bar{K},x_1),\ldots,g(\bar{K},x_S))$. Every investor has $1/(1 + \bar{K})$ initial shares in the risky asset and A units of the sure asset. If $N(K,B)$ is sufficiently small relative to $N_C(K,B)$ when $K \neq \bar{K}$, it may be possible to interpret this asset market equilibrium as a CSMEE with the given N function. In this CSMEE, the only firms ever created will be those employing $\bar{K}$ units of operating capital. Because $N(\bar{K},B) = N_C(\bar{K},B)$, every individual will be indifferent between remaining a capitalist and creating a firm operating at $\bar{K}$.

To demonstrate that we have in fact a CSMEE, it remains to be shown that it is not to any agent's advantage to set up a firm (or several firms) with $K \neq \bar{K}$ and hold them completely. We conjecture that a way of constructing an equilibrium with this property is to take $\bar{K}$ close to a K level obtained in a CSMEE with $N = N_C$. Then, the equilibrium interest rate $\bar{r}$ should be close to r, the interest rate associated with the CSMEE, with $N = N_C$, and we can be assured, by taking $\bar{K}$ close enough to K, of obtaining a utility level for i which is higher than what i can obtain by himself.

Finally, it is worth noting that there is no guarantee that a CSMEE with nonclassical expectations is Pareto superior to the equilibrium obtained without a stock market (Kihlstrom and Laffont 1979).

5.8   Fixed Costs, Uncertainty, and the Need for a Stock Market

In this section we will argue, using the present model, that the necessity for a stock market arises from the existence of the fixed costs incurred in setting up a firm and from the presence of uncertainty. As mentioned in the introduction, the fact that the stock market plays a nontrivial role in the economy studied here follows from a comparison of the equilibrium of the stock market economy with the equilibrium of the same economy without a stock market. In Kihlstrom and Laffont (1979), we studied the equilibrium achieved in the non–stock market economy. That equilibrium differs in several ways from the one achieved with a stock market. First, without a stock market, some individuals strictly prefer to be capitalists rather than entrepreneurs while others strictly prefer to be entrepreneurs. In contrast, in the stock market model of this paper, all individuals are indifferent about their role as entrepreneurs or nonentrepreneurs. This is true because without a stock market only entrepreneurs bear the risks associated with the firms they create. Nonentrepreneurs bear no risks. As a result of the lack of risk sharing opportunities, the marginal condition (61) does not hold in the non–stock market economy. Furthermore, in contrast to the stock market economy in which $N = N_C$, the non–stock market economy is inefficient in Diamond's second-best sense. If, in addition, there is only one type of individual, a stock market equilibrium in which $N = N_C$ is efficient in the unrestricted sense while the non–stock market equilibrium is not. These observations imply that the introduction of the stock market plays an essential role in improving the efficiency of the economy's operation.[1] As we shall now show, this is not true if there is neither uncertainty nor a fixed cost to setting up a firm.

In the model discussed above, the fixed cost is borne in the form of the one unit of entrepreneurial capital required to create a firm. In general, we could have assumed that the fixed cost was c units of capital, where $c \neq 1$. In order to extend the analysis to this trivially different case, it would of course be necessary to assume that there exists a $K(x)$ at which

$$(88) \qquad g(K(x),x) = g_K(K(x),x)[K(x) + c].$$

Thus, figure 5.1 would be replaced by figure 5.4.

In this case $N_C(K,B)$ would, of course, equal $K + c - B$.

If $c = 0$, the assumption that a $K(x)$ exists which satisfies (88) implies that $g(K,x) = Kx$. Thus, g not only must exhibit stochastic constant returns to scale, but must, in fact, be a constant returns to scale function. In this case figure 5.4 becomes figure 5.5, and $K(x)$ is not unique. As a result, the equilibrium K^* will not be unique. There will also be no need for a stock market in which to sell firm shares. This is true since any $(\hat{\gamma}_i, \hat{K}_i)$ choice which is optimal for i will be indifferent to some other choice $(\check{\gamma}_i, \check{K}_i)$ with $\check{\gamma}_i = 1$ and $\check{K}_i = \hat{\gamma}_i \hat{K}_i$. Specifically, i's state x wealth from $(\hat{\gamma}_i, \hat{K}_i)$ is $A + r[1 + \hat{\gamma}_i \hat{K}_i] + \hat{\gamma}_i \hat{K}_i x$ and this equals $A + r[1 + \check{K}_i] + \check{K}_i x$ if $\check{K}_i = \hat{\gamma}_i \hat{K}_i$.

When $\check{\gamma}_i = 1$, the stock market is unnecessary. Every individual can simply create his own firm and hold it. This is feasible since there are no fixed costs to setting up the firm. This point has also been made in the context of a sharecropping model by Stiglitz (1974) and Newbery (1977).

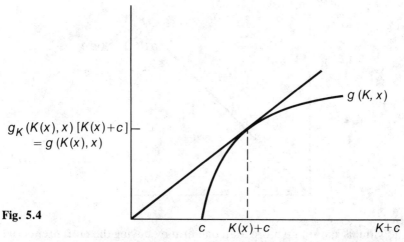

$g_K(K(x),x)[K(x)+c]$
$= g(K(x),x)$

Fig. 5.4

With $c > 0$ and $N(K,B) = K + c - B$, $\hat{\gamma}_i$ will in general differ from one. Because fixed costs are positive, it is not feasible for every investor to set up his own firm. Thus, the stock market is essential for the exchange of shares between entrepreneurs and capitalists, i.e., between those who do not create firms but who want to hold firm shares.

It should also be added that the need for a stock market is eliminated when there is no uncertainty. This is true even if there are fixed costs, i.e., even if c is positive.

Without stock trading, $1/(1 + K^*)$ individuals create firms and raise all operating capital by issuing debt. Their profits are

$$h(K^*) - rK^* = h(K^*) - \frac{h(K^*)}{1 + K^*}K^* = \frac{h(K^*)}{1 + K^*} = r.$$

The remaining $K^*/(1 + K^*)$ capitalists each receive their marginal product $h'(K^*) = r$ by selling their capital in the debt market. Thus, without a stock market all capitalists and all entrepreneurs have a final wealth which equals $A + r$.

This same result can also be obtained with a stock market, but it cannot be improved on. If there were a stock exchange in which some individual sold $(1 - \gamma)$ capital units in the debt market while investing γ units in firm shares, his return would be

$$r(1 - \gamma) + \gamma[h(K^*) - rK^*] = r.$$

As noted, this is the same wealth he would obtain as an entrepreneur or as a capitalist when there is no stock market.

The need for a stock market is also eliminated if all type 1 individuals are risk neutral and if there are sufficiently many of these individuals to result in the satisfaction of (55). For the stock market to be superfluous in this case, however, it may be necessary to assume that risk neutral

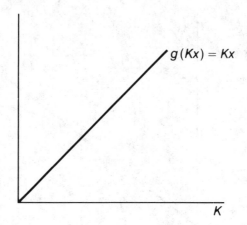

Fig. 5.5

individuals can set up more than one firm by buying the entrepreneurial capital in the debt market. If this is possible, the argument just given for the case of no uncertainty can be modified by replacing $h(K)$ with $Eg(K,\tilde{x})$. With this modification it can be shown that all risk neutral individuals can receive an expected wealth of $A + r$ by becoming entrepreneurs (possibly for more than one firm) and retaining all firm shares or by being capitalists. It can also be shown that all risk averse individuals receive a sure wealth of $A + r$ by remaining capitalists and holding no shares. Again, the introduction of a stock market fails to permit an improvement on this allocation of final wealth.

In Kihlstrom and Laffont (1979), entrepreneurs cannot set up more than one firm by buying entrepreneurial capital in the debt market. Thus, in the equilibrium of that paper it is possible that not all firms are held by the risk neutral individuals even though (55) holds.

5.9   Survey of Related Literature

The survey of this section describes the post-Diamond literature and relates it to the present paper. We first consider the literature on the possibility of stockholder unanimity.

As mentioned in the introduction, Leland (1974) used Diamond's framework to show that the production plan which maximizes stock market value receives unanimous shareholder approval. The same result was obtained for a slightly broader class of technologies—specifically, those which satisfy a condition referred to as spanning—by Ekern and Wilson (1974) and Radner (1974). Grossman and Stiglitz (1977) subsequently clarified the role of the competitivity assumption in the discussion of unanimity.

Hart (1979) has shown that even without spanning, unanimous agreement on market value maximization can be achieved in economies with a large number of firms. A similar result obtains in our model. Even if the production function does not satisfy a spanning condition, all equilibrium shareholders of every firm are unanimous about the goals of the firm. This unanimity is achieved because of the clientele effect described in proposition 4. This effect arises because of a process of market self-selection that results in firms each of which are held by identical stockholders who therefore agree completely on the firm's operation. Except in special cases, which, of course, include spanning and stochastic constant returns to scale, there is not, however, unanimity across firms. This happens because firms held by individuals of different types, in general, choose different operating capital levels. One case, not mentioned earlier, in which there is always unanimity across firms occurs when the utility functions of all agents are from a class for which portfolio separation holds. If, for example, the utility functions $u(\bullet, i)$ are all risk averse and all exhibit constant absolute risk aversion, then they will all choose to hold firms operated at the same K level which will in general differ from K^{*}.[2]

The post-Diamond stock market literature on efficiency includes contributions by Hart (1975, 1977, 1979), Drèze (1974), Grossman and Hart (1979), Helpman and Razin (1978), Stiglitz (1972, 1975), Jensen and Long (1972), and Merton and Subrahmanyam (1974). In addition, the literature on sharecropping contains the closely related work of Stiglitz (1974) and Newbery (1977) discussed in section 5.8.

Hart (1975) showed that Diamond's results could not be extended to the case in which there were several goods traded in spot markets which opened after the resolution of uncertainty.

Drèze (1974) proposed a criterion for firm behavior which was implementable even when the technology failed to satisfy stochastic constant returns to scale. Drèze's approach was suggested by his observation that the firm's choices of production plans are, in general, public goods for the shareholders. Firms, in effect, choose the assets available to investors. This observation had been made earlier by Smith (1970) and is also the basis for a later contribution by Helpman and Razin (1978). Drèze exploited the public good interpretation by defining an equilibrium in which the firm used the stockholder's "Lindahl prices" to compute a value of each production decision. It is this value which he assumed the firm maximized, *taking the distribution of ownership as given*. He observed a nonconvexity in the consumption space implied by the stock market model. Drèze's criterion for firm maximization avoided the difficulties usually created by nonconvexities precisely because firms treated ownership shares parametrically and because investors took production decisions as given when choosing a portfolio of ownership shares. The cost of decentralized decision making in Drèze's model is the possibility of inefficient equilibria.

The justification for Drèze's approach varies. Gevers (1974) provides a rationale based on majority voting without side-payments. Grossman and Hart (1979) give an argument in favor of a closely related criterion. Their argument is in the spirit of Hart's earlier paper (1977) and is based on the possibility of a takeover.

One important point to be observed is that the public good externality observed by Drèze fails to arise when there are stochastic constant returns to scale. In this case, the firms have no control over the assets which will be available to investors. An alternative method by which constrained efficiency can be restored is to devise a framework in which the separation of production and investment decisions is eliminated, i.e., in which the externality is internalized. In our model each individual can, if he finds it necessary, jointly make the production and investment decisions by becoming an entrepreneur. As pointed out earlier, not all individuals find it necessary to exercise this option in our equilibrium. For any given individual, there are many individuals who become entrepreneurs and run firms in accordance with the given individual's desires.

There is a potential problem which must be faced in any attempt to coordinate production and investment decisions. Specifically, such coordination reintroduces the nonconvexity Drèze avoided by decentralization. In our model, this nonconvexity enters in the objective function of entrepreneurs. Fortunately, the problem created by this nonconvexity is not fundamental. This is demonstrated in our lemma 2, which establishes the uniqueness of the solution to the entrepreneurs' maximization problem.

Hart (1977) shows that the inefficient Drèze equilibria can be eliminated in large economies by permitting takeovers. A situation qualifies as a takeover bid equilibrium if it is a Drèze equilibrium for which no takeover is possible. In Hart's model, the agent who takes over internalizes the externality by buying the firm, reorganizing production, and selling shares. This agent plays the role of our entrepreneur. The possibility of a takeover becomes a force which results in efficiency. In our model, this force is provided by the possibility of entry.

Helpman and Razin (1978) suppress the separation of decisions by setting up a (participation) noncooperative game in which each agent contributes a share of input. However, in this game the contribution of an agent creates an externality of the atmosphere type (since the production depends on the *sum* of individual inputs). Then a uniform subsidy on the input contribution activity financed by lump sum transfers helps restore efficiency. However, there seems to be no reason why an agent should take the value of the firm (i.e., here the value of future outputs) as independent of his actions (since he provides inputs); a large-number assumption seems to be required to justify this "competitive" behavior.

Sticking to the public good analogy, Hart's takeover bid equilibrium is analogous to a Foley politico-equilibrium, Helpman and Razin's participation equilibrium is analogous to an equilibrium with subscription made efficient by an appropriate tax system, and our entrepreneurial equilibrium is similar to a Tiebout equilibrium.

There exists, in financial economics, a closely related literature which uses a special model, the mean-variance model.

Two cases must be distinguished, the case of independently distributed production functions where a general technology is used and the case of partially correlated returns where the assumption of multiplicative uncertainty is made.

Let us first consider the case where some correlation exists. The mean-variance model permits the derivation of the equilibrium value of the firm as a function of its investment policy. Using such a model, Stiglitz (1972) showed that the stock market equilibrium was inefficient. The inefficiency can be attributed to noncompetitive behavior on the part of firms which take into account the nonproportional effect of their investment policy on their equilibrium value. The externality argument cannot be invoked here to explain the inefficiency since multiplicative uncertainty is assumed. Jensen and Long (1972) have shown that in this model the equilibrium converges to a Pareto optimum as the number of firms goes to infinity. Indeed, as the number of firms goes to infinity, the noncompetitive value maximization behavior is transformed into competitive behavior, so that in the limit we are in a special case of Diamond (1967).

Merton and Subrahmanyam (1974) have argued that perfect competition requires perfect correlation since all technologies should be available to all individuals. It is also the point of view we have taken in this paper. Allowing free entry at a zero cost, they show that Jensen and Long's model (with noncompetitive behavior) is unstable with respect to the number of firms. Free entry is shown to lead to an infinite number of firms and Pareto optimality. The case of positive set up costs was subsequently considered by Stiglitz (1975).

There remains the case of *completely independent* firms. Without (Stiglitz 1972) or with (Jensen and Long 1972) multiplicative uncertainty, one does not obtain efficiency in the limit. This shows that the difficulty comes from the fact that in this case noncompetitive behavior is not transformed into competitive behavior in the limit. In fact, Merton and Subrahmanyam have argued that with free entry the limit of these noncompetitive equilibria does not even exist. They also considered the case of competitive behavior and multiplicative uncertainty. In this case, they showed that the economy was Diamond efficient in the small-numbers case as well as in the limit. This result is to be expected from Diamond's analysis.

Finally, we mention the paper of Novshek and Sonnenschein (1978), who consider a model without uncertainty but with free entry, fixed costs, and noncompetitive behavior. They show that when fixed costs are small relative to demand and when demand curves slope down, the noncompetitive Cournot equilibrium exists and approximates the perfectly competitive equilibrium in which price equals minimum average cost. Thus, when there is no uncertainty, the Novshek-Sonnenschein equilibrium will approximate the equilibrium described in this paper if the demand curves slope down.

Appendix 1

The proof of proposition 2 is based on the two simple lemmas which follow.

Lemma A1. If $\alpha \in E$ and $\alpha' \in C$, if $u(\cdot, \alpha) = u(\cdot, \alpha')$, and if (18) holds, then (17) holds. If α and α' are in E, if $u(\cdot, \alpha) = u(\cdot, \alpha')$, and if (19) holds, then for some k,

$$\text{(A1)} \quad k = N(K(\alpha), B(\alpha)) + B(\alpha) - K(\alpha) = N(K(\alpha'), B(\alpha'))$$
$$+ B(\alpha') - K(\alpha').$$

Proof. Consider first the case in which $\alpha \in E$ and $\alpha' \in C$. The equilibrium choice, call it $(\hat{K}(\alpha), \hat{B}(\alpha))$, is α's maximizing choice for these values. Once $(K(\alpha), B(\alpha))$ is fixed at these values, the equilibrium $\Gamma(\alpha)$ is chosen to solve

$$\max_{\Gamma(\alpha)} Eu(\widetilde{W}_E(\hat{K}(\alpha), \hat{B}(\alpha), \Gamma(\alpha)), \alpha)$$

and

$$\text{(A2)} \quad \max_{\Gamma(\alpha)} Eu(\widetilde{W}_E(\hat{K}(\alpha), \hat{B}(\alpha), \Gamma(\alpha)), \alpha)$$

$$= \max_{\substack{\Gamma(\alpha) \\ K(\alpha) \\ B(\alpha)}} Eu(w_E(K(\alpha), B(\alpha), \Gamma(\alpha)), \alpha).$$

If now

$$\text{(A3)} \quad N(\hat{K}(\alpha), \hat{B}(\alpha)) < 1 + \hat{K}(\alpha) - \hat{B}(\alpha),$$

then

$$\text{(A4)} \quad \max_{\Gamma(\alpha)} Eu(\widetilde{W}_E(\hat{K}(\alpha), \hat{B}(\alpha), \Gamma(\alpha)), \alpha) < \max_{\Gamma(\alpha')} Eu(\widetilde{W}_C(\Gamma(\alpha')), \alpha').$$

This is so as a result of two facts. First, each portfolio that α is able to choose can also be chosen by α'. Second, for each portfolio $\Gamma(\alpha)$, (A3) will imply that

$$\widetilde{W}_E(\hat{K}(\alpha), \hat{B}(\alpha), \Gamma(\alpha)) < \widetilde{W}_C(\Gamma(\alpha))$$

with probability one. Taken together (A2) and (A4) assert that (18) fails. As a consequence (18) implies

$$N(K(\alpha), B(\alpha)) \geq 1 + K(\alpha) - B(\alpha),$$

which together with proposition 1 implies (17). A similar argument establishes (A1). QED.

Lemma A2. Suppose that $u(\cdot, \alpha) = u(\cdot, \alpha')$. *If* $\alpha' \in C$ *and* $\alpha \in E$ *and if* $\Gamma(\alpha', \{\alpha\}) = 0$, *then* (18) *holds. If* α *and* α' *are in* E *and* $\Gamma(\alpha', \{\alpha\}) = 0$, *then*

(A5)
$$\max_{\substack{\Gamma(\alpha') \\ K(\alpha') \\ B(\alpha')}} \mathrm{E}u(\widetilde{W}_E(K(\alpha'), B(\alpha'), \Gamma(\alpha')), \alpha')$$

$$\geq \max_{\substack{\Gamma(\alpha) \\ K(\alpha) \\ B(\alpha)}} Eu(\widetilde{W}_E(K(\alpha), B(\alpha), \Gamma(\alpha)), \alpha).$$

Proof. If $\Gamma(\alpha', \{\alpha\}) = 0$, then α's firm is not significant in the portfolio of α'. If the right side of (18) was exceeded by the left, α would prefer to switch his role from entrepreneur to capitalist. Since his firm is not significant in $\Gamma(\alpha')$, he can imitate α' and purchase this portfolio. This would yield him a higher utility than he has in the equilibrium. But then the equilibrium condition (12) must fail for α, a contradiction. This contradiction implies that the right side of (18) must exceed or equal the left side. The opposite inequality is obtained by a similar argument as is the inequality (A5). QED.

Proof of Proposition 2. The proof proceeds by treating each type i separately. We first consider those types in which there are capitalists. For such a type, we choose a specific capitalist α' and consider the set

$$P_{\alpha'} = \{\alpha : \alpha \text{ is an entrepreneur of type } i \text{ and } \Gamma(\alpha', \{\alpha\}) > 0\},$$

which is the set of entrepreneurs of type i in whose firms α' makes a significant investment. This set is of Lebesgue measure zero. Thus, for almost all entrepreneurs of type i, $\Gamma(\alpha', \{\alpha\}) = 0$. Because of this, lemmas A1 and A2 imply that (17) and (18) hold for almost all entrepreneurs of type i.

If there are capitalists of every type, the proof is completed by the above argument. Suppose, however, that there is some type i which contains no capitalists. If we choose an arbitrary entrepreneur α' of this type, it will again be true that $\mu(P_{\alpha'}) = 0$. Thus, again $\Gamma(\alpha', \{\alpha\}) = 0$ except for a set of type i entrepreneurs of measure zero. Since α' was chosen arbitrarily, lemma A2 implies that for any α' of type i, (A5) holds for almost all entrepreneurs α of type i. But this can only happen if (19) holds for almost all α and α' of type i. Thus, almost all entrepreneurs of type i must have the same expected utility in equilibrium. Then because of lemma A1 there must be a k such that (A1) holds for almost all α and α' of type i.

It now remains to be shown that $k = 1$. To accomplish this, we will show that if $k < 1$, then almost any entrepreneur of type i can raise his extended utility over that which he obtains in equilibrium by becoming a capitalist. The only problem that may arise in this argument is that by becoming capitalists and eliminating their firms, the type i entrepreneurs might lose significant investment opportunities.

To see how this possibility can be avoided, we must again choose some representative type i entrepreneur α'. He can be chosen so that (19) and (A1) hold for almost all other α of type i. As before, $\Gamma(\alpha',\{\alpha\}) = 0$ for almost all type i entrepreneurs α. Thus, almost any type i entrepreneur α can still buy the portfolio $\Gamma(\alpha')$ after exiting as an entrepreneur. If α does exit to become a capitalist and does buy $\Gamma(\alpha')$, his random income will be

$$A + r[1 - \int_E N(K(\beta), B(\beta))\Gamma(\alpha', d\beta)] + \int_E \tilde{\pi}(K(\beta), B(\beta))\Gamma(\alpha', d\beta).$$

With probability one this will exceed, by $1 - k$, the random equilibrium income of α', which is

$$A + r[k - \int_E N(K(\beta), B(\beta))\Gamma(\alpha', d\beta)] + \int_E \tilde{\pi}(K(\beta), B(\beta))\Gamma(\alpha', d\beta).$$

Thus, by becoming a capitalist and buying $\Gamma(\alpha')$, almost every entrepreneur α of type i can obtain a higher expected utility than α' does. But recall that the equilibrium expected utility of α' is equal to that of almost all entrepreneurs α of type i. Thus, when $k < 1$, almost all entrepreneurs of type i will prefer to be capitalists rather than entrepreneurs. Thus, $k < 1$ is not consistent with equilibrium. QED.

Appendix 2

Proof of Lemma 3. Note first that

(A6) $$F^i_{K_i}(K_i, C_i) = Eu'(\tilde{t}, i) \left[\frac{g_{K_i}(K_i, \tilde{x})}{(1 + K_i)} - \frac{g(K_i, \tilde{x})}{(1 + K_i)^2} \right]$$

and

(A7) $$F^i_{K_i K_i}(K_i, C_i) = Eu''(\tilde{t}, i) \left[\frac{g_{K_i}(K_i, \tilde{x})}{(1 + K_i)} - \frac{g(K_i, \tilde{x})}{(1 + K_i)^2} \right]^2$$
$$+ Eu'(\tilde{t}, i) \left[\frac{g_{K_i K_i}(K_i, \tilde{x})}{(1 + K_i)} - 2\frac{g_{K_i}(K_i, \tilde{x})}{(1 + K_i)^2} + 2\frac{g(K_i, \tilde{x})}{(1 + K_i)^3} \right],$$

where

$$\tilde{t} = A + r[1 - C_i] + C_i \frac{g(K_i,\tilde{x})}{1 + K_i}.$$

Also, notice that (A6) and (A7) imply that

(A8) $F^i_{K_i K_i}(K_i, C_i) = Eu''(\tilde{t},i)\left[\dfrac{g_{K_i}(K_i,\tilde{x})}{(1 + K_i)} - \dfrac{g(K_i,\tilde{x})}{(1 + K_i)^2}\right]^2$

$$+ Eu'(\tilde{t},i)\left[\frac{g_{K_i K_i}(K_i,\tilde{x})}{(1 + K_i)}\right] < 0,$$

if $F^i_{K_i}(K_i, C_i) = 0$. Since $g_{KK} < 0$ for all $x \ne \underline{x}$, the strict inequality in (A8) holds even if type i individuals are risk neutral and $u''(\bullet,i) = 0$. Thus, if there exists $\bar{K}_i(C_i)$ such that

$$F^i_{K_i}(\bar{K}_i(C_i), C_i) = 0,$$

then $\bar{K}_i(C_i)$ must be a unique global maximizer of $F^i(K_i, C_i)$.

We now prove that for each C_i and r, there exists a K_i satisfying $F^i_{K_i} = 0$, which, because of (A6), is equivalent to

(A9) $Eu'(\tilde{t},i)[g_{K_i}(K_i,\tilde{x})(1 + K_i) - g(K_i,\tilde{x})] = 0.$

Now under our assumptions

$$g_K(0,x)[1 + 0] - g(0,x) = g_K(0,x)\begin{cases} > 0 \text{ if } x \ne \underline{x} \\ = 0 \text{ if } x = \underline{x} \end{cases}.$$

By continuity, there exists a $\underline{K} > 0$ such that $K \le \underline{K}$ implies

$$g_K(K,x)[1 + K] - g(K,x) > 0 \text{ if } x \ne \underline{x}.$$

Thus $K_i \le \underline{K}$ implies

$$Eu'(\tilde{t},i)[g_{K_i}(K_i,\tilde{x})[1 + K_i] - g(K_i,\tilde{x})] > 0.$$

In addition, there exists a $\hat{K}$ such that $K_i \ge \hat{K}$ implies that

(A10) $g_{K_i}(K_i,x)[1 + K_i] - g(K_i,x) < 0$

for all $x \ne \underline{x}$. If $x = \underline{x}$, the difference on the left side of (A10) is zero. Thus, $K_i \ge \hat{K}$ implies

(A11) $Eu'(\tilde{t},i)[g_{K_i}(K_i,\tilde{x})(1 + K_i) - g(K_i,\tilde{x})] < 0.$

Now the continuity of u and g implies that there exists $\bar{K}_i(C_i) \in (\underline{K}, \hat{K})$ at which (A9) holds and $F^i(\bar{K}_i(C_i), C_i) = 0$. Implicit function theorem arguments guarantee that $\bar{K}_i(C_i)$ is a differentiable function of C_i and r.

If $u(\bullet,i)$ is linear, $u'(t,i)$ is independent of the value t taken by $\tilde{t}$. Thus, (A9) reduces to (49). If (47) holds, (A9) becomes

(A12) $Eu'(\tilde{t},i)[h'(K_i)(1+K_i)-h(K_i)]\tilde{x}$,

which is zero when (51) holds. As noted in the text, (51) and (49) are equivalent when g satisfies (47).

To prove that

(A13) $\lim_{C_i \to 0} \bar{K}_i(C_i) = K^*$,

recall that $\bar{K}_i(C_i)$ must be in the interval $[\underline{K},\hat{K}]$. If (A13) fails, there will be a sequence $\{C_i^m\}$ converging to zero such that

$$\lim_{m \to \infty} \bar{K}_i(C_i^m) = K^{**} \neq K^*,$$

where $K^{**} \in [\underline{K},\hat{K}]$. Since $F^i_{K_i}$ is continuous in K_i and C_i,

$$\lim_{m \to \infty} F_{K_i}(\bar{K}_i(C_i),C_i) = F_{K_i}(K^{**},0)$$

$$= \frac{1}{(1+K^{**})}u'(A+r,i)E[g_{K_i}(K^{**},\tilde{x})(1+K^{**})-g_{K_i}(K^{**},\tilde{x})] \neq 0.$$

But for each m,

$$F^i_{K_i}(\bar{K}_i(C_i^m),C_i^m) = 0,$$

so that

$$\lim_{m \to \infty} F_{K_i}(\bar{K}_i(C_i^m),C_i^m) = 0.$$

As a result of this contradiction, (A13) must hold. QED.

Proof of Lemma 4. We consider the risk neutral case first. In this case, lemma 3 and (52) imply

$$F^i(\bar{K}_i(C_i),C_i) = E[A + E\frac{g(K^*,\tilde{x})}{(1+K^*)}(1-C_i) + C_i\frac{g(K^*,\tilde{x})}{(1+K^*)}]$$

$$= A + E\frac{g(K^*,\tilde{x})}{(1+K^*)},$$

which is independent of C_i. Thus, C_i can be chosen arbitrarily. If (53) holds,

$$\frac{\partial}{\partial C_i}F^i(\bar{K}_i(C_i),C_i) = -r + \frac{Eg(K^*,\tilde{x})}{(1+K^*)} > 0.$$

Since the marginal utility of C_i is always positive for risk neutral individuals, they will choose C_i to equal the upper bound, $(A/r) + 1$, imposed by the constraint that the probability of bankruptcy must be zero. Finally, suppose that (54) holds. In this case,

$$\frac{\partial}{\partial C_i}F^i(\bar{K}_i(C_i),C_i) = -r + \frac{Eg(K^*,\tilde{x})}{(1+K^*)} < 0$$

and the optimal C_i is zero.

Now suppose that i is risk averse and consider first the cases in which (52) and (54) hold. Fix K_i at any level and note that

$$(A14) \qquad F^i_{C_i}(K_i,0) = u'(A + r,i)\left[-r + \frac{Eg(K_i,\tilde{x})}{(1 + K_i)}\right].$$

Since $u'(\bullet,i) > 0$ and K^* maximizes $(Eg(K,\tilde{x})/(1 + K))$, the expression for the derivative in (A14) is nonpositive if

$$r \geq \frac{Eg(K^*,\tilde{x})}{(1 + K^*)},$$

i.e., if (52) or (54) hold. Since

$$F^i_{C_iC_i}(K_i,C_i) = Eu''(\tilde{t},i)\left[-r + \frac{Eg(K_i,\tilde{x})}{(1 + K_i)}\right]^2 < 0,$$

it will never be optimal to let C_i be positive regardless of K_i. Thus, $\hat{C}_i = 0$ and $\hat{K}_i$ is arbitrary.

Finally, we consider the case in which (53) holds. First, recall that it was shown in lemma 3 that

$$\lim_{C_i \to 0} \bar{K}_i(C_i) = K^*.$$

Because of this and the continuity assumptions made about $u(\bullet,i)$ and g,

$$\lim_{C_i \to 0} F^i(\bar{K}_i(C_i),C_i) = F^i(K^*,0) = u(A + r,i).$$

For $C_i \in (0,(A/r) + 1]$, lemma 3 implies that $\bar{K}_i(C_i)$ is differentiable and therefore continuous. Thus, $F^i(\bar{K}_i(C_i),C_i)$ is continuous on the entire interval $[0, (A/r) + 1]$. It therefore attains a maximum $\bar{C}_i$ on this interval. We let $\hat{K}_i = \bar{K}_i(\bar{C}_i)$ and $\hat{C}_i = \bar{C}_i$.

It remains to be shown that $\hat{C}_i > 0$. If $(\partial/\partial C_i) F^i(\bar{K}_i(C_i),C_i)$ exists at $C_i = 0$, the positivity of $\hat{C}_i > 0$ can be established by proving

$$(A15) \qquad \frac{\partial}{\partial C_i} F^i(\bar{K}_i(0),0) > 0.$$

Unfortunately, even the differentiability of $u(\bullet,i)$ and of g together with (50) does not imply the existence of $(\partial/\partial C_i) F^i(\bar{K}_i(0),0)$. As a result, a more complicated proof is required.

First, recall that, because of lemma 3, $\bar{K}_i(C_i)$ is a differentiable function of C_i on $(0,(A/r) + 1]$. Thus, the differentiability of $u(\bullet,i)$ and g imply that $(\partial/\partial C_i) F^i(\bar{K}_i(C_i),C_i)$ exists on this interval. Furthermore, when this derivative exists, the envelope theorem implies that

$$(A16) \qquad \frac{\partial}{\partial C_i} F^i(\bar{K}_i(C_i),C_i) = Eu'(\tilde{t},i)\left[-r + \frac{g(\bar{K}_i(C_i),\tilde{x})}{(1 + \bar{K}_i(C_i))}\right].$$

The continuity of $u'(\cdot,i)$ and of g, the limiting result (50), and the expression (A16) imply that, for C_i sufficiently small, $(\partial/\partial C_i)$ $F^i(\bar{K}_i(C_i), C_i)$ is approximately

$$(A17) \qquad u'(A + r, i)\left[-r + \frac{Eg(K^*, \tilde{x})}{(1 + K^*)}\right],$$

which is positive because of (53). Thus, $F^i(K_i(C_i), C_i)$ is a strictly increasing function near zero. As a result, $\hat{C}_i$ cannot equal zero; i.e., $\hat{C}_i > 0$.

It should be noted that when $(\partial/\partial C_i)$ $F^i(\bar{K}_i(0), 0)$ exists, it equals the expression in (A17) and is therefore positive as required in (A15). QED.

Notes

1. As mentioned in section 5.7, the introduction of a stock market may not improve efficiency if $N \neq N_C$. This can occur because the stock market may not be Diamond efficient in this case.

2. If, specifically, $u(I, i) = -\exp(-a_i I)$, then it is easily verified that for each i, $K_i = \bar{\bar{K}}$, where $\bar{\bar{K}}$ satisfies

$$E\left\{\left[g_K(\bar{\bar{K}}, \tilde{x}) - \frac{g(\bar{\bar{K}}, \tilde{x})}{(1 + \bar{\bar{K}})}\right] \exp\left[\left(\sum_{i=1}^{n} \mu_i a_i^{-1}\right)^{-1} \frac{g(\bar{\bar{K}}, \tilde{x})}{(1 + \bar{\bar{K}})}\right]\right\} = 0.$$

The equilibrium is completely described if we now let $\nu = 1/(1 + \bar{\bar{K}})$,

$$\gamma_1 = \left[\sum_{i=1}^{n} \mu_i a_i^{-1}\right]^{-1} \frac{a_1^{-1}}{(1 + \bar{\bar{K}})},$$

$$\gamma_i = \frac{a_1 \gamma_1}{a_i},$$

and

$$r = \frac{E\left\{g_K(\bar{\bar{K}}, \tilde{x}) \exp\left[\left(\sum_{i=1}^{n} \mu_i a_i^{-1}\right)^{-1} \frac{g(\bar{\bar{K}}, \tilde{x})}{(1 + \bar{\bar{K}})}\right]\right\}}{E\left\{\exp\left[\left(\sum_{i=1}^{n} \mu_i a_i^{-1}\right)^{-1} \frac{g(\bar{\bar{K}}, \tilde{x})}{(1 + \bar{\bar{K}})}\right]\right\}}.$$

Note that $\bar{\bar{K}}$ is not equal to K^*.

References

Arrow, K. J. 1953. Le role des valeurs boursieres pour la repartition la meilleure des risques. *Econometrie*. Colloques Internationaux du Centre National de la Recherche Scientifique, vol. 11, pp. 41–47. Paris. English translation: 1963. The role of securities in the optimal allocation of risk-bearing. *Review of Economic Studies* 31, no. 4: 91–96.

Aumann, R. J. 1964. Markets with a continuum of traders. *Econometrica* 32: 39–50.

Baron, D. 1979. Investment policy, optimality, and the mean-variance model. *Journal of Finance* 34: 206–32.

Debreu, G. 1959. *Theory of value*. New York: Wiley.

Diamond, P. 1967. The role of a stock market in a general equilibrium model with technological uncertainty. *American Economic Review* 57: 759–76.

Drèze, J. 1974. Investment under private ownership: Optimality, equilibrium, and stability. In Drèze, J., ed., *Allocation under uncertainty: Equilibrium and optimality*, chap. 9. London: Macmillan.

Ekern, S., and Wilson, R. 1974. On the theory of the firm in an economy with incomplete markets. *Bell Journal of Economics and Management Science* 5: 171–80.

Gevers, L. 1974. Competitive equilibrium of the stock exchange and Pareto efficiency. In Drèze, J., ed., *Allocation under uncertainty: Equilibrium and optimality*, chap. 10. London: Macmillan.

Grossman, S., and Hart, O. 1979. A theory of competitive equilibrium in stock market economies. *Econometrica* 47: 293–330.

Grossman, S., and Stiglitz, J. 1977. On value maximization and alternative objectives of the firm. *Journal of Finance* 32: 389–402.

Hart, O. 1975. On the optimality of equilibrium when markets are incomplete. *Journal of Economic Theory* 11: 418–43.

————. 1977. Takeover bids and stock market equilibrium. *Journal of Economic Theory* 16: 53–83.

————. 1979. On shareholder unanimity in large stock market economies. *Econometrica* 47: 1057–84.

Helpman, E., and Razin, A. 1978. Participation equilibrium and the efficiency of the stock market allocation. *International Economic Review* 19: 129–40.

Jensen, M. C., and Long, J. B. 1972. Corporate investment under uncertainty and Pareto optimality in the capital markets. *Bell Journal of Economics and Management Science* 3: 151–74.

Kihlstrom, R., and Laffont, J. J. 1979. A general equilibrium entrepreneurial theory of firm formation based on risk aversion. *Journal of Political Economy* 87: 719–48.

————. 1980. General equilibrium in a labor managed economy with uncertainty and incomplete markets. CARESS Working Paper 80–19, University of Pennsylvania.

Leland, H. 1974. Production theory and the stock market. *Bell Journal of Economics and Management Science* 5: 125–44.

Merton, R., and Subrahmanyam, M. 1974. The optimality of a competitive stock market. *Bell Journal of Economics and Management Science* 5: 145–70.

Modigliani, F., and Miller, M. 1958. The cost of capital, corporation finance, and the theory of investment. *American Economic Review* 48: 433–43.

Newbery, D. M. G. 1977. Risk sharing, sharecropping, and uncertain labor markets. *Review of Economic Studies* 44: 585–94.

Novshek, W., and Sonnenschein, H. 1978. Cournot equilibrium and Walras equilibrium. *Journal of Economic Theory* 19: 223–55.

Radner, R. 1974. A note on unanimity of stockholder's preferences among alternative production plans: A reformulation of the Ekern-Wilson model. *Bell Journal of Economics and Management Science* 5: 181–86.

Smith, V. 1970. Corporate financial theory under uncertainty. *Quarterly Journal of Economics* 84: 451–72.

Stiglitz, J. 1972. On the optimality of the stock market allocation of investment. *Quarterly Journal of Economics* 86: 25–60.

———. 1974. Incentives and risk in sharecropping. *Review of Economic Studies* 41: 219–55.

———. 1975. Monopolistic competition and the capital market. Technical Report 161, IMSSS. Stanford University.

Comment   David Levhari

The paper by Kihlstrom and Laffont is another example of the efficient use of the continuum of traders model to show the optimality of competition. In this particular application it is shown that stock market equilibrium provides a constrained optimum in Diamond's sense without having to use the special assumptions on production and uncertainty that Diamond adopts in his paper. Kihlstrom and Laffont allow firms to possess a regular U-shaped cost function, and yet the equilibrium generated possesses the properties of social optimum in Diamond's sense. Somehow, the existence of a continuum of traders allows us to use some sort of a "law of large numbers" so that the ensuing equilibrium is socially efficient.

The assumptions of Kihlstrom and Laffont are also somewhat special. All individuals have identical abilities, and all of them face identical random variables. There are no learning possibilities, and no changing of subjective probability distributions is allowed. All individuals are similarly endowed. There is no distinction between control and ownership. Thus, there is no distinction between the entrepreneurs and the firms they establish in the aims of maximization.

David Levhari is professor of economics at Hebrew University, Jerusalem.

With respect to the Aumann-like continuum of traders model, one wonders whether there is also a limiting theorem that as the number of traders tends to infinity in a regular fashion, the market equilibrium becomes efficient. That is, the question is whether a Debreu-Scarf structure can be established to prove that as the number of traders grows in some regular fashion, the market equilibrium tends to an optimal allocation.

Some of the questions that come to mind are as follows: What are the essential simplifications in Diamond that allow him to obtain his results without invoking a continuum of traders? Is the assumption in Kihlstrom and Laffont that firms face identical random variables not oversimplistic? Is it possible to build a framework of similar nature in which firms' ownership and control are not identical and the attitudes of the firms toward risky ventures cannot be identified with those of the entrepreneurs?

The paper is thus an interesting use of the continuum of traders model to show equivalence, in the Aumann sense, between equilibrium and efficiency of allocation, and one may just wonder whether other realistic and possibly more complex assumptions can be incorporated in the present model.

6   Multiperiod Securities and the Efficient Allocation of Risk: A Comment on the Black-Scholes Option Pricing Model

David M. Kreps

6.1 Introduction

Over the past six years, a great stir in academic financial theory (sometimes spilling over into practice) has been caused by the option pricing model originally advanced by Black and Scholes (1973) and by Merton (1973b).[1] The reason for this stir is that strong results are derived from what seem at first to be weak assumptions. While the weakness of these assumptions is illusory, the model does make an important point: The ability to trade securities frequently can enable a "few" multiperiod securities to span "many" states of nature. In the Black-Scholes model there are two securities and uncountably many states of nature, but because there are infinitely many trading opportunities and, what is crucial, because uncertainty resolves "nicely," markets are effectively complete. Thus the punchline: Perhaps even though there are far fewer securities than states of nature, nonetheless there is a complete (or nearly complete) set of contingent claims markets. Perhaps, therefore, risk is allocated efficiently.

The purpose of this paper is to explore this idea and to attempt to see what is important in determining the number of securities "needed" to have complete markets. In this regard, the following two questions will be addressed to some extent: (1) The Black-Scholes model has been criticized on the grounds that it takes as given that which any good

David M. Kreps is professor in the Graduate School of Business at Stanford University.

Discussions with J. M. Harrison, O. Hart, P. Milgrom, and especially R. Wilson have been very helpful to the author. This research was supported in part by National Science Foundation Grant SOC 77–07741 A01 to the Institute for Mathematical Studies in the Social Sciences, Stanford, by the Mellon Foundation, by the Churchill Foundation, and by a grant from the Social Sciences Research Council of the UK to the Department of Applied Economics, Cambridge.

economist would want endogenously determined: equilibrium prices of the few multiperiod securities. This is a valid criticism because those prices are the critical data in determining whether markets are complete. To what extent, then, is it reasonable to suppose that equilibrium prices will have the property required for complete markets? (2) In what sense, if any, is the Black-Scholes result robust? It will be seen that the property required for complete markets concerns the very delicate fine structure of the model. Other models that approximate the Black-Scholes model in a standard sense do not possess this property. Do these other models have "approximately complete" markets? One hopes that the answer is yes. Otherwise, one either must be able to discern the critical fine structure or must discard the conclusions of the Black-Scholes model for practical purposes.

The paper is divided into two parts. The first part contains an analysis of the basic issues in the spirit of Radner (1972). In section 6.2 a multiperiod exchange economy with uncertainty is formulated. The economy is specified by a finite state space Ω, a collection of agents, a finite set of dates $t = 0, 1, \ldots, T$ at which agents consume, and an exogenously specified information structure, which describes what information (all) agents know at each date. Formally, the information structure is a sequence of nondecreasingly finer partitions of Ω, $\{F_t; t = 0, \ldots, T\}$. The interpretation is that at date t, all agents know which cell of F_t contains the true state and no more. There is a single consumption good which serves as numeraire. Finally, there are N "long-lived" securities that allow agents to trade consumption between dates and states. Each security is a contingent claim to consumption at the terminal date T. Markets where these securities can be exchanged for each other and for the consumption good open at each date t, with $p = \{p_n(t, \omega); n = 1, \ldots, N, t = 0, \ldots, T, \omega \in \Omega\}$ the price process of the securities. A definition of an equilibrium for this economy is given, exactly as in Radner (1972). Every such equilibrium is given an alternate characterization, as an equilibrium in a Debreu-style economy where a (possibly incomplete) set of contingent claims markets opens at date zero.

The basic question is posed and answered in section 6.3: Under what conditions will the corresponding Debreu-style economy be one with a complete set of markets (so that the equilibrium allocation is Pareto efficient)? A necessary and sufficient condition for this is: For $t < T$ and $A \in F_t$, let $K(t, A)$ be the cardinality of $\{A' \in F_{t+1}; A' \subseteq A\}$. Then it is necessary and sufficient that for every t and $A \in F_t$, the span of the conditional support of $p(t + 1)$ given $\omega \in A$ has dimension $K(t, A)$. Therefore, a necessary condition is that N, the number of securities, must be at least $K = \max\{K(t, A)\}$. This is illustrated by a simple example that makes the basic point: With N securities and T trading dates ($t = 0, \ldots, T - 1$), up to N^T states of nature can be spanned.

While it is necessary for complete markets that $K \leq N$, this is not sufficient. The necessary and sufficient conditions involve the equilibrium prices p, and this is clearly less than satisfactory on economic grounds. A refinement is given in section 6.4 that is more satisfactory. Fixing everything except the terminal payoffs of the securities (that is, fixing the state space, information structure, and agents), "almost every" selection of K or more securities (determined by their terminal payoffs) gives an economy with a complete markets equilibrium. (This presumes that an equilibrium with a complete set of contingent claims markets exists.) Here, "almost every" means a generic result in the sense of Radner (1979). Thus, in determining whether markets are "likely" to be complete in an economy with long-lived securities, the crucial comparison is K versus the number of securities N. This section closes with several embellishments on the basic model.

The qualitative insight to be gained from the analysis in sections 6.2, 6.3, and 6.4 is clear: A few securities that are frequently traded *may* span a very large dimensional space of contingent claims. Markets *may be* complete, and it is *possible* that risk is allocated efficiently. But how are these "may be's" to be converted into more positive statements? What value of K is appropriate for modeling purposes? Might it be that K is very much larger than N, and yet markets are approximately complete and risk is allocated approximately efficiently? These questions concerning the robustness of the analysis are extremely difficult for two related reasons. The analysis does not indicate what (if anything) will suffice for "approximately complete markets" and "approximately efficient allocations." The analysis identifies K as the crucial piece of data, and K is a property of the fine structure of the model. If conditions necessary for "approximate completeness/efficiency" involve the datum K, then one is unlikely to be able to apply this analysis with any confidence—the task of discerning the "true" value of K defies the imagination.

The following sort of result is therefore sought. If one economy approximates a second idealized economy in a coarse sense and if the idealized economy has "complete markets," then the first economy has approximately efficient equilibrium allocations. The key is to make the sense of approximation as coarse as possible, in order to make the analysis as robust as possible. The remainder of the paper is devoted to discussion of this type of result and in particular to convergence to the Black-Scholes model that dominates the financial literature. The issues raised are very delicate and difficult mathematically, and therefore the analysis given is preliminary at best.

Section 6.5 concerns the idealized economy to which other economies will converge: the Black-Scholes model. The use of continuous time creates difficulties. Both the sense in which this model represents a Radner equilibrium and the sense in which it is a "complete markets" equilibrium are not straightforward. These difficulties are resolved as in Harrison and Kreps (1979), and the section closes with brief discussion on the inadequacies of this resolution.

A convergence result is proved in section 6.6. Within a certain framework, sequences of models that converge to the Black-Scholes model have asymptotically efficient equilibrium allocations. The mode of convergence required is such that a sequence can converge without convergence of the "fine structure" of the economies: In each economy along the sequence, K is very much larger than N. (In fact, $K = \infty$ and $N = 2$ for each economy.) This shows that for approximate efficiency, the K versus N comparison may be misleading.

This convergence result is a step in the right direction, but it suffers from some severe deficiencies. Chief among these is that the framework of the result is very restrictive—the state space, information structure, and agents are all fixed along the sequence. (What changes along the sequence are the dates at which trading takes place and, perhaps, the equilibrium prices.) It *ought* to be the case that this sort of convergence result holds in a much less restrictive setting. But when one attempts to obtain analogues in wider contexts, difficulties arise. For example, if the state space changes along the sequence, then so does the commodity space and so (perforce) must the agents. How then is one to define "asymptotic efficiency"? Section 6.7 discusses where these difficulties lie, why in some sense they cannot be completely overcome, and how they *might* be partially finessed. "Answers" are not provided in this section. Rather, the aim of the discussion is to indicate limitations of both the result in section 6.6 and any possible extension and to spur research that will culminate in an approximation theory more adequate than that which is given here.

Section 6.8 presents a brief summary of the main points of the paper, together with a list of weaknesses and questions left unanswered by the analysis.

The general topic addressed here has a long history in the literature, and a review of pertinent contributions may help put things in perspective. The mode of analysis of a multiperiod exchange economy follows Radner (1972) and his definition of an equilibrium of plans, prices, and price expectations. This definition is implicit as well in the simpler setting of Arrow (1964). Arrow (1964) and Guesnerie and Jaffray (1974) discuss circumstances under which a Radner economy has a "complete" set of markets—Arrow analyzes a two-period economy, and Guesnerie and Jaffray extend Arrow's idea (that at each date there should be a complete set of financial claims for the next date) to a multiperiod setting. When a Radner economy does not have "complete markets," inefficiencies may result, and these may be inefficiencies even relative to the existing market structure. On this and other points concerning incomplete Radner economies, see Hart (1975). Several papers, noting that there are "fewer securities than states," have discussed the role of options on those securities for completing markets. On this point, see Breeden and Litzenberger (1978), Friesen (1979), and Ross (1976).

There is a chunk of literature that seeks to show how efficient allocations can arise with few securities using arguments very different from those used here. In these papers, agents are assumed to be "sufficiently alike" (for example, identical subjective probability estimates, no non-market income, and HARA class utility functions with identical risk cautiousness) so that complete markets are unnecessary. See, for example, Wilson (1968).

When some of the information may be privately held and/or information is endogenously generated and is costly, a host of difficulties arise: Grossman (1977) and Grossman and Stiglitz (1976) are two excellent examples of the huge literature on this topic.

Throughout this paper only exchange economies are considered. Extending the analysis to questions of production and productive efficiency involves nontrivial complications, even in the simple models of the first half of the paper. These problems are roughly those pointed to in the "spanning" literature: see Diamond (1967), Stiglitz (1972), and the Bell Journal Symposium on the Optimality of Competitive Capital Markets (1974). Because of the multiperiod setting here, where agents are constantly changing their portfolio holdings, the papers of Grossman and Stiglitz (1980) and Hart (1979) are especially important.

6.2 Equilibrium in a Multiperiod Exchange Economy

Consider the following model of an exchange economy with uncertainty. There is a finite number of states of the world, indexed by $\omega \in \Omega$. There is a finite number of time periods, indexed by $t = 0, 1, \ldots, T$. All agents in this economy have access to the same information which is exogenously specified. This information is represented by a sequence of partitions of Ω, $\{F_t; t = 0, \ldots, T\}$. The interpretation is that at time t agents know which cell of F_t contains the true state. Information increases through time: F_{t+1} is at least as fine as F_t. For simplicity, it is assumed that F_0 is trivial and that F_T is the discrete partition. The σ-field of events generated by F_t is denoted $\boldsymbol{F}_t$.

There is a single consumption good which cannot be stored. This good is consumed at each date, and the amount consumed at date t can vary across cells of F_t; thus, the consumption space for agents is $X = X_{t=0}^{T} R^{(\Omega, F_t)}$, where $R^{(\Omega, F_t)}$ is the space of F_t measurable real valued functions on Ω. The notation $x = (x(0), \ldots, x(T))$ is used for a generic element of

X, with $x(t,\omega)$ denoting the value of $x(t)$ in the state ω. Vectors x will be interpreted as net trade (rather than total consumption) vectors for agents.

The agents in this economy are indexed by $i = 1,\ldots,I$. Each agent is characterized by a subset $X^i \subseteq X$, representing feasible net trades for agent i, and by a complete and transitive binary relation $\gtrsim^i$ on X^i, representing agent i's preferences among net trades. It is assumed throughout that each X^i is "comprehensive upwards," in the sense that if $x \in X^i$ and if $x' \in X$ are such that $x'(t,\omega) \geq 0$ for all t and ω, then $x + x' \in X^i$. Moreover, it is assumed that each X^i contains the origin, and that each $\gtrsim^i$ is strictly increasing in the sense that for x and $x' \neq 0$ as above, $x + x' >^i x$.

There are N assets or securities in this economy. These are claims to (state contingent) consumption at date T. They are indexed by $n = 1,\ldots,N$. Security n entitles the bearer (on date T) to $d_n(\omega)$ units of the consumption good at date T if the state is ω. The net supply of these securities is zero. It is assumed that for every state there is one of these securities that pays off a nonnegative amount in every state and a strictly positive amount in that state.

At each date $t \leq T$ and in every state, markets open in which these N securities can be traded for one another and for the consumption good. The price (in units of the consumption good) of security n at date t in state ω will be denoted by $p_n(t,\omega)$. These markets are frictionless—there are no transaction costs and no restrictions on short sales. A *price system* is a vector stochastic process $p = \{p_n(t,\omega); n = 1,\ldots,N, t = 0,\ldots,T, \omega \in \Omega\}$ with $p(t)$ F_t measurable for each t.

The agent's problem in this economy is to manage a portfolio of these N securities in order to obtain for himself the best possible net trade vector of state contingent consumption. This is formalized as follows. A trading strategy is an N dimensional vector stochastic process $\theta = \{\theta_n(t,\omega)\}$ such that $\theta(t)$ is F_t measurable for each t. The interpretation is that $\theta_n(t,\omega)$ is the number of shares of security n held from date t until $t+1$ in state ω. (For $t = T$, $\theta_n(T,\omega)$ is the number of shares from which the dividend is received.) The constraint that $\theta(t)$ is F_t measurable is the natural information constraint. If prices are given by $p = \{p_n(t)\}$, then the strategy θ results in the following net trade vector in state contingent consumption:

(2.1) $x(\theta,p) = (x(0;\theta,p),\ldots,x(T;\theta,p))$, where

$$x(0;\theta,p) = -\theta(0){\cdot}p(0) \text{ (the dot means dot product)},$$

$$x(t;\theta,p) = (\theta(t-1) - \theta(t)){\cdot}p(t) \text{ for } t = 1,\ldots,T-1, \text{ and}$$

$$x(T;\theta,p) = (\theta(T-1) - \theta(T)){\cdot}p(T) + \theta(T){\cdot}d.$$

A net trade bundle $x \in X$ is said to be feasible for agent i at prices p if $x \in X^i$ and if there exists a trading strategy θ such that $x \leq x(\theta, p)$. The set of feasible net trade bundles for i at prices p is denoted $X^i(p)$. Note that this definition contains an implicit assumption of free disposal and that $x \in X^i(p)$ implies that x satisfies the appropriate budget constraints on net trades.

An equilibrium for the economy described above is a price system p and, for $i = 1, \ldots, I$, net trade bundles x^i and trading strategies θ^i such that

(2.2a) $\qquad\qquad x^i \leq x(\theta^i, p)$ and $x^i \in X^i$ for all i,

(2.2b) $\qquad x^i$ is $\gtrsim^i$ maximal among all $x \in X^i(p)$ for each i,

and

(2.2c) $\qquad\qquad\qquad \sum_i \theta^i = 0.$

Condition (a) says that x^i is a feasible net trade for i and that x^i is feasible if i adopts the trading strategy θ^i. Condition (b) says that taking prices p as given, agent i can do no better than x^i. Condition (c) is the market clearing condition. It says that securities markets clear exactly. Note that this together with (2.2a) and (2.1) imply that $\sum_i x^i \leq 0$, or markets for the consumption good clear. This is an equilibrium of plans, prices, and price expectations in the sense of Radner (1972), assuming rational expectations on the part of agents as to the prices that will prevail at subsequent dates contingent on states.[2]

The following alternative characterization of an equilibrium will be useful. Fix a price system p. Define

$$M' = \{x \in X : x = x(\theta, p) \text{ for some trading strategy } \theta\}.$$

Suppose it is true that

(2.3) $\qquad\qquad M' \cap \{x \in X : x \geq 0, x \neq 0\} = \phi.$

(As shall be claimed in the following proposition, (2.3) is necessary for any equilibrium where agents' preferences are strictly increasing in the sense above.) Then define

(2.4) $\quad M = \{x \in X : x = m' + (r, 0, \ldots, 0) \text{ for } m' \in M' \text{ and } r \in R\}$

and

(2.5) $\qquad \pi(m' + (r, 0, \ldots, 0)) = r \text{ for } m' \in M' \text{ and } r \in R.$

Clearly, M is a subspace of X. Moreover, (2.3) guarantees that $\pi : M \rightarrow R$ is a well-defined, strictly positive linear functional.

Proposition 1. If $\{p, (x^i, \theta^i)^I_{i=1}\}$ is an equilibrium, then (2.3) holds, and

(2.6) $x^i \in M \cap X^i$, $\pi(x^i) \leq 0$, and x^i is $\gtrsim^i$ maximal in $\{x \in M \cap X^i : \pi(x) \leq 0\}$.

Conversely, if p satisfies (2.3) and if there exist x^i satisfying (2.6) (for M and π defined from p) and $\Sigma_i x^i = 0$, then there exist θ^i such that $\{p, (x^i, \theta^i)\}$ is an equilibrium.

The proof is straightforward and is left to the reader with one hint. In the converse half, suppose x^i and p are given. By strict monotonicity of $\gtrsim^i$, there exist $\bar{\theta}^i$ such that $x^i = x(\bar{\theta}^i, p)$. Let $\theta^i = \bar{\theta}^i$ for $i \neq 1$ and $\theta^1 = -\Sigma_{i \neq 1} \bar{\theta}^i$—then verify that $x(\theta^1, p) = x(\bar{\theta}^i, p) = x^1$. Of course, $\Sigma_i \theta^i = 0$.

The interpretation of this proposition is clear. Fix an equilibrium $\{p, (x^i, \theta^i)\}$, and define M and π from p by (2.4) and (2.5). Imagine an economy in the style of Debreu (1959) where at date zero agents can purchase any net trade bundle $x \in M$ at the price $\pi(x)$. Note well that if $M \neq X$, this is not an economy with a complete set of contingent claims markets. Of course, agent i faces two constraints in this Debreu-style economy: The x he selects must lie in X^i and must satisfy the budget constraint $\pi(x) \leq 0$. Then (2.6) says that prices π are equilibrium prices in this economy with corresponding equilibrium allocation (x^i).

Interpreting the converse half is a little trickier. Fix a Debreu-style economy with contingent claims markets for claims in some M, and let π be equilibrium prices and (x^i) the corresponding equilibrium allocation. The proposition does not guarantee that there are prices p that give the same equilibrium allocations in an economy with the given long-lived securities. Rather, *if* there are prices p that give rise to M and the equilibrium π via (2.4) and (2.5), then they are equilibrium prices (with corresponding allocation (x^i)).

6.3   Complete Markets Equilibria

Suppose that for an equilibrium price system p, the corresponding space M is X. Then the equilibrium allocation (x^i) is an equilibrium allocation for a Debreu-style economy with a complete set of contingent claims markets and therefore is Pareto efficient. Thus, it is natural to seek conditions that yield $M = X$.

Define for $t < T$ and $A \in F_t$

(3.1) $\qquad K(t, A) = \text{cardinality}\{A' \in F_{t+1} : A' \subseteq A\}$,

$\qquad\qquad$ and $K = \max\{K(t, A); t < T, A \in F_t\}$.

In words, $K(t, A)$ is the number of "subcells" of A in F_{t+1}. This is a measure of the amount of information that might be received by date $t+1$ if at date t the event A is known to prevail: If $K(t, A) = 1$, then no new information will be received. If $K(t, A) = 2$, then new information of an either/or type will be received, and so on.

Proposition 2. Let p be an equilibrium price system, and let M be defined from p by (2.4). A necessary and sufficient condition for $M = X$ is that for each $t < T$ and $A \in F_t$,

(3.2)   dimension$\{$ span $\{p(t+1, \omega); \omega \in A\}\} = K(t, A)$.

A paraphrase of this condition is that the conditional support of $p(t+1)$ given that $\omega \in A$ consists of $K(t, A)$ linearly independent vectors. There are at most $K(t, A)$ vectors in this conditional support (because $p(t+1)$ is F_{t+1} measurable). Thus, $K(t, A)$ is an upper bound on dim $\{$ span $\{p(t+1, \omega); \omega \in A\}\}$. The condition is that this upper bound is hit in every instance. The proof of this proposition involves straightforward induction on T. Rather than work through the details, a full example will be given which should make both the proposition and its proof transparent.

Example. Suppose that there are six states $\{\omega_1, \ldots, \omega_6\}$ and four dates $t = 0, \ldots, 3$. The exogenous information structure is given by the partitions

$$F_0 = \{\Omega\}, F_1 = \{\{\omega_1, \omega_2\}, \{\omega_3, \omega_4, \omega_5, \omega_6\}\},$$

$$F_2 = \{\{\omega_1, \omega_2\}, \{\omega_3, \omega_4\}, \{\omega_5, \omega_6\}\},$$

$$F_3 = \{\{\omega_1\}, \{\omega_2\}, \{\omega_3\}, \{\omega_4\}, \{\omega_5\}, \{\omega_6\}\}.$$

Thus, $K(1, \{\omega_1, \omega_2\}) = 1$ while $K(2, \{\omega_1, \omega_2\}) = 2$. Suppose that there are two securities whose dividends at date 3 are as in table 6.1.

Consider two possible equilibrium price systems arising from these data, as depicted in figures 6.1a and 6.1b. The column vectors in these event trees give the prices of the two securities as a function of the date and state. For example, in figure 6.1a the column vector $(9, 4.2)'$ which is starred is interpreted to mean $p_1(2, \omega_4) = .9$ and $p_2(2, \omega_4) = 4.2$. Note that the tree structure corresponds to the information structure.

Does $M = X$ in either or both cases? The answer is yes if and only if for every $t > 0$ and $A \in F_t$, the vector $x = (x(0), \ldots, x(T))$ that is given by $x(s) = 0$ for $s \neq t$ and $x(t) = 1_A$ is in M. That is, there must exist a trading strategy that produces one unit of consumption in event A at date t and nothing at any other date-event pair. Begin by asking if this is true for $t = 1$ and for every $A \in F_1$. In each case the answer is yes—the two possible values of $p(1)$ are linearly independent; thus, there exist (θ_1, θ_2) and (θ_1', θ_2') such that $(\theta_1, \theta_2) \cdot (p_1(1), p_2(1))' = 1_{\{\omega_1, \omega_2\}}$ and $(\theta_1', \theta_2') \cdot (p_1(1), p_2(1))' = 1_{\{\omega_3, \omega_4, \omega_5, \omega_6\}}$. This clearly suffices. Now proceed to ask the question for $t = 2$. For $A = \{\omega_1, \omega_2\}$ there is no problem in either case. But matters are not so simple for $A = \{\omega_3, \omega_4\}$. In case a it can be done: First, solve

Table 6.1

State	ω_1	ω_2	ω_3	ω_4	ω_5	ω_6
Payoff of security #1—$d_1(\cdot)$	1	1	1	1	1	1
Payoff of security #2—$d_2(\cdot)$	1	2	3	6	4	5

$$(\theta_1,\theta_2)\cdot(.9,4.2)' = 1 \text{ and } (\theta_1,\theta_2)\cdot(.909,4.1)' = 0.$$

This can be done because the two column vectors are linearly independent. Let (θ_1^*,θ_2^*) be the solution. Next, solve

$$(\theta_1,\theta_2)\cdot(.81,1.26)' = 0 \text{ and } (\theta_1,\theta_2)\cdot(.81,3.75)' = (\theta_1^*,\theta_2^*)\cdot(.81,3.75)'.$$

This can be done by the first step—the solution, denote it $(\theta_1^{**},\theta_2^{**})$, is just a scalar multiple of (θ_1',θ_2'). Then the strategy of starting with $(\theta_1^{**},\theta_2^{**})$ at date zero, changing to $(0,0)$ at date one if $\{\omega_1,\omega_2\}$ occurs and to (θ_1^*,θ_2^*) if $\{\omega_3,\omega_4,\omega_5,\omega_6\}$ occurs, and then consuming everything at date two yields one unit of consumption at date two if and only if $\{\omega_3,\omega_4\}$ occurs.

But consider case b. One cannot solve

$$(\theta_1,\theta_2)\cdot(.9,4.2)' = 1 \text{ and } (\theta_1,\theta_2)\cdot(.909,4.242)' = 0,$$

because the two column vectors are linearly dependent. Thus, if one consumes one unit at date two and nothing at date three when $\{\omega_3,\omega_4\}$ occurs, one must consume something either at date two or at date three when $\{\omega_5,\omega_6\}$ occurs.

By inductively applying this sort of logic, one can see that $M = X$ in case a (as predicted by proposition 2), but that $M \neq X$ in case b.

Example a makes the basic idea clear. In this economy there are six states of nature and only two securities, yet markets are complete. This is because the process of learning which of the six states is the true state takes place not all at once but in three steps. Agents can revise their portfolios after each step in the learning process. At each step, at most *two* "signals" are possible. And the equilibrium prices of the two securities are "well behaved"—they are "linearly independent" in a fashion that enables agents to take full advantage of new information as it is received.

6.4   Genericity of the case $M = X$ with K or more securities

Condition (3.2) in proposition 2 can be viewed as two nested conditions. First, the number of securities N must be at least as large as $\max_{t,A} K(t,A) = K$. In addition to this, the equilibrium prices must be "sufficiently independent." In case b of the example, $N = K (= 2)$, but because $p(2,\omega_3)$ and $p(2,\omega_5)$ are not independent, markets are not com-

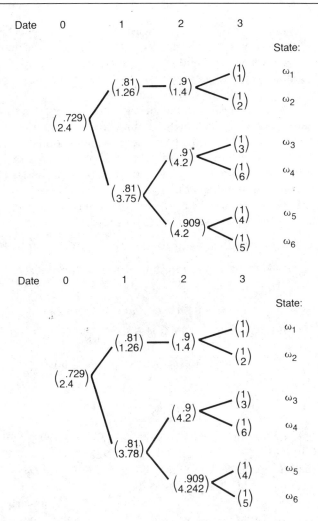

Fig. 6.1a (*top*) **and** *b* (*bottom*)

plete. This second part of (3.2) is less than satisfactory on economic grounds, because it involves endogenous data, the equilibrium prices p. It cannot be completely dispensed with—not *every* set of K or more securities will have equilibrium prices that satisfy (3.2). Consider, for example, K securities whose dividends at date T are scalar multiples of one another. (That is, $d_n = r_n d_1$ for $r_n \in R$.) But a result almost this strong is possible. Fix the economic setting; that is, fix the state space, information structure, and agents. Suppose N securities are selected at "random." By a selection of N securities is meant a selection of a point d from the set $(R^{(\Omega, F T)})^N$, which hereafter is denoted by D. A subset of D will be called *sparse* if its closure has Lebesgue measure zero. If the selection of d is done "randomly enough," there is zero probability that the outcome will land in a given sparse set. Following the terminology of Radner (1979), a result that holds off of a sparse set is called *generic*. The next proposition therefore gives the title of this section.

Proposition 3. Fix the economic setting. Suppose that if in this setting a Debreu-style regime of complete contingent claims markets is set up, then there is an equilibrium with equilibrium allocation $\{x^i\}$. Then if $N \geq K$, there is a sparse set in D such that for all d not in that set, the economy with N long-lived securities paying d admits an equilibrium with $M = X$ and with equilibrium allocation $\{x_i\}$.

Proof. In the Debreu-style economy, there is a linear functional $\phi : X \to R$ that is strictly positive and that satisfies

(4.1) $x^i \in X^i, \phi(x^i) \leq 0$, and x^i is $\geq^i$ maximal in $\{x \in X^i : \phi(x) \leq 0\}$.

(That is, ϕ gives the equilibrium prices.) Normalize ϕ so that $\phi((1,0,\ldots,0)) = 1$. For $t = 0,\ldots,T$ and $A \in F_t$, define $\chi_{t,A}$ by

$$\chi_{t,A}(s) = 0 \text{ for } s \neq t \text{ and } \chi_{t,A}(t) = 1_A.$$

That is, $\chi_{t,A}$ is the claim that pays one unit of consumption at date t in the event A.

For any $d \in D$, define p from d and ϕ as follows. For $t \leq T$ and $\omega \in \Omega$, let $A \in F_t$ be such that $\omega \in A$. Then let

(4.2) $$p_n(t,\omega) = \sum_{\omega \in A} d_n(\omega) \phi(\chi_{T,\{\omega\}}) / \phi(\chi_{t,A}).$$

Two things, once demonstrated, give the result. First, except for d from a sparse subset of D, p so defined satisfies (3.2), and thus $M = X$. Second, for all such d, the linear functional π defined in (2.5) is ϕ.

For the first result, it is necessary to show that except for d from a sparse set, the set $\{p(t+1,\omega); \omega \in A\}$ contains $K(t,A)$ linearly independent vectors for every t and $A \in F_t$. Since there are finitely many such pairs (t,A) and since the union of a finite number of sparse sets is sparse, it suffices to show that for every t and A the set of $d \in D$ for which the corresponding $\{p(t+1,\omega); \omega \in A\}$ does not contain $K(t,A)$ linearly independent vectors is sparse. Using (4.2), the set $\{p(t+1,\omega); \omega \in A\}$ can be written

$$\{ \sum_{\omega \in A'} d(\omega) \phi(\chi_{T,\{\omega\}}) / \phi(\chi_{t+1,A'}); A' \in F_{t+1}, A' \subseteq A\},$$

which, letting $\alpha(t,\omega)$ denote the strictly positive scalar $\phi(\chi_{T,\{\omega\}}) / \phi(\chi_{t,A})$ is

$$\{ \sum_{\omega \in A'} d(\omega) \alpha(t+1,\omega); A' \in F_{t+1}, A' \subseteq A\}.$$

The set of d for which this set of $K(t,A)$ vectors is linearly dependent is clearly closed. That it has Lebesgue measure zero is also apparent as follows: Let $Y : D \to (R^N)^{K(t,A)}$ be the map

$$Y(d) = [\sum_{\omega \in A'} d(\omega) \alpha(t+1,\omega)]_{A' \in F_{t+1}, A' \subseteq A},$$

and let λ denote Lebesgue measure on D. Then the measure $\lambda \circ Y^{-1}$ on $(R^N)^{K(t,A)}$ is absolutely continuous with respect to Lebesgue measure because the $\alpha(t+1,\omega)$ are strictly positive. And the Lebesgue measure in $(R^N)^{K(t,A)}$ of vectors $[(r)_{n=1}^N]_{k=1}^{K(t,A)}$ such that the $(r)_n$ are linearly dependent is zero, if $N \geq K$.

For the second result, it suffices to show that for all strategies θ, $\phi(x(\theta,p)) = 0$. There is nothing to do but grind this out:

$$\phi(x(\theta,p)) = \phi(\chi_{0,\Omega}) x(o; \theta,p) + \sum_{t=1}^{T-1} \sum_{A \in F_t} \phi(\chi_{t,A}) x(t,A; \theta,p) +$$

$$\sum_{\omega \in \Omega} \phi(\chi_{T,\{\omega\}}) x(T,\omega; \theta,p)$$

$$= \phi(\chi_{0,\Omega})(-\theta(0) \cdot p(0)) + \sum_{t=1}^{T-1} \sum_{A \in F_t} \phi(\chi_{t,A}) [\theta(t-1,A) -$$

$$\theta(t,A)] \cdot p(t,A) + \sum_{\omega \in \Omega} \phi(\chi_{T,\{\omega\}}) [(\theta(T-1,\omega) -$$

$$\theta(T,\omega)) \cdot p(T,\omega) + \theta(T,\omega) \cdot d]$$

$$= \sum_{t=0}^{T-1} \sum_{A \in F_t} [-\theta(t,A) \cdot p(t,A) \phi(\chi_{t,A}) +$$

$$\sum_{A' \in F_{t+1}, A' \subseteq A} \theta(t,A) \cdot p(t+1,A') \phi(\chi_{t+1,A'})]$$

(note that $d \equiv p(T)$)

$$= \sum_{t=0}^{T-1} \sum_{A \in F_t} \theta(t,A) \cdot [- \sum_{\omega \in A} p(T,\omega) \phi(\chi_{T,\{\omega\}}) +$$

$$\sum_{A' \in F_{t+1}, A' \subseteq A} p(T,\omega) \phi(\chi_{T,\{\omega\}})]$$

$$= \sum_{t=0}^{T-1} \sum_{A \in F_t} \theta(t,A) \cdot [0] = 0. \qquad \text{QED}$$

A remark may help the reader through this maze. If the security prices p are to be the "same" as ϕ, then (4.2) is required. This can be seen as follows. In the Debreu-style economy, for $A \in F_t$ a claim to $d_n 1_A$ (contingent) units of consumption at date T costs $\sum_{\omega \in A} d_n(\omega) \phi(\chi_{T,\{\omega\}})$ units of date zero consumption, or $\sum_{\omega \in A} d_n(\omega) \phi(\chi_{T,\{\omega\}}) / \phi(\chi_{t,A})$ units of date t, event A consumption. If expectations are rational and an equilibrium is in force, then this must be the price in units of date t consumption of security

n at date t in the event A. This is (4.2). As to the genericity of condition (3.2), the reader may find it helpful to take the economic structure of the example, make up a set of equilibrium prices for a Debreu-style economy with complete markets, and then see what is entailed in picking d so that p defined from (4.2) does not satisfy (3.2).

Several remarks about this proposition and the previous analysis are worth making.

1. A by-product of the proposition is a result concerning the "generic existence of equilibrium": If $N \geq K$ and if the economic setting is such that an equilibrium exists with a Debreu-style regime of complete contingent claims markets, then for all d except from a sparse subset of D, the economy admits an equilibrium.

2. The proposition does not show that for $N \geq K$ and generic d, all equilibria are Pareto efficient. It only shows that there are efficient equilibria. But it seems likely that the stronger result is true, at least for "most" economic settings.

3. The following result complementary to the proposition might be imagined: Fixing Ω and $\{F_t\}$, for every $d \in D$ where $N \geq K$ the set of "communities of agents" that do not admit an equilibrium in which $M = X$ is sparse among all communities of agents. The concept of a community of agents is ambiguous here, but what is intended is something like the treatment in Radner (1979), where agents are parametrized by their subjective probability assessments. Such a result is impossible—as already noted, if the d_n are collinear and Ω has more than one state, then $M = X$ cannot result. It is conjectured that the result is true, however, if this and similar trivially pernicious choices of d are disallowed. (It seems likely that the technology developed in Radner (1979) would work excellently in this context.)

4. In sections 6.2 through 6.4 it has been assumed that there is a single perishable consumption good. It should be clear that the results given hold if there is a finite number of consumption goods, as long as there are spot markets in the consumption goods at each date and if securities pay off in a good whose relative price is strictly positive in the date T spot market.

5. It has been assumed that all securities "live" from date zero to T and that securities pay off only on date T. Clearly, the basic results do not change if securities pay off on other dates as well and/or if securities live for other sets of dates. The important thing is that for any time period t to $t+1$ and event $A \in F_t$, at least $K(t,A)$ securities must be "alive."

6. For the sake of completeness, a result from Harrison and Kreps (1979) is repeated here. Suppose that one is given a state space Ω, a time index set $\{0, \ldots, T\}$, an information structure $\{F_t\}$, and a set of N securities $\{d_n; n = 1, \ldots, N\}$. Moreover, suppose that a price system p is given and it

is claimed that p is the equilibrium price system for an economy as above. That is, the claim is that there exists a population of agents meeting the requirements above such that p is part of an equilibrium in the economy that houses them. Under what conditions is this claim true? For simplicity, assume that one of the securities, say, the first, pays out a strictly positive amount in every state of nature. One necessary and sufficient condition for an affirmative answer is that (2.3) is true. A second is that there exists a probability measure Q on Ω such that $Q(\{\omega\}) > 0$ for every $\omega \in \Omega$, and if $E[\cdot]$ denotes expectation with respect to Q, then

$$E[p_n(t+1)/p_1(t+1)\,|\,F_t] = p_n(t)/p_1(t),$$

for every $t < T$ and n. (Also, $p(T)$ must be proportional to d.) Moreover, $M = X$ if and only if there exists exactly one such probability measure.

6.5 The Black-Scholes Model

The Black-Scholes model is a continuous time, infinite state version of the model in section 6.2 that comes to a similar and striking conclusion: With a "simple enough" information structure, a small finite number (two) of securities can span an infinite dimensional space of contingent claims, owing to the infinite number of trading opportunities. The sense in which this is true is not entirely straightforward, so a review of the model is now presented.

A probability space (Ω, F, P) is given. On this space is defined a standard (mean zero, variance one) Brownian motion $\{B(t); t \in [0,1]\}$. The information available to agents at date t ($t \in [0,1]$) is the history of the Brownian motion up to that date: $F_t = F\{B(u); 0 \le u \le t\}$. It is assumed that $F = F_1$ as before.

For simplicity it will be assumed that agents consume only at dates zero and one and that they have endowment of the consumption good only at those dates.[3] A consumption bundle is therefore a pair $x = (r, y)$, where $r \in R$ is consumption at date zero and y is state contingent consumption at date one, an F measurable real valued function. The space of consumption bundles is denoted $X = R \times Y$ and is assumed to be a linear space of such pairs.[4] Agents are described by a feasible net trade set $X^i \subseteq X$ and a preference ordering $\succeq^i$ on X^i. It is assumed that each X^i is "comprehensive upward" and that $\succeq^i$ is strictly increasing in the following sense: If $x' = (r', y') \in X$ is such that $r' \ge 0$ and $y' \ge 0$ P-a.s., and either $r' > 0$ or $P(y' > 0) > 0$, then for all $x \in X^i$, $x + x' \in X^i$ and $x + x' \succ^i x$.

There are two long-lived securities in this world, which (as before) are claims to date one consumption. The first yields e^r units of consumption independent of the state, while the second yields $\exp\{\mu + \sigma B(1, \omega)\}$ units in state ω. (Here, r, μ, and $\sigma > 0$ are given constants.) Trading in the two securities can take place at any date between zero and one (as better information about the true state of the world is received), with relative equilibrium prices

(5.1) $p_1(t) = e^{rt}$ and $p_2(t) = \exp\{\mu t + \sigma B(t)\}$.

At date zero, the two securities and the consumption good are traded at relative prices one apiece.

In saying that these are equilibrium prices, the following is meant. Given the price process $p = \{p(t)\}$, agents seek to manage a portfolio of the two securities so as to obtain the best possible net trade vector. A *trading* strategy is formally represented as a vector stochastic process $\theta = \{\theta_n(t); n = 1,2, t \in [0,1]\}$, where $\theta_n(t,\omega)$ represents the number of shares of security n held at time t if the state is ω. The obvious informational constraint on θ is that for every t, $\theta(t)$ must be F_t measurable. But more qualifications are necessary. One must say what sorts of trading strategies represent actions that agents are physically capable of. Moreover, because no consumption takes place between dates zero and one, because agents' preferences are strictly increasing, and because (by assumption) agents do not receive fresh funds for investment between those two dates, any trading strategy θ should be *self-financing*. That is to say, any changes in the composition of an agent's portfolio at dates $t \in (0,1]$ should involve zero net cost of transaction. Any purchases should be financed by a corresponding sale, and the proceeds from any sale should be reinvested elsewhere. (Date one is included in this constraint as it is imagined that date one consumption takes place *after* date one markets close.)

One possibility is to say that agents can employ any strategy θ such that $t \rightarrow \theta_n(t,\omega)$ is of bounded variation for every n and a.e. ω. Such θ correspond to trading strategies that have the representation: The amount held at date t is the difference between a total amount bought during $[0,t]$ and an amount sold during that period. It is clear that such a strategy θ should be called self-financing if $0 = d\theta(t) \cdot p(t)$ for all $t \in (0,1]$. In this case θ yields the net trade vector $x(\theta,p) = (r(\theta,p), y(\theta,p))$ given by

(5.2) $r(\theta,p) = -\theta(0) \cdot p(0)$ and $y(\theta,p) = \theta(T) \cdot d$.

A second, less generous possibility is to say that agents are capable of employing only *simple* trading strategies, defined as follows. A trading strategy θ is called simple if there exist a finite integer J and dates $0 = t_0 < t_1 < t_2 < \ldots < t_J \leq 1$ such that $\theta(t,\omega)$ is constant over intervals of the form $t \in [t_j, t_{j+1})$. In words, agents rearrange their portfolios only finitely many times, where the number of times and the dates are fixed in advance. A simple strategy θ is self-financing if $[\theta(t_j) - \theta(t_{j-1})] \cdot p(t_j) = 0$ for all $j \geq 1$, in which case (5.2) gives $x(\theta,p)$.

Having defined what strategies agents are capable of, the definition of an equilibrium proceeds exactly as before. An equilibrium is an ensemble $\{p,(x^i,\theta^i)\}$ such that $p(t)$ is F_t measurable for all t, $x^i = x(\theta^i,p) \in X^i$ for each i, x^i is $\geq^i$ maximal in $\{x(\theta,p)\} \cap X^i$ for each i, and $\Sigma_i\,\theta^i = 0$.

Does the Black-Scholes model give prices which for some community of agents are equilibrium prices in this sense? The answer to this question depends on what trading strategies are allowed to agents. If bounded variation strategies as defined above are permitted, then the answer is no. This is because there is a bounded variation strategy θ such that for p the Black-Scholes prices, $r(\theta,p) > 0$ and $y(\theta,p) \geq 0$ P-a.s. That is, the condition analogous to (2.3) does not hold. See Harrison and Kreps (1979), section 6) for the basic idea. Note that this phenomenon is not peculiar to the Black-Scholes model. It occurs in virtually every continuous time model with frictionless markets and two or more securities. But if simple trading strategies only are allowed, then the answer is yes. To show this, show that (2.3) does hold in this case. (A direct proof is not difficult.) The discussion in Kreps (1981, section 6) shows that this is sufficient.

Take then the case where only simple trading strategies are allowed. A result analogous to proposition 1 is immediate. Defining

$$M' = \{x \in X : x = x(\theta,p) \text{ for a simple trading strategy } \theta\},$$

$$M = \{x \in X : x = m' + (r,0) \text{ for } m' \in M' \text{ and } r \in R\}, \text{ and}$$

$$\pi(m' + (r,0)) = r \text{ for } m' \in M' \text{ and } r \in R,$$

it follows that M is a subspace of X and π is a well-defined, strictly positive linear functional on M. Moreover, if $\{p,(x^i,\theta^i)\}$ is an equilibrium, then

$$\pi(x^i) \leq 0, x^i \in X^i \cap M, \text{ and } x^i \text{ is } \geq^i \text{ maximal in } \{x \in X^i \cap M : \pi(x) \leq 0\}.$$

That is, $\{x^i\}$ is an equilibrium allocation in a Debreu-style economy where claims in M can be bought at prices π.

Is this a "complete markets" equilibrium? It can be shown that $M \neq X$ (for any reasonable choice of X), so the answer seems to be no. But there is a sense in which the answer is yes. Suppose that $X = R \times L^2(\Omega,F,P)$; strategies θ must satisfy $\theta_n(t)p_n(t) \in L^2(\Omega,F,P)$ for all t and $n = 1,2$, $X^i = X$ for each i, and each agent's preferences are continuous in the Euclidean $\times$ L^2-norm product topology on X. Then following the results in Harrison and Kreps (1979) and Kreps (1981, especially theorem 5), there exists a strictly positive linear functional $\psi : X \to R$ such that if $\{p,(x^i,\theta^i)\}$ is an equilibrium (where p are the Black-Scholes prices, of course), then

(5.3) $\psi(x^i) \leq 0, x^i \in X^i, \text{ and } x^i \text{ is } \geq^i \text{ maximal in } \{x \in X^i : \psi(x) \leq 0\}.$

(The linear functional ψ turns out to be the unique continuous, strictly positive extension of π from M to all of X, and it is the uniqueness of this extension that yields (5.3).)

This is the sense in which two long-lived securities can yield a complete set of contingent claims for uncountably many contingencies if there are infinitely many trading opportunities. One feels uneasy about both this model and the conclusion arrived at on several grounds, among which are the following:

1. The restriction to simple trading strategies is unnatural. There are other more natural ways to exorcise trading strategies that violate (2.3). For example, the requirement that $\theta(t) \cdot p(t) \geq -L$ for some finite L will suffice for the Black-Scholes model. This can be interpreted as a credit constraint. But no theory has been developed along these lines to the author's knowledge.

2. The twin assumptions that each $X^i = X$ and that each $\succeq^i$ is Euclidean $\times L^2$ continuous are hardly palatable. (To some extent, the use of the L^2 topology can be foregone. See Harrison and Kreps 1979, section 7.) It would be nice to be able to widen the class of trading strategies so that $M = X$ *and* p is part of an equilibrium. The extant literature on the Black-Scholes model, especially Merton (1977), suggests that the former can be done by allowing trading strategies that are Ito integrals, and it has been conjectured by Harrison (1978) that the entire program is feasible if a restricted class of Ito integrals is allowed.

3. Most important is that no intuitive feeling has been developed for why two securities suffice to give "complete markets" in this model, nor whether this result is generic in any sense. How does one generalize K to a continuous time setting, and why (if a generalization is possible) does $K = 2$ in this case? The proof of theorem 3 in Harrison and Kreps (1979) is the key step in obtaining the result that markets are "complete" in the Black-Scholes model, and in that proof the key step is the use of the remarkable result of Kunita and Watanabe (1967) that every martingale on the Brownian information structure can be written as a stochastic integral of Brownian motion. Intuitive comprehension of that result is necessary if one is to feel comfortable using the Black-Scholes model.

6.6   A Convergence Result

Begin with the following pieces of the Black-Scholes model: (Ω, F, P), $\{F_t; t \in [0,1]\}$; a finite collection of agents with $X^i = X = R \times L^2(\Omega, F, P)$ and preferences that are Euclidean $\times L^2$ continuous and strictly increasing. Assume that if these agents are placed in a Debreu-style economy with a complete set of contingent claims markets, then the linear functional $\psi : X \to R$ that is introduced in section 6.5 is an equilibrium set of prices, with corresponding equilibrium allocation (x^i).

Now consider placing these agents in a sequence of economies like those in section 6.2 except that Ω as above remains fixed and so is infinite. Index the economies by $H = 1, 2, \ldots$ In economy H, trading in two securities takes place at the $H + 1$ dates $t = 0, 1/H, \ldots, 1$. The information available at date h/H is $F_{h/H}$ (for F_t as above), and thus "$K = \infty$" in each of these economies. Let $\{p_n(t; H); n = 1, 2, t = 0, 1/H, \ldots, \}$ denote the equilibrium prices in economy H, and let $(x^i(H))$ denote the corresponding equilibrium allocation. Assume for simplicity that $d_1(H) = e^r$ for all H, so that $p_1(t; H) > 0$ for all t and H by (2.3), and that $p_1(0; H) = 1$ for all H.

Of course, in economy H it is not true that $M = X$. Thus, the allocation $(x^i(H))$ may be Pareto inefficient. To measure the degree of this inefficiency, the allocations $(x^i(H))$ will be compared with the efficient allocation (x^i). Write $x^i(H) = (r^i(H), y^i(H))$ and $x^i = (r^i, y^i)$. Define $\delta^i(H)$ by

(6.1) $\qquad \delta^i(H) = \inf \{\delta > 0 : (r^i(H) + \delta, y^i(H)) >^i (r^i, y^i)\}.$

That is, $x^i(H)$ augmented by $\delta^i(H)$ units of date zero consumption is at least as good as x^i. If agent i prefers $x^i(H)$ to x^i, then $\delta^i(H)$ is set equal to zero. If no δ can be found to make i better off with $x^i(H) + (\delta, 0)$ than with x^i, then $\delta^i(H)$ is set equal to $+\infty$. Define

(6.2) $\qquad \Delta(H) = \overset{I}{\underset{i=1}{\Sigma}} \delta^i(H).$

In words, $\Delta(H)$ units of date zero consumption can be distributed among agents after they trade to equilibrium in economy H so that each agent is at least as well off as in the efficient allocation (x^i). If $\Delta(H)$ is "small," then economy H is "nearly" efficient.

Proposition 4. Let $\{p(t); t \in [0, 1]\}$ be the Black-Scholes price system. If the equilibrium prices $\{p(t; H)\}$ converge to $\{p(t)\}$ in the sense that

(6.3) $\qquad \underset{H \to \infty}{\lim} p_2(t; H)/p_1(t; H) = p_2(t)/p_1(t)$ in L^2 uniformly in t,

then $\lim_{H \to \infty} \Delta(H) = 0$.

Proof. (This proof makes heavy use of the technology of Harrison and Kreps 1979 and Kreps 1981, and it is probably unintelligible to readers unfamiliar with those papers.)

Without loss of generality, it can be assumed that $r = 0$ and $p_1(t) \equiv p_1(t; H) \equiv 1$ for all H. (See Harrison and Kreps 1979, section 7.) In this case (6.3) becomes: $\lim_{H \to \infty} p_2(t; H) = p_2(t)$ in L^2 uniformly in t.

It will suffice to show that for every $x \in X$ such that $\psi(x) \le 0$ there exists a sequence of (self-financing) trading strategies $\theta(H)$ that involve trading at dates $0, 1/H, \ldots, 1$ only and a sequence $\{x(H)\} \subseteq X$ such that

(6.4) $\qquad x(\theta(H), p(H)) \ge x(H)$ for every H, and $\underset{H \to \infty}{\lim} x(H) = x.$

(Limits in X are always in the Euclidean $\times L^2$ product topology.) For if this is true for all x, it is true in particular for x^i. Thus, as H gets large, it is feasible in economy H for agent i to obtain an $x^i(\theta(H), p(H))$ which is at least as good as some $x(H)$ which in turn is close in terms of $\succeq^i$ to x^i. (Recall the continuity of $\succeq^i$.) By revealed preference, $x^i(H) \succeq^i x(\theta^i(H), p(H))$, and thus $\delta^i(H) \to 0$ as $H \to \infty$.

Fix $x \in X$. From Harrison and Kreps (1979) and Kreps (1981) it is known that there exist simple trading strategies $\theta(\ell)$ that are self-financing for p and $x(\ell)$ ($\ell = 1, 2, \ldots$) such that

(6.5) $x(\theta(\ell), p) \geq x(\ell)$ for every ℓ and $\lim\limits_{\ell \to \infty} x(\ell) = x$.

In Harrison and Kreps (1979), such θ are assumed to satisfy the condition $\theta_n(t) p_n(t) \in L^2$ for each t and n. But in fact one can *add* the condition that $\theta_2(t) \in L^\infty$ for all t, and still there exist $\theta(\ell)$ and $x(\ell)$ as in (6.5). (To see this, review the proof of theorem 2 in Harrison and Kreps 1979 with this additional condition on simple trading strategies, and verify that it remains a valid proof.) For the remainder of this proof, simple trading strategies will be assumed to satisfy this additional condition.

Let θ be any simple trading strategy that is self-financing for p. Define from θ a trading strategy θ^H (for economy H) by

$$\theta_2^H(h/H) = \theta_2(h/H) \text{ for } h = 0, \ldots, H, \theta_1^H(0) = \theta_1(0), \text{ and}$$

$$\theta_1^H(t) \text{ for } t > 0 \text{ defined so that } \theta^H \text{ is self-financing for } \{p(t; H)\}.$$

Note that if θ changes values at dates $0 = t_0 < t_1 < \ldots < t_J \leq 1$, then θ^H changes values at dates $t_0^H, t_1^H, \ldots, t_J^H$, where for $t \in [0,1]$, $t^H = \inf\{u \geq t;$ $u = h/H$ for some integer $h\}$.

To show that (6.4) is true, it will suffice to show that for any simple θ (self-financing for p),

(6.6) $$\lim\limits_{H \to \infty} x(\theta^H, p(H)) = x(\theta, p).$$

For this combined with (6.5) yields (6.4) by an easy argument. To show (6.6), note first that $\theta^H(0) = \theta(0)$ and therefore $r(\theta^H, p(H)) = -\theta(0) \cdot p(0; H)$. Since F_0 is trivial, the constant $p(0; H) \to p(0)$ by assumption, and thus $r(\theta^H, p(H)) \to -\theta(0) \cdot p(0) = r(\theta, p)$. Next note that

$$y(\theta, p) = \theta(1) \cdot d = \theta(t_J) \cdot d = \theta(t_J) \cdot [d - p(t_J)] + \theta(t_J) \cdot p(t_J)$$

$$= \theta(t_J) \cdot [d - p(t_J)] + \theta(t_{J-1}) \cdot p(t_J)$$

(because θ is p self-financing)

$$= \theta(t_J) \cdot [d - p(t_J)] + \theta(t_{J-1}) \cdot [p(t_J) - p(t_{J-1})] + \theta(t_{J-1}) \cdot p(t_{J-1})$$

$$= \theta(t_J) \cdot [d - p(t_J)] + \sum_{j=0}^{J-1} \theta(t_j) \cdot [p(t_{j+1}) - p(t_j)] + \theta(0) \cdot p(0)$$

(by iterating the above argument)

$$= \theta_2(t_J)[d_2 - p_2(t_J)] + \sum_{j=0}^{J-1} \theta_2(t_j)[p_2(t_{j+1}) - p_2(t_j)] + \theta(0) \cdot p(0)$$

(since $d_1 \equiv p_1(t) \equiv 1$). Similarly,

$$y(\theta^H, p(H)) = \theta_2^H(t_J^H)[d_2(H) - p_2(t_J^H; H)] +$$

$$\sum_{j=0}^{J-1} \theta_2^H(t_j^H)[p_2(t_{j+1}^H; H) - p_2(t_j^H; H)] + \theta^H(0) \cdot p(0; H).$$

For H large enough that $t_{j+1} - t_j > 1/H$ for all j, it follows that $\theta_2^H(t_j^H) = \theta_2(t_j)$ for all j. By assumption, $\theta_2(t) \in L^\infty$ for all t, and by previous argument, $\theta(0) \cdot p(0) = \lim_H \theta^H(0) \cdot p(0; H)$. Thus, $y(\theta, p) = \lim_H y(\theta^H, p(H))$ follows from $\lim_H d_2(H) = d_2$ in L^2 (note that d is proportional to $p(1)$ and $d(H)$ is proportional to $p(1; H)$, and by assumption $d_1 \equiv d_1(H) \equiv 1$), and

$$\lim_{H \to \infty} [p_2(t^H; H) - p_2(t)] = \lim_{H \to \infty} [p_2(t^H; H) - p_2(t^H)] +$$

$$\lim_{H \to \infty} [p_2(t^H) - p_2(t)] = 0 + 0 = 0 \text{ in } L^2 \text{ uniformly in } t,$$

the first by the hypothesis of the proposition and the second because $t^H - t < 1/H$ and geometric Brownian motion is L^2 uniformly continuous. QED.

Proposition 4 shows that it is possible to have K much larger than N (∞ versus 2), and yet equilibrium allocations are "nearly" efficient. This in itself is not remarkable—Wilson (1968) shows that this is possible by making strong assumptions concerning agents' preferences. But here much weaker assumptions about preferences are made. Instead, there are strong assumptions on the ability to trade securities frequently, the way in which uncertainty resolves, and the approximate behavior of equilibrium security prices. It would be preferable, of course, not to make assumptions about equilibrium prices. A possible direction would be to take as given Ω, F, P, $\{F_t\}$, and agents, assume that $\psi : X \to R$ gives equilibrium prices for a Debreu-style economy with complete markets, and then show that (1) for each H, or for H sufficiently large, there is an equilibrium in the long-lived securities economy with two securities that pay off exactly (or approximately) what the Black-Scholes securities pay, and (2) these equilibrium prices converge to the Black-Scholes prices in the sense of (6.3). But even if this is true, it is a result predicated on very strong assumptions.

A number of extensions can be obtained cheaply. The reliance on the exact distributions of the Black-Scholes price processes is unnecessary—the methodology works for any diffusion process covered by theorem 3 in Harrison and Kreps (1979). This includes, for more than two securities, multidimensional diffusions. The diffusion assumption is not particularly necessary, except insofar as it is a case where "markets are complete" in the limit. Other stochastic processes, such as the jump process model of Cox and Ross (1976), could be used. Finally, the use of the space of square integrable claims and the L^2 topology is not necessary—see the discussion in Harrison and Kreps (1979, section 7). Of course, if preferences are continuous in another topology, then (6.3) will have to be modified appropriately.

It is worth noting that what is a flaw in the Black-Scholes model, namely, the need to restrict attention to simple trading strategies, becomes a virtue here. If one takes the view (implicit in proposition 4) that the Black-Scholes model is to be regarded as an ideal approximation to economies with many, but only finitely many, trading dates, then the restriction makes sense. In the "limit" economy, agents should not be able to employ strategies that cannot be approximated (in terms of preference) by strategies available in the economies approaching the limit. The trading strategies of bounded variation that turn nothing into one unit of consumption do not pass this test for agents of the sort discussed here. So from this perspective, these strategies can reasonably be excluded from the set of strategies available in the limit economy.

6.7 Extending the Convergence Result

Perhaps the least satisfactory aspect of proposition 4 is that in it, Ω, F, P, $\{F_t\}$, and the agents do not change along the sequence. A more satisfactory treatment of the problem would cover the following example.

Fix a positive integer H and imagine an economy with 3^H states of nature. Every state ω has H coordinates $(\omega_1, \ldots, \omega_H)$ where each ω_h takes on one of three possible values: -2; 0; 2. Think of each ω_h as being determined by an independent experiment, where the probabilities of the outcomes 2 and -2 are $\frac{1}{8}$ apiece and the probability of outcome 0 is $\frac{3}{4}$. Let Ω^H denote this state space and P^H this probability measure on Ω^H. In this economy, agents consume at dates zero and one and trade at dates $t = 0, 1/H, \ldots, 1$. The information available at date h/H, denoted $F^H_{h/H}$, is the σ-field generated by the first h coordinates of the state. (That is, at date h/H the first h coordinates of the state have been revealed to agents.) Note that this yields $K = 3$. There are two securities traded in this economy, paying the following dividends at date one:

$$d^H_1 = e^r \text{ and } d^H_2(\omega) = \exp[\sigma(\sum_{h=1}^{H} \omega_h)/\sqrt{H} + \mu].$$

Here $\omega = (\omega_1, \ldots, \omega_H)$, and r, μ, and $\sigma > 0$ are given constants. These are traded together with the consumption good at date zero at relative prices one apiece. The two securities are also traded for each other at dates $1/H, \ldots, 1$ with relative equilibrium prices

$$p_1^H(h/H, \omega) = e^{rh/H} \text{ and } p_2^H(h/H, \omega) = \exp\left[\sigma\left(\sum_{g=1}^{h} \omega_g\right)/\sqrt{H} + \mu h/H\right].$$

(No matter what values r, μ, and σ take on as long as $\sigma > 0$, for large enough H these prices are equilibrium prices for some agents. That is, for all sufficiently large H they satisfy (2.3).)

Because $K = 3$ and $N = 2$, this economy has incomplete markets. Yet for large H, the equilibrium price system in this economy is "very much like" the Black-Scholes price system. A more precise statement is that as H goes to infinity, the price systems p^H converge weakly to the Black-Scholes price system (in the sense of Billingsley 1968).[5] Does this imply that as H goes to infinity, the equilibrium allocations are asymptotically Pareto efficient?

Proposition 4 offers no concrete guidance on this question. Here, unlike there, as H changes so do state spaces and information structures. Since the state spaces change, so must the commodity spaces, and therefore so must the agents. There is a sense in which proposition 4 offers evidence that the answer to this question is yes: It is possible to define on the Black-Scholes probability space a sequence of vector stochastic processes $\{\hat{p}^H(h/H); h = 0, \ldots, H\}$ that have the same distribution as the processes $\{p^H(h/H)\}$ given above and that converge to the Black-Scholes prices in the sense of (6.3).[6] Therefore, if for large H one seeks to approximate in $M'(H)$ (the set of budget feasible net trades in economy H) the individual agents' parts of an allocation that is budget feasible at the Black-Scholes prices (on the presumption that one such allocation is Pareto efficient), then proposition 4 suggests that this is possible.

But for a number of reasons, the quality of this evidence is low.

1. As noted above, the agents must change with H. In what sense can an allocation from the Black-Scholes economy be Pareto efficient for economy H? There can be no sense in which this is true, because for agents in economy H, their piece of any such allocation does not lie in the domain of their preferences. What would make sense is a statement such as:

(7.1) In economy H there is a Pareto efficient allocation $(x^i(H)) \in (X(H))^I$ such that as H goes to infinity, each $x^i(H)$ is approximated by some bundle from $M'(H)$.

2. Assuming that (7.1) is to be sought, how is the notion of "approximate" to be formalized? Proposition 4 suggests the following:

(7.2) For each $x^i(H) = (r^i(H), y^i(H))$ there exists $(s^i(H), z^i(H)) \in M'(H)$ such that $\lim_{H\to\infty} \{|r^i(H) - s^i(H)| + E^H[(y^i(H) - z^i(H))^2]\} = 0$.

This type of criterion worked in proposition 4 because the agents (and P^H) did not change with H, and the agents' preferences were assumed continuous and their net trade sets open in the corresponding topology. Thus, from (7.2) it was easy to conclude that $\Delta(H) \to 0$. Here, because agents change with H, (7.2) alone will not suffice to guarantee "asymptotic efficiency," even if every agents' preferences are Euclidean $\times$ L^2 continuous. An assumption of *equicontinuity* (measured in date zero consumption) will clearly be required. That is, as H changes the agent who "plays role i" in economy H cannot be varying too wildly with H in terms of the continuity of his preferences.

3. Assume that (7.1) is to be sought, formalized as in (7.2). This in general will be false. Because agents change with H, the allocation $(x^i(H))$ that is being "chased" may change with H sufficiently quickly to frustrate convergence. (This was not a problem in proposition 4 because there a single unchanging allocation was being chased.) For example, suppose that for efficiency in economy H it is necessary to trade the contingent claim $y(H)$ given by

$$y(\omega; H) = 1_{\{\omega_1 \neq 2\}}, \text{ where } \omega = (\omega_1, \ldots, \omega_H).$$

Trade in this claim would be necessary for efficiency if, for example, two agents disagreed about the probability distribution of ω_1, even if they agreed about all other probabilities. It can be shown that for this claim $y(H)$ there does *not* exist $z(H) \in Y(H)$ such that for some $s(H)$, $(s(H), z(H)) \in M'(H)$ and

$$(7.3) \qquad \lim_{H \to \infty} E^H[(y(H) - z(H))^2] = 0.$$

Thus, if these claims appear in the allocations $(x^i(H))$ being chased, (7.2) cannot hold.

Compare this with the following situation. Suppose that for efficient allocation in economy H only the following two claims are required (in addition to those in $M(H)$):

$$y'(\omega; H) = \sup_h \left\{ \exp\left[\sum_{g=1}^h \omega_g / \sqrt{H} \right]; h = 0, \ldots, H \right\}$$

and

$$y''(\omega; H) = [d_2^H(\omega) - a]^+$$

For these claims the statement corresponding to (7.3) is true, and there is some hope that (7.2) may prove to be true.

What distinguishes $y'(H)$ and $y''(H)$ from $y(H)$? Why does (7.3) hold for the first two and not the third? Recall that the price systems p^H converge to the Black-Scholes prices in a very coarse fashion, in the weak topology.[7] The claims $y'(H)$ and $y''(H)$ depend on the state only via "coarse" features of the price history. More precisely, they are given by weak topology continuous functions of prices.[8] This is not true of the claims $y(H)$. They depend on the "fine features" of the price history.

Since convergence takes place in the weak topology, it is reasonable to expect that at *best* sequences of claims corresponding to weak topology continuous functions will be approximated by marketed claims. In general, (7.1) and (7.2) will be false, unless (perhaps) the allocations $(x^i(H))$ being chased "settle down" in this fashion. Since $(x^i(H))$ is meant to be a Pareto efficient allocation for the agents in economy H, it seems likely that in order to ensure that the $(x^i(H))$ "settle down" it will be necessary to assume that agents "settle down." (No general formulation of this can be offered here. But the reader may wish to ponder the following example that seems to work: For $i = 1, \ldots, I$ fix real numbers α^i and a utility function $u^i : R \times R \to R$. In economy H, let agent i's preferences for (r, y) be given by the index $E^H[u^i(r, \alpha^i d_2^H(\omega) + y(\omega))]$. That is, agents are expected utility maximizers whose date one endowments are proportional shares of the second security.)

4. In proposition 4 the information structure does not change with H—at time h/H agents possess all the Brownian information to that date. Thus, in the proposition, trading strategies θ can have $\theta(h/H)$ depending on more than the history of prices up to time h/H. In the sequence of economies given above, this extra information is not available. It can be shown in the setting of proposition 4 that for some claims this extra information is extraneous: For a claim whose value depends continuously on finitely many values of prices, (6.4) remains true when agents can base portfolio holdings on past price information only. This suggests that with some further restrictions on the allocations $(x^i(H))$ being chased, (7.1) and (7.2) will not be rendered false by the changing information structure. But what those restrictions are in general remains an open question. (A good place to start is probably with the work of Aldous 1978 concerning the relation between weak convergence à la Billingsley 1968 and "convergence of information.")

The somewhat disjointed discussion of this section can be summarized as follows. Proposition 4 is a first step toward a general theory of approximation of the sort discussed in the introduction. But it takes too many things as fixed. A more satisfactory theory would subsume the example with which this section began. Proposition 4 suggests that such a theory can be created, but subject to the very important qualifications noted above.

6.8 Concluding Remarks

To sum up what has been said: Frequent trading makes it *possible* for a few securities to span many states of nature. Whether markets are "perfectly" complete depends critically on the fine structure of the way in which uncertainty resolves. But the condition required for complete markets is not "nearly" required for "approximately" complete markets.

If equilibrium prices approximate an ideal model in a fairly coarse sense and if that ideal model has perfectly complete markets, then markets in the original model will give nearly efficient equilibrium allocations. Thus, if actual security prices behave "like" those in the Black-Scholes model (meaning here the general class of diffusion process models for which markets are complete), risk is allocated approximately efficiently.

A number of caveats to this argument have already been noted. The analysis in the second half of the paper relies on unpalatable assumptions concerning agents' net trade sets and preferences. The approximation analysis takes equilibrium prices as exogenously given, which is certainly an unhappy state of affairs. And the approximation result that is derived is preliminary at best—a more satisfactory theory will require qualifications that may turn out to be unpalatable. To this list the following more general caveats should be added:

1. The final conclusion given above rests on a very large supposition. Do actual security prices behave (even coarsely) "like" those in the Black-Scholes model? One can point to incidents where sudden bits of news have caused security prices to jump discontinuously, which the Black-Scholes prices do not do. In Merton (1976) it is argued that such jumps *may* be unimportant for the efficient allocation of risk because they may be "diversifiable" components of uncertainty. But to make this argument, it is at least necessary to assume that agents hold portfolios that are "diversified" enough to make such risk negligible. This in turn requires strong assumptions on preferences. Moreover, "continuous sample paths" are not (as is sometimes naively believed) sufficient for Black-Scholes type behavior: Harrison (1978) observes that if prices act in precisely the Black-Scholes model except that the diffusion coefficient changes with, say, the political party of the occupant of the White House (and if it is impossible to make book on the results of presidential elections), then sample paths are continuous yet markets are not complete. The question of whether prices do behave approximately like Black-Scholes prices (even coarsely) is very difficult, and nothing here should be construed as an assertion that they do.

2. For efficient allocation of risk, *all* uncertainty must be "spanned." In the Black-Scholes model, the only uncertainty is security price uncertainty. But phenomena such as differential information, moral hazard, individual uncertainty about future tastes, etc., represent uncertainty the resolution of which is not reflected (completely) in any security price. At best, there are complete markets only in uncertainty which is so reflected.

3. Adding production decisions to the story causes major difficulties. A firm contemplating a new and uncertain production process cannot (necessarily) observe prices for claims contingent on the outcome of that uncertainty—the problems addressed in the "spanning" literature (Diamond 1967; Stiglitz 1972; Ekern and Wilson 1974; Leland 1974; Merton

and Subrahmanyam 1974; Radner 1974; Grossman and Stiglitz 1980) all arise. Note that adding firms is "easy" only when they are "competitive" (see Grossman and Stiglitz 1980), and Hart (1979) indicates that with short sales, "competitive" firms will be difficult to find.

4. Still, suppose security prices do behave "nearly" like the Black-Scholes prices. Then at least, it seems, markets are "nearly" complete for purposes of pure exchange in the security price uncertainty. Even this is suspect. The arguments used here put tremendous strain on the assumptions of rational expectations and zero transaction costs. In a world with transactions costs and even slightly "irrational" expectations, there will be a place for markets where agents can purchase at the outset sundry "standard" packages of claims contingent on security price histories. The CBOE need not go out of business owing to the arguments put forward here.

Notes

1. Besides these two seminal papers, the following make significant contributions from the perspective taken here: Cox and Ross (1976), Harrison and Kreps (1979), Kreps (1981), Merton (1977), and Ross (1978). Smith (1976) provides a survey of the literature through 1976. Diffusion models were introduced into financial theory in Merton (1971, and 1973a).

2. Two technical points are worth making. First, unlike in Radner (1972), no bound is placed on the magnitude of θ. This is not necessary here, as general existence of equilibria will not be an issue. Second, the definition of an equilibrium of plans, prices, and price expectations presumes that agents will carry out plans that they embark on (or, more to the point, they believe that they will carry them out). Implicit in this is an "unchanging tastes" assumption, which can be used to motivate restrictions on preferences, notably weak separability across states. See Donaldson, Rossman, and Selden (1978). If agents' preferences "changed" in the sense of Hammond (1976), the analysis here would be significantly different.

3. See Harrison and Kreps (1979, section 7) for a discussion of this restriction.

4. If $y = y'$ P-a.s., then y and y' are assumed to be indistinguishable as time one contingent claims. Note that for the first time the probability measure P has entered the story. It will continue to do so, and the reader should note where and how it does.

5. To be more formal about this, define $p_1^H(t) = e^{rt}$ and $p_2^H(t, \omega) = p_2^H(h/H, \omega)$ for $t \in [h/H, (h+1)/H)$. Then weak convergence in $D^2[0, 1]$ (with the Skorohod topology) to the process given in (5.1) follows from Donsker's theorem and the continuous mapping theorem. See Billingsley (1968) for definitions and details.

6. More generally, a theorem of Skorohod (1956) ensures that weak convergence and *almost sure* convergence are compatible in roughly this sense: If $p(H)$ converges weakly to $\hat{p}$, then there exists a probability space on which are defined processes $\hat{p}(H)$ and $\hat{p}$ such that each $\hat{p}(H)$ has the same distribution as $p(H)$ and $\hat{p}$ has the same distribution as p, and $\hat{p}(H)$ converges a.s. to $\hat{p}$. Note that the convergence criterion in (6.3) is neither necessary nor sufficient for almost sure convergence in the Skorohod topology on $D^2[0, 1]$. Moreover, replacing (7.3) by a.s. convergence in the Skorohod topology would be insufficient for purposes here, for roughly the same reason that a.s. convergence does not imply L^p convergence for random variables. Therefore, in a general treatment of the convergence problem, convergence in the weak topology would not be the "correct" criterion.

7. Caveat emptor: As noted above in note 6, convergence in the weak topology is apt to turn out to be too weak a criterion for the results being sought. Throughout this section, the weak topology is used for purposes of discussion, to indicate the *general* sort of convergence/ topology that one would like to use in extending proposition 4.

8. That is, they correspond to a function $f : D^2[0,1] \to R$ that is continuous in the Skorohod topology.

References

Aldous, David. 1978. Weak convergence of stochastic processes for processes viewed in the Strasbourg manner. University of Cambridge Applied Statistical Laboratory. Mimeographed.

Arrow, Kenneth J. 1964. The role of securities in the optimal allocation of risk bearing. *Review of Economic Studies* 31: 91–96.

Billingsley, Patrick. 1968. *Convergence of probability measures*. New York: John Wiley & Sons.

Black, Fischer, and Scholes, Myron. 1973. The pricing of options and corporate liabilities. *Journal of Political Economy* 81: 637–59.

Breeden, Douglas, and Litzenberger, Robert. 1978. Prices of state-contingent claims implicit in option prices. *Journal of Business* 51: 621–51.

Cox, John, and Ross, Stephen. 1976. The valuation of options for alternative stochastic processes. *Journal of Financial Economics* 3: 145–66.

Debreu, Gerard. 1959. *The theory of value*. New York: John Wiley & Sons.

Diamond, Peter. 1967. The role of a stock market in a general equilibrium model with technological uncertainty. *American Economic Review* 57: 759–76.

Donaldson, J.; Rossman, Michael; and Selden, Larry. 1978. Dynamic consumption choice with changing time and risk preferences. Columbia University. Mimeographed.

Ekern, Steiner, and Wilson, Robert. 1974. On the theory of the firm in an economy with incomplete markets. *Bell Journal of Economics and Management Science* 5: 171–80.

Friesen, Peter. 1979. The Arrow-Debreu model extended to financial markets. *Econometrica* 47: 689–708.

Grossman, Sanford. 1977. The existence of futures markets, noisy rational expectations, and informational externalities. *Review of Economic Studies* 44: 431–49.

Grossman, Sanford, and Stiglitz, Joseph. 1976. Information and competitive price systems. *American Economic Review* 66: 246–53.

———. 1980. On stockholder unanimity in making production and financial decisions. *Quarterly Journal of Economics* 94: 543–66.

Guesnerie, Roger, and Jaffray, J.-Y. 1974. Optimality of equilibrium of plans, prices, and price expectations. In Drèze, J., ed., *Allocation under uncertainty*. London: MacMillan.

Hammond, Peter. 1976. Changing tastes and coherent dynamic choice. *Review of Economic Studies* 43: 159–73.

Harrison, J. Michael. 1978. Lecture notes.

Harrison, J. Michael, and Kreps, David. 1979. Martingales and arbitrage in multiperiod securities markets. *Journal of Economic Theory* 20: 381–408.

Hart, Oliver. 1975. On the optimality of equilibrium when the market structure is incomplete. *Journal of Economic Theory* 11: 418–43.

———. 1979. On shareholder unanimity in large stock market economies. *Econometrica* 47: 1057–84.

Kreps, David. 1981. Arbitrage and equilibrium in economies with infinitely many commodities. *Journal of Mathematical Economics* 8: 15–35.

Kunita, H., and Watanabe, S. 1967. On square integrable martingales. *Nagoya Mathematical Journal* 30: 209–45.

Leland, Hayne. 1974. Production theory and the stock market. *Bell Journal of Economics and Management Science* 5: 125–44.

Merton, Robert. 1971. Optimal consumption and portfolio rules in a continuous-time model. *Journal of Economic Theory* 3: 373–413.

———. 1973a. An intertemporal capital asset pricing model. *Econometrica* 41: 867–87.

———. 1973b. Theory of rational option pricing. *Bell Journal of Economics and Management Science* 4: 141–83.

———. 1976. Option pricing when underlying stock returns are discontinuous. *Journal of Financial Economics* 3: 125–44.

———. 1977. On the pricing of contingent claims and the Modigliani-Miller theorem. *Journal of Financial Economics* 5: 241–49.

Merton, Robert, and Subrahmanyam, M. 1974. The optimality of a competitive stock market. *Bell Journal of Economics and Management Science* 3: 145–70.

Radner, Roy. 1972. Existence of equilibrium of plans, prices, and price expectations in a sequence of markets. *Econometrica* 40: 289–303.

———. 1974. A note on unanimity of stockholders' preferences among alternative production plans: A reformulation of the Ekern-Wilson model. *Bell Journal of Economics and Management Science* 3: 181–86.

———. 1979. Rational expectations equilibria: Generic existence and the information revealed by prices. *Econometrica* 47: 655–78.

Ross, Stephen. 1976. Options and efficiency. *Quarterly Journal of Economics* 90: 75–89.

———. 1978. A simple approach to the valuation of risky streams. *Journal of Business* 51: 453–75.

Skorohod, A. V. 1956. Limit theorems for stochastic processes. *Theory of Probability and Its Application* 1: 261–90.

Smith, Clifford. 1976. Option pricing: A review. *Journal of Financial Economics* 3: 3–52.

Stiglitz, Joseph. 1972. On the optimality of the stock market allocation of investment. *Quarterly Journal of Economics* 86: 25–60.

Wilson, Robert. 1968. The theory of syndicates. *Econometrica* 36: 119–32.

7 The Matching Process as a Noncooperative Bargaining Game

Dale T. Mortensen

7.1 Introduction

The term "matching" refers to any process by which persons and/or objects are combined to form distinguishable entities with some common purpose that none can accomplish alone. The allocation of apartments to tenants, the assignment of jobs to workers or factories to sites, the pairing of men and women in marriage, and the formation of collections of agents known as firms are all examples. Problems of interest are those in which matchings take place voluntarily, substitution possibilities exist in the sense that no individual agent is an essential member of any coalition, and the "value" of the joint activity engaged in by a coalition can be divided among its members in many ways. There are two questions of interest. First, for a given environment described by the set of agents, the "value" of each possible coalition, and the technology by which coalitions can form, what is the "equilibrium" coalition structure? Second, is an equilibrium coalition structure "efficient" in any meaningful sense?

At this level of generality, there is a small but diverse literature. The topics include location problems, the theory of coalition production economies, labor managed firms, marriage and divorce, and the theory of local public goods. That the value of a coalition's activities depends on the identities of its members and that the willingness of the members of a coalition to participate depends on the division of that value are essential ingredients. A further complication arises when the identities and/or locations of potential members are not known with certainty ex ante. In this case the existence of recruiting and search costs create quasi rents. How these are divided affects the incentives that individual agents have

Dale T. Mortensen is professor of economics at Northwestern University.

to allocate resources to the process of coalition formation. The focus of the paper is on this aspect of the problem.

The problem of coalition formation under conditions of imperfect and costly information is most closely related to the search theoretic approach to market analysis. There are two recent papers on the topic, one by the author (1978) and another by Diamond and Maskin (1979). Both papers are attempts to extend existing search theory in ways that allow equilibrium analysis. The relatively simple problem of bilateral matching, pairing, is treated. The divisions of the surplus attributable to the existence of a match is by nature a bilateral bargaining problem. A particular solution to this problem determines the value of the match to each member of a pair. If values associated with the potential pairings are not identical, then an individual agent neither holds out for the best possible match nor sticks with an existing one if a better opportunity presents itself. In the absence of a requirement to compensate each other in the event of a separation, separations occur too frequently. In a partial equilibrium context, I show that any matched pair maximizes their joint wealth, however they choose to divide it, if each is required to compensate the other for the lost share of the surplus in the event of a separation initiated by the former.

Diamond and Maskin, using the descriptive language of contract law, call an agreement concerning the division of the value of a match a "contract," a separation initiated by one of the two parties a "breach of contract," and required compensation equal to lost rent "compensatory damages." Compensation for breach voluntarily written into a contract is called "liquidated damages." By taking into account interactions that I ignore, they show that liquidated damages are sometimes greater than compensatory damages. They also study the issue of the efficiency of the matching process under both damage regimes when the surplus attributable to any match is divided equally between the members of the pair.

The focus of the paper is on the relationship between the bargaining outcome expected by the as yet unmatched pairs and the incentive of each unmatched agent to invest in the process of forming matches. This focus is resolved by using a model based on two distinguishing assumptions. First, no search by matched agents is allowed. Second, the aggregate rate at which matches form is endogenously determined by the search intensities chosen by individual unmatched agents. The breach of contract issue is ignored given the first assumption, but the divisions of the value of a match that agents expect to be written into contracts are crucial as a consequence of the second. Finally, following Diamond and Maskin, both "linear" and "quadratic" matching technologies are considered.

The method of analysis follows. Given a particular individually rational solution to the bargaining problem that any two agents of opposite type face when they meet, the problem of determining the search intensity choices is formulated as a many-person repeated game. The game is played by all the unmatched agents of the two types. A constant steady state fraction of matched agents of each type exists given a bargaining outcome, any solution to the game, and a specification of the technology. Each agent's payoff function is the discounted flow of expected future net benefits, and benefits are transferable across agents. The noncooperative Nash solution to the game of search intensity choice is imposed.

Not surprisingly the joint Nash search intensity choices and hence the matching process that is induced by it are generally inefficient in the sense that another possibility exists which would make all players better off. If the probability that a match will form in a short time interval is independent of the number of unmatched agents—the "linear" technology case—no unmatched agent searches intensively enough given any fixed division of the value of a match. The externality involved can be described as follows. If an unmatched agent searches more intensely, he and *some agent of the opposite type* will form a match more quickly on average. However, in contemplating his search intensity choice, the agent only takes account of his own expected benefit, which is proportional to his share of the surplus obtained in the future match. The share to be obtained by his future partner is ignored. An alternative contract exists that will solve this incentive problem. Specifically, when the agent responsible for the formation of a particular match is allocated all the surplus attributable to it, the joint wealth of all players is maximized by the Nash solution to the game of search intensity choice.

Given a "quadratic" technology, the probability that a match will form in a short time interval is proportional to the number of unmatched pairs. The contingent contract just described does not yield an efficient matching outcome in this case. Although the externality discussed still exists, more intensive search by all other agents reduces the number of agents of the opposite type that each individual can expect to find in the future. As a consequence of this second externality alone, unmatched agents search too intensively. Interestingly, the effects of the two externalities in combination cancel, given an appropriate bargaining outcome. In one limiting case of the model, the Nash solution to the game of search intensity choice maximizes the total wealth of all the searching agents if every partnership divides the surplus equally. More generally, the agent responsible for the formation of each match must be allocated a share of its surplus that lies between one-half and unity.

In sum, matching outcomes depend on the bargains that agents not yet matched expect to negotiate. Although there is no reason to believe that one individually rational outcome will occur rather than another, the incentives induced by virtually all motivate inefficient search. However, a particular bargaining outcome does exist that yields an efficient matching process in each example considered in the paper. The imposition of this contract can be viewed as an assignment of property rights that would induce a cooperative solution to the game of matching.

7.2 Matching Technologies

In this section we sketch an aggregate matching model, formally a stochastic process of the "birth/death" type. Following Diamond and Maskin, the problem is one of forming pairs composed of agents of two different types for the special case in which the numbers of agents of both types are equal. Let m denote the common number of agents of the two types or, equivalently, the number of possible pairs. Let n denote the number of unmatched pairs. The state space for the matching process is the set of all possible values that n can take on, the set $\{0, 1, \ldots, m\}$.

Let $a(n)$ denote the average instantaneous rate at which new matches form and $b(n)$ denote the average instantaneous rate at which new unmatched pairs enter the process given that there are n unmatched pairs at the moment. (Both of these functions are specified in detail later.) Hence, the probability that exactly one new match will form in a short time interval of length Δt is approximately $a(n)\Delta t$ and the probability that one new unmatched pair will enter the system is $b(n)\Delta t$. Since either or neither of these two possibilities will occur during the interval with virtual certainty for sufficiently small values of Δt, we have

$$P_{t+\Delta t}(0) = \Delta t a(1) P_t(1) + (1 - \Delta t b(0)) P_t(0) + 0(\Delta t)!,$$

$$P_{t+\Delta t}(n) = \Delta t a(n+1) P_t(n+1) + \Delta t b(n-1) P_t(n-1)$$
$$+ [1 - \Delta t a(n) - \Delta t b(n)] P_t(n) + 0(\Delta t)!, \; n = 1, 2, \ldots, m,$$

$$\sum_{n=0}^{m} P_t(n) = 1,$$

where $P_t(n)$ is the probability that there will be n unmatched pairs at time t and $0(\Delta t)!/\Delta t \to 0$ as $\Delta t \to 0$. The first equation reflects the fact that there can be no unmatched pairs at the end of the interval $(t, t + \Delta t)$ only if either there were one at the beginning and a match formed during the interval or there were none at the beginning and none entered during the interval. The second equation reflects the fact that either a "birth" or a "death" can occur or neither does when $n > 0$. The last requirement reflects the fact that $[P_t(0), P_t(1), \ldots, P_t(m)]$ is the probability distribution over possible states at time t.

Divide both sides of the first two equations by Δt, rearrange terms appropriately, and take the limits as $\Delta t \to 0$. The result is the system of differential equations

$$\dot{P}(0) = a(1)P(1) - b(0)P(0),$$

$$\dot{P}(n) = a(n+1)P(n+1) + b(n-1)P(n-1) - [a(n) + b(n)]P(n),$$

$$n = 1, 2, \ldots, m,$$

$$\sum_{n=0}^{m} P(n) = 1.$$

It is well known that the solution to this system converges to a unique steady state as $t \to \infty$ if $(a(n), b(n)) \geq 0$. (See Feller 1968, pp. 454–58.) The limiting distribution is the particular solution to the difference equation

(1) $a(n+1)P(n+1) + b(n-1)P(n-1) = [a(n)+b(n)]P(n)$

associated with the boundary conditions

(2a) $a(1)P(1) = b(0)P(0)$

and

(2b) $\sum_{n=0}^{m} P(n) = 1.$

For each n, the limiting probability is the relative frequency with which the process is in state n along any sample path of infinite length.

I consider two alternative specifications of the matching rate $a(n)$, linear and quadratic. In the linear case, the probability that some one of the n unmatched pairs will meet in a short time interval is independent of the number of unmatched pairs. Hence, the average instantaneous rate at which pairs form is proportional to n; i.e.,

(3) $a(n) = \alpha n,$

where $\alpha \Delta t$ is the probability that a particular pair of the n possibilities will form a match. In the quadratic case, the probability that a particular unmatched pair will form a match during a short time interval is proportional to the fraction of agents of either type that are not matched. Hence,

(3′) $a(n) = \alpha(n/m)n = \alpha n^2/m.$

These alternative specifications can be interpreted as follows. Let α_1 denote the frequency with which each unmatched agent of type 1 meets agents of type 2, and let α_2 denote the frequency with which each unmatched agent of type 2 meets agents of type 1. The contact frequency per unmatched pair is the sum

(4) $\alpha = \alpha_1 + \alpha_2.$

If matched agents of the opposite type are never met, (3) obtains. However, if all matched and unmatched agents of the opposite type are contacted with equal probability, then (3′) obtains because n/m is the probability that a contact made will be unmatched. Hence, in the quadratic case, matched and unmatched agents cannot be distinguished ex ante.

For the specification of $b(n)$, the rate at which new unmatched pairs enter the system, we suppose that existing matches dissolve at an exogenous average rate β. Hence,

(5) $$b(n) = \beta(m-n),$$

where $1/\beta$ is the expected duration of a match. In other words, β is the "turnover" rate.

In principle one can solve (1) for the explicit functional form of the limiting probability distribution over the states of the process for each specification of $a(n)$ and $b(n)$. For our purpose, it is enough to derive an expression for the expected fraction of unmatched pairs. Since we are primarily interested in the large numbers of agents case, this task is facilitated by an appeal to the law of large numbers.

Given (2a), an inductive argument applied to (1) yields

(6) $$P(n) = [b(n-1)/a(n)]P(n-1), \qquad n = 1,\dots,m,$$

in general. Of course,

$$En \equiv \sum_{n=0}^{m} nP(n) = \sum_{n=1}^{m} nP(n) = \sum_{n=1}^{m+1} nP(n) = \sum_{n=0}^{m} (n+1)P(n+1)$$

by virtue of the fact that (2b) implies $P(m+1) = 0$. Hence, in the linear case, (3), (5), and (6) imply

$$En = \sum_{n=0}^{m} (n+1)[\beta(m-n)/\alpha(n+1)]P(n)$$

$$= (\beta/\alpha) \sum_{n=0}^{m} (m-n)P(n) = (\beta/\alpha)[m - En]$$

or, equivalently,

(7) $$E(n/m) = \beta/(\alpha+\beta).$$

Indeed, experts will recognize that $P(n)$ is the binomial distribution with "probability of success" $\beta/(\alpha+\beta)$ and "sample" size m. Hence, the variance of n/m,

$$\frac{m}{m^2}[\beta/(\alpha+\beta)][1-\beta/(\alpha+\beta)],$$

vanishes as $m \to \infty$.

The explicit form of the distribution function is not so transparent in the quadratic case, but the law of large numbers still applies. The latter fact allows us to derive the limiting value of $E(n/m)$ using the following argument. First, note that

$$En^2 \equiv \sum_{n=0}^{m} n^2P(n) = \sum_{n=1}^{m} n^2P(n) = \sum_{n=1}^{m+1} n^2P(n) = \sum_{n=0}^{m} (n+1)^2P(n+1)$$

by virtue of (2b). Consequently, (3'), (5), and (6) imply

$$En^2 = \sum_{n=0}^{m} (n+1)^2[m\beta(m-n)/\alpha(n+1)^2]P(n)$$

$$= (m\beta/\alpha) \sum_{n=0}^{m} (m-n)P(n) = (m\beta/\alpha)(m-En)$$

or, equivalently,

$$E(n/m)^2 = (\beta/\alpha)[1 - E(n/m)].$$

As the variance of n/m, $E\,(n/m)^2 - [E\,n/m]^2$, vanishes as $m \to \infty$, the mean is approximately equal to the positive root of the quadratic

$$[E\,n/m]^2 + (\beta/\alpha)E(n/m) - (\beta/\alpha) = 0$$

when m is large. In other words,

$$(7')\qquad E\,(n/m) = \frac{1}{2}\left[(\beta/\alpha)^2 + 4(\beta/\alpha)\right]^{1/2} - \frac{1}{2}(\beta/\alpha).$$

Equations (7) and (7') imply that

$$(8)\qquad E(n/m) = f(\beta/\alpha)$$

in both cases where $f(x)$ is a strictly increasing concave function such that $f(0) = 0$ and $f(\infty) = 1$. Furthermore, the elasticity $\eta(x) = xf'(x)/f(x)$ is decreasing and tends to zero as $x \to \infty$ in both cases, but

$$\eta(0) = \begin{cases} 1 & \text{if linear,} \\ \dfrac{1}{2} & \text{if quadratic.} \end{cases}$$

In other words, the expected fraction of unmatched agents is approximately β/α in the linear case and $(\beta/\alpha)^{1/2}$ in the quadratic when the turnover rate β is small relative to the contact rate α. The specification assumed by Diamond and Maskin (1979) is equivalent to this approximation. As the observed fraction of unmatched agents is small in many contexts (the unemployment rates in labor markets and the vacancy rates in the markets for apartments are examples), its consideration is not without interest.

7.3 Matching Equilibria

An equilibrium theory of search intensity choice by unmatched agents is developed in this section. Since these choices determine the stochastic rate at which matches form (specifically the parameter α in the previous section), the theory provides a behavioral foundation for studying bilateral matching processes. The model is special in the sense that only unmatched agents are permitted to search. This restriction is imposed to permit a clearer view of issues relating to efficiency of matching processes.

An agent's search intensity is defined as the expected frequency with which agents of the opposite type are contacted. The cost of search per unit time period $c_i(s)$, $i = 1$ and 2, is an increasing strictly convex function defined on the positive real line with the property that $c_i(0) = 0$. The argument s_i is the expected number of contacts made by the agent per unit time period. Hence, $s_i \Delta t$ is (approximately) equal to the probability that agent i will initiate a contact with an agent of type $j \neq i$ in a short time interval of length Δt. Hence, $\Delta t(s_1 + s_2)$ is the probability that a particular unmatched pair will meet during the interval in the linear matching technology case. In the quadratic case, $\Delta t(s_1 + s_2)n/m$ is the same probability.

Ex ante all unmatched pairs are identical in the sense that the expected total value of any match is the same for all possible pairings. Prior to a face to face meeting no one has information on which to base an inference concerning how the value of a particular match will differ from that of any other. However, ex post a statistic $x \in [0,1]$, which we interpret as the "quality" or "fit" of the match, is observed. It determines the value of the match $w(x)$. In other words, at the actual meeting of the two agents the "goodness of fit" is determined. This process of "getting to know one another" is viewed as a random draw from a distribution characterized by the c.d.f. $F(x)$. This formalization of ex post heterogeneity is from Wilson (1979).

Consistent with the interpretation of x as an indicator of quality, $w(x)$ is a positive increasing continuous function on $[0,1]$. The distribution function $F(x)$ is also assumed to be continuous.

A division of the value of a match between the members of a partnership contingent on the fit realized is a vector function $(w_1(x), w_2(x))$, where $w_i(x)$, $i = 1$ and 2, is the allocation obtained by the agent of type i. Ultimately, the division is determined as an outcome of the bargaining that takes place between the members of actual pairs after they meet. For now, the division and the c.d.f. $F(x)$ are regarded as given, the same for all potential pairs, and known to all unmatched agents.

Let $v_i(t)$, $i = 1$ and 2, denote the expected present value of an agent's future net stream of benefits given that he pursues an optimal search strategy. The agent's choice problem is one of dynamic programming, and $v_i(t)$ is the value of the agent's optimal program at time t. We wish to apply Bellman's principle of dynamic optimality. To do so, we must specify the outcomes of all events that can occur during a small future time interval of length Δt.

I start with the case of a linear matching technology. The probability that a particular agent of type i will meet some unmatched agent of type j is $\Delta t(s + s_j(t))$, $j \neq i$, where s is the search intensity to be chosen and $s_j(t)$ is the search intensity common to all agents of the opposite type. Suppose that the latter is known to our agent and is regarded as given. If the agent does not meet another of opposite type during the interval, then he continues to search, which has expected value $v_i(t + \Delta t)$ by definition. If a prospective partner is met during the interval, then a fit $x \in [0,1]$ is realized and the pair considers the split $(w_1(x), w_2(x))$. An individually rational match is consummated if and only if

(9) $(w_1(x), w_2(x)) \geq (v_1(t+\Delta t), v_2(t+\Delta t))$.

Call $A(t+\Delta t) \subset [0,1]$, the subset of qualities defined by these inequalities, the set of acceptable fits. Bellman's principle then requires that our agent's optimal strategy and its value, given the same for agents of the opposite type, satisfy

$$(10) \quad v_i(t) = \max_{s \geq 0} \{ -\Delta t c_i(s) + \frac{\Delta t}{1 + r\Delta t} (s + s_j) [\Pr\{x \in A(t+\Delta t)\}$$

$$\times E\{w_i(x) | x \in A(t+\Delta t)\} + \Pr\{x \notin A(t+\Delta t)\} v_i(t+\Delta t)]$$

$$+ \frac{1}{1 + r\Delta t} [1 - \Delta t(s + s_j)] v_i(t+\Delta t)\}, \quad j \neq i, i = 1 \text{ and } 2,$$

where $\Delta t c_i(s)$ is the cost of search incurred by the agent during the interval and r is the discount rate common to all agents.

A joint search strategy $(s_1^0(t), s_2^0(t))$ that solves (10) for both $i = 1$ and 2 is a candidate for a Nash solution to the game of search strategy choice played by unmatched agents. Because the supergame is a sequence of the same instantaneous game continuously repeated, the solution is stationary. By requiring $v(t) = v(t+\Delta t)$ for all $(t, \Delta t)$ and by making the obvious limiting argument, (10) can be made to yield the following necessary and sufficient conditions for a noncooperative stationary Nash search intensity pair denoted as (s_1^0, s_2^0). Letting (v_1^0, v_2^0) denote the associated payoffs obtained,

$$(10a) \quad rv_1^0 = \max_{s_1 \geq 0} [(s_1 + s_2^0) \Pr\{x \in A^0\} [E\{w_1(x) | x \in A^0\} - v_1^0] - c_1(s_1)]$$

and

$$(10b) \quad rv_2^0 = \max_{s_2 \geq 0} [(s_1^0 + s_2) \Pr\{x \in A^0\} [E\{w_2(x) | x \in A^0\} - v_2^0] - c_2(s_2)],$$

where A^0 is the set of acceptable fits defined by (9) when $v_i(t+\Delta t) = v_i^0$, $i = 1$ and 2. In a Nash equilibrium every unmatched agent selects his own search intensity to maximize the expected net benefit flow attributable to his own search given the optimal choices made by all other unmatched agents.

Now consider the bilateral bargaining problem that two agents of opposite type face when they meet. Because the division $(w_1(x), w_2(x))$ is arbitrary at this point, it can happen that the realized fit x is not in the acceptable set A^0 even though $w(x)$, the total value of a match, exceeds the sum of both agents' values of continued search, $v_1^0 + v_2^0$. However, in this situation an alternative division of the value of the match exists which would make both agents better off by inducing a consummation of the match even if both expect the division $(w_1(x), w_2(x))$ to obtain for any alternative matching opportunity. In other words, only divisions that are feasible and both individually and jointly rational, i.e.,

(11a) $$w(x) = w_1(x) + w_2(x)$$

and

(11b) $w(x) \geq v_1^0 + v_2^0 \Rightarrow (w_1(x), w_2(x)) \geq (v_1^0, v_2^0), \qquad \forall x \in [0,1],$

can be equilibrium outcomes of the bilateral bargaining problem that unmatched agents face when they meet.

The existing theory of symmetric bilateral bargaining does not provide any generally accepted restrictions on outcomes beyond those given in (11). Hence, we must be content with the following definition of equilibrium.

Definition 1. An allocation of the value of every possible match $(w_1^0, w_2^0) : [0,1] \rightarrow \mathbf{R}_+^2$ and a search strategy pair $(s_1^0, s_2^0) \in \mathbf{R}_+^2$ is an equilibrium solution to the combined noncooperative/bargaining game of matching if they satisfy

(12a) $$rv_1^0 = \max_{s_1 \geq 0}[(s_1 + s_2^0)E\max[w_1^0(x) - v_1^0, 0] - c_1(s_1)],$$

(12b) $$rv_2^0 = \max_{s_2 \geq 0}[(s_1^0 + s_2)E\max[w_2^0(x) - v_2^0, 0] - c_2(s_2)]$$

and

(13a) $$w_1^0(x) + w_2^0(x) = w(x), \qquad \forall x \in [0,1],$$

(13b) $$w(x) \geq v_1^0 + v_2^0 \Rightarrow (w_1^0(x), w_2^0(x)) \geq (v_1^0, v_2^0)$$

given a linear matching technology. The equations of (12) are implied by (10) and (11), and the equations of (13) are a restatement of feasibility and individual rationality, respectively. In sum, an equilibrium search intensity pair is a Nash strategy relative to a bargaining outcome and the bargaining outcome is feasible and individually rational given the noncooperative Nash payoffs induced by it.

Because (13a) implies that the converse of (13b) is true, the set of equilibrium acceptable fits is

$$A^0 = \{x \in [0,1] \mid w(x) \geq v_1^0 + v_2^0\}.$$

Because $w(x)$ is nondecreasing in x, a critical reservation fit $x^0 \leq 1$ exists such that all fits $x \geq x^0$ are acceptable. The minimally acceptable fit is the smallest solution to

(14) $$w(x^0) = v_1^0 + v_2^0.$$

As a consequence of the well-known indeterminacy of the bilateral bargaining problem, many equilibria exist in general. To illustrate this point, consider the following family of divisions of the value of every possible match as candidates for equilibrium bargaining outcomes:

(15a) $$w_1^0(x) = v_1^0 + \theta[w(x) - v_1^0 - v_2^0], \qquad \forall x \in [0,1],$$

(15b) $w_2^0(x) = v_2^0 + (1-\theta)[w(x) - v_1^0 - v_2^0]$, $\forall x \in [0,1]$.

This rule satisfies both conditions of (13) for every choice of $\theta \in [0,1]$. Obviously the family is the class of rules—divide the surplus of the match between the two types of agents according to the shares θ and $(1-\theta)$. The special case of $\theta = \frac{1}{2}$ is Nash's (1950) solution to symmetric bilateral bargaining problems.

Proposition 1. Given a linear matching technology, a unique nontrivial matching equilibrium exists for every $\theta \in [0,1]$ if either (i) $c_1'(0) < \theta E$ $w(x)$ or (ii) $c_2'(0) < (1-\theta)E\, w(x)$.

Proof. Combine (12) and (15) to obtain

(16a) $rv_1^0 = \max_{s_1 \geq 0}[(s_1 + s_2^0)\theta E \max[w(x) - v^0, 0] - c_1(s_1)]$,

(16b) $rv_2^0 = \max_{s_2 \geq 0}[(s_1^0 + s_2)(1-\theta)E \max[w(x) - v^0, 0] - c_2(s_2)]$,

where $v^0 \equiv v_1^0 + v_2^0$. Since every element of the class of rules defined by (15) satisfies (14), we need only show that unique strategy/payoff pairs exist that solve (16) for every $\theta \in [0,1]$. As the cost functions are strictly convex, the solutions to the two optimization problems implicit in (16) are unique for an arbitrary value of v^0, call it v. Let $(s_1, s_2) = (\sigma_1(v), \sigma_2(v))$ denote the functions implicitly defined by the following sufficient conditions for optimality:

(17a) $c_1'(s_1) \geq \theta E \max[w(x) - v, 0]$,   equality if $s_1 > 0$,

(17b) $c_2'(s_2) \geq (1-\theta)E \max[w(x) - v, 0]$,   equality if $s_2 > 0$.

Since $c_1'(s_1)$ and $c_2'(s_2)$ are both continuous and increasing, the implicit functions defined by (17), $\sigma_1(v)$ and $\sigma_2(v)$, are both continuous and nonincreasing. Furthermore, $c_1'(s_1) \geq 0$, $c_2'(s_2) \geq 0$, and $w(1) \geq w(x) \forall x \in [0,1]$ together with (17) imply $\sigma_1(w(1)) = \sigma_2(w(1)) = 0$. Finally, the hypothesis implies either $\sigma_1(0) > 0$, $\sigma_2(0) > 0$, or both.

An inspection of (16) and (17) reveals that $v^0 = v_1^0 + v_2^0$ is a fixed point of the continuous function $\phi(v)$ defined by

(18) $r\phi(v) = \max_{s_1 \geq 0} [(s_1 + \sigma_2(v))\theta E[w(x) - v, 0] - c_1(s_1)]$

$\qquad + \max_{s_2 \geq 0} [(\sigma_1(v) + s_2)(1-\theta) E[w(x) - v, 0] - c_2(s_2)]$.

Since $(s_1^0, s_2^0) = (\sigma_1(v^0), \sigma_2(v^0))$, it suffices to establish that $\phi(v)$ has a unique fixed point. Because $Ew(x) > 0$ and $c_1(0) = c_2(0) = 0$, the fact that either $\sigma_1(0) > 0$, $\sigma_2(0) > 0$, or both implies $\phi(0) > 0$. Furthermore, $\phi(w(1)) = 0$ because $\sigma_1(w(1)) = \sigma_2(w(1)) = 0$. Hence, the continuity of $\phi(v)$ is sufficient to guarantee a $v^0 = \phi(v^0) \in (0, w(1))$. Finally, the fixed point is unique because (18) and $\sigma_1(v)$, $i = 1$ and 2, nonincreasing imply that $\phi(v)$ is decreasing.

The hypothesis is necessary as well as sufficient for a nontrivial equilibrium. If both (i) and (ii) fail, then the equilibrium is $(s_1^0, s_2^0) = 0$. No unmatched agent searches because the marginal cost is too high relative to the expected benefit of trying to find a match.

In equilibrium, the matching rate is

$$(19) \qquad \alpha^0 = (s_1^0 + s_2^0) \Pr\{x \in A^0\} = (s_1^0 + s_2^0)[1 - F(x^0)],$$

where x^0 is the marginally acceptable fit as defined by (14). In other words, the equilibrium matching rate is equal to the product of the equilibrium meeting rate and the equilibrium probability that a random meeting of an unmatched pair will yield an acceptable match. Both of these and, hence, the equilibrium steady state fraction of unmatched agents $E(n/m) = \beta/(\alpha + \beta)$ vary with θ, the shares of the surplus obtained by the two agent types.

Given an appropriate modification of the equations of (12), the existence of a matching equilibrium can also be established for the quadratic matching technology. During a short interval of length Δt, the probability that an individual agent of type i will either find or be found by some unmatched agent of the other type, $j \neq i$, is

$$\Delta t [s + s_j](n/m).$$

Here s is the agent's own search intensity, s_j is the common intensity at which agents of the other type search, and n/m, the fraction of unmatched agents of each type, is both the probability that an agent found by our individual is not matched and the probability that some one of the n unmatched agents of the other type will find our individual. With large numbers of agents, n/m is (almost) nonstochastic and equal to $f(\beta/\alpha)$ in a steady state, where $f(\cdot)$ is the function defined by (7′).

By virtue of Bellman's principle, a particular agent of type i selects an intensity that solves

$$v_i = \max_{s \geq 0} \left\{ -\Delta t c_i(s) + \frac{\Delta t}{1 + r\Delta t}(s + s_j)f(\beta/\alpha)E\max[w_i(x), v_i^0] \right.$$
$$\left. + \frac{1}{1 + r\Delta t}[1 - \Delta t(s + s_j)f(\beta/\alpha)]v_i \right\},$$

providing that bargaining outcomes are individually rational. If the search intensities chosen by all other agents are known and regarded as given, then the joint solution for all agents is the noncooperative Nash search intensity pair (s_1^0, s_2^0) with associated payoff that satisfy

$$(20a) \qquad rv_1^0 = \max_{s_1 \geq 0} [(s_1 + s_2^0)f(\beta/\alpha^0)E\max[w_1(x) - v_1^0, 0] - c_1(s_1)],$$

$$(20b) \qquad rv_2^0 = \max_{s_2 \geq 0} [(s_1^0 + s_2)f(\beta/\alpha^0)E\max[w_2(x) - v_2^0, 0] - c_2(s_2)],$$

where

(21a)
$$\alpha^0 = (s_1^0 + s_2^0)[1 - F(x^0)]$$

and

(21b)
$$x^0 = w^{-1}(v^0).$$

Replacing the conditions of (12) with (20), we obtain sufficient conditions for a matching equilibrium in the quadratic case.

Consider again the family of feasible and individually rational bargaining outcomes that divide the surplus of every match according to fixed shares, those defined by (15) for all values of $\theta \in [0,1]$.

Proposition 2. Given a quadratic matching technology, a nontrivial equilibrium exists for every $\theta \in [0,1]$ if either (i) $c_1'(0) < \theta Ew(x)$ or (ii) $c_2'(0) < (1-\theta)Ew(x)$.

Proof. Given (15), the equations of (20) can be rewritten as

(22a) $$rv_1^0 = \max_{s_1 \geq 0} [(s_1^0 + s_2)f(\beta/\alpha^0)\theta E\max[w(x) - v^0, 0] - c_1(s_1)],$$

(22b) $$rv_2^0 = \max_{s_2 \geq 0} [(s_1^0 + s_2)f(\beta/\alpha^0)(1 - \theta)E\max[w(x) - v^0, 0] - c_2(s_2)],$$

where $v^0 = v_1^0 + v_2^0$. Again, consider the necessary and sufficient conditions for an optional pair (s_1, s_2) given an arbitrary v^0, denoted as v. These are

(23a) $c_1'(s_1) \geq f(\beta/\alpha)\theta E\max[w(x) - v, 0]$,   equality if $s_1 > 0$,

(23b) $c_2'(s_2) \geq f(\beta/\alpha)(1 - \theta)E\max[w(x) - v, 0]$,   equality if $s_2 > 0$.

Because $f(\beta/\alpha)$ is increasing and $\alpha = (s_1 + s_2)[1 - F(w^{-1}(v))]$, the equations define continuous functions $(\sigma_1(v), \sigma_2(v))$ such that $(\sigma_1(0), \sigma_2(0)) > 0$ and $\sigma_1(w(1)) = \sigma_2(w(1)) = 0$. Hence, $v(w(1)) = 0$ and $v(0) > 0$ so that a fixed point $v^0 = \varphi(v^0) \in (0, w(1))$ exists, where $\varphi(v)$ is the function defined by

$$r\varphi(v) = \max_{s_1 \geq 0} [(s_1 + \sigma_1(v))f(\beta/\alpha(v))\theta E\max[w(x) - v, 0] - c_1(s_1)]$$

$$+ \max_{s_2 \geq 0} [(\sigma_1(v) + s_2)f(\beta/\alpha(v))(1 - \theta)E\max[w(x) - v, 0] - c_2(s_2)]$$

and

$$\alpha(v) = [\sigma_1(v) + \sigma_2(v)][1 - F(w^{-1}(v))].$$

Because the functions $(\sigma_1(v), \sigma_2(v))$ need not be nonincreasing, the argument used to establish uniqueness in proposition 1 does not go through. Nevertheless, for every fixed point $v^0, (s_1^0, s_2^0) = (\sigma_1(v^0), \sigma_2(v^0))$ is an equilibrium search intensity pair.

7.4 Matching Efficiency

In the linear matching technology case, unmatched agents do not search intensively enough in any of the equilibria identified in the previous section. Specifically, an intensity pair $(s_1, s_2) > (s_1^0, s_2^0)$ exists that is strictly preferred by every unmatched couple. Because the matching frequency is determined by the search intensities of all agents, an increase in that of one type augments the value of search to every member of the other type. However, no individual agent takes account of this external economy. In this section, I show that this externality is internalized by the bargaining outcome that allocates all the surplus attributable to every match to the agent responsible for making the match.

Although this same externality is present given a quadratic technology, there is another with a countervailing effect. It arises because the expected meeting rate is proportional to the fraction of unmatched pairs which is itself endogenously determined as a decreasing function of the sum of the intensities with which the two agent types search. In the absence of the first externality, more intensive search by all other agents reduces the return to search for each individual by reducing the probability that an agent met will be unmatched. Interestingly, if the surplus attributable to every match is shared equally, then the effect of the second externality just cancels that of the first in the limit as the fraction of unmatched agents tends to zero. In the general case, joint wealth maximization requires that the matchmaker receive the larger share of the surplus attributable to each match.

The principal purpose of this section, then, is to show that most equilibria are inefficient but that joint wealth maximizing equilibria exist if a more general class of feasible and individually rational bargaining outcomes is allowed. The class includes those that make the division of the surplus attributable to every match between the partners contingent on the identity of the agent responsible for making the match.

To formally establish that every equilibrium identified in the previous section is inefficient given a linear technology, we use the fact that the conditions of (16) implicitly define two functions $v_1(s_2)$ and $v_2(s_1)$ such that $(v_1^0, v_2^0) = (v_1(s_2^0), v_2(s_1^0))$. Both are clearly continuous and strictly increasing because of the external economy already discussed. If $(s_1^0, s_2^0) > 0$, then these functions and the first-order conditions for a Nash strategy choice by members of each agent type implicitly define the equilibrium intensity pair (s_1^0, s_2^0) as the intersection of the two reaction curves. Formally, (16) and (17) imply

$$c_1'(s_1^0) = E \max [w_1^0(x) - v_1(s_2^0), 0]$$

and

$$c_2'(s_2^0) = E \max [w_2^0(x) - v_2(s_1^0), 0].$$

Let $g_i(s_j), j \neq i$, denote the two reaction curves implicitly defined by these two equations. As $c_i'(s_i)$ and $v_i(s_j)$ are all strictly increasing, the optimal choice by one type given the other's intensity $g_i(s_j)$ is continuous and decreasing as illustrated in figure 7.1. The curves labeled v_1^0 and v_2^0 in the figure represent the intensity pairs that yield the same value of search to agents of type $i = 1$ and 2 as that obtained at (s_1^0, s_2^0). Since the payoff realized by each type increases with the other's search intensity, all intensity pairs in the shaded region in figure 7.1 are strictly preferred by agents of both types to the equilibrium (s_1^0, s_2^0).

The average quality of the matches that form in equilibrium is also too low. Since $v = v_1 + v_2 > v^0 = v_1^0 + v_2^0$ for any intensity pair in the preferred region, the minimally acceptable fit $w^{-1}(v)$ is larger than in equilibrium. As a consequence, the matching rate $\alpha = (s_1 + s_2)[1 - F(w^{-1}(v))]$ can be too small even though $(s_1 + s_2) > (s_1^0 + s_2^0)$. In other words, the existence of the externality does not unambiguously imply that the equilibrium fraction of unmatched agents $\beta/(\alpha^0 + \beta)$ is too large except in the special case in which all matches have identical values ex post ($w(x) = w \; \forall x \in [0,1]$).

No unmatched agent searches intensively enough because none expects to receive the net social benefit attributable to the formation of a match, $w(x) - v_1^0 - v_2^0$, in the future in return for the marginal investment

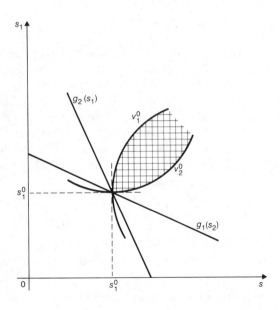

Fig. 7.1   Nash equilibrium.

required to seek out some agent of the opposite type. Viewed from this perspective, it would appear that the externality could be internalized by allocating the entire net benefit, the surplus attributable to such a match, to the agent who succeeded in making the contact responsible for the formation of the match. This particular allocation rule is a special case of the class of bargaining outcomes that are contingent on this random event.

Let $w_{ij}(x)$ denote the value of a match with fit $x \in [0,1]$ to the agent of type i given that the pair met as a consequence of a contact made by the agent of type j. The argument provided in the previous section justifies the following generalization of the equilibrium concept.

Definition 2. An allocation rule $(w^0_{1j}, w^0_{2j}) : [0,1] \rightarrow \mathbf{R}^2_+, j = 1$ and 2, and a search intensity pair $(s^0_1, s^0_2) \in \mathbf{R}^2_+$, is an equilibrium solution to the noncooperative bargaining game of matching given a linear technology if

$$(24a) \quad rv^0_1 = \max_{s_1 \geq 0} \{s_1 E \max[w^0_{11}(x) - v^0_1, 0] + s^0_2 E \max[w^0_{12}(x)$$

$$- v^0_1, 0] - c_1(s_1)\},$$

$$(24b) \quad rv^0_2 = \max_{s_2 \geq 0} \{s^0_1 E \max[w^0_{21}(x) - v^0_2, 0] + s_2 E \max[w^0_{22}(x)$$

$$- v^0_2, 0] - c_2(s_2)\}$$

and for $j = 1$ and 2,

$$(25a) \quad w(x) = w^0_{1j}(x) + w^0_{2j}(x), \quad \forall\, x \in [0,1],$$

$$(25b) \quad w(x) \geq v^0_1 + v^0_2 \Rightarrow (w^0_{1j}(x), w^0_{2j}(x)) \geq (v^0_1, v^0_2), \quad \forall\, x \in [0,1].$$

The conditions of (24) define a noncooperative Nash search intensity pair and reflect the fact that the surplus obtained by each party to a match is contingent on who made the contact. The conditions of (25) require that the contingent allocation of the value be feasible and individually rational. One can easily establish existence in the sense of proposition 1 for every rule that divides the surplus attributable to every match according to shares contingent on the name of the agent making the match.

An inspection of (24) reveals that the externality is still present except in the special case

$$(26) \quad w^0_{ij}(x) = \begin{cases} v^0_i + w(x) - v^0_1 - v^0_2 & \text{if } j = i, \\ v^0_i & \text{if } j \neq i. \end{cases}$$

This rule obviously allocates all the surplus of every match to the agent responsible for the contact that led to its formation. Given (24) and (26), we have

$$rv^0 = \max_{(s_1, s_2) \geq 0} [(s_1 + s_2) E \max[w(x) - v^0, 0] - c_1(s_1) - c_2(s_2)],$$

where $v^0 = v^0_1 + v^0_2$. Hence,

Proposition 3. Given a linear technology, the joint wealth of every unmatched couple is maximum in equilibrium if and only if all the surplus associated with every match is allocated to the agent responsible for its formation.

Given a quadratic matching technology, the analogous definition of an equilibrium is obtained by replacing the conditions of (24) by

$$(27a) \qquad rv_1^0 = \max_{s_1 \geq 0} \{s_1 f(\beta/\alpha^0) E \max[w_{11}^0(x) - v_1^0, 0] - c_1(s_1)$$

$$+ s_2^0 f(\beta/\alpha^0) E \max[w_{12}^0(x) - v_1^0, 0]\},$$

$$(27b) \qquad rv_2^0 = \max_{s_2 \geq 0} \{s_2 f(\beta/\alpha^0) E \max[w_{22}^0(x) - v_2^0, 0] - c_2(s_2)$$

$$+ s_1^0 f(\beta/\alpha^0) E \max[w_{21}^0(x) - v_2^0, 0]\},$$

where $f(\beta/\alpha)$ is the increasing function defined by (7') and

$$(28) \qquad \alpha^0 = (s_1^0 + s_2^0)[1 - F(w^{-1}(v^0)]$$

is the equilibrium rate at which acceptable matches form. Again, equilibrium can be established for any rule that allocates the surplus according to shares contingent on the name of the agent responsible for the contact using the argument of proposition 2.

An inspection of (27) reveals the following fact. Were the efficient allocation rule for the linear case ($w_{ij}^0 = v_i^0, j \neq i$) adopted, then every agent searches too intensely. The reduction of the probability that an agent contacted in the future will be unmatched attributable to more intensive search by all ($f'(\cdot) > 0$) is not taken into account by any individual. This observation suggests that some rule that allocates less than the entire surplus to the agent responsible for making a particular match might have the desired incentive properties.

The joint wealth maximizing problem is

$$(29a) \qquad rv^* = \max_{(s_1, s_2) \geq 0} \{(s_1 + s_2) f(\beta/\alpha) E \max[w(x) - v^*, 0]$$

$$- c_1(s_1) - c_2(s_2)\}$$

$$= (s_1^* + s_2^*) f(\beta/\alpha^*) E \max[w(x) - v^*, 0] - c_1(s_1^*) - c_2(s_2^*),$$

where

$$(29b) \qquad \alpha = (s_1 + s_2)[1 - F(w^{-1}(v^*))].$$

As $f(\cdot)$ is an increasing concave function such that $f(0) = 0$ by virtue of (7'), the right-hand side of (29a) is strictly concave in (s_1, s_2). Hence, the following first-order conditions are sufficient to determine the search strategy pair (s_1^*, s_2^*) that maximize the sum of the values of search $v_1 + v_2$:

(30) $$c'_i(s^*_i) \geq \left[f(\beta/\alpha^*) + (s^*_1 + s^*_2)f'(\beta/\alpha^*)\frac{\partial(\beta/\alpha)}{\partial(s_1 + s_2)} \right]$$

$$\times \frac{\partial(s_1 + s_2)}{\partial s_i} E\max[w(x) - v^*, 0]$$

$$= [1 - \eta(\beta/\alpha^*)]f(\beta/\alpha^*) E\max[w(x) - v^*, 0],$$

with strict equality holding if $s^*_i > 0$, $i = 1$ and 2, where $\eta(x) = xf'(x)/f(x)$ is the elasticity of $f(\cdot)$. As $\eta(0) = \frac{1}{2}$ and $f(0) = 0$ while $\eta(\infty) = 0$ and $f(\infty) = 1$ by virtue of $(7')$, one can establish that v^* exists by applying the now familiar fixed point argument.

Equations (29) and (30) imply that the joint wealth maximizing intensity pair is a Nash solution given the following feasible and individually rational contingent bargaining outcome:

(31) $$w_{ij}(x) = \begin{cases} v^0_i + [1 - \eta(\beta/\alpha^*)][w(x) - v^0_1 - v^0_2] & \text{if } j = i, \\ v^0_i + \eta(\beta/\alpha^*)[w(x) - v^0_1 - v^0_2] & \text{if } j \neq i, \end{cases}$$

$i = 1$ and 2. Given this rule, every Nash solution (s^0_1, s^0_2) satisfies

(32) $$rv^0 = \max_{(s_1, s_2) \geq 0} \{(s_1 + s_2)[1 - \eta/\beta/\alpha^*)]f(\beta/\alpha^0)$$

$$\times E\max[w(x) - v^0, 0] - c_1(s_1) - c_2(s_2)\}$$

$$+ (s^0_1 + s^0_2)\eta(\beta/\alpha^*)f(\beta/\alpha^0) E\max[w(x) - v^0, 0],$$

where $v^0 = v^0_1 + v^0_2$ by virtue of (27). Consequently,

(33) $$c'_i(s^0_i) \geq [1 - \eta(\beta/\alpha^*)]f(\beta/\alpha^0) E\max[w(x) - v^0, 0]$$

with strict equality holding if $s^0_i > 0$, $i = 1$ and 2.

Clearly, every solution to (29) and (30) satisfies (32) and (33). Hence,

Proposition 4. Given a quadratic technology and a contingent bargaining outcome that allocates to the agent responsible for making every match the share $1 - \eta(\beta/\alpha^*)$ of its surplus, a search intensity pair that maximizes the joint wealth of every unmatched couple is a Nash solution to the game of search intensity choice.

Because of the possibility of multiple equilibria (see proposition 2), the converse is not guaranteed. However, if there is an inefficient equilibrium, neither agent type searches intensively enough.

Proposition 5. Given the hypothesis of proposition 4, the joint wealth maximizing search intensity pair (s^*_1, s^*_2) is unique and at least as large as (s^0_1, s^0_2), any Nash solution associated with the allocation rule (31).

Proof. Because $\frac{1}{2} \geq \eta(\beta/\alpha) \geq 0$ and $c'_1(s_1)$ and $c'_2(s_2)$ are continuous and strictly increasing, the functions $v(s_1, s_2)$ defined by

$$rv(s_1, s_2) = [s_1 c'_1(s_1) + s_2 c'_2(s_2)]/[1 - \eta(\beta/\alpha^*)] - c_1(s_1) - c_2(s_2)$$

are continuous and strictly increasing,

$$v^* = v(s_1^*, s_2^*),$$

and

$$c_1'(s_1^*) = c_2'(s_2^*) \qquad \text{if } (s_1^*, s_2^*) > 0$$

by virtue of (29) and (30), while

$$v^0 = v(s_1^0, s_2^0)$$

and

$$c_1'(s_1^0) = c_2'(s_2^0) \qquad \text{if } (s_1^0, s_2^0) > 0$$

by virtue of (32) and (33). Hence, the fact that v^* is unique and such that $v^* \geq v^0$ by definition implies (s_1^*, s_2^*) unique and $(s_1^*, s_2^*) \geq (s_1^0, s_2^0)$. QED.

Furthermore, proposition 5 provides the means needed to establish the following converse of proposition 4.

Proposition 6. Given the hypothesis to proposition 4, a Nash solution to the game of search intensity choice maximizes the joint wealth of every unmatched couple if all matches are identical ex post ($w(x) = w \; \forall \, x \in [0, 1]$).

Proof. Because all matches are acceptable ($w \geq v^0$) in equilibrium $\alpha^0 = (s_1^0 + s_2^0)[1 - F(w^{-1}(v^0))] = s_1^0 + s_2^0$. Hence, under the hypothesis, (33) can be rewritten as

$$(34a) \quad c_1'(s_1^0) \geq [1 - \eta(\beta/\alpha^*)]f(\beta/(s_1^0 + s_2^0))[w - v^0], \qquad \text{equality if } s_1^0 > 0,$$

and

$$(34b) \quad c_2'(s_2^0) \geq [1 - \eta(\beta/\alpha^*)]f(\beta/(s_1^0 + s_2^0))[w - v^0], \qquad \text{equality if } s_2^0 > 0.$$

Because $f(\beta/\alpha)$ is strictly increasing and continuous and $c_1'(s_1)$ and $c_2'(s_2)$ are both strictly increasing and continuous, the solution to (34) is unique for every choice of v^0 and decreases as v^0 increases. As (s_1^*, s_2^*) solves (34) when $v^0 = v^*$, $v^* > v^0$ implies $(s_1^*, s_2^*) < (s_1^0, s_2^0)$, which contradicts proposition 5.

One way to interpret these results follows. When the agent who makes each match receives the entire surplus, a joint wealth maximizing equilibrium is possible if the agent's share $[w(x) - v^0]$ is taxed at the proportional rate $\eta(\beta/\alpha^*)$ and if the proceeds of the tax are redistributed to the other agent. The optimal tax rate depends on the joint wealth maximizing meeting rate $\alpha^* = (s_1^* + s_2^*)[1 - F(w^{-1}(v^*))]$. To calculate it, one would have to solve explicitly the joint wealth maximizing problem. However, because $E(n/m) = f(\beta/\alpha)$, $f(0) = 0$ and $\eta(0) = \frac{1}{2}$, and $f(\infty) = 1$ and $\eta(\infty) = 0$, the optimal tax rate is approximately $\frac{1}{2}$ (the surplus is shared equally) if the equilibrium fraction of unmatched agents is near zero and unique and is zero (the agent who makes a match gets all the surplus) if the equilibrium fraction of unmatched agents is near one and unique. Finally, uniqueness of equilibrium is guaranteed if matches are not too heterogeneous ex post.

7.5   A Summary and a Reinterpretation

A unique feasible and individually rational division of the surplus attributable to every match that motivates all unmatched agents to search efficiently exists given either technology. The allocation has the property that a larger share is received by the agent responsible for making the match. The sum of the ex ante present values of the future net incomes accruing to the members of the typical unmatched pair is maximum when they expect this allocation rule to obtain. However, no individual once contacted by another has an incentive to agree to that division ex post. Furthermore, the agent who made the contact has no special bargaining position as a consequence once the meeting takes place. Hence, there is no reason to believe that ex post bilateral bargaining will yield the efficient agreement.

Agents who are as yet unmatched might precommit. Each may well be willing to agree ex ante to assign the unknown agent who will make the match the appropriate share of the surplus. However, there exists no means by which the typical unmatched pair can meet ex ante for this purpose. Once the pair meets, the two no longer have the incentives required to obtain the agreement that might have motivated their meeting. The fact of having met only presents them with the bilateral bargaining problem as we formulated it in the text.

This paradox might be resolved by introducing a class of third parties, brokers or middlemen, who supply matching services and by so doing have a continuing interest in the bargaining outcomes. Of course, brokers exist in many market contexts in which matching is important. Labor markets, markets for housing, and at various times and places the "marriage market" all serve as examples. The presumed ability of specialists to provide matching services of better quality and at a lower cost is the usual explanation given for the existence of such middlemen. Although these advantages may be necessary to explain the existence of brokers, another possible role is suggested by the following reinterpretation of the model.

Suppose that there are two types of principals that can be matched as pairs for some purpose. However, assume that the cost of self-search by each principal is prohibitive relative to the expected benefit attributable to a future match. A principal can hire a broker to search in his stead at a reasonable price because the latter can search more economically. Given that none of the principals search for themselves, $w(x)$ is the difference between the total value of a match with fit x and the sum of the opportunity cost that the two would incur were they matched. Given this interpretation, any match with fit x such that $w(x) - p(x) \geq 0$ is acceptable to the pair, where $p(x)$ is the sum of the contingent commissions that the two principals pay to their brokers. If the sum of the opportunity costs of being matched is the same for every unmatched pair, then competition among the many unmatched principals for the scarce matching services supplied by brokers would bid the sum of the commission up to $w(x)$. Given this price structure, the agents in our model can be interpreted as the brokers who represent the $2n$ unmatched principals.

Because all the matches are equivalent from each principal's perspective and each is indifferent to the length of time required to obtain a match, the search intensities and the criterion for an acceptable match are discretionary decisions taken by the brokers. Hence, s_i is the intensity of search chosen by a broker who represents a principal of type i and v_i is the present value of the profit that the broker can expect in return for his effort to locate a match for that principal. An allocation of $w(x)$ between the two agents who meet to form a match is now a division of the commission, that both principals are willing to pay, between their respective brokers.

The one difference is that the brokers have a continuing interest in the market for matching services that principals searching for themselves would not have. Having formed one match, they look forward to the prospect of doing the same for other principals in the future. They not only have an incentive to precommit themselves to the efficient allocation rule; as third parties they also have the means to do so. The fact that in some market contexts the broker responsible for creating a match receives the entire finder's fee while in others commissions are split between the principals' brokers in a prescribed manner is suggestive in the light of our results concerning the dependence of the efficient allocation rule on the form of the matching technology.

This reinterpretation of the model is obviously a very special case once brokers are introduced. The opportunity costs of being matched is not the same for all principals of the same type. This kind of heterogeneity will create inframarginal rents for some and hence an interest in the intensity with which the broker searches. A general model must also allow for search by the principals as well as the brokers. These complications may yield quite different results. Nevertheless, the reinterpretation suggests a fruitful path for further research.

References

Diamond, Peter, and Maskin, Eric. 1979. An equilibrium analysis of search and breach of contract, I: Steady states. *Bell Journal of Economics* 10: 282–316.

Feller, William. 1968. *An introduction to probability theory and its applications*, vol. 1, 3d ed. New York: John Wiley & Sons.

Mortensen, Dale T. 1978. Specific capital and labor turnover. *Bell Journal of Economics* 9: 572–86.

Nash, J. F. 1950. The bargaining problem. *Econometrica* 18: 155–62.

Wilson, Charles. 1979. Equilibrium employment and wage levels in some models with job matching and moral hazard. Paper presented at Northwestern University, 30 April 1979.

Comment   Peter Diamond

Dale Mortensen's analysis of matching equilibrium focuses on the incentives for search effort. Each individual chooses a rate at which he tries to contact potential partners. With the quadratic technology the rate of success depends on the number of potential partners available. The quality of any potential match is a random variable. Mortensen assumes that matches are made (contracted) if and only if the value of the match exceeds the (dynamic programming) value of continued search by the pair of potential partners. Matches are not broken for better alternatives.

Mortensen's analysis of efficient incentives for search takes this contracting rule as given. Interestingly, this contracting rule is not socially efficient with the quadratic technology. Passing up a match that is just worthwhile improves the search process for others, at no cost to the pair passing up a match. This external economy implies that the efficient contracting rule involves passing up matches that are privately worthwhile.[1] This result is shown below.

This issue did not arise in my work with Maskin since we assumed that individuals could break a contract to form a better match with no resource cost. Once one assumes a setup cost for creation of a match, the same inefficiency in private contracting appears in a model with breach of contract.

To focus on the issue of contracting, Mortensen's model is simplified by eliminating search intensity as a decision variable. Let s_1 and s_2 be the (positive) rates of search of the two types of agents. Search is assumed to be costless. Since search does not vary with the division of the surplus from a match, we can assume that the surplus is divided evenly between partners, with no loss in generality.

With these simplifications, the equilibrium with a quadratic technology (Mortensen equations (20)–(21)) becomes

Peter Diamond is professor of economics at Massachusetts Institute of Technology.

$$rv_1^0 = (s_1 + s_2)f(\beta/\alpha^0)\frac{1}{2}E\max[w(x) - v_1^0 - v_2^0, 0],$$

(1) $$rv_2^0 = (s_1 + s_2)f(\beta/\alpha^0)\frac{1}{2}E\max[w(x) - v_1^0 - v_2^0, 0],$$

$$\alpha^0 = (s_1 + s_2)(1 - F(x^0)),$$

$$x^0 = w^{-1}(v_1^0 + v_2^0),$$

where r is the interest rate; v_i^0, the value of the search process; $w(x)$, the value of a match of quality x; $F(x)$, the distribution of the random variable x; β, a constant of the search process; f a positive increasing function determined by the search process; and 2, an integer lying between 1 and 3. With the equal division rule, we have $v_1^0 = v_2^0$, further simplifying the analysis.

Let us make the minimum acceptable quality of match a control variable. Denoting it by x^*, we can write the value equation as

(2) $$rv_1^0 = (s_1 + s_2)f(\beta/(s_1 + s_2)(1 - F(x^*)))\frac{1}{2}\int_{x^*}^{\infty}(w(x) - 2v_1^0)dF.$$

Individual incentives call for accepting any worthwhile match, i.e., having $w(x^*) = 2v_1^0$. If f did not vary with x^*, this would also be efficient for the matching process. However, since f increases in x^*, there is an external diseconomy in forming a match and v_1^0 is maximized at a higher level of x^*, one with $w(x^*) > 2v_1^0$. The level of x^* maximizing the steady state value satisfies

(3) $$w(x^*) - 2v_1^0 = \frac{\beta f'F'}{f(s_1 + s_2)(1 - F)^2}\int_{x^*}^{\infty}(w(x) - 2v_1^0)dF.$$

As long as match quality is variable, this expression is positive.

Note

1. Unemployment compensation is one method of inducing individuals to pass up matches that would otherwise be worthwhile.

Reference

Diamond, P., and Maskin, E. 1979. An equilibrium analysis of search and breach of contract, I: Steady states. *Bell Journal of Economics* 10: 82–105.

Comment   Steven A. Lippman

In the game-theoretic spirit of two earlier papers (Diamond and Maskin 1979; Mortensen 1978) with costly and imperfect information, Mortensen considers an environment in which homogeneous agents of two types meet pairwise via a search process in order to form a match. (We shall utilize marriage, apartment rentals, and the labor markets as prototypical examples.) The matches provide the sole source of benefits, search is the only cost, and each agent's payoff function is the expected discounted flow of net benefits. The focus of Mortensen's equilibrium analysis is on the incentives of unmatched agents for engaging/investing in search. Presumably, the incentives vary directly with the number n of unmatched pairs. We shall refer to n as the *state* of the system.

An important feature of Mortensen's approach is that the aggregate matching model is set up as a birth/death process. This structure, which is hinted at in Diamond and Maskin (1982) and Mortensen (1978), is quite general and admits a hearty mix of examples; employed in full-blown generality, however, the ensuing analysis would be nearly intractable. As formulated by Mortensen, a birth—an increase in the state n—occurs whenever a new unmatched pair is created; dissolution of an extant match (e.g., divorce) and immigration (e.g., entry into the labor force and creation of a new job) are the obvious means of increasing n, with the latter possibility explicitly excluded in this paper (and included in Diamond and Maskin 1979). A death occurs when a match is formed. This leads Mortensen to posit the birth and death rates

$$(1) \qquad\qquad\qquad \lambda_n = (m - n)\beta$$

$$(2) \qquad\qquad \mu_n = \begin{cases} \alpha n\ , & \text{the linear technology,} \\ \alpha\binom{n}{2}, & \text{the quadratic technology,} \end{cases}$$

where β is the dissolution (or turnover or divorce) rate and m is the number of each type of agent in the total population. Using these rates, the expected fraction of unmatched pairs is calculated and this quantity is then utilized in deriving properties of the equilibrium solution(s).

With the above setup an analysis different from Mortensen's could be pursued. Assuming that signals effective in revealing individual agents' existence and availability are in place—viz., absence of a wedding ring and presence at a singles bar, vacancy sign, or help wanted ad—a searching unmatched agent can avoid contacting an already matched agent. Moreover, these signals reveal the state of the system to all interested

Steven A. Lippman is professor, Graduate School of Management, University of California, Los Angeles.

parties, including potential entrants. With knowledge of the state of the system as revealed by the agents (or even their brokers), markets with system dynamics such as agglomerative and imitative effects can be included. For example, there are many contexts in which the immigration as well as the turnover rate should be modeled as increasing in n, for n is a measure of matching opportunities.

Further complications are presented by the fact that the birth and death rates are not exogenously given but rather affected (in a nonlinear manner) by the agents' strategies. We illustrate this and other complications in the following example.

Assume that the contract flow rate for each agent associated with any given contact is a random variable X with cumulative distribution function F, and X is independent of the past history of the system. To simplify matters, assume that the agents in any match must evenly divide the contract benefits, thereby eliminating the bargaining aspects of the model. In such a simple system with agglomeration, the agent's optimal strategy is characterized by two increasing sequences $\langle d_n \rangle$ and $\langle v_n \rangle$ as follows. When the state of the system is n, an unmatched agent will accept a match with flow rate in excess of v_n; matched agents will willingly (attempt to) separate when their current benefit is less than $d_n \, (\geq v_n)$. It is clear that

$$\mu_n = n(1 - F(v_n)),$$

but the birth rate is a function not only of n but also of the set of existing contracts. In order to maintain the Markovian nature of the process we can utilize Mortensen's assumption that matches are not voluntarily broken for better alternatives, though "involuntary" dissolutions are allowed; that is, dissolution for a particular match is not dependent upon the contract flow rate for that particular match. In this case we have

$$\lambda_{n,m} = \beta_n(m - n) + g_n,$$

where $2m$ is the total population of agents, β_n is the dissolution rate, and g_n is the immigration rate. As exposited we assume that β_n and g_n increase in n, with β_n serving as measure of population "malaise."

Now the value $V_{n,m}(v)$ of a match with flow v when there are n and $m - n$ unmatched and matched agents of each type is given by

$$
(3) \quad V_{n,m}(v) = \frac{v}{\alpha + \Lambda_{n,m}} + \frac{\Lambda_{n,m}}{\alpha + \Lambda_{n,m}} \left\{ \frac{\mu_n}{\Lambda_{n,m}} V_{n-1,m}(v) + \frac{g_n}{\Lambda_{n,m}} V_{n+1,m+1}(v) \right.
$$

$$
\left. + \frac{(m-1-n)\beta_n}{\Lambda_{n,m}} V_{n+1,m}(v) + \frac{\beta_n}{\Lambda_{n,m}} V_{n+1,m}(0) \right\}
$$

and

(4) $V_{n,m}(0) = \dfrac{\Lambda_{n,m}}{\alpha + \Lambda_{n,m}} \left\{ \dfrac{\mu_n/n}{\Lambda_{n,m}} \displaystyle\int_{v_n}^{\infty} V_{n-1,m}(x), dF(x)/[1 - F(v_n)] \right.$

$\left. + \dfrac{\frac{n-1}{n}\mu_n}{\Lambda_{n,m}} V_{n-1,m}(0) + \dfrac{(m-n)\beta_n}{\Lambda_{n,m}} V_{n-1,m}(0) + \dfrac{g_n}{\Lambda_{n,m}} V_{n+1,m+1}(0) \right\},$

where α is the discount factor, $\Lambda_{n,m} = \mu_n + \lambda_{n,m}$, $\Lambda_{n,m}/(\alpha + \Lambda_{n,m}) = Ee^{-\alpha T}$ is the expected discount factor,

$$\frac{v}{\alpha + \Lambda_{n,m}} = vE \int_0^T e^{-\alpha t} dt$$

is the expected discounted earnings till a change of state, and T is an exponential random variable with parameter $\Lambda_{n,m}$.

The difficulty in determining the existence and qualitative properties of $\langle v_n \rangle$ is apparent; nevertheless, success in such an undertaking would surely provide valuable insights.

References

Diamond, P., and Maskin, E. 1979. An equilibrium analysis of search and breach of contract, I: Steady states. *Bell Journal of Economics* 10: 282–316.

———. 1982. An equilibrium analysis of search and breach of contract II: A non–steady state example. *Journal of Economic Theory* 25:165–95.

Mortensen, D. 1978. Specific capital and labor turnover. *Bell Journal of Economics* 9: 572–86.

8   The Capacity Expansion Process in a Growing Oligopoly: The Case of Corn Wet Milling

Michael E. Porter and A. Michael Spence

A central aspect of the dynamic problem facing the firm in an evolving industry is the decision about additions to productive capacity. Particularly in capital intensive industries, capacity decisions have long lead times and involve commitments of resources which may be large in relation to firms' total capitalization. If the firm fails to add capacity at the appropriate time, it not only loses immediate sales and market shares but also may diminish its long-run competitive position—if the firm adds too much capacity, it can be burdened with unmet fixed charges for long periods of time. From a competitive standpoint, additions to capacity can pose major problems since the matching of capacity to demand is often a major determinant of industry rivalry and profits. The problem is most acute in industries producing standardized products, where product differentiation does not protect firms against mistaken capacity decisions of others.

The capacity decision not only involves high stakes, but also is fraught with subleties. In the presence of lead times and lumpiness, it requires expectations about future demand. It also involves the oligopolistic interdependence problem, since the capacity decisions of competitors over the

A. Michael Spence is professor of economics and business administration at Harvard University. Michael E. Porter is associate professor of business administration at Harvard.

The authors would like to thank George Rozanski for his invaluable help with the computing of the model. His skill, speed, and patience contributed greatly to this effort. We have benefited also from comments at seminars at MIT, the Antitrust Division, the Harvard Business School, the University of Montreal, the UCLA Business School, the Harvard Economics Department, and the Yale School of Management. We thank participants in these seminars for their patience and constructive input. The members of the NBER seminar (whose papers appear in this volume) and especially Professor Sidney Winter provided extremely useful insights into the relationship between this type of model and the models of general equilibrium theory.

259

planning horizon will determine the profitability of decisions by a single firm. These complexities suggest that modeling the capacity expansion process in an industry may have a high payout in understanding the structural conditions which drive it, the nature of equilibria, and the implications for the optimal capacity decisions of individual firms.

This paper attempts to model the capacity expansion process through the analysis of a specific recent case: the corn wet milling industry. The corn wet milling industry is typical of many large, undifferentiated product industries in the economy and provides a useful setting for such a study. While the model developed here uses data from corn wet milling, its structure and the principles that emerge are applicable to the capacity expansion process generally. Part of our purpose, however, has been to show how economic analysis can play a role in setting corporate investment decisions. For this purpose, the case study seemed well suited.

In carrying out this case study, we had several objectives. The analysis done here is similar to the analysis that would be carried out by a firm doing a careful job of corporate planning leading up to a major investment decision. We wanted to understand what the ingredients in such a problem looked like from the decision maker's standpoint. Of central concern was the predictability of the behavior of rivals and the analysis that would go into such predictions. It is our tentative conclusion that starting from common views about the nature of the market opportunity, firms can develop consistent views about their rivals' behavior and the returns to their own investment. Part of our purpose is to set out one version of the analytical model that would give rise to these shared and consistent predictions. This aspect of the study could be titled "The Structure of the Dynamic Equilibrium."

In addition to the model itself, we have been interested in the way in which the dynamic equilibrium varies with the underlying structural attributes, particularly the amount of uncertainty about demand for the product. The paper contains several observations about the impact of uncertainty on investment decisions and industry evolution. These are thoughts that could be developed further, using a theoretical model.

There are interesting differences in the ways in which firms respond to risks that emerge in the case study and that influence their investment decisions.

These and related issues need not be studied exclusively in the context of a case study. Indeed, they would not, but we found that the case study which forces one to attend to what the decision maker would find important and does not allow one to ignore relevant features of the problem is a useful way of locating the central conceptual issues and of shedding some light on the determinants of the evolution of industries in what (from a static point of view) is a disequilibrium situation. It is our hope that researchers in economics and business administration will find the approach useful and provocative.

The paper can be read in a number of ways, depending upon the reader's interest in the details of the analysis of the corn wet milling case. Section 8.1 describes the corn wet milling industry and a major investment opportunity presented by high fructose corn syrup. Section 8.2 discusses the model used to analyze the capacity expansion process in the market. The next six sections (8.3 through 8.8) present the details of corn wet milling economics and the assumptions of the model. Section 8.9 describes the equilibrium in the market. Sections 8.10 and 8.11 discuss the effects of varying degrees of uncertainty on the capacity expansion process and the sources of the expectations of firms in the industry.

Some readers may be interested more in the approach and the model than in the corn wet milling industry. Our suggestion would be to read section 8.1 as an introduction, and then read section 8.2, 8.9, 8.10, and 8.11.

8.1 The Corn Wet Milling Industry

The corn wet milling industry[1] converts corn into two major end products: cornstarch and corn syrup.[2] Except for a small fraction of industry output, cornstarch and corn syrup are commodity products, sold primarily to the food, textile, paper, and adhesives industries. Starch is used primarily as a stiffening and texturizing agent, while corn syrup is used as a texturizer, thickener, and sweetener.

Corn is ground into starch slurry (this operation is termed "basic grind"), which can be either further processed into finished starch or converted into corn syrup through a chemical process. Industry production uses continuous process technology, and the size of efficient increments to capacity is large. The minimum efficient scale plant processes 30,000 bushels of corn per day and represents an investment cost in excess of $30 million. Efficient increments to capacity are equally large. To put this in perspective, the total grind capacity of the industry in 1972 was 108 million bushels per day, the equivalent of thirty-six minimum efficient scale plants.

The corn wet milling industry had been a stable industry for decades, dominated by Corn Products Company (now CPC International) and consisting of approximately a dozen firms. Competition in the industry historically could be described as "gentlemanly." Through the 1960s and early 1970s, however, the industry was rocked by the entry of three "outsiders," all large commodity processing and trading firms (Grain Processing, Cargill, and Archer-Daniels-Midland). A period of intense industrial warfare and severe price competition periodically characterized the industry from the late 1960s until 1972 as the new entrants were assimilated; a few firms left the industry in the process. By 1972 and into 1973, however, industry capacity utilization had risen back to high levels and the industry consisted of eleven firms.

In 1972, however, this old industry was confronted by a potentially revolutionary development—the commercialization of high fructose corn syrup (HFCS). HFCS, a commodity product, is a corn syrup very high in fructose, or sweetness. It is made by further conversion of conventional corn syrup to add to its sweetness content. HFCS is a substitute for sugar and is intrinsically somewhat cheaper to produce than sugar. If HFCS were to replace a significant proportion of sugar, this new product would approximately double the size of the corn wet milling industry. Thus, the exogenous shock of HFCS's commercialization in 1972, proved a reality by initial sales of the product to the food industry by corn wet millers Standard Brands, and Staley Manufacturing Company, confronted every firm in the industry with an important decision about adding capacity to produce the new product.

8.1.1   The HFCS Capacity Decision

The firms confronting the decision about HFCS faced a myriad of issues. The first was the expected level of demand and the rate at which users would convert from sugar to HFCS. The principal market for HFCS is the liquid sugar market of which soft drinks are the dominant end use. The growth of the HFCS market depended on the rate at which users reformulated their products to allow the use of HFCS, and hence on the level of sugar prices and the consequent inducement to reformulate. Although HFCS was believed to be almost completely substitutable for sugar, small and subjective changes in the taste of some products occurred. This required additional care in product reformulation, and though this was not costly, fears about not duplicating the taste of products was a barrier to changeover. Also, the somewhat different physical properties of HFCS required some product reformulation in some cases.

The incentive of the user to change over to HFCS depended on the spread between the cost of HFCS and the price of sugar. HFCS costs less to produce than sugar, but sugar prices were highly volatile. Sugar was traded in a very politicized world market, with less developed countries as major suppliers. Sugar prices were supported above world market prices by legislation in the United States. It was believed that the trend in sugar prices would be up reflecting increased costs of production, though predicting sugar prices over the long run was difficult.

HFCS demand also depended to some extent upon the HFCS capacity that was actually built. Large users of sugar were unlikely to convert to HFCS unless enough capacity was on-stream that they could be assured of gaining adequate supplies and would not be at the mercy of only one or two HFCS suppliers. Thus, demand and supply were interdependent; this guaranteed some temporary excess capacity if high demand for HFCS was to occur.

The second major issue facing a corn wet miller in deciding about HFCS capacity was what way to participate in HFCS. If a firm decided to begin HFCS production at all, it had a number of alternatives. Because high fructose production involved further conversion of corn syrup, a firm would enter the HFCS market by diverting capacity it had used for corn syrup production into HFCS. Alternatively, it could divert basic corn grinding capacity, but build additional facilities to produce corn syrup and convert it into HFCS. Finally, the firm could construct fully integrated HFCS capacity, consisting of corn grinding capacity, corn syrup refining capacity, and HFCS conversion capacity.

If a firm chose to divert either grind capacity or integrated corn syrup capacity into the production of HFCS, it was necessarily removing capacity from the corn syrup or starch markets. Thus, if enough corn wet millers diverted capacity, supply would be insufficient to meet demand in these other markets and prices in them would rise. As a result, the corn syrup and starch profits of each firm depended on the HFCS capacity decision of all the other firms.

Conversely, the fact that HFCS production was at the end of the continuous process technology with starch slurry and corn syrup as intermediate products meant that the construction of integrated HFCS capacity was not without risk for the starch and corn syrup markets. If the integrated capacity constructed by firms in the industry significantly exceeded demand for HFCS, then the output of the upstream stages of the HFCS production process could be diverted into the starch or corn syrup markets. What is more, grind and corn syrup capacity diverted for use in HFCS production could be put back into the starch and corn syrup markets. Thus, if the HFCS capacity exceeded demand, not only would HFCS prices be depressed, but the starch and/or corn syrup markets would deteriorate. Even if a firm chose not to enter into the production of HFCS, it could not escape the effects of HFCS if this scenario occurred, and its profits depended on the HFCS capacity decisions of its rivals.

The profitability of HFCS would depend on the spread between HFCS costs and prices. Prices would be a function of the capacity utilization in the industry and of the price of sugar. If the demand for HFCS were close to or exceeded the HFCS capacity put on-stream, then HFCS would be expected to be priced relative to sugar (at approximately a 15 percent discount). However, if there were substantial excess HFCS capacity, then HFCS would likely be priced relative to cost. A significant part of HFCS costs were variable, the major element being the cost of corn. However, there were fixed operating overhead and significant capital costs. Judging from experience in the starch and corn syrup markets, in periods of substantial overcapacity the price of HFCS was likely to be near variable costs.

Other issues were access to HFCS production technology and the likely future changes in that technology. HFCS production technology was being licensed in 1972 by Standard Brands, the pioneer producer. However, other firms were also offering technology, and it was believed to be within reach of all the participants in the corn wet milling industry in 1972, though they might face a modest delay if they chose not to license from Standard Brands. HFCS technology was sure to improve, but there were no predictions that the basic process would change so that firms could gain significantly by waiting to invest.

Finally, a firm choosing not to enter into HFCS production faced a number of risks besides those described above. It would forego having a full line of corn sweeteners, all of which were sold to basically the same group of customers who might value dealing with a full-line firm. It would also give up the sales revenue and cash flow of participation in this potentially large market. This could increase vulnerability to price wars and might have a cost in terms of less capital to invest in the industry.

In 1972 there were eleven major firms in the corn wet milling industry. A list of the competitors and their capacities for producing HFCS and other products (starch and corn syrup) is given in table 8.1. The analysis that follows is conducted in terms of operating profits and margins. For the record, however, the costs of HFCS are roughly as in table 8.2.

8.2 The Approach to Assessing Competitor Behavior and the Evolution of the Market

In modeling the evolution of the corn wet milling industry, one is faced (as an analyst and as a competitor) with complexity created by the very

Table 8.1   Firms and Capacities in 1972 (millions of pounds)

Firm	Capacity in Starch and Corn Syrup	HFCS Capacity
American Maize	761	0
Anheuser-Busch	317	0
Archer-Daniels-Midland	951	0
Cargill	1,193	0
CPC International	3,439	0
Grain Processing	1,396	0
Hubinger	634	0
Pennick & Ford	825	0
National Starch	571	0
Staley	2,021	200
Standard Brands	1,196	200
Total	13,304	400

Table 8.2   **Costs of HFCS**

Cost Component	Cost per lb. (¢)
Raw materials (net of by-products)	2–4
Variable processing costs	2–4
Overhead	1–2
Capital cost at full capacity utilization	2.5–4

large number of possible outcomes. Such complexity is often dealt with by using scenarios, and we employ that procedure here. Scenarios simply aggregate continuously varying outcomes into a manageable number of interestingly different groupings. Thus, instead of describing demand by its level each year, for example, one can approximate the full range of outcomes with low, medium, and high demand scenarios. There is of course a risk in proceeding in this way. The scenarios, being approximations, can be incorrectly chosen so as to obscure important differences. The alternative, however, is an unmanageably large number of variables that make rigorous analysis impractical.

The second reason for employing scenarios relates to the sequential character of capacity decisions. Capacity decisions are not made on a once-for-all basis at a single point of time by every competitor. There is in fact a sequence of decisions through time, with information from the market about demand, prices, and competitors' behavior pouring in. As a practical matter, this must also be simplified. The approach taken here is to characterize the industry's evolution in terms of scenarios for purposes of predicting the "first round" decisions of competitors. The alternative is to try to deal with the full sequence of decisions, a procedure that also quickly becomes impractically complicated.

The modeling effort is guided by the following broad structure. For the individual firm, the profitability of its operations and its HFCS capacity decisions are determined by two sets of factors: (*a*) the evolution of demand and sugar prices, the latter being a predominant influence on HFCS prices, and (*b*) the capacity expansion decisions of its competitors. The demand-related factors are subject to uncertainty. And as noted earlier, they are not independent of capacity expansion. The decisions of competitors and the implications of those decisions for industry capacity are to be predicted.

Competitor analysis and the prediction of the pattern of industry capacity expansion are the central focus of our analysis. The fundamental principle we employ in searching for equilibrium is that the predicted industry capacity and the predicted behavior of rivals must be *consistent*. Consistency involves the following chain of reasoning.

The capacity decisions of individual competitors will depend in part upon the industry capacity expansion path that they anticipate. These decisions will also depend upon their preferences, their attitudes toward risk, their financial resources, and other factors. While firms' decisions depend upon anticipated capacity in the industry, actual industry capacity clearly depends upon firms' capacity decisions. Consistency requires that the anticipated pattern of industry capacity expansion is that which results from the predicted capacity decisions of the firms in the industry, whose decisions are in turn conditional on the anticipated industry capacity. This consistency requirement is an equilibrium in the sense that expectations converge on outcomes that are consistent with the behavior of rivals.

There is of course no *logical* reason why firms could not have expectations that were inconsistent with the likely behavior of rivals. But it does seem reasonable to assume that as part of the process of generating and refining their expectations, firms will *check* their projections for aggregate industry capacity against their analysis of competitors' decisions in the light of industry capacity. Anticipating that other firms are engaged in the same process, a single firm should expect industry capacity expansion to be the result of predicted choices about rivals behavior, and it should expect rivals to come to the same or similar conclusions. Consistency then simply summarizes the idea that intelligent rivals will converge in their expectations about each others' behavior.[3]

The ingredients in the model are illustrated in figure 8.1. The figure can be read as follows. We begin at (A) with an assumption about the expansion of industry capacity over time. That, combined with random

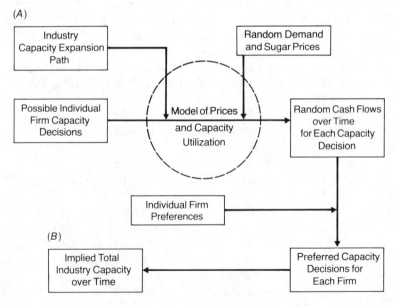

Fig. 8.1   Components of capacity expansion model.

demand, gives random net cash flows for each possible capacity expansion decision for each firm. The combining of demands, investment decisions by individual firms, and industry capacity expansion into cash flows over time involves an economic model of the industry. That model for corn wet milling is laid out in sections 8.3 to 8.8. The model takes capacity, demand, and sugar prices and generates prices, profit margins, and capacity utilization rates. The latter are then used to project cash flows for various possible investment decisions. The point is that there is a static industry model built in here.

In the language of microeconomics, the random cash flows that go with investment decisions can be thought of as the opportunity set, or, rather, the opportunity set, conditional on the industry capacity expansion scenario. In selecting a level of investment, the firm is selecting a random sequence of cash flows. Those random cash flows combined with firm preferences with respect to risk, return, and financial resources determine optimal capacity decisions for each firm. The individual firm investment decisions add up each year to give a time path for industry capacity (B). Note that the entire sequence is conditional on the starting assumption at (A). The consistency check is whether (A) and (B) are the same. A shared assumption about industry capacity which failed, via the process shown in figure 8.1, to generate the same industry capacity expansion path would not result from rational firm choices. It would therefore not be the assumption that careful firms would make. The expected evolution of industry capacity is that path that reproduces itself in figure 8.1. Then individual firm decisions and implied (uncertain) cash flows are the ones associated with that capacity expansion path.

From this description, it is easy to see that competitor analysis is the central feature of this model. The equilibrium is really the industry path that will withstand careful competitor analysis. Of course, if firms fail to check their assumptions in this way, then other paths could result. The hypothesis here is that they do.

This equilibrium assumption can be modified in a variety of ways to take into account the fact that firms' perceptions of uncertain events may differ and that their perceptions may be erroneous. The model allows firms' preferences, capabilities, and financial resources to influence their decisions. But the central organizing principle remains that anticipated growth must be consistent with rival firms' decisions, conditional on anticipated capacity growth.

It is worth noting that part of the economic structure of the model includes the assumption that there are no futures markets for high fructose corn syrup. Thus, firms cannot (and as far as we could tell did not) engage in futures contracts that assured both the quantity and price of future output from the plants they built. It is an interesting question why these markets did not exist. We will not try to give a complete answer here. We suspect that informational asymmetrics between the producers and buyers of HFCS concerning the completeness of the substitutability of HFCS for sugar made it difficult to structure contracts that would shift part of the risk to buyers or to third parties. Given that futures contracts did not exist, the planning process outlined in figure 8.1 can be thought of as a partial substitute for the price mechanism that would arbitrate these investment decisions in a general equilibrium world with a complete set of markets.

As Professor Winter points out in his insightful remarks in the comment to this paper, our hypothesis is that the evolving oligopoly, deprived of the full complement of markets required to guide investment decisions, *calculates* the equilibrium in the market and then makes the associated investment decisions. This calculated equilibrium is not the same one that would result with the full set of futures markets, because of the increased uncertainty that is created by the absence of those markets.

The detailed development of the model for the HFCS problem includes the following steps. First, a range of possible scenarios for demand and sugar prices is set out, with some assessment of their likelihoods. Next, a range of possible capacity expansion paths for the industry is constructed. Third, we assess the implications for profitability of a variety of capacity addition strategies for individual firms, conditional on demand and industry capacity expansion. Fourth, taking into account uncertainty about demand and individual firm characteristics, we determine the decisions the firms are likely to take, conditional on each of the industry capacity expansion scenarios. Finally, we ask which of the capacity expansion scenarios is most consistent with the sum of the capacity decisions of the firms. That becomes the predicted evolution of the industry and a prediction of the associated decisions for each firm. This sequence is carried out for the decisions taken in 1972 and checked against the historical record.

8.3 Demand and Sugar Price Scenarios

The potential demand for HFCS over the planning horizon depended on the proportion of sugar users who could be converted to HFCS. The 1972 demand for sugar was 14.3 billion pounds, of which 5.3 billion pounds was liquid sugar.[4] HFCS substituted for sugar on approximately a pound for pound basis. On the basis of the range of expert opinion in 1972, we can construct three scenarios for HFCS demand by 1980, as shown in table 8.3.

Demand is uncertain in two respects. The long-run size of the market and the rates at which actual demand would approach the long-run levels were matters of opinion. In constructing the scenarios depicted in table 8.3, we averaged over subgroups of a richer menu of scenarios consisting

Table 8.3	HFCS Demand in 1980 (pounds)		
Sugar Prices	Low Demand (2.5 billion)	Medium Demand (5.0 billion)	High Demand (10.0 billion)
Low (8¢)	Scenario A	Scenario B	X
Medium (18¢)	X	Scenario C	Scenario E
High (28¢)	X	Scenario D	Scenario F

of various long-run demands and rates of adoption of HFCS by the major potential users.

Demand over the 1973–80 time period was assumed to be an S-shaped function of time, and the time paths for demand in each of the low, medium and high scenarios are shown in table 8.4. The S-shaped function was chosen to reflect the path of adoption usually followed by new products such as HFCS. Given uncertainties and the costs of changeover, users convert slowly in the early years, with changeovers occurring at an accelerated rate once large-scale changeover begins to occur. Actual HFCS demand in 1972 was approximately 400 million pounds.

Sugar prices over the planning horizon could also vary. We simplify by abstracting from the short-run variation in sugar prices and creating three scenarios for average sugar prices between 1972 and 1980, also shown in table 8.3. Sugar prices were widely expected to be in the eighteen cent range, and this is taken as the medium sugar price scenario. The low sugar price scenario represents the floor of industry estimates and past history, with the high scenario an arbitrary figure selected on the basis of past sugar price movements and expectations in 1972. It was assumed that although sugar prices would fluctuate in the short run, these fluctuations could be ignored, and the average figures were used in calculations over the planning horizon.[5]

Demand for HFCS and sugar prices are not independent, however, as discussed above. Therefore, all the possible combinations of demand and sugar prices portrayed in table 8.3 are not in the feasible set. Demand for HFCS is very unlikely to be high unless sugar prices are high, and vice versa. Using this principle, three of the nine combinations in table 8.3 were eliminated, leaving six demand/sugar price scenarios. These six scenarios became the exogenous environment or states of nature in the

Table 8.4	HFCS Demand Scenarios (billions of pounds)							
	1973	1974	1975	1976	1977	1978	1979	1980
High demand	1.1	2.0	3.0	4.4	7.2	8.8	9.5	10.0
Medium demand	.7	1.0	1.4	1.8	3.0	4.0	4.5	5.0
Low demand	.66	.92	1.18	1.44	1.7	1.96	2.22	2.5

model. Firms' expectations over these scenarios were an important part of their decision making problem.

One might suspect that if the demand for HFCS were high and began to cut into the liquid sugar market, then the price of sugar would be cut as a response. Our view is that the HFCS market was not big enough to affect worldwide sugar prices significantly. Moreover, sugar prices appear to be set as a first approximation by raw sugar prices and a relatively stable refining cost and profit margin. Hence, the model takes sugar prices as random, but exogenous with respect to the development of the HFCS market. This is an approximation, one we felt did not do excessive violence to the facts.

One additional aspect of HFCS demand is built into the model, reflecting buyer behavior for this important input to their products. As described above, major buyers are unlikely to change over to HFCS unless sufficient capacity is on-stream to serve their needs without making them vulnerable to interruptions and bargaining power by a few suppliers. As a result, it is assumed that the high demand scenario cannot occur unless substantial capacity is added. This interdependence of supply and demand will be further reflected in the capacity/conversion scenarios described below.

Demand for products in the traditional corn milling markets—cornstarch and corn syrup—is assumed to be constant at 1972 levels. This corresponds to our use of 1972 figures for sugar demand. While both sugar demand and corn syrup/cornstarch demand were expected to grow, their expected rates of growth were similar and introducing growth into the analysis would needlessly complicate the model. The growth rates in the conventional markets were expected to be in the range of 3 percent per year.

8.4 Capacity Decisions of Competitors

To rationally make its own capacity decision, each firm had to predict the HFCS capacity that other corn wet millers would put on-stream and the degree to which they would convert capacity presently used in the other markets to HFCS. To do this, the firm had to assess each competitor's situation and predict the decision that the competitor would make. For purposes of the model, we simplify by assuming that the firm makes *aggregate* predictions about the behavior of its rivals. It predicts (*a*) the total HFCS capacity its competitors will add over the planning horizon and (*b*) the degree to which that capacity will be converted from uses in the corn syrup and cornstarch markets. The latter is critical because it will influence the supply/demand balance and hence prices in the markets for cornstarch and corn syrup.

We further simplify by abstracting the firm's predictions about the total capacity additions of its competitors into three capacity scenarios and into two scenarios about the extent of conversion. The scenarios for total capacity added are chosen to correspond to the demand scenarios described above. High total capacity additions by competitors will meet the total 1980 demand for HFCS in the high demand scenario, while medium and low total capacity additions by competitors will meet the medium and low 1980 HFCS demands, respectively. For the conversion scenarios, it is assumed either that competitors will convert no capacity—add all HFCS capacity on a fully integrated basis—or that 25 percent of the total HFCS capacity added by competitors will be converted from other markets. Moreover, since capacity equaled demand in 1972 for cornstarch and corn syrup, 25 percent conversion appeared to be the upper limit of the amount of capacity that would be converted in view of the profit potential in the other markets and the need to maintain customer relationships by serving their needs in the other markets. Heavy conversion of capacity increased the risk of alienation of customers in the other markets, many of whom would also be HFCS purchasers, and this could be especially serious if HFCS demand did not materialize.

The three scenarios for total competitor capacity additions are shown in table 8.5. The time path of competitor capacity additions was chosen to reflect lead times in capacity addition and the interdependence of demand and supply. Given the two-year lead time in adding integrated HFCS capacity and the one year needed to convert capacity, very little capacity could come on-stream in 1973 and 1974, which is reflected in all three scenarios. To achieve medium and especially high demand, much capacity would have to be put on-stream early in the planning period. Thus, we assume that capacity is put on-stream on an accelerated basis in 1975 and 1976, ahead of demand.

Where the capacity scenario did not match the actual HFCS demand scenario, excess or deficient capacity would become apparent in the

Table 8.5   **Capacity Expansion Scenarios (billions of pounds)**

	1973	1974	1975	1976	1977	1978	1979	1980	Demand
High capacity	.6	2.0	6.0	7.25	8.1	9.25	10	10	High
				6.0	6.0	6.0	6.0	6.0	Medium
				6.0	6.0	6.0	6.0	6.0	Low
Medium capacity	.6	1.5	3.5	5.75	7.75	9.25	10	10	High
				4.25	4.75	4.85	5.0	5.0	Medium
				3.5	3.5	3.5	3.5	3.5	Low
Low capacity	.5	1.0	2.0	NA	NA	NA	NA	NA	High
				3.0	4.25	4.85	5.0	5.0	Medium
				2.1	2.2	2.3	2.4	2.5	Low

industry by 1975 or 1976. Therefore, from 1976 onward, the assumed capacity expansion is chosen to reflect and is conditional on the level of demand in the HFCS markets. In table 8.5 each capacity expansion path branches into three subpaths in 1976, depending upon the observed level of demand. Thus, the pattern of capacity expansion from 1976 onward depends upon the demand-growth scenario that actually occurred.[6] Further, as argued earlier, high demand growth was very unlikely when capacity was low because the major buyers of HFCS were reluctant to switch over from sugar until there was sufficient capacity in the HFCS market to meet their needs. Later, in assigning probabilities to demand scenarios, we make the probability of high demand zero when capacity expansion is low.

8.5   Alternative Strategies

Each firm has a number of strategies available to it in HFCS. In the model, we allowed six possible strategies as shown in table 8.6. If the firm chose to do nothing, it simply continued to operate in the cornstarch and corn syrup markets. It could benefit if capacity was diverted into HFCS through conversion that removed capacity from those other markets, and it was vulnerable if excess capacity in HFCS caused the dumping of HFCS capacity into the traditional markets.

The most conservative strategy for entering HFCS production was to convert capacity from the other markets to HFCS by appending HFCS refining facilities to an existing plant. While a firm could theoretically choose to convert less, we assumed that the conversion option involved one minimum efficient scale, or MES. An MES plant has the capacity to grind 30,000 bushels per day of corn. A 30,000 bushel per day plant was capable of producing 357 million pounds of HFCS per year. The investment cost of adding HFCS refining capacity to an existing plant was estimated through industry interviews at $9 million, and conversion could take place in one year.[7]

More aggressive strategies were to build fully integrated HFCS capacity by either constructing a separate "greenfield" plant or adding another production unit to an existing corn wet milling complex. All options of constructing integrated capacity had an assumed lead time of two years. Firms could actually speed up construction slightly at an added cost. Two years was the most likely construction time, and the possibility of accelerated construction was eliminated from the model for simplicity.

The strategy of adding another production unit to an existing complex enabled the firm to economize on investment costs, because certain investments in infrastructure such as railroad sidings, storage facilities, and maintenance facilities could be shared. We have assumed that only one MES production unit could be added to an existing facility before

Table 8.6 Capacity Decision Options in HFCS

Strategy	Total HFCS Capacity On-Stream (millions of pounds)				Required Capital Investment (millions)				Total Investment (millions)	Change in Cornstarch/Corn Syrup Capacity (millions of pounds)
	1973	1974	1975	1976	1973	1974	1975	1976		
1. Do nothing	0	0	0	0	0	0	0	0	0	0
2. Convert one MES plant	0	357	357	357	$ 9	0	0	0	$ 9	−357
3. Add on one MES plant	0	0	357	357	$18	$18	0	0	$ 36	0
4. Construct one greenfield MES plant	0	0	357	357	$25	$25	0	0	$ 50	0
5. Select one add-on + one greenfield plant	0	0	714	714	$43	$43	0	0	$ 86	0
6. Select one add-on + two greenfield plants	0	0	714	1,071	$43	$68	$25	0	$136	0

new investment in infrastructure would have to be made, and we have further assumed initially that each firm had at least one existing corn wet milling complex where one such plant could be added at low investment cost. The investment cost for one MES greenfield production unit was estimated at $50 million, while the investment for an add-on unit was $36 million. These investment outlays were spread over the two years of construction. While the add-on strategy clearly dominated adding a greenfield plant if each firm was assumed to have one production complex where an add-on could be made, this assumption was easily relaxed later in the analysis.

The fifth strategy involved adding two MES units of integrated production capacity for HFCS. As in the previous options, the firm was assumed to have the ability to add on one unit at lower investment cost. It added the other MES sized unit through a greenfield plant at correspondingly higher investment. The final strategic option was to add three MES units of capacity, of which two were greenfield and one was add-on. This final strategy spread investment costs over three years, and capacity came on-stream in 1975 and 1976. All the strategies are described in table 8.6.

It was assumed that three MES sized production units was the maximum capacity any one firm could add in the HFCS market. This was based on the massive investment cost of HFCS capacity, but the option of adding a fourth HFCS production unit could be easily added to the model. We further assumed that mixed strategies involving conversion and construction of integrated HFCS capacity would not be adopted. This was because the conversion option was a low risk, low investment way to participate in HFCS which appeared to be inconsistent with making major investment outlays in constructing integrated HFCS capacity. While a firm might convert capacity in the short run to speed HFCS output onto the market, at the same time building capacity which would take a year longer to come on-stream, this tactical step was not allowed in the model for simplicity.

8.6   Expectations concerning Demand and Sugar Prices

How a particular investment appears to a firm will depend heavily upon the expectations with respect to demand and sugar prices described above in terms of scenarios. These expectations evolve over time as new information becomes available. It is possible for firms to have divergent expectations about these events, though there are forces that tend to produce convergent expectations (see section 8.11).

Initially, we have attributed to the firms the same views with respect to demand and sugar prices. We have also tested the sensitivity of the results to changes in these expectations. What actually occurred in the corn wet milling industry was a combination of unexpectedly high sugar prices in the 1973–75 period and an extraordinarily optimistic set of projections not only by firms, but also by securities analysts and other observers of the industry.

Table 8.7 gives the probabilities that were used for the purpose of calculating the expected present value and the standard deviations of returns to the various capacity expansion strategies. Note that when capacity is low, the probability of a high demand is zero. When capacity is low, the probabilities for the remaining demand and sugar price scenarios are the probabilities conditional on demand not being high.

Later, we report the effects of changing these probabilities. Those shown in table 8.7 reflect what appears to have been an optimistic view of the future, one that was widely held in the industry at the time. Little weight was given to low sugar prices, in part because the failure of Congress to extend the sugar price support legislation in 1974 was not anticipated. By 1974 sugar prices proved to be so high that the enactment of support legislation would have been politically infeasible. The long-run cost of refined sugar was believed to be in the neighborhood of eighteen cents per pound. The cost of HFCS, at 1972 prices of corn, was approximately ten cents per pound. Thus, while sugar prices could fluctuate significantly in the short run and while HFCS demand could develop slowly, the longer-term economics of HFCS success seemed reasonably assured.

8.7 Pricing, Capacity Utilization, and Supply/Demand in Starch and Corn Syrup

The next step in the model is to translate the demand and capacity scenarios into product prices and capacity utilization rates, in both high fructose corn syrup and the other markets for starch and corn syrup. We begin with HFCS. The capacity utilization rate in HFCS is the ratio of demand to capacity or the value one, whichever is smaller. HFCS is priced in relation to sugar unless there is considerable excess capacity in

Table 8.7   **Demand and Sugar Price Risks**

Demand/Sugar Price Scenario		Probability	
Demand	Sugar Price	Medium or High Capacity	Low Capacity
Low	Low	.05	.077
Low	Medium	.1	.154
Medium	Medium	.4	.615
Medium	High	.1	.154
High	Medium	.219	0
High	High	.131	0

HFCS. In the latter case, HFCS is priced close to operating cost.[8] With these principles in mind, we drew up the following pricing rules for the model: (*a*) If HFCS capacity utilization is less than 70 percent, then the HFCS operating margin is 2¢ per pound of output regardless of the level of sugar prices. This represents a loss, since capital costs are 2–2.5¢ per pound and overhead conservatively an additional 1¢ per pound. (*b*) If HFCS capacity utilization is greater than 70 percent, then the HFCS is priced in relation to sugar. Thus, if sugar prices are medium (18–20¢), the operating margin for HFCS is 10¢. If sugar prices are high, the operating margin for HFCS is 18¢ per pound. If sugar prices are low, the operating margin is 2¢ per pound of output.

With respect to the markets for starch and corn syrup, two possibilities arise. If capacity has been diverted to HFCS and is being used there, then there will be a capacity shortage in starch and corn syrup, putting upward pressure on prices. If on the other hand there is significant excess capacity in HFCS, that capacity can be diverted back into corn syrup, creating excess capacity and downward pressure on prices. With these principles, the specific assumptions are as follows.

Let H be HFCS capacity and c be HFCS capacity utilization. From the previous discussion let S be .25 if there was significant conversion (i.e., 25 percent) and zero otherwise. Excess capacity in starch and corn syrup is

$$E = H(1 - c - S).$$

The pricing rules are as follows: (i) if $E > 500$ million pounds, then operating margins on starch and corn syrup are one cent per pound, (ii) if $-500 < E < 500$, operating margins are three cents per pound, and (iii) if $E < -500$ million, there is a capacity shortage and operating margins are five cents per pound.

It remains to determine the operating profit for a typical firm in a given year. To do so, we need to specify how demand is allocated to capacity in each of the markets. In doing this, we have treated capacity in other products and excess HFCS capacity asymmetrically. The reasoning is that, provided prices are comparable, buyers of starch and corn syrup will stay with their regular suppliers rather than buy from an HFCS plant that has been opportunistically diverted back to starch and corn syrup because of excess capacity in HFCS. Thus, in starch and corn syrup, the old capacity, minus that which was converted, has first shot at the demand. Only if there remains some unsatisfied demand does the excess HFCS capacity get used to supply corn syrup and starch.

Suppose a firm has z units of HFCS capacity and t units of other capacity. Let c be the HFCS capacity utilization, m the HFCS operating margin, and q the starch operating margin. If there has been no conversion, there is no excess demand in starch and corn syrup. The profits of the firm are therefore $mzc + qt$. Here it is assumed that the firm's capacity utilization matches that of the industry. If there is substantial conversion (i.e., 25 percent of H), then there will be excess demand in starch relative to industry capacity. The excess demand is $.25H$. The capacity left over in HFCS is $H(1-c)$; thus, capacity utilization for the leftover capacity is

$$\min\left\{1, \left[\frac{.25H}{(1-c)H}\right]\right\} = \min\left\{1, \frac{.25}{1-c}\right\}.$$

The firm then gets additional profits of

$$qz(1-c)\min\left\{1, \left[\frac{.25}{(1-c)}\right]\right\} = qz\min[.25, 1-c].$$

Therefore, for the high conversion scenarios the operating profits for the firm with z units of HFCS capacity and t units of other capacity are

$$mzc + q[t + z\min(.25, (1-c))].$$

This, in conjunction with the pricing rules and capacity-demand scenarios described earlier, permits one to calculate the operating profits and cash flows through time for each firm, for various combinations of industry capacity expansion, demand, and specific decisions by the firms.

8.8 The Calculation of Returns to Investment for Firms and Strategies

Using the probabilities described in the previous section, the assumptions about pricing and capacity utilization, and the firms' initial positions, we calculated for each firm the net cash flows of investment for each combination of capacity, demand, and strategy. Using a discount rate of 10 percent, the present values of the cash flows were calculated for each strategy-capacity-demand combination. Next, with the probabilities as in section 8.6, we calculated the expected present value of the net cash flows and standard deviation of the present value of the net cash flows for each strategy-capacity combination. Note that investment in starch and corn syrup capacity is taken as sunk; depreciation on this investment is not added back to cash flows, nor is depreciation subtracted from operating profit. Thus, we have a true measure of cash flows. These will be higher than reported profits because the latter have depreciation on old plant and equipment subtracted out.

The results are reported in appendix A, where there is one table per firm, each containing thirty-six boxes corresponding to strategy-capacity pairs. Thus, in table A-1 for American Maize, the upper left-hand box corresponds to the strategy of converting one minimum efficient scale facility and to the high capacity, high conversion scenario for the industry. Within each box in the tables there are five numbers. They are (a) the expected value of the present value of the net cash flows of investment (EPDV), (*b*) the standard deviation of the present value of the cash flows (SD), (*c*) the maximum present value across demand scenarios (PVMAX), (*d*) the minimum present value across demand scenarios (PVMIN), and (*e*) the smallest cumulative cash flow for any demand scenario for any year (CUMMIN). The fifth item requires brief comment. It is included as a measure of the financial resources the firm may have to mobilize in this market if demand is weak and things do not go well. As one would expect, these negative cash flows usually occur in the second or third year of the process when the major investments have been made, but before the majority of the returns are in. The figures differ from one company to the next because of initial differences in 1972 in overall grind capacity and in HFCS capacity. These initial capacities were reported in section 8.1.

The tables are to be thought of as summarizing the financial implications for each firm of combinations of their own strategy and the behavior in the aggregate of rivals. They do not tell us without further analysis what the behavior of rivals, individually or collectively, will be. Rather, they provide data on which to base judgments about competitor behavior and, hence, the most likely pattern of industry capacity expansion. We turn to that task next.

8.9   Analysis of Competitor Behavior, Expectations, and Market Equilibrium

In this section the principles described in section 8.2 are applied to the case at hand. We are looking for a hypothesis about industry capacity expansion which, when shared by the firms in the market, will lead to capacity expansion decisions that in the aggregate add up to that contained in the initial hypothesis.

The choices facing the firms are those described in the previous section and summarized in appendix A. The next step is to determine what choices the firms will make. This can be done in a variety of ways. One way is to apply decision criteria, such as mean-variance tradeoffs, relatively mechanically. We did not proceed in this way. Rather, we used the information that was available to us concerning each firm to make judgments about their strategic choices. The judgments about each firm's choice from its alternatives are based upon several kinds of information: (*a*) the financial consequences of alternative strategies, (*b*) the firm's size, financial resources, and strength, and (*c*) the historical behavior of the firm and the implications of that behavior for corporate goals, tolerance for risk, and aggressiveness.

In appendix B we have summarized the relevant characteristics of the firms with respect to deciding among risky investment alternatives. Using these facts and judgments, the "best" decisions for each firm conditional upon industry capacity expansion were assessed and are reported in table 8.8. At the foot of each column, the total HFCS capacity implied by the firms' collective decisions is reported, along with the fraction of that capacity generated by converting corn syrup and starch facilities.

Given our best estimate of the then-prevailing expectations about future demand, the equilibrium capacity expansion path in the industry is the medium capacity, high conversion scenario. If that outcome is anticipated, firms in the aggregate will choose to install fourteen MES HFCS plants, which would provide 4,998 million pounds per year of HFCS capacity over the first three to four years. Of that capacity, three to five MES plants will be converted so that conversion is in the range of 21 to 35 percent of HFCS capacity—with four conversions, the percentage is 28.

The medium capacity scenario has 3,800–4,250 million pounds per year of capacity by 1976, depending on actual demands. By 1977 that becomes 6,500 million pounds. Thus, the medium capacity, high conversion scenario had the required consistency property; the predicted behavior of firms is close enough to the initial hypothesis to be an equilibrium.

The other five capacity-conversion scenarios all generate behavior that is not consistent with the assumed scenario. The high capacity scenario leads to less than 3,000 million pounds of capacity, all of it converted. Neither the total nor the conversion rate matches the assumption of low capacity result. The medium capacity, low conversion scenario generates (through firms' decisions) 4,284 million pounds of capacity, which is consistent with the medium capacity hypothesis. However, the conversion rate is 66 percent, pointing back to the medium capacity, high conversion scenario as the most likely equilibrium.

In view of the expectations that were widely held in 1972 and that proved to be confirmed in the first two years thereafter, the equilibrium analysis suggests that fairly rapid expansion of capacity was predictable and consistent with informed strategic choices by rival firms in the industry. This is not to say that the choices that firms actually made (which proved to be close to those reported in table 8.8) were based upon precisely this kind of analysis. We do not know enough about the decision making process to be able to make that assertion.

However, we can examine the decisions firms actually took in the initial phases of the market's growth to the extent that we have data on them. Table 8.8a shows the capacity expansion in the industry through 1976.

The medium capacity scenario has higher capacity levels than those actually observed in 1973–76. However, this is partly a matter of timing. By 1976 the industry had under construction over 4 billion pounds of capacity, which came on-stream in the period following 1976. The medium capacity scenario is therefore reasonably accurate, though it

Table 8.8 Firm Strategies in HFCS, Conditional on Assumed Industry Capacity Expansion and Conversion Scenarios

| | Assumed Capacity | | | | | |
| | High | | Low | | Medium | |
	Low Conversion (25%)*	High Conversion (0%)*	High Conversion (25%)*	Low Conversion (0%)*	High Conversion (25%)*	Low Conversion (0%)*
Company:						
American Maize	Convert	Convert	1 add-on + 1 greenfield	Convert	1 add-on	Convert
Anheuser-Busch	Convert	Convert	1 add-on	Convert	Convert	Convert
Archer-Daniels-Midland	Convert	Convert	1 add-on + 2 greenfields	1 add-on + 1 greenfield	1 add-on + 2 greenfields	1 add-on + 1 greenfield
Cargill	Convert	Convert	1 add-on + 2 greenfields	1 add-on + 1 greenfield	1 add-on + 1 greenfield	Convert
CPC International	Convert	Nothing	1 add-on + 1 greenfield	1 add-on + 2 greenfields	Convert	Convert
Grain Processing	Nothing	Nothing	Convert	Convert	Convert	Convert
Hubinger	Nothing	Nothing	Convert	Convert	Convert	Convert
Penick & Ford	Nothing	Nothing	Convert	Convert	Convert	Convert
Staley	Convert	Convert	1 add-on + 2 greenfields	1 add-on + 1 greenfield	1 add-on + 1 greenfield	Convert
Standard Brands	Convert	Convert	1 add-on + 2 greenfields	1 add-on + 1 greenfield	1 add-on + 1 greenfield	1 add-on + 1 greenfield
Implied outcome	7MES = 2,499Mlbs. 100% conversion	6MES = 2,142Mlbs. 100% conversion	20MES = 7,104Mlbs. 15% conversion	16MES = 5,712Mlbs. 31% conversion	14MES = 4,998Mlbs. 28% conversion EQUILIBRIUM	12MES = 4,284Mlbs. 66% conversion

*Amount H from conversion.

Table 8.8*a*   **Industry Capacity Expansion (billions of pounds)**

	1973	1974	1975	1976
Actual industry capacity (estimated)*	0.6	1	1.4	2.2
Medium capacity scenario	.6	1.5	3.5	3.5

*Based on sales, assuming full capacity utilization during 1973–75.

predicts the building of capacity somewhat earlier than it actually occurred.

We cannot be sure of the individual company capacity decisions. Archer-Daniels-Midland had close to 1 billion pounds of capacity by 1976.[9] The other predictions in table 8.8 generally correspond to what we know about the behavior of other competitors.[10]

This history of the events in the market is interesting. In 1973 the industry capacity expansion began accelerating. There was great enthusiasm on the part of industry participants and analysts. Demand growth was aided by a tremendous surge in sugar prices in 1974. Amstar, a leading sugar producer, entered HFCS to protect itself in the sweetener market. However, at the end of 1974 the sugar price support legislation in the United States lapsed and was not renewed because of high sugar prices. The latter then tumbled to the eight cent per pound level. This adversely affected the HFCS market. By 1976 the capacity planned in 1973–74 was coming on-stream, while demand was falling off. By late 1976 industry capacity utilization was low (in the neighborhood of 60 percent) and the profits had been squeezed out of the margins in the industry. By 1977 analysts were predicting a return to full capacity only by the end of the decade.

8.10   The Effect of Expectations, Risk, and Uncertainty on the Evolution of the Market

The behavior of the firms, the nature of the equilibrium, and the character of the evolutionary process depend upon the underlying expectations about demand. This section is devoted to the relation between uncertainty and the equilibrium expansion path for the industry.

Uncertainty acts as a stabilizing and leveling force in the capacity expansion process. In the HFCS problem there was considerable uncertainty about demand. As a firm increased its level of investment in HFCS capacity, it increased its mean return, but it also increased its risk and exposure to very poor outcomes, as is readily apparent in the tables in appendix A. This exposure causes even the less risk-averse firms to choose to limit their investment, even when the expected return is high. Under different circumstances involving lower risk, a strategy of aggressively preempting more of the market might have been desirable. But with significant downside risks, taking a dominant market share was not a prudent strategy.

We can illustrate the role of uncertainty in firm behavior by examining the effects of changes in the expected probability distribution of demand on the risk-return trade-off of alternative strategies under various assumed capacity scenarios. Figures 8.2, 8.3, and 8.4 plot the undominated strategies in risk-return space for firm 1 (American Maize) for several probability distributions and the low, medium, and high capacity addition scenarios (all with high conversion). The horizontal axis is the expected present value, and the vertical axis is the standard deviation. The strategy option corresponding to each point on the graph is the circled number, and the bracketed numbers are the probabilities assumed.

In the low and medium capacity scenarios, more aggressive strategies generally increase return but always increase risk. In the high capacity scenario, more aggressive strategies often lead to lower expected returns and higher risk. Increasing uncertainty raises the risk for each strategic option and rotates the risk return frontier leftward. This makes more conservative strategies more likely, holding firms' risk-return trade-offs constant. Where firms have varying risk postures, uncertainty thus makes firms' optional choices increasingly dependent on their tolerance for risk.

In the analysis in table 8.8, where the equilibrium is portrayed, the largest projected share of capacity for a single firm is 21.4 percent. It belongs to Archer-Daniels-Midland. The original two firms that were participants in HFCS, Standard Brands and Staley, end up with 18.2 percent of capacity each, while the fourth largest firm is Cargill with 14 percent of the market. The resulting four-firm concentration ratio is 70 percent. This is high, but is not the industry dominance one would expect if one or two firms aggressively preempted the market. Uncertainty, then, represents a significant qualification to the strategy of preemptive capacity expansion and growth.

To see just how central the role of uncertainty is, it is useful to consider how the strategic opportunities would appear when risks are significantly lower. It is not difficult to see that with little or no exogenous risk, the ultimate size of the market is known almost with certainty. Under these circumstances, the strategies can be ordered unambiguously. Depending on the known demand, the firm will either do nothing or build to the limit. This can be readily seen in figures 8.2, 8.3, and 8.4, where removing uncertainty makes the risk-return lines horizontal.

With no uncertainty, preemptive investment, limited only by the financial resources available to the firm, becomes the appropriate strategy because it clearly maximizes discounted cash flow. The issue in the capacity expansion process becomes one of who can move first and fastest to occupy dominant positions in the industry, because there is only so

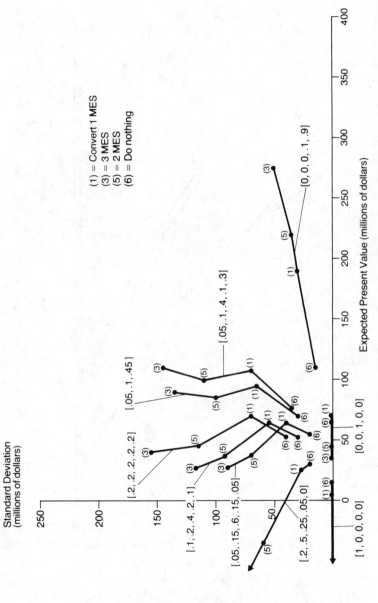

Fig. 8.2 Expected values and variances of strategic options with alternative expectations about future demand. Firm: American Maize. Capacity scenario: high capacity, high conversion.

Standard Deviation
(millions of dollars)

Expected Present Value (millions of dollars)

(1) = Convert 1 MES
(3) = 3 MES
(5) = 2 MES
(6) = Do nothing

[0, 0, 0, .1, .9]

[.05, .1, .4, .1, .3]

[.05, .1, .45]

[.2, .2, .2, .2, .2]

[.1, .2, .4, .2, .1]

[.05, .15, .6, .15, .05]

[0, 0, 1, 0, 0]

[.2, .5, .25, .05, 0]

[1, 0, 0, 0]

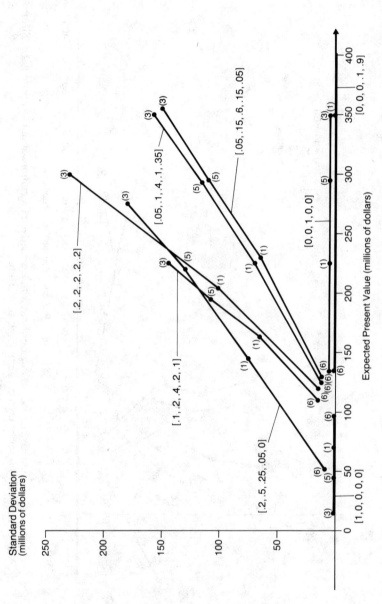

Fig. 8.3 Expected values and variances of strategic options with alternative expectations about future demand. Firm: American Maize. Capacity scenario: low capacity, high conversion.

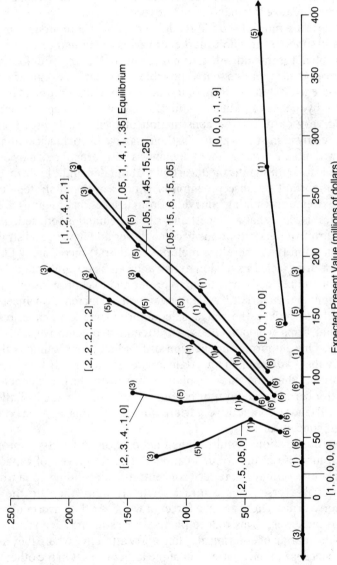

Fig. 8.4

Expected values and variances of strategic options with alternative expectations about future demand. Firm: American Maize. Capacity scenario: medium capacity, high conversion.

much known demand to serve. Under these circumstances, however, the firm faces the problem of other firms with the same idea.

In formal terms, the reduction of uncertainty transforms the game from one with a single equilibrium to one with many equilibria. Without uncertainty, the optimal strategy for each firm is to expand capacity so as to supply whatever demand is not covered by rivals' known capacity. Thus, there are multiple equilibria depending on whether one firm gets a jump and supplies the whole market or various combinations of firms do. The problem for the individual firm is to ensure that the equilibrium that is achieved is as favorable to it as possible. That entails expanding as fast as possible itself, but ensuring that others do not. This requires trying to preempt by means of public announcements of major capacity and contracting very early for the construction of facilities. If preemption is attempted by many firms and fails, then massive overcapacity will result. Thus, with no uncertainty about demand, a new form of risk may emerge to replace it. With significant uncertainty about demand, this form of risk is not important because preemption is not a rational strategy except under extreme risk-taking behavior. From inspection of figures 8.2, 8.3, and 8.4, it is clear that as uncertainty about demand is reduced, a firm's risk-return frontiers or options become flatter and flatter, and strategies of preemption (and therefore multiple equilibria) increasingly likely.

Unless firms lack an aversion to risk and can bear significant drains on cash, uncertainty will cause them to prefer and to choose lower levels of investment in the market.[11] At least over a range, increases in uncertainty are likely to reduce the range of equilibrium market shares because individual firms will not choose to attempt a preemptive investment strategy. One important implication of this line of reasoning is that an industry that evolves in an uncertain environment is likely to end up less concentrated than one whose evolutionary growth phase is characterized by greater certainty about future demand. Certainty in the evolutionary phase will lead to competitive warfare, the exit of firms, and the potential for high concentration.

These observations require some qualification. As a first approximation, an increase in uncertainty causes the desired levels of capacity to fall. That may or may not reduce concentration depending upon whether the less risk-averse firms contract relatively more than do the more risk-averse firms. There are two forces at work. As the uncertainty about demand increases, firms reduce planned investment. As a result, firms just on the margin of entering may find entry attractive where they did not before, because of the contraction of the larger firms. On the other hand, when investments of firms that were in the market are held constant, an increase in risk reduces the attractiveness of the market. It seems reasonable to hypothesize (and Spence 1979b has been able to show) that under certain conditions, concentration is a U-shaped function of risk. That is, as demand uncertainty increases, beginning at a low level, the number of firms that find it attractive to enter at some scale rises. But as the risk increases further, the market becomes unattractive to the more risk-averse firms in spite of the reduced levels of investment of the larger, less risk averse rivals.

In these terms, the HFCS case would be regarded as an intermediate one. The risks were high enough to prevent any firm from making a large enough investment to achieve a dominant share (40 percent or more of the market). But the risks and costs were not so large as to prevent smaller firms from entering the HFCS market at relatively small scales.

The model assumes constant returns to scale in HFCS production beyond a one-MES add-on strategy, and no reduction in costs owing to a learning curve, for early entrants. This is because most observers believed these assumptions were largely accurate in the corn wet milling industry. However, such cost behavior could be added to the model. The effect would be to flatten the risk-return trade-offs of alternative strategies and increase the attractiveness of larger investments by individual firms, particularly those that were more prepared to take risks.

The HFCS market was in some sense an intermediate case. Risk was high, but not so high as to force everyone into adopting the most conservative strategies. Also, in HFCS as in other markets firms differed in their attitudes toward, and tolerance for, risk. Thus, their choices ranged from no investment, to a small-scale conservative entry, to modest commitment to a leadership position. No one could justify a preemptive attempt to capture a dominant share.

8.10.1   Different Expectations and Equilibrium

Apart from uncertainty and risk, different expectations could have caused a dramatically different evolution in the HFCS market. For example, with less optimistic expectations, the low capacity scenario with a substantial amount of conversion would have been the outcome. With the probabilities shown in table 8.9, the model yields a low capacity expansion outcome with 50 percent conversion, as shown in table 8.10. As was the case earlier, the strategies adopted by firms are based upon the calculated present values and cash flows for each firm, and an assessment of their attitudes toward risk and their financial resources.

Similarly, with very optimistic probabilities, a high capacity equilibrium could have developed in the market. However, with probabilities attached to high demand sufficiently elevated to justify investing in the

Table 8.9   Probabilities Yielding a Low Capacity Equilibrium

Demand	Low	Low	Medium	Medium	High	High
Sugar price	Low	Medium	Medium	High	Medium	High
Probability	0.3	0.55	0.15	0.0	0.0	0.0

Table 8.10 Low Capacity Equilibrium

	High Capacity		Low Capacity		Medium Capacity	
	25% Conversion	0 Conversion	25% Conversion	0 Conversion	25% Conversion	0 Conversion
American Maize	Nothing	Nothing	Convert	Convert	Nothing	Nothing
Anheuser-Busch	Nothing	Nothing	Convert	Nothing	Nothing	Nothing
Archer-Daniels-Midland	Nothing	Nothing	1 add-on	1 add-on	1 Convert	1 Convert
Cargill	Nothing	Nothing	1 add-on	1 add-on	1 Convert	1 Convert
CPC International	Nothing	Nothing	Convert	Convert	Nothing	Nothing
Grain Processing	Nothing	Nothing	Nothing	Nothing	Nothing	Nothing
Hubinger	Nothing	Nothing	Convert	Nothing	Nothing	Convert
National Starch	Nothing	Nothing	Nothing	Nothing	Nothing	Nothing
Pennick & Ford	Nothing	Nothing	Convert	Convert	Nothing	Nothing
Staley	Nothing	Nothing	1 add-on	1 add-on	Nothing	Convert
Standard Brands	Nothing	Nothing	1 add-on	1 add-on	Nothing	Convert
Total	0 capacity	0 capacity	9 MES = 3,213M lbs.	7 MES = 2,499M lbs.	2 MES = 714M lbs.	5 MES = 1,785M lbs.
			55% conversion	42% conversion	100% conversion	100% conversion
				EQUILIBRIUM		

face of a large total industry capacity, the variance of returns tends to fall. As the earlier discussion of risk indicated, this will push firms toward preemption, and the market toward multiple equilibria. Applying the technique used in the previous section will not guarantee an equilibrium. There is too much "doing the same thing": either very large expansions or doing nothing. This, of course, is exactly what one would expect. With demand uncertainty hypothetically reduced, the principal differentiating feature of firms, their attitudes to and tolerance for risk, becomes less and less relevant.

8.11   Expectations and Risk Aversion
   in the Capacity Expansion Process

Our model has treated firms' expectations about future demand and competitor behavior as exogenous and independent. We have treated the risk aversion of firms as independently and exogenously determined as well, and our judgments about each firm's trade-off of risk and return were based on assessments of the backgrounds of each firm's management, the place of the corn wet milling operation in each firm's overall operations, and other factors described earlier. Yet neither firms' expectations about the future nor their risk aversion is necessarily independent and exogenous in the capacity expansion process. There are strong reasons to suspect that both are generated endogenously through a variety of processes that will be crucial to further understanding the capacity expansion decisions that actually take place.

8.11.1   Expectations about Future Demand

Firms form their expectations about future demand in part through independent analysis and discussions with customers. However, all firms in the industry obtain information about future prospects directly or indirectly from many common sources. There are mechanisms which cause expectations to converge and perhaps also to inflate.

One common information source used by firms is the limited number of prospective customers, most of whom firms already serve with other products. Through these common buyers all firms will have access to essentially similar views of customer needs.

A second common source of information comes from the interaction between firms and the capital markets, where the security analysts play a major role in information flow and expectations creation. Security analysts are in business to recommend purchases of stock based on company research. They develop predictions of future demand that are published and widely read by industry participants. Analysts rely heavily on interviews with industry participants in information gathering, and hence provide another mechanism for the circulation of predictions about the future among firms and thus for the convergence of expectations.

They also interview customers and other industry observers, from whom many of the firms also gather information.

Embedded in this argument is a view that capital markets are imperfect in an informational sense. Lacking full information about the future, the capital markets react to signals about future conditions of firms. These signals take the form of statements by management and historical firm results, filtered through security analysts. Major investment decisions are also signals, taken in the context of a general overview about the propriety of making them, as portrayed by analysts and the financial press. There is therefore a significant role for security analysts and the capital markets in the capacity expansion process.

Through analysts, firms can play a role in creating an optimistic bias in judgments about future demand. Firms seek to maximize the price of their shares. They do this by portraying the future as optimistically as they can to analysts. While overoptimistic predictions by firms about the future carry the risk of failure to deliver, it can be argued that investors have short memories and that rationalizations for results below forecast are usually available. Thus, the increase in stock prices generated by optimistic predictions about the future are greater than the negative movements in stock price caused by unrealized predictions. If firms attempt to portray themselves optimistically, then this information is circulated through the security analysts to other firms, tending to inflate other firms' predictions through a risk aversion process that will be described below.

Firms also communicate with one another through their public statements in the press, through their annual reports and other public documents, and through appearances by management before groups of security analysts. This communication provides a mechanism for expectations to converge.

Finally, firms communicate expectations to one another through actual decisions to commit resources. If one firm announces a capacity decision, this communicates that firm's implicit expectations about demand to the other firms in a particularly credible fashion. Thus, there is a wide variety of mechanisms to aid in convergence of expectations about future demand.

A firm might try to use these mechanisms to create mistaken expectations about the future. A firm would gain, for example, if every other firm thought future demand would be low when it really would be high. The bluffer could build capacity sooner, and reap the benefits while its rivals caught up. However, communicating such mistakenly negative expectations worsens the firm's position with the capital markets and thus carries a cost to the firm. Perhaps as a result, one rarely observes firms making bearish statements about future demand. At worst, demand is expected to be "temporarily" depressed or "temporarily" modest, while the future holds great promise.

In most markets, including the corn wet milling industry, it makes little sense for the firm to create mistakenly high expectations about demand in its rivals. This is because doing so will create excess capacity, hurting the firm as well as its rivals, though its rivals will be hurt more if they build mistakenly. Such an incentive not to overinflate rivals' expectations goes directly against the pressure to paint an optimistic picture of the future to the capital markets.

A final factor to be noted about future expectations is that many managers seem to prefer progress and making positive moves to pessimism and inaction. It is also human nature to be optimistic about the future if possible. This may create an additional optimistic bias in future expectations.

8.11.2   Risk Aversion

A firm's risk-return trade-off function is due in part to a wide range of factors specific to its particular situation. However, there is a sense in which the risk aversion of firms in a market is partially endogenous. Consider a situation where there are long lead times in building capacity. Suppose a manager has the choice of building capacity or not building it, with future demand being either high or low. As table 8.11 shows, if the manager chooses not to build, his best outcome is satisfactory profits in the event that demand proves to be low. But suppose he chooses not to build, demand proves to be high, and all of his competitors build capacity. Here the manager is in difficulty; his incorrect decision is hard to explain. On the other hand, if he builds capacity along with all his competitors, if demand proves to be low, then blame can be shared or attributed to industrywide factors out of his control. Thus, the risk averse manager may well build capacity even if doing so would not be justified by the firm's true expectations about the future and risk-return indifference curve, provided other firms in the industry are building capacity. If no other firm builds capacity, it will be a rare manager who builds unless his beliefs about the future are extremely strong (or he ignores uncertainty).

This analysis would suggest that once a few firms have announced capacity additions in a market, particularly if they have at the same time

Table 8.11   Outcomes of Building Decisions

	Future Demand	
	High	Low
Build	High profits	Low profits
Don't build	Lost profits	Medium profits

communicated optimistic expectations about future demand through the mechanisms described earlier, many firms will rapidly announce capacity additions. This bandwagon effect would tend to produce excess capacity in the industry and work against any but a high capacity equilibrium in our sense.

The bandwagon effect is reinforced by the capital markets if security analysts hold positive expectations about the future. Pressure from analysts and stockholders on management to build capacity will grow within firms which have not announced capacity additions. In fact, announcements of capacity additions may become key signals to the stock market which result in share price increases. Thus, in the face of generally optimistic expectations about future demand, even though there may be great uncertainty there will be a strong tendency toward overbuilding of capacity through shifts in the shape of firms' indifference curves.

If this bandwagon process is present, then a preemptive strategy by one or more firms can be disastrous. A preemptive strategy, accompanied by aggressive language about future expectations and planned behavior, can virtually guarantee upward-spiraling capacity additions.

8.12   Conclusions

It may be useful to conclude this analysis by underscoring the major points and by identifying areas in which further research would yield a high payoff.

The main point is that it is possible to calculate the most likely capacity decisions for firms in an expanding market. Those calculations are based upon the assumption that firms will come to a common view about each other's decisions. They will do this by analyzing their competitors' decisions, conditional upon hypotheses about the rate of capacity expansion in the industry, thereby finding the capacity expansion hypothesis that is consistent with the decisions that are expected, conditional on that hypothesis. Capacity expansion scenarios that are consistent with individual firm decisions are referred to as "equilibria."

As a prediction about what will happen in a market, such equilibria seem to us a natural focus of attention. Using the beliefs about the market potential that prevailed in the industry, the resulting medium capacity, high conversion equilibrium is a reasonable approximation to actual behavior in the corn wet milling industry. But several qualifications are in order. First, firms may make mistakes about their competitors' preferences, capabilities, and financial resources. This introduces some slippage, in the form of increased uncertainty, into the process. Second, firms may fail to analyze rivals carefully; they may make assumptions about industry capacity that would not be borne out by a careful analysis of competitor decisions based on a shared industry capacity assumption.

Third, firms may have different views about demand: its expected level and the uncertainty surrounding it. This may cause their behavior to diverge from that predicted by a rival which approaches the demand side of the capacity decision problem with different judgments about the future.

The second point that emerges is that the equilibrium outcome varies with expectations concerning demand and market potential. The entire equilibrium analysis rests upon assumptions about the likelihood of various rates of growth of the market. We have argued in section 8.11 that there are factors at work that cause expectations about demand to converge among competitors and other interested parties such as customers and security analysts. Nevertheless, the model takes these expectations as a datum.[12] There is little doubt in our minds that a high research priority should be accorded to the problem of how these expectations are determined. While the expectations represent subjective judgments, they are influenced by signals from the environment, by past experience, and by the expectations of others. It is not, therefore, beyond the realm of possibility that the processes that influence the formation of expectations can be subjected to analysis similar to that presented above. Expectations formation would be a function of the actual decisions by competitors embodied in our model, the information content in those decisions, and other signaling behavior of competitors.

The third major area of interest is the effect of uncertainty on the evolution of the industry and on its ultimate structure. Business strategy analysis has emphasized the importance of large shares and of achieving dominant positions by making preemptive investments under the right circumstances. The question of the desirability of dominant shares aside, this leaves unanswered how a firm should go about achieving a dominant share. The analysis above suggests that the presence of exogenous uncertainty makes preemptive investments unattractive. Nevertheless, there may be profitable investment opportunities, contemplated at more modest scales, in markets with high uncertainty.

From an economic standpoint, the effect of uncertainty is to shrink the set of equilibria, eliminating the points characterized by large shares for a few firms. In the absence of uncertainty, the set of equilibria is large.[13] Other considerations, such as who is able to move first or credibly commit themselves to these moves, then determine the outcome from the expanded equilibrium set. One of the effects of uncertainty in the growth phase is thus to reduce the concentration of the mature industry. That in turn can affect the profitability and performance of the industry in other dimensions after the period of rapid growth is over.

The observation that uncertainty reduces the incentive to make preemptive investments raises another research topic. In those markets where uncertainty either is not especially large or is rapidly resolved, the equilibrium analysis does not tell us what will happen. Further analysis of the preemption process is required to determine who will move first, how commitments are made credible, and what signals effectively communicate intentions. Attention to constraints on growth, to the possible advantages of diversified firms with internal financial resources, and to other influential factors will be required.

The high fructose corn syrup problem is not atypical of the expansion problem in general. As with any market, there are some unique features, but the problem is similar to that encountered in many other industries. With a commodity product, the strategic decisions focus upon capacity, scale, and costs. Compared with consumer products or capital goods, the problem is less complicated in that the product policy, marketing, and related decisions are less intricate. Applying this framework to the more complex situations will require careful attention to cross-elasticities of demand and market segmentation. But there seems no reason to expect that the basic approach will be less applicable in these more complex environments.

Appendix A.   Financial Implications
of Strategic Choices

American Maize
(SCENARIO)

(STRATEGY)				1	2	3	4	5	6
CONVERT	1 MES	1	EPDV	105.705500	75.255425	217.756630	182.672950	173.048920	135.495980
			SD	71.981062	65.431276	71.093882	66.468371	89.484487	87.192668
			PVMAX	198.333480	162.297080	349.481220	309.750970	283.889000	245.947760
			PVMIN	4.476020	0.116301	68.503765	38.140455	31.061796	7.117709
			CUMMIN	3.549640	−2.405120	6.220000	6.220000	6.220000	5.220400
	1 MES	2	EPDV	79.635483	29.452691	200.889430	137.700330	160.947510	97.114125
			SD	71.378952	55.959538	65.547177	56.377765	90.911728	82.280129
GREENFIELD			PVMAX	167.651350	103.242940	312.710510	242.147750	269.246390	199.005200
			PVMIN	−34.802979	−38.351336	64.695863	15.305580	3.371634	−32.323563
			CUMMIN	−38.057260	−43.119520	−9.780000	−19.560000	−19.667100	−36.565000
	3 MES	3	EPDV	108.821170	48.844504	344.982830	278.217410	276.928860	205.004730
			SD	145.321180	130.863460	159.930710	149.405060	188.716410	183.418720
			PVMAX	289.143670	217.614600	642.741430	564.714320	492.296260	420.162360
			PVMIN	−116.096120	−126.003580	14.790971	−46.728548	−63.009955	−108.882100
			CUMMIN	−129.340860	−143.635140	−27.780000	−104.274800	−105.774200	−125.135400
	1 MES Add-on	4	EPDV	92.999119	42.816327	214.253070	151.063970	174.311150	110.477760
			SD	71.378952	55.959538	65.547176	56.377765	90.911727	82.280129
			PVMAX	181.014980	116.606570	326.074140	255.511390	282.610020	212.368840
			PVMIN	−21.439344	−24.987700	78.059499	28.669217	16.735271	−18.959928
			CUMMIN	−24.057260	−29.119520	−2.780000	−5.560000	−5.667100	−22.565000
	2 MES	5	EPDV	98.606624	43.158096	287.353180	221.269520	229.517370	161.243990
			SD	108.673140	93.723911	117.969270	108.016980	146.598950	139.777450
			PVMAX	233.278700	164.941160	501.784850	426.383520	402.278100	330.647990
			PVMIN	−71.462323	−78.559036	45.627756	−10.933550	−25.351020	−66.503490
			CUMMIN	−77.334520	−87.459041	−27.780000	−55.560000	−55.774200	−74.350000
DO NOTHING		6	EPDV	74.027977	29.110922	127.789320	67.494781	105.741290	46.347896
			SD	34.371860	18.930135	16.805031	6.898354	36.015186	25.834557
			PVMAX	115.387630	54.908348	136.999800	71.275620	149.578310	80.726044
			PVMIN	15.220000	15.220000	97.127604	54.908348	45.457924	15.220000
			CUMMIN	15.220000	15.220000	15.220000	15.220000	15.220000	15.220000

Anheuser-Busch
(SCENARIO)

		1	2	3	4	5	6
1	EPDV	62.514403	58.270865	143.198860	143.293600	111.354920	108.454630
	SD	52.434287	54.702539	64.383616	63.935645	69.046122	72.568240
	PVMAX	131.011400	130.261200	269.549670	268.165710	196.618600	198.848730
	PVMIN	-4.403980	-8.763699	11.835360	6.104573	4.539695	-1.762291
	CUMMIN	-5.330360	-11.285120	-2.660000	-2.660000	-2.660000	-3.659600
2	EPDV	36.444388	12.468132	126.331670	98.320985	99.253515	70.072778
	SD	51.501729	45.358345	57.935739	58.624499	70.379729	67.839882
	PVMAX	100.329260	71.207054	232.778960	200.562500	181.975990	151.906170
	PVMIN	-43.682980	-47.231337	8.027456	-16.730301	-23.150466	-41.203563
	CUMMIN	-46.937260	-51.999521	-18.660000	-37.320000	-37.427100	-45.445000
3	EPDV	65.630073	31.859945	270.425060	238.838070	215.234870	177.963380
	SD	125.585240	120.464170	152.998070	146.857840	168.608380	169.451060
	PVMAX	221.821580	185.578720	562.809880	523.129080	405.025860	373.063330
	PVMIN	-124.976110	-134.883580	-41.877433	-78.764428	-89.532055	-117.762100
	CUMMIN	-138.220860	-152.515140	-36.660000	-122.034800	-123.534200	-134.015400
4	EPDV	49.808025	25.831768	139.695310	111.684620	112.617150	83.436415
	SD	51.501729	45.358345	57.935739	53.624499	70.379729	67.839882
	PVMAX	113.692900	84.570691	246.142590	213.926140	195.339630	165.269800
	PVMIN	-30.319344	-33.867700	21.391093	-3.366665	-9.786830	-27.839928
	CUMMIN	-32.937260	-37.999520	-11.660000	-23.320000	-23.427100	-31.445000
5	EPDV	55.415530	26.173537	212.795420	181.890170	167.823370	134.202640
	SD	88.888815	83.259592	110.771790	105.362550	126.253730	125.514170
	PVMAX	165.956620	132.905280	421.853300	384.798270	315.007700	283.548960
	PVMIN	-80.342323	-87.439037	-11.040650	-42.969431	-51.873119	-75.383491
	CUMMIN	-86.214520	-96.339040	-36.660000	-73.320000	-73.534200	-83.230000
6	EPDV	30.836884	12.126363	54.231557	28.115434	44.047292	19.306548
	SD	14.317845	7.885483	7.000256	2.873559	15.002383	10.761570
	PVMAX	48.065542	22.872465	57.068247	29.690370	62.307917	33.627011
	PVMIN	6.340000	6.340000	40.459199	22.872465	18.935824	6.340000
	CUMMIN	6.340000	6.340000	6.340000	6.340000	6.340000	6.340000

(STRATEGY)

Archer-Daniels-Midland
(SCENARIO)

(STRATEGY)			1	2	3	4	5	6
	1	EPDV	124.188170	82.523592	249.661980	199.524470	199.449500	147.067720
		SD	80.422020	70.052410	74.176192	67.596433	98.304666	93.494411
		PVMAX	227.142480	176.006130	383.686160	327.546450	321.234440	266.102750
		PVMIN	8.276020	3.916301	92.753758	51.849504	42.411343	10.917709
		CUMMIN	7.849640	1.394880	10.020000	10.020000	10.020000	9.020400
	2	EPDV	98.118158	36.720858	232.794780	154.551850	187.348100	108.685870
		SD	79.911966	60.544544	68.973741	57.601696	99.759135	88.523990
		PVMAX	196.460350	116.951990	346.915450	259.943240	306.591820	219.160190
		PVMIN	-31.002980	-34.551336	88.945856	29.014630	14.721182	-28.523564
		CUMMIN	-34.257259	-39.319520	-5.980000	-11.960000	-12.067100	-32.765000
	3	EPDV	127.303840	56.112671	376.888180	295.068940	303.329450	216.576480
		SD	153.791890	135.344850	162.987520	150.514800	197.378800	189.447650
		PVMAX	317.952670	231.323640	676.946370	582.509830	529.641700	440.317350
		PVMIN	-112.296110	-122.203580	39.040964	-33.019500	-51.660408	-105.082100
		CUMMIN	-125.540860	-139.835140	-23.980000	-96.674800	-98.174200	-121.335400
	4	EPDV	111.481800	50.084494	246.158420	167.915490	200.711730	122.049510
		SD	79.911966	60.544544	68.973741	57.601696	99.759135	88.523990
		PVMAX	209.823990	130.315620	360.279090	273.306880	319.955460	232.523830
		PVMIN	-17.639344	-21.187699	102.309490	42.378266	28.084819	-15.159928
		CUMMIN	-20.257260	-25.319520	1.020000	1.020000	1.020000	-18.765000
	5	EPDV	117.089300	50.426263	319.258530	238.121040	255.917960	172.815740
		SD	117.167420	98.240712	121.161120	109.178500	155.359550	145.930850
		PVMAX	262.087710	178.650210	535.989800	444.179010	439.623540	350.802990
		PVMIN	-67.662323	-74.759036	69.877749	2.775499	-14.001472	-62.703491
		CUMMIN	-73.534520	-83.659040	-23.980000	-47.960000	-48.174200	-70.550000
	6	EPDV	92.510653	36.379089	159.694670	84.346302	132.141880	57.919643
		SD	42.953534	23.656451	21.000168	8.620676	45.007151	32.284709
		PVMAX	144.196630	68.617396	171.204740	89.071110	186.923750	100.881030
		PVMIN	19.020000	19.020000	121.377600	68.617396	56.807472	19.020000
		CUMMIN	19.020000	19.020000	19.020000	19.020000	19.020000	19.020000

Cargill
(SCENARIO)

(STRATEGY)			.1	2	3	4	5	6
	1	EPDV	147.729260	91.780942	290.299320	220.987990	233.075510	161.806480
		SD	91.211169	75.957018	78.252175	69.068748	109.579230	101.547830
		PVMAX	263.836050	193.467130	427.252460	350.212290	368.800740	291.773850
		PVMIN	13.116021	8.756301	123.640590	69.310502	56.867084	15.757709
		CUMMIN	12.189640	6.234880	14.860000	14.860000	14.860000	13.860400
	2	EPDV	121.659250	45.978207	273.432130	176.015370	220.974110	123.424630
		SD	90.793614	66.413087	73.453767	59.196527	111.061570	96.515990
		PVMAX	233.153920	134.412980	390.481750	282.609080	354.158120	244.831290
		PVMIN	-26.162980	-29.711336	119.832690	46.475628	29.176921	-23.683565
		CUMMIN	-29.417261	-34.479521	-1.140000	-2.280000	-2.387100	-27.925001
	3	EPDV	150.844930	65.370021	417.525520	316.532450	336.955460	213.315230
		SD	164.597540	141.075880	166.952590	151.944790	208.452370	197.165210
		PVMAX	354.646240	248.784650	720.512680	605.175660	577.207990	465.988450
		PVMIN	-107.456110	-117.363580	69.927797	-15.558501	-37.204669	-100.242100
		CUMMIN	-120.700860	-134.995140	-19.140000	-86.994802	-88.494201	-116.495400
	4	EPDV	135.022890	59.341844	286.795760	189.379010	234.337740	136.788260
		SD	90.793615	66.413087	73.453767	59.196526	111.061570	96.515992
		PVMAX	246.517560	147.776620	403.845390	295.972710	367.521760	258.194920
		PVMIN	-12.799344	-16.347700	133.196330	59.839265	42.540558	-10.319928
		CUMMIN	-15.417261	-20.479521	5.860000	5.860000	5.860000	-13.925001
	5	EPDV	140.630390	59.683611	359.895870	259.584560	289.543960	187.554490
		SD	128.003340	104.020650	125.312240	110.679070	166.553500	153.803540
		PVMAX	298.781280	196.111210	579.556090	466.844840	487.189830	376.474080
		PVMIN	-62.822324	-69.919037	100.764580	20.236498	0.454267	-57.863493
		CUMMIN	-68.694520	-78.819042	-19.140000	-38.280000	-38.494200	-65.710000
	6	EPDV	116.051740	45.636438	200.332010	105.809820	165.767880	72.658396
		SD	53.883875	29.676283	26.344810	10.814371	56.460073	40.500165
		PVMAX	180.890190	86.078395	214.771040	111.736940	234.490050	126.552130
		PVMIN	23.860000	23.860000	152.264430	86.078395	71.263211	23.860000
		CUMMIN	23.860000	23.860000	23.860000	23.860000	23.860000	23.860000

CPC International
(SCENARIO)

(STRATEGY)		1	2	3	4	5	6
1	EPDV	366.213940	177.698330	667.454130	420.190720	545.158220	298.596720
	SD	192.108270	131.258010	120.891100	84.244514	215.119260	177.003520
	PVMAX	604.388760	355.522520	831.590900	560.573720	810.263140	530.027060
	PVMIN	58.036022	58.676301	410.301040	231.365890	191.030680	60.677711
	CUMMIN	57.109642	51.154881	59.780001	59.780001	59.780001	58.780401
2	EPDV	340.143920	131.895600	650.586940	375.218110	533.056820	260.214870
	SD	192.050130	121.586790	118.500960	75.446725	216.714550	171.698970
	PVMAX	573.706630	296.468380	794.820180	492.970500	795.620530	483.084500
	PVMIN	18.757021	15.208665	406.493140	208.531020	163.340520	21.236437
	CUMMIN	15.502740	10.440481	43.780001	43.780001	43.780001	16.995001
3	EPDV	369.329610	151.287410	794.680340	515.735180	649.038170	368.105470
	SD	265.372410	195.097160	206.736310	166.013740	312.533290	270.196210
	PVMAX	695.198940	410.840030	1124.851100	815.537080	1018.670400	704.241660
	PVMIN	-62.536112	-72.443578	356.588250	146.496890	96.958935	-55.322096
	CUMMIN	-75.780858	-90.075141	25.780001	2.845201	1.345802	-71.575399
4	EPDV	353.507560	145.259230	663.950580	388.581740	546.420460	273.578510
	SD	192.050130	121.586790	118.500960	75.446725	216.714550	171.698970
	PVMAX	587.070260	309.832010	808.183820	506.334140	808.984170	496.448140
	PVMIN	32.120656	28.572301	419.856780	221.894660	176.704160	34.600074
	CUMMIN	29.502740	24.440481	50.780001	50.780001	50.780001	30.995001
5	EPDV	359.115070	145.601000	737.050700	458.787300	601.626680	324.344740
	SD	228.999980	158.518470	167.104560	125.582430	271.477090	228.026660
	PVMAX	639.333980	358.166600	983.894540	677.206280	928.652240	614.727300
	PVMIN	-17.902321	-24.999035	387.425030	182.291890	134.617870	-12.943491
	CUMMIN	-23.774518	-33.899039	25.780001	25.780001	25.780001	-20.789999
6	EPDV	334.536420	131.853830	577.486830	305.012550	477.850600	209.448640
	SD	155.328290	85.546303	75.942837	31.174032	162.754560	116.747750
	PVMAX	521.442910	248.133790	619.109470	322.098370	675.952450	364.805340
	PVMIN	68.780001	68.780001	438.924880	248.133790	205.426810	68.780001
	CUMMIN	68.780001	68.780001	68.780001	68.780001	68.780001	68.780001

Grain Processing
(SCENARIO)

(STRATEGY)			1	2	3	4	5	6
1		EPDV	167.476540	99.546404	324.387660	238.992510	261.282450	174.169980
		SD	100.285160	80.923154	81.784009	70.332795	119.063080	108.322160
		PVMAX	294.616190	208.114170	463.797740	369.225360	408.701390	313.307870
		PVMIN	17.176021	12.816301	149.549800	83.957540	68.993179	19.817709
		CUMMIN	16.249640	10.294880	18.920000	18.920000	18.920000	17.920400
2		EPDV	141.406530	53.743670	307.520470	194.019890	249.181050	135.788130
		SD	99.929805	71.355315	77.296544	60.563236	120.564440	103.247080
		PVMAX	263.934060	149.060020	427.027030	301.622150	394.058770	266.365310
		PVMIN	-22.102980	-25.651335	145.741890	61.122665	41.303017	-19.623564
		CUMMIN	-25.357260	-30.419520	2.920000	2.920000	2.920000	-23.865000
3		EPDV	170.592210	73.135485	451.613870	334.536980	365.162400	243.678730
		SD	173.673820	145.901250	170.336800	153.158270	217.771620	203.669080
		PVMAX	385.426380	263.431680	757.057960	624.188740	617.108640	487.522460
		PVMIN	-103.396110	-113.303580	95.837002	-0.911463	-25.078573	-96.182096
		CUMMIN	-116.640860	-130.935140	-15.080000	-78.874800	-80.374200	-112.435400
4		EPDV	154.770160	67.107307	320.884110	207.383530	262.544680	149.151760
		SD	99.929805	71.355315	77.296544	60.563236	102.564440	103.247080
		PVMAX	277.297700	162.423660	440.390670	314.985790	407.422410	279.728940
		PVMIN	-8.739344	-12.287699	159.105530	74.486302	54.666653	-6.259927
		CUMMIN	-11.357260	-16.419520	9.920000	9.920000	9.920000	-9.865000
5		EPDV	160.377670	67.449076	393.984220	277.589080	317.750910	199.917990
		SD	137.104530	108.889160	128.862180	111.955450	175.969170	160.434010
		PVMAX	329.561420	210.758250	616.101370	485.857920	527.090490	398.008090
		PVMIN	-58.762323	-65.859035	126.673790	34.883535	12.590364	-53.803492
		CUMMIN	-64.634521	-74.759039	-15.080000	-30.160000	-30.374200	-61.650000
6		EPDV	135.799020	53.401901	234.420360	123.814340	193.974820	85.021895
		SD	63.052715	34.725977	30.827624	12.654537	66.067278	47.391644
		PVMAX	211.670330	100.725430	251.316320	130.750020	274.390700	148.086150
		PVMIN	27.920000	27.920000	178.173630	100.725430	83.389307	27.920000
		CUMMIN	27.920000	27.920000	27.920000	27.920000	27.920000	27.920000

Hubinger
(SCENARIO)

(STRATEGY)		1	2	3	4	5	6
1	EPDV	93.351286	70.397228	196.430420	171.409030	155.402210	127.761170
	SD	66.359077	62.351208	69.099026	65.728722	83.609303	82.993167
	PVMAX	179.076940	153.133670	326.617920	297.856080	258.926520	232.475740
	PVMIN	1.936020	-2.423699	52.294559	28.977038	23.475519	4.577709
	CUMMIN	1.009640	-4.945120	3.680000	3.680000	3.680000	2.680400
2	EPDV	67.281273	24.594494	179.563230	126.436420	143.300810	89.379326
	SD	65.682376	52.908692	63.308449	55.574398	85.014847	78.125295
	PVMAX	148.394810	94.079519	289.847200	230.252870	244.283910	185.533180
	PVMIN	-37.342979	-40.891336	48.486656	6.142164	-4.214642	-34.863563
	CUMMIN	-40.597260	-45.659521	-12.320000	-24.640000	-24.747100	-39.105000
3	EPDV	96.466956	43.986308	323.656620	266.953500	259.282160	197.269930
	SD	139.666740	127.877840	157.916650	148.669790	182.944030	179.405200
	PVMAX	269.877130	208.451180	619.878140	552.819450	467.333780	406.690340
	PVMIN	-118.636120	-128.543580	-1.418235	-55.891964	-70.596231	-111.422100
	CUMMIN	-131.880860	-146.175140	-30.320000	-109.354800	-110.854200	-127.675400
4	EPDV	80.644910	37.958131	192.926860	139.800050	156.664440	102.742960
	SD	65.682376	52.908692	63.308451	55.574398	85.014846	78.125295
	PVMAX	161.758440	107.443160	303.210840	243.616500	257.647540	198.896810
	PVMIN	-23.979344	-27.527700	61.850292	19.505800	9.148994	-21.499928
	CUMMIN	-26.597260	-31.659520	-5.320000	-10.640000	-10.747100	-25.105000
5	EPDV	86.252414	38.299900	266.026980	210.005610	211.870660	153.509190
	SD	103.003460	90.716690	115.871480	107.249000	140.759460	135.679760
	PVMAX	214.022160	155.777750	478.921550	414.488640	377.315620	317.175970
	PVMIN	-74.002323	-81.099037	29.418550	-20.096967	-32.937296	-69.043490
	CUMMIN	-79.874520	-89.999042	-30.320000	-60.640000	-60.854200	-76.890000
6	EPDV	61.673768	24.252726	106.463110	56.230868	88.094584	38.613096
	SD	28.635689	15.770967	14.000511	5.747118	30.004767	21.523139
	PVMAX	96.131084	45.794931	114.136490	59.380740	124.615830	67.254023
	PVMIN	12.680000	12.680000	80.918399	45.744931	37.871648	12.680000
	CUMMIN	12.680000	12.680000	12.680000	12.680000	12.680000	12.680000

National Starch
(SCENARIO)

(STRATEGY)		1	2	3	4	5	6
1	EPDV	87.222821	67.987257	185.851280	165.821430	146.648330	123.924230
	SD	63.577790	60.826310	68.130616	65.366228	80.702233	80.914318
	PVMAX	169.524480	148.588040	315.276280	291.955470	246.543560	225.792770
	PVMIN	0.676021	−3.683699	44.253772	24.431467	19.712248	3.317709
	CUMMIN	−0.250360	−6.205120	2.420000	2.420000	2.420000	1.420400
2	EPDV	61.152808	22.184524	168.984080	120.848810	134.546930	85.542378
	SD	62.859189	51.400138	62.214921	55.180451	82.095735	76.070703
	PVMAX	138.842350	89.533889	278.505570	224.352260	231.900950	178.850210
	PVMIN	−38.602979	−42.151336	40.445869	1.596533	−7.977913	−36.123563
	CUMMIN	−41.857259	−46.919520	−13.580000	−27.160000	−27.267100	−40.365000
3	EPDV	90.338490	41.576338	313.077480	261.365890	250.528280	193.432980
	SD	136.864300	126.399910	156.926550	148.307020	180.086340	177.419420
	PVMAX	260.334670	203.905550	608.536490	546.918840	454.950820	400.007370
	PVMIN	−119.896110	−129.803580	−9.459023	−60.437595	−74.359503	−112.682100
	CUMMIN	−133.140860	−147.435140	−31.580000	−111.874800	−113.374200	−128.935400
4	EPDV	74.516444	35.548161	182.347720	134.212450	147.910560	98.906014
	SD	62.859188	51.400138	62.214921	55.180451	82.095734	76.070703
	PVMAX	152.205980	102.897530	291.869200	237.715900	245.264580	192.213850
	PVMIN	−25.239343	−28.787699	53.809505	14.960170	5.385724	−22.759928
	CUMMIN	−27.857260	−32.919520	−6.580000	−13.160000	−13.267100	−26.365000
5	EPDV	80.123948	35.889929	255.447830	204.418000	203.116790	149.672240
	SD	100.193750	89.228816	114.842030	106.870590	137.868150	133.652040
	PVMAX	204.469710	151.232110	467.579910	408.588030	364.932660	310.493000
	PVMIN	−75.262323	−82.359036	21.377763	−24.642598	−36.700567	−70.303491
	CUMMIN	−81.134520	−91.259040	−31.580000	−63.160000	−63.374200	−78.150000
6	EPDV	55.545303	21.842755	95.883973	50.643259	79.340706	34.776148
	SD	25.790187	14.203821	12.609293	5.176032	27.023221	19.384405
	PVMAX	86.578627	41.199300	102.794860	53.480131	12.232870	60.571053
	PVMIN	11.420000	11.420000	72.877612	41.199300	34.108378	11.420000
	CUMMIN	11.420000	11.420000	11.420000	11.420000	11.420000	11.420000

Pennick & Ford
(SCENARIO)

(STRATEGY)			1	2	3	4	5	6
1		EPDV	111.931240	77.703650	228.503690	188.349250	181.941750	139.393830
		SD	74.820756	66.986230	72.119586	66.845519	92.451797	89.312994
		PVMAX	208.037570	166.914870	361.002890	315.745230	296.468510	252.736810
		PVMIN	5.756020	1.396301	76.672184	42.758240	34.884801	8.397709
		CUMMIN	4.829640	−1.125120	7.500000	7.500000	7.500000	6.500000
2		EPDV	85.861226	31.900916	211.636500	143.376630	169.840340	101.011980
		SD	74.251978	57.501405	66.691570	56.787148	93.888838	84.379858
		PVMAX	177.355430	107.860720	324.232170	248.142020	281.825900	205.794250
		PVMIN	−33.522979	−37.071336	72.864282	19.923366	7.194640	−31.043564
		CUMMIN	−36.777259	−41.839520	−8.500000	−17.000000	−17.107100	−35.285000
3		EPDV	115.046910	51.292730	355.729900	283.893710	285.821700	208.902580
		SD	148.173050	132.371080	160.954650	149.777580	191.630880	185.446360
		PVMAX	298.847760	222.232380	654.263110	570.708600	504.875780	426.951410
		PVMIN	−114.816110	−124.723580	22.959390	−42.110763	−59.186949	−107.602100
		CUMMIN	−128.060860	−142.355140	−26.500000	−101.714800	−103.214200	−123.855400
4		EPDV	99.224862	45.264552	225.000140	156.740270	183.203980	114.375610
		SD	74.251978	57.501405	66.691571	56.787148	93.888838	84.379859
		PVMAX	190.719070	121.224360	337.595810	261.505660	295.189540	219.157890
		PVMIN	−20.159343	−23.707699	86.227918	33.287003	20.558277	−17.679928
		CUMMIN	−22.777260	−27.839520	−1.500000	−3.000000	−3.107100	−21.285000
5		EPDV	104.832370	45.606320	298.100250	226.945820	238.410200	165.141840
		SD	111.532880	95.243089	119.037460	108.406566	149.546820	141.847230
		PVMAX	242.982790	169.558950	513.306530	432.377790	414.857610	337.437040
		PVMIN	−70.182323	−77.279037	53.796175	−6.315765	−21.528014	−65.223491
		CUMMIN	−76.054520	−86.179040	−26.500000	−53.000000	−53.214200	−73.070000
6		EPDV	80.253720	31.559146	138.536390	73.171082	114.634120	50.245748
		SD	37.262529	20.522157	18.218331	7.478505	39.044057	28.007240
		PVMAX	125.091710	59.526133	148.521460	77.269891	162.157830	87.515093
		PVMIN	16.500000	16.500000	105.296020	59.526133	49.280931	16.500000
		CUMMIN	16.500000	16.500000	16.500000	16.500000	16.500000	16.500000

Staley
(SCENARIO)

(STRATEGY)		1	2	3	4	5	6
1	EPDV	287.418790	178.898830	533.599920	396.963190	435.565940	296.300640
	SD	161.952080	130.500320	135.220580	117.298450	191.729960	174.269260
	PVMAX	491.218180	352.844080	766.398440	615.136910	671.145320	518.426160
	PVMIN	30.699001	23.896862	241.852070	137.131910	113.251070	34.820627
	CUMMIN	29.253640	19.962880	33.420000	33.420000	33.420000	31.860400
2	EPDV	261.348770	133.096100	516.732730	351.990570	423.464540	257.918790
	SD	161.585750	120.990210	130.304350	107.357240	193.212330	169.231660
	PVMAX	460.536050	293.789930	729.627720	547.533690	656.502700	471.483600
	PVMIN	-8.580000	-14.570775	238.044170	144.297040	85.560905	-4.620646
	CUMMIN	-12.353260	-20.751520	17.420000	17.420000	17.420000	-9.925000
3	EPDV	290.534460	152.487910	660.826130	492.507660	539.445890	365.809390
	SD	235.431390	195.541900	223.789350	200.142680	290.332780	269.442500
	PVMAX	582.028380	408.161590	1059.658600	870.100270	879.552570	692.640760
	PVMIN	-89.873132	-102.223020	188.139280	52.262909	19.179316	-81.179179
	CUMMIN	-103.636860	-121.267140	-0.580000	-49.834800	-51.494201	-98.495400
4	EPDV	274.712410	146.459730	530.096370	365.354220	436.828180	271.282430
	SD	161.585750	120.990210	130.304350	107.357240	193.212330	169.231660
	PVMAX	473.899680	307.153570	742.991360	560.897330	669.866340	484.847240
	PVMIN	4.783637	-1.207139	251.407800	127.660670	98.924542	8.742991
	CUMMIN	1.646740	-6.751520	24.420000	24.420000	24.420000	4.075000
5	EPDV	280.319920	146.801500	603.196480	435.559760	492.034400	322.048660
	SD	198.837600	158.560910	182.260750	158.898120	248.677670	226.416470
	PVMAX	526.163410	355.488160	918.702070	731.769470	789.534420	603.126400
	PVMIN	-45.239343	-54.778475	218.976060	88.057907	56.838252	-38.800572
	CUMMIN	-51.630520	-65.091040	-0.580000	-1.480000	-1.494200	-47.710000
6	EPDV	255.741270	132.754330	443.632620	281.785030	368.258320	207.152560
	SD	124.438280	83.757279	79.660269	56.221810	138.129970	112.602890
	PVMAX	408.272330	245.455340	553.917010	376.661560	536.834630	353.204440
	PVMIN	41.442980	39.000561	270.475910	153.899810	127.647200	42.922918
	CUMMIN	40.924000	37.588000	42.420000	42.420000	42.420000	41.860000

Standard Brands
(SCENARIO)

(STRATEGY)			1	2	3	4	5	6
1		EPDV	207.165070	147.339680	395.063540	323.792110	320.931820	246.054900
		SD	125.181110	110.510440	121.406250	112.322870	153.398180	146.959410
		PVMAX	366.126480	293.317940	617.876980	537.867020	508.987490	430.911070
		PVMIN	14.199001	7.396861	136.556050	77.605779	63.970138	18.320627
		CUMMIN	12.753641	3.462880	16.920000	16.920000	16.920000	15.360400
2		EPDV	181.095050	101.536950	378.196340	278.819490	308.830420	207.673040
		SD	124.627740	101.093840	115.658460	102.147020	154.818350	142.056320
		PVMAX	335.444340	234.263800	581.106260	470.263800	494.344880	383.968510
		PVMIN	-25.079999	-31.070776	132.748150	54.770905	36.279975	-21.120646
		CUMMIN	-28.853261	-37.251521	0.920000	0.920000	0.920000	-26.425000
3		EPDV	210.280740	120.928760	522.289740	419.336580	424.811770	315.563650
		SD	198.630280	175.946980	210.225380	195.258990	252.455000	242.919070
		PVMAX	456.936660	348.635460	911.137200	792.830380	717.394740	605.125670
		PVMIN	-106.373130	-118.723020	82.843254	-7.263224	-30.101615	-97.679179
		CUMMIN	-120.136860	-137.767140	-17.080000	-82.834800	-84.494201	-114.995400
4		EPDV	194.458690	114.900590	391.559980	292.183130	322.194050	221.036680
		SD	124.627750	101.093840	115.658460	102.147020	154.818350	142.056320
		PVMAX	348.807980	247.627430	594.469900	483.627440	507.708510	397.332150
		PVMIN	-11.716363	-17.707139	146.111780	68.134542	49.643612	-7.757009
		CUMMIN	-14.853260	-23.251520	7.920000	7.920000	7.920000	-12.425000
5		EPDV	200.066190	115.242360	464.660090	362.388680	377.400280	271.802910
		SD	161.970160	138.843200	168.237710	153.842040	210.515690	199.504560
		PVMAX	401.071700	295.962020	770.180600	654.499570	627.376590	515.611310
		PVMIN	-61.739343	-71.278475	113.680040	28.531775	7.557322	-55.300572
		CUMMIN	-68.130520	-81.591040	-17.080000	-34.480000	-34.494200	-64.209999
6		EPDV	175.487550	101.195180	305.096230	208.613950	253.624200	156.906810
		SD	87.356640	63.577345	63.687723	50.586615	99.393394	84.988533
		PVMAX	283.180620	185.929210	405.395550	299.391670	374.676800	265.689350
		PVMIN	24.942981	22.500561	165.179890	94.373672	78.366266	26.422918
		CUMMIN	24.424000	21.088000	25.920000	25.920000	25.920000	25.360000

Appendix B.   Summary of Considerations in Predicting Individual Firm Decisions

American Maize. This company is committed to the corn milling industry because of long participation and the background of top management. It cannot withstand very large negative cumulative cash flows, but it will want to participate in the HFCS market. American Maize is one of the older CWM companies that had been damaged by the entry into CWM of Cargill and Archer-Daniels-Midland, both of which entered with large, efficient operations.

Anheuser-Busch. Primarily a beer company, AB developed its own enzyme technology for HFCS production. It will enter if the opportunity is right. The financial resources are large enough to absorb risk, but AB is far from committed to CWM. The AB corn milling operation reports to a Busch executive also responsible for the St. Louis Cardinals and Busch Gardens, other AB operations. Busch has been in corn milling primarily as a by-product of technological capability drawn from its brewing operations.

Archer-Daniels-Midland. A closely held company with large financial resources, ADM had successfully entered CWM in 1970–71. The company's experience is in agricultural commodities, and it is used to low margins and wide earnings swings, and to surviving through competing with large, highly efficient facilities. ADM can absorb risk and is known as a risk taking company. Short-run dips in stock prices are of less concern to ADM than to less closely held firms. ADM was likely to invest heavily, as it had in basic CWM in 1970–71.

Cargill. Cargill is an extremely large, privately held, very successful grain trading company that was diversifying into other commodity products much like ADM. Cargill has much in common with ADM: it is a risk taker, it has significant financial resources, it is experienced with cyclical commodities, and it is used to competing on cost and scale. Our feeling is that Cargill is slightly more conservative in taking risks than ADM.

CPC International. Long the historical leader in CWM, CPC had relinquished a substantial share of the market by 1972. Managerial and financial resources had been devoted to a successful program of international expansion and diversification into consumer products. CPC had the financial resources to compete vigorously in HFCS, was very conservatively managed, and was attempting to achieve steady growth in sales and earnings. In 1972, HFCS was likely to appear too risky to justify a major commitment of resources. CPC therefore would enter tentatively and in a small way.

Grain Processing. This is a privately held company with a history similar to that of ADM and Cargill. We know very little about GP, and hence their behavior is hard to predict. They entered CWM in the mid-sixties before Cargill and ADM. That entry seemed less aggressive than the later moves by Cargill and ADM.

Hubinger. Hubinger is a small old-line corn wet miller. It is totally dependent on CWM and in financial difficulty as a result of the price wars accompanying ADM's entry into CWM in 1970–71. Hubinger will want to participate in HFCS, but with limited financial resources could not mount a major effort. At most they would be likely to convert. As a matter of history the H. J. Heinz Company bought Hubinger in 1975 (having failed in a bid to acquire Staley), and with Heinz's considerable resources, Hubinger did move into HFCS in 1976.

National Starch. This company is a relatively small, enormously successful specialty starch and adhesives company whose strategy consists of R&D and product differentiation. NS has consistently avoided undifferentiated commodities and the need for high volume, low cost operations by producing only specialty starches among CWM products. NS is well managed and would not regard HFCS as either a threat or an appropriate opportunity. It was the least vulnerable of any firm to excess capacity in the traditional HFCS markets.

Pennick & Ford. A relatively small old-line CWM company, P&F, like Hubinger, was hurt by the ADM entry. P&F was purchased by R. J Reynolds in the mid-1960s and then sold under Federal Trade Commission pressure to VWR Corporation. VWR was experiencing profitability problems, and the P&F operation was losing money in 1972. P&F could want to play the HFCS game, but lacked the financial resources for a large, risky commitment and perhaps even for a modest commitment.

Staley. Staley was a major participant in CWM and the only firm to license the HFCS technology from Standard Brands before 1972. In 1972, Staley had 200 million pounds of HFCS capacity on-stream, about the same as Standard Brands. Staley is heavily committed to HFCS and possesses significant financial resources. But a very large investment in HFCS may strain Staley's financial situation depending upon how the HFCS market develops.

Standard Brands. SB is a diversified consumer food products company. It purchased Japanese technology for HFCS production and pioneered the commercial introduction of HFCS in the United States. SB had significant financial resources and is not heavily dependent on CWM. It like CPC had turned its attention away from corn wet milling into other businesses in recent years and offered to license the technology to any firm that wanted it. Its initial strategy seemed to be to encourage development of the HFCS market while aggressively leading the development. Thus, it will probably invest, but not attempt to preempt the market.

As a matter of historical record, Amstar, the largest sugar refiner in the United States, also entered HFCS, to hedge against the obvious threat HFCS presented to the traditional sugar markets. It was believed, and still is to some extent, that HFCS is, in the long run, at least as inexpensive a liquid sweetener as sugar and is probably lower in cost than sugar.

Notes

1. All data used in this paper are taken from Michael E. Porter and Margaret Lawrence, *Note on the Corn Wet Milling Industry in 1972* (Intercollegiate Case Clearinghouse, Boston, 1978, Case 1–378–186, and *Note on the Corn Wet Milling Industry, 1973–1977* (Intercollegiate Case Clearinghouse, Boston, 1978, Case 1–378–206).

2. The industry also produced other products, including dextrose and dextrins. They are not nearly so important as starch and corn syrup, and are omitted from the discussion for simplicity.

3. This Nash equilibrium concept has been criticized in static models on the grounds that it involves mistaken assumptions about rivals' behavior. The point there is that an oligopoly game is played repeatedly or continuously. This creates a situation in which learning about rivals' behavior can occur and behavior can adapt. However, the capacity expansion game is played once. The issue of whether to assume firms will continue doing what they are doing now (a poor assumption in the pricing problem) does not arise here. In the capacity expansion situation, the problem for the firm is to avoid errors about rivals' behavior. That, we argue, involves finding a pairing of individual firm choices and aggregate outcomes that is internally consistent.

4. All demand figures are taken from United States Department of Agriculture *Sugar and Sweetener Reports*.

5. More precisely, this involves making the following approximation: Our interest will be in the mean and variance of the present value of net cash flows. Since the cash flow in period t depends on sugar price in period t, the expected value or mean of the present value is not affected by our implicit assumption that sugar prices are perfectly correlated over time. The variance, however, is affected. Let $Vt(pt)$ be the discounted present value of the derivation of the cash flow in period t, as a function of the sugar price in period t. The variance of the present value of net cash flows is

$$V = \sum_{\tau,t=1}^{T} E(Vt(pt)V\tau(p\tau)).$$

Taking a linear approximation $Vt(pt) = Vt'(\bar{p})(pt - \bar{p})$,

$$V = \sum_{\tau,t=1}^{T} Vt'(\bar{p})V\tau'(\bar{p})\,\text{cov}\,(pt,p\tau).$$

What we did is set $pt = p$, a random variable. Thus, our calculated variance is

$$\hat{V} = \sum_{\tau,t=1}^{T} Vt'(\bar{p})V\tau'(\bar{p})\,\text{var}\,(p).$$

Letting $s\tau t$ be the correlation coefficient for pt and $p\tau$,

$$V = \sum_{s;t=1}^{T} Vt'(\bar{p})V\tau'(\bar{p})\,s t\tau\,\text{var}\,(p).$$

Thus, $\hat{V}$, the measure we used, overstates the variance of the present value of cash flows by an amount that depends inversely on the closeness of the serial correlation $\hat{V}$ and V. With no serial correlation, all the terms in V with $t \neq \tau$ are zero. With more time and a larger budget one would want to estimate an autoregressive model for sugar prices and use that in calculating V. But that was not done here. The result is an overstatement of the variance of present value of net cash flows.

6. Making capacity expansion adapt to demand is in lieu of a full dynamic programming treatment in which one would work backward from future to present decisions.

7. We have ignored for simplicity the option of adding corn syrup and HFCS refining capacity to existing grind capacity.

8. We recall that the specific assumptions about HFCS demand are as follows: (a) In the long run, liquid sugar and HFCS are close substitutes, and as a result HFCS will be priced close to sugar. (b) Demand for HFCS is also a function of industry capacity. (c) In the short and medium term, HFCS demand may be substantially below its long-run equilibrium level, because of changeover costs and possible taste effects for bottlers.

9. *Business Week*, 15 November 1976.

10. For a listing of the announced capacity decisions, see "Note on the Corn Wet Milling Industry, 1973–1977," Harvard Business School, Case 1–376–206.

11. One might interpret the preemptive investment prescription in a different way. Admitting that uncertainty may make such a strategy unacceptably risky to a single firm, one could use it as a screening device: put resources preemptively into markets where the risks are not imprudently high. Or more bluntly, do not play risky competitive games. Whether that is good advice depends upon the menu of investment opportunities that are open to the firm. It has the luxury of choosing among low risk, high return investments; few would argue that it should accept the risks involved in markets like HFCS, but not all firms have this option.

12. The model takes expectations about demand as exogenous. Expectations about capacity expansion and competitor behavior are endogenous, and emerge from the equilibrium analysis.

13. This problem of large numbers of equilibria is reminiscent of the oligopoly problem in the mature industry, where reasonable concepts of equilibrium do not delimit the outcomes sufficiently for predictive purposes.

References

Boston Consulting Group. 1968. *Perspectives on experience*. Boston, Massachusetts.

Porter, Michael E. 1978a. A note on the corn wet milling industry, 1973–1977. Harvard Business School. Case 1–378–206.

———. 1978b. Note on the corn wet milling industry in 1972. Harvard Business School. Case 1–378–186.

Spence, A. Michael. 1979a. Investment, strategy, and growth in a new market. *Bell Journal of Economics*. Spring issue.

———. 1979b. Investment in an uncertain environment. Harvard University. Mimeographed.

Comment   Sidney G. Winter

There are clearly good reasons to regard the Porter and Spence paper as being in a different genre from the others presented at this conference—for example, the others say very little about corn syrup.

At a higher level of abstraction also, the paper has a unique orientation. In my comments, I want to view the paper in perspective from a high level of theoretical generality, and in so doing to emphasize some of its distinctive features more than the authors themselves have done. The "perspective" I offer is not a critical one, for I find myself much in sympathy with the sort of inquiry that Porter and Spence have undertaken. Their willingness to plunge into the detail of a specific industry in a specific historical setting and to organize that detail in a coherent theoretical framework seems to me quite laudable. The resulting analysis illuminates not merely the specific situation studied, but also the broad and fundamental problem of the role of prices and markets in coordinating activity. On the other hand, I am skeptical about some details of their approach. In the final section of my comment, I suggest an alternative view of how oligopolists might succeed in coordinating their investment behavior in the sort of situation they describe.

In his 1968 presidential address to the Econometric Society, F. H. Hahn reviewed some basic problems in analysis of the adjustment dynamics of market systems. He closed with an elegant and concise statement of our central theoretical task: "The most intellectually exciting question of our subject remains: is it true that the pursuit of private interest produces not chaos but coherence, and if so, how is it done?" (Hahn 1970, p. 12). To study economic dynamics is, of course, to appreciate the particular importance of the query, *How is it done*? The result of Hahn's survey was a rather gloomy appraisal of the progress that economic theorists had made in understanding the mechanism of the "invisible hand": "I see no support for the view that any of the traditional methods of response of various agents to their economic environment makes the 'hand' perform as it is often taken to perform." (Hahn 1970, p. 1).

Although there have been many important advances in economic theory since Hahn's address, a similar survey today would no doubt reach much the same conclusion. Progress toward understanding the active coordinating function of the market mechanism has been minimal. This is a consequence of the overwhelmingly dominant role of equilibrium analysis in the research method of most economic theorists. As practiced by economists, equilibrium analysis involves the application of consistency tests to limit the range of situations that are regarded as actually realizable in economic life. The great power of the method lies precisely

Sidney G. Winter is professor of economics and of organization and management at Yale University.

in the fact that it obviates the need to study the complicated and probably situation-specific dynamic processes by which "inconsistencies" in the system are identified and eliminated. However, it is hardly surprising that economists remain uninformed about the answers to questions they have chosen to suppress. The question, *How is it done?* remains largely unanswered because it remains largely unexplored.

That equilibrium analysis, as usually practiced, fails to illuminate disequilibrium processes is inherent in the logic of the method. That the failure is an important one—perhaps so important as ultimately to force the sacrifice of the great simplifications the method yields—is a feature of economic reality. More specifically, the importance of the failure can be attributed to the following four features of reality, taken singly and in combination.

—Futures markets and contingent markets exist only in negligible proportion to the scope envisaged for these institutional devices in abstract models of efficient intertemporal allocation under uncertainty.
—The institutional reality does not include a *tatônnement*; more broadly, it includes no device for systematically checking the consistency of tentative plans formulated by a large fraction of economic actors *before* actual implementation of those plans has begun.
—The existence of specialized producers' durables and the cost conditions characteristic of processes of information acquisition, transfer, and storage contribute an important degree of irreversibility to many economic decisions; i.e., with all prices held constant there are large present value sacrifices involved in reverting to an initial state after having taken certain sorts of actions.
—Technological change continually generates new, imperfectly anticipated allocational possibilities, and at the same time destroys the viability of old allocations; more broadly, such processes of long-term historical change as population growth, industrialization, resource depletion, waste accumulation, and naturally occurring climatic change all combine with advancing technology to present a continually novel context for all economic choice.

But for the first two considerations, the market mechanism would in fact be the sort of planning system to which economists often compare it. Currently functioning markets would signal the future consequences of proposed current action, conditioned by the proposed current actions of others. But in fact, it is overwhelmingly the case that it is steps actually *taken* by each actor that impinge on the others, not steps *contemplated*. And the implications of steps actually taken may remain latent and obscured for a long time, before they affect prices in a functioning market. Such a system does not necessarily produce "chaos," but to represent it as a system that checks plans for mutual consistency is to employ a loose and misleading metaphor.

Were it not for the third consideration, the consequences of imperfect coordination would be ephemeral, and the distinction between consistency testing of plans and consistency testing of actual actions would evaporate. As inconsistencies appeared, revealing some past choices as mistaken, there would be quick reversals and redirections of action. The stability properties of such a multiactor, frictionless quest for a consistent solution are problematic, but at least the social learning process would not be complicated and slowed by the accumulating, slowly depreciating "debris of the actual groping process" (Hahn 1970, p. 4). As it is, the actor who has made an economically irreversible mistake has presumably learned something about the problem he faced, but he now faces a new problem. And the actor who has somehow stumbled on the (or "an") equilibrium action will fail to find corroboration of his choice as the durable consequences of the mistaken choices of others shape his environment.

Finally, the reality of nonrepetitive historical change mocks the equilibrium theorist's last-resort comforting thought, the proposition that, if the problem stands still, the social learning process will surely find the right answer to it. Given enough time, even slow learners making slowly depreciating mistakes should be able to grope their way to a solution. Again, acceptance of this hypothetical proposition is qualified by concerns about the stability of the adjustment process; also, information cost considerations provide reason to doubt the supposition that the accumulation of sufficient experience is the only requisite of perfect learning. But the important point is that these sorts of questions arise only in models. In reality, the problem is not standing still at all.

I should emphasize that the foregoing considerations do not directly imply any judgment on the merits of market mechanisms and the pursuit of private interest as against any concrete organizational alternative for dealing with the social coordination problem. The invisible hand has many strengths, and in many contexts those strengths may confer a decisive superiority relative to other arrangements. Rather, the judgment is about the adequacy of equilibrium analysis in the neo-Walrasian tradition, and it is one of skepticism about the ability of that sort of analysis to reveal the true character of the institutional arrangements it purports to analyze. The insights of Hayek (1948) and Schumpeter (1950), though admittedly undeveloped by contemporary standards, may have a more direct bearing on the "most intellectually exciting question of our subject" than the modern theorist's storehouse full of existence and optimality results.

Now consider, from this point of view, the situation in the corn wet milling industry that Porter and Spence describe. A technological advance—the development of a commercially viable production method for high fructose corn syrup—faced the firms of the industry with a novel decision context. The market for their products had expanded in a relatively *unanticipated and discontinuous* manner, an aspect of the situation underemphasized by the title of the Porter and Spence paper. It was clear that the new product represented a profit opportunity, but the size of the market would ultimately depend on the degree to which HFCS could displace sugar in various applications. Also, and fundamentally, it was not at all clear to whom the profit opportunity "belonged." If all firms were to respond aggressively by adding new capacity to produce HFCS, they might all regret it—even in the event of strong demand. On the other hand, very timid responses all around would mean high profits per unit, but low total profit. Thus, from the point of view of industry profitability, and of course also from a social welfare point of view, a significant coordination problem existed. By making investment decisions without a proper allowance for the contemporaneous actions of others, firms could easily sacrifice profits and waste resources. Overresponse in particular posed the threat of prolonged overcapacity not just in HFCS, but in all markets involving the same upstream processes. (The standard of a "proper allowance" for the actions of others depends of course on whether one is concerned about profits sacrificed or resources wasted.)

An organized futures market in HFCS, extending several years into the future, could have performed a valuable social role. The commodity itself was sufficiently standardized to present no serious obstacles to such an arrangement. Although producers might have been reluctant to enter into unconditional contracts to deliver a commodity they had never produced before, a more flexible standard contract could have been devised to shift a part of the production risk to the buyer. An active market in such futures contracts would have registered in price movements the developing information on the relationship of capacity and demand. Producers could have guided their capacity decisions accordingly. Soft-drink manufacturers and other potential HFCS buyers would have faced a clear measure of their incentive to convert from sugar to HFCS, and could have laid off to speculators most of the risk associated with their own investments in learning about the new sweetener. Of course, a functioning futures market is not a *tatônnement* on intertemporal prices; there is more to coordination than aggregating available information about actions taken. But there was no futures market, let alone a *tatônnement*. Perhaps there is a generalizable lesson here, a pessimistic principle that says that economic change rarely goes forward in an institutional context well suited for its guidance and control. Rather, the lag of institutional adaptations behind the need for them is a part of the problem of change.

It seems unlikely that the investment response of the corn wet milling industry to the HFCS opportunity came close to some plausible standard of ex ante optimality, but of course such questions are almost as difficult to judge in retrospect as in prospect. From the Porter and Spence account, it does seem clear that the investment choices of the industry as a whole did at least display a good deal of coherence. Viewed in a Schumpeterian perspective, their case study might even be appraised as a typical success story for the market mechanism, only slightly qualified by reference to the generalized (and perhaps unavoidable) failure to appreciate the depths to which the sugar price might sink. In the neo-Walrasian framework, however, the story hardly fits at all. The market mechanisms analyzed by Porter and Spence operate on different principles and perform different functions than the stylized market mechanisms of general equilibrium theory.

Starkly put, their explanation of how "coherence" was achieved and "chaos" avoided is that all firms computed the Cournot solution to the HFCS investment problem and acted accordingly. The Cournot model involved has a number of sophisticated elements, including demand uncertainty, mutual recognition of differentiating features of the oligopolistic rivals, and a range of qualitatively different investment options. But the basic coordinating force is the assumed general principle that the course of industry development anticipated by each individual firm is one it expects would be realized if it were generally anticipated. As the authors rightly remark, the acceptability of the Cournot equilibrium analysis in the context of the single-move investment game is considerably higher than it is in the more familiar context of output determination. It is important to emphasize, also, that they resort to equilibrium analysis not merely as a convenient theoretical device, but as a plausible abstraction of actual decision process in the industry—an answer to the question, *How is it done?*"

The most fundamental contrast between their analysis and neo-Walrasian equilibrium theory involves the informational role of prices. Prices are not sustaining equilibrium; they are signaling disequilibrium. The steps taken in response to disequilibrium are coordinated, imperfectly, by a variety of *nonprice* information flows and by actors' anticipating each other's behavior. The results of those steps are only tardily reflected in price movements, when it is too late to reconsider the steps but not to adapt to the new disequilibrium that they have produced. The players in the game need to know as much as possible about the details of each other's situation. In the Porter and Spence account *all* firms are performing the functions of the commissar for corn wet milling—a perspective sharply different not only from neo-Walrasian theory, but also from the Hayekian picture of the information processing economies of the market.

A number of features of the specific situation in the corn wet milling industry contribute to the plausibility of the explanation offered for the degree of coordination achieved.

—The situation involves a relatively short list of actors, all of whom are known to each other. A flood of *de novo* entry into the industry, from unidentified sources, is apparently not a sufficiently likely prospect to be taken into consideration. The firms involved evidently think, with reason, that they collectively "own" the new profit opportunity, although it is not immediately obvious what the ownership shares are.

—The actors can draw on a large fund of shared information about each other. The scale of past participation and previously revealed attitudes toward risks are particularly important indicators of likely future behavior. Prediction efforts based on this sort of information are not severely complicated by product differentiation or by secret development efforts proceeding simultaneously in several laboratories.

—Similarly, the actors share a fund of information about the demand side of the picture, derived from contacts with potential buyers and public sources. Again, the absence of product differentiation simplifies the problem of drawing inferences from this sort of information.

—Security analysts act as independent arbiters of expectations regarding the future prospects of the industry as a whole. Provided that the expectation thus certified is reasonably accurate and consistent with the reactions to it, this can make for improved coordination; otherwise, it can mean the investing firms are all wrong together.

—Firms communicate with each other through public statements, financial reports, and observable actions taken.

—Risk aversion and perhaps financial constraints limit recourse to preemptive strategies. These considerations operate to restrain and stabilize the aggregate industry investment to a degree that depends on the size of the contemplated investment opportunity relative to the size of the investing firms.

Any attempt to assess the generality of the mechanisms described, or to apply similar logic to other cases, might well focus on the extent to which these features of the original case are replicated.

I close these comments with a sketch of an alternative model of investment coordination in the situation studied by Porter and Spence, a model that seems to me to have somewhat greater behavioral plausibility than the Cournot-style computation they impute to the firms. In this alternative view, firms focus initially not on the capacity expansion path of the industry but on the full cost of production (including target return) of HFCS. This calculation would determine a price level just low enough to eliminate incentives for further additions to capacity. Consideration of the uncertain demand for HFCS would follow, resulting in a best estimate of the capacity likely to be ultimately installed, perhaps with a qualifying indication of high and low values. The first-cut answer to the question how the opportunity would be shared in the industry would be provided by reference to prevailing market shares in corn syrup. This preliminary estimate would then be modified by each individual firm according to its view of the special attributes and circumstances—including financial constraints, atypical cost conditions, and attitudes toward risk—of its rivals and itself. Such modifications would be constrained by the technical indivisibility of investment and would not be likely to go outside the range of plus or minus one MES plant. In finally carrying out its own plan, each firm would view itself as laying claim to its appropriate, historically based share of the new industry opportunity.

Like the Porter and Spence scheme, this alternative one has the central property that it would not, in many circumstances, produce "chaos" in the sense of a vast disproportion between the aggregate investment undertaken and the estimated size of the aggregate opportunity. Also like their scheme, there is a list of considerations that are highly relevant to its efficacy as a coordination device, but there is only a partial overlap between the two lists. In particular, the role played in their model by risk aversion is here played by the assumption that firms roughly scale their ambitions in the new market to their historical shares in the old one. This change amounts to a more explicit recognition of the fact that what the firms need to roughly coordinate their behavior is a Schelling (1960) focal point. Although the carrying out of the same Cournot equilibrium calculation by all parties might well provide the focal point if economic theorists were doing the calculating, I suspect that the historical shares approach would more readily come to the mind of the businessman.

References

Hahn, F. H. 1970. Some adjustment problems. *Econometrica* 38: 1–17.
Hayek, Friederich A. 1948. *Individualism and economic order*. South Bend, Ind.: Gateway Editions.
Schelling, Thomas C. 1960. *The strategy of conflict*. Cambridge, Mass.: Harvard University Press.
Schumpeter, Joseph A. 1950. *Capitalism, socialism, and democracy*. 3d ed. New York: Harper & Brothers.

Contributors

William A. Brock
Department of Economics
University of Wisconsin
Madison, Wisconsin 73706

Dennis W. Carlton
Law School
University of Chicago
Chicago, Illinois 60637

Peter Diamond
Department of Economics
Massachusetts Institute of
   Technology
Cambridge, Massachusetts 02139

Jerry R. Green
Department of Economics
Harvard University
Cambridge, Massachusetts 02138

Sanford J. Grossman
Department of Economics
University of Chicago
Chicago, Illinois 60637

Oliver D. Hart
Churchill College
Cambridge, England

Richard E. Kihlstrom
Department of Economics
University of Pennsylvania
Philadelphia, Pennsylvania 19104

David M. Kreps
Graduate School of Business
Stanford University
Stanford, California 94305

Jean-Jacques Laffont
Université des Sciences Sociales de
   Toulouse
Place Anatole France, 31042
Toulouse, France

Hayne E. Leland
School of Business Administration
University of California
Berkeley, California 94720

David Levhari
Department of Economics
Hebrew University
Jerusalem, Israel

Steven A. Lippman
Graduate School of Management
University of California
Los Angeles, California 90024

John J. McCall
Department of Economics
University of California
Los Angeles, California 90024

Dale T. Mortensen
Department of Economics
Northwestern University
Evanston, Illinois 60201

Joseph M. Ostroy
Department of Economics
University of California
Los Angeles, California 90024

Michael E. Porter
Graduate School of Business
  Administration
Harvard University
Cambridge, Massachusetts 02138

Andrew Postlewaite
Wharton School
University of Pennsylvania
Philadelphia, Pennsylvania 19104

Edward C. Prescott
Department of Economics
University of Minnesota
Minneapolis, Minnesota 55455

John G. Riley
Department of Economics
University of California
Los Angeles, California 90024

A. Michael Spence
Department of Economics
Harvard University
Cambridge, Massachusetts 02138

Sidney G. Winter
School of Organization and
  Management
Yale University
New Haven, Connecticut 06520

Author Index

Subject Index